Women Writing About Money addresses the paradoxical situation
of the women of Jane Austen's time who had no legal access to
money yet were held responsible for domestic expenditure. In
this context, money becomes the major issue in women's fiction,
as well as the legal disabilities suffered by women and the
restrictions imposed by rank. The book translates the fictional
money of the novels of Jane Austen's day into the power of
contemporary spendable incomes. From the perspective of what
the British pound could buy at the market, the economic lives of
women in the novels emerge as part of a general picture of
women's economic disability. Through the work of both well-
known and less canonical writers such as Jane Austen and Maria
Edgeworth, Eliza Parsons and Sarah Green, as well as writers of
magazine fiction, *Women Writing About Money* examines the
professional lives of women authors, the kinds of publishers who
would publish their work, the profits they could expect to
receive, and the specific demands of their different reading
publics. By linking authorship to the economic lives of contemporary women, *Women Writing About Women* links the fantasy
worlds of women's fiction with the social and economic realities
of both readers and writers.

CAMBRIDGE STUDIES IN ROMANTICISM 9

WOMEN WRITING ABOUT MONEY

CAMBRIDGE STUDIES IN ROMANTICISM

General editors
Professor Marilyn Butler   Professor James Chandler
University of Oxford   *University of Chicago*
Editorial board
John Barrell, *University of York*   Paul Hamilton, *University of Southampton*
Mary Jacobus, *Cornell University*   Kenneth Johnston, *Indiana University*
Alan Liu, *University of California, Santa Barbara*
Jerome McGann, *University of Virginia*
David Simpson, *University of Colorado*

This series aims to foster the best new work in one of the most challenging fields within English literary studies. From the early 1780s to the early 1830s a formidable array of talented men and women took to literary composition, not just in poetry, which some of them famously transformed, but in many modes of writing. The expansion of publishing created new opportunities for writers, and the political stakes of what they wrote were raised again and again by what Wordsworth called those "great national events" that were "almost daily taking place": the French Revolution, the Napoleonic and American wars, urbanization, industrialization, religious revival, an expanded empire abroad and the reform movement at home. This was an enormous ambition, even when it pretended otherwise. The relations between science, philosophy, religion and literature were reworked in texts such as *Frankenstein* and *Biographia Literaria*; gender relations in *A Vindication of the Rights of Woman* and *Don Juan*; journalism by Cobbett and Hazlitt: poetic form, content and style by the Lake School and the Cockney School. Outside Shakespeare studies, probably no body of writing has produced such a wealth of response or done so much to shape the responses of modern criticism. This indeed is the period that saw the emergence of those notions of "literature" and of literary history, especially national literary history, on which modern scholarship in English has been founded.

The categories produced by Romanticism have also been challenged by recent historicist arguments. The task of the series is to engage both with a challenging corpus of Romantic writings and with the changing field of criticism they have helped to shape. As with other literary series published by Cambridge, this one will represent the work of both younger and more established scholars, on either side of the Atlantic and elsewhere.

TITLES PUBLISHED

Romantic Correspondence: Women, Politics and the Fiction of Letters
by Mary A. Favret
British Romantic Writers and the East: Anxieties of Empire
by Nigel Leask
Edmund Burke's Aesthetic Ideology
Language, Gender and Political Economy in Revolution
by Tom Furniss
Poetry as an Occupation and an Art in Britain, 1760–1830
by Peter Murphy
In the Theatre of Romanticism: Coleridge, Nationalism, Women
by Julie A. Carlson
Keats, Narrative and Audience
by Andrew Bennett
Romance and Revolution: Shelley and the Politics of a Genre
by David Duff
Literature, Education, and Romanticism: Reading as Social Practice, 1780–1832
by Alan Richardson
Women Writing about Money: Women's Fiction in England, 1780–1820
by Edward Copeland
Shelley and the Revolution in Taste: The Body and the Natural World
by Timothy Morton
William Cobbett: The Politics of Style
by Leonora Nattrass
The Rise of Supernatural Fiction, 1762–1800
by E. J. Clery

Passion subdued by Reason.

WOMEN WRITING ABOUT MONEY

Women's Fiction in England, 1790–1820

EDWARD COPELAND

Pomona College, Claremont, California

CAMBRIDGE
UNIVERSITY PRESS

Published by the Press Syndicate of the University of Cambridge
The Pitt Building, Trumpington Street, Cambridge, CB2 1RP
40 West 20th Street, New York, NY 10011-4211, USA
10 Stamford Road, Oakleigh, Melbourne 3166, Australia

First published 1995

Printed in Great Britain at the University Press, Cambridge

A catalogue record for this book is available from the British Library

Library of Congress cataloguing in publication data

Copeland, Edward.
Women writing about money: women's fiction in England, 1790–1820 / Edward Copeland.
p.   cm. – (Cambridge studies in Romanticism)
Includes bibliographical references (p.).
ISBN 0 521 45461 1
1. English fiction – 19th century – History and criticism.   2. Money in literature.   3.
English fiction – Women authors – History and criticism.   4. English fiction – 18th century
– History and criticism.   5. Women and literature – England – History – 18th century.   6.
Women and literature – England – History – 19th century.   7. Women novelists, English –
Economic conditions.   8. Women – England – Economic conditions.   9. Women –
England – Social conditions.   10. Economics in literature.   11. Romanticism – England.
I. Title.   II. Series.
PR868.M65C66   1995
823'.709355–dc20   94-10269   CIP

ISBN 0 521 45461 1 hardback

For
Margaret Mathies

Contents

xi

Contents

Illustrations

Acknowledgments

My grateful thanks are due to those friends and relations who have listened to me, assisted me, and encouraged me. Some have been helpful in particular ways that demand more than general thanks: Philip Copeland, Jan Fergus, Will Jones, Deborah Kaplan, Deirdre Le Faye, Helen Lefroy, Robert Maccubbin, Mitzi Myers, James Robinson, Rich Schmidt, and Dru Sherrod. Ruth Perry supplied the title. I must here record my special gratitude to the late J. David Grey of the Jane Austen Society of North America and to the late Dean Robert Voelkel of Pomona College for significant moral support. I am especially grateful to colleagues who read and offered suggestions on all or portions of the manuscript: Isobel Grundy, Thomas Pinney, Judith Stanton, and Jonathan Veitch.

Librarians of the following institutions have been unfailingly kind and helpful at every stage of my research: Sterling Library and the Beinecke Library at Yale University; Rice University Library; Honnold Library of the Claremont Colleges; the Library of the University of California at Santa Barbara; the University of Chicago Library; the Pforzheimer Library; the Berg Collection of the New York Public Library; and in London, the British Library, the Fawcett Library, the Institute for Historical Studies, and the Senate House Library of the University of London; in Bath, the Library of the City of Bath; in Winchester, the Hampshire County Archives. In particular, I am grateful for the unstinting assistance I received in the early days of the project from Virginia Renner, Elsa Sink, and Mary Wright of Reader Services at the Henry E. Huntington Library, San Marino, California.

My research has been generously supported by grants administered through Pomona College: faculty research grants, the Wig Fund, Pew Seminars, and a Mellon Foundation grant for a leave of absence to study art history at the University of California, Riverside.

The Graves Foundation supplied support for a sabbatical leave for research in London. The NEH Summer Fellowship Program at the Yale Center for British Arts, 1985, enabled me to explore the illustration of women's periodicals with the helpful advice of David Solkin and colleagues in the seminar. I would like especially to record my thanks to John Brewer and the Center for Seventeenth and Eighteenth Century Studies at the Clark Library, UCLA, for the endless treasures of its seminar on "Culture and Consumption in the Seventeenth and Eighteenth Centuries."

My deepest debt of gratitude goes to the person to whom the book is dedicated.

Abbreviations and notes

Citations from Jane Austen's minor works, the juvenilia and the fragmentary novels, are from *Minor Works*, volume VI of R. W. Chapman, *The Works of Jane Austen*, 1st ed. 1954, reprinted with revisions by B. C. Southam 1966, 6 vols. (Oxford University Press, 1982). This volume is referred to as *MW*.

All citations to Jane Austen's novels are to Chapman's *The Works of Jane Austen*.

Citations from Jane Austen's correspondence are taken from *Jane Austen's Letters*, 2nd ed., ed. R. W. Chapman (Oxford University Press, 1979). This volume is referred to as *Letters*.

Introduction

> "Oh! mother, how happy I should be" said she, as she passed a
> toy shop, "if I had all those pretty things!"
> "What, all! Do you wish for them all, Rosamund?"
> "Yes, mamma, all."
>
> Maria Edgeworth, "The Purple Jar" (1796)

I made my first acquaintance with the subject of this study, the
consumer agenda of women's fiction, 1790–1820, early. Of all the
stories my grandmother read, Maria Edgeworth's "The Purple Jar"
was far and above the one my cousin and I liked the best.[1] She would
read of little Rosamund, of wise spending and careful budgets, and
we would see bloody feet in the snow. It was our favorite story. Every
time we heard it, it enchanted us, it terrified us, it disappointed us,
but it was still the one story in Grandmother's collection that truly
touched our souls – F. W. Woolworth's and Sunday School packed
into one disturbing tale.

The best part of "The Purple Jar," the part that really drew us in,
was the heroine's total, dizzy delight in shopping. Everything that
Rosamund sees on her trip to London enchants her: artificial flowers,
jewelry, pretty buckles, and some beautifully colored jars in the
window of a chemist's shop. The jewelry, "ranged in drawers behind
glass," stops her in mid-step: "Mamma, you'll buy some of these?"
"Which?" asks her mother, but Rosamund doesn't care: "Which, –
I don't know which; – but any of them, for they are all pretty." She
looks only to take some small part in the great consumer spectacle
before her. Her mother tells her patiently that she has no "use" for
these objects, that they are in town to buy her some new shoes.
Rosamund, however, yearns for a purple vase she has seen in the
chemist's shop. When her mother gives her the choice between shoes
and the vase, she takes the vase. Now for the sad part. When she gets
home, she finds that the vase is not the beautiful object she thought

it was at all, but an ordinary glass jar filled with a disgusting purple liquid. She wants to return to town for the shoes. "No, Rosamund, you must abide by your own choice," says her mother, "and now the best thing you can possibly do, is to bear your disappointment with good humour." Rosamund repents and promises to do better next time, but Edgeworth, brilliantly, leaves her story of consumer desire open ended: "I am sure, no not quite sure," Rosamund confesses to her mother, "but, I hope, I shall be wiser another time."

"The Purple Jar" has it all: passion, happiness, heartbreak, suffering, and redemption. More than that, it speaks to the self-awareness of a generation of women, who in 1796 were reading "The Purple Jar" to their daughters both for their own instruction and for their daughters'. Recent studies shed particular light on Edgeworth's story by demonstrating that a strong retail culture had developed in England from the seventeenth through the eighteenth centuries, and that by the end of the eighteenth century the country posssessed a large network of retail shops.[2] In other words, Edgeworth's story turns its attention to an already done thing. Shopping was an established fact of middle-class life. Edgeworth's contribution was in bringing to children's literature her perception of a market culture that, as Chandra Mukerji notes ominously, owed its existence to the disturbing fact that "material interests are not ... subservient to other social goals."[3]

I began reading women's novels, 1790–1820, thinking that "money in Jane Austen's novels" was to be my subject, that I would read the lesser fry to illuminate her, and that whatever I found, Jane Austen would remain the primary focus of the study. Instead, a discourse in women's fiction presented itself that had shape, direction, and a consistency of engagement that merited attention on its own.[4] As one critic of women's fiction from the late eighteenth to the early nineteenth centuries has wisely remarked: "The unread is not necessarily the unreadable."[5]

My concurrent discovery of yet a different literature, the equally heady excitements of Terry Eagleton, Fredric Jameson, and Mikhail Bakhtin, along with feminists like Elizabeth Janeway, Terry Lovell, Mary Poovey, Nancy Armstrong, and Teresa de Lauretis, has left its unmistakable tracks on the study as well, together with provocative essays and studies of consumerism by Jean Baudrillard, Pierre Bourdieu, and Colin Campbell.[6] As one might suppose from such tutors, this study inevitably assumes that late eighteenth- and early nineteenth-century women's fiction, including fiction in the popular magazines and Minerva Press novels, comes ideologically freighted, that it speaks in codes loud enough to contemporary ears, if faint to ours. As I now read "The Purple Jar," I wonder where the greatest burden of anxiety really rests in that story: with Rosamund, or with her poor author, whose earnest labor to attach "use" to consumption provides so feeble a dam against the enchanting powers that attract her heroine.

Women's fiction between 1790 and 1820 turned its attention to the "meaning" of consumption, especially its meaning for women, as a concern of defining importance. Although emulation, as Lorna Weatherill argues, was a doubtful contributor to the retail economy of the eighteenth century,[7] "fashion" – not always the same as emulation[8] – emerges in the last quarter of the century as a certain attraction for women of the middling ranks: in fiction as a focus of comic revelation, as in Frances Burney's novel *Evelina* (1778), and in the *Lady's Magazine*, a popular woman's journal of fashion, fiction, and news that flourished from 1770 to 1832, as a focus of monthly temptations.[9]

The *Lady's Magazine* with its emphasis on the doings of the *haut ton* marked "fashion" as a structure around which middling rank women could mount their conversation about consumption. The *Lady's Magazine* tapped a grass-roots response to the subject, too, since it drew on its eager readers for the contributions that filled its pages. The magazine offered women the opportunity to speak to other women, to argue with one another, and often to provide one another with specialized information otherwise hard to come by. The *Lady's*, together with other women's magazines at the end of the century, nurtured a culture for women centered on material culture. Year by year, the women's conversation in the magazines intensified, as it did in women's novels, charting a narrative of shifting ideologies devoted to explaining just what it meant to be female and middle class in a market economy.[10]

One of the most fragile lines of evidence in the history of eighteenth-century consumption, as all researchers admit, lies in the scanty evidence available on the relation of women and money.[11] But "the limited ability of women everywhere to control capital," as Carole Shammas describes it, affects any reading of women's literature of the period.[12] Lorna Weatherill, in citing the sheer hard work expected of women in managing households, notes that conduct books continued to advise that husbands should control the spending of the money.[13] But Amanda Vickery finds ample evidence that women of the lesser gentry at mid-century exercised control over routine spending decisions in their households.[14]

And Hoh-Cheung Mui and Lorna H. Mui's study of shopkeeping demonstrates that women, particularly those in urban areas, had day-to-day experience with consumption in their relations with "petty" shopkeepers, a not insignificant part of the retailing trade. These operators of small shops, often no more than the corner of a room, catered to the daily needs of families ("subsistence purchasing") with such groceries and staples as tea, sugar, flour, coffee, soap, candles, and salt. Many of the shopkeepers were women themselves, according to the Muis, since the small amounts of capital needed to set up shop did not automatically place such activity out of their reach. In addition, they catered to customers also likely to be women, who in their day-to-day shopping had the hands-on management of the family's daily budget for consumption. Here, at this most localized level of domestic spending, with the shillings and pence for the immediate needs of the family's subsistence in their control, women seem to have been granted significant, if limited, economic responsibility.[15] Debts to petty shopkeepers are in fact the debts that most often wring cries of desperation from women authors applying for help from the Royal Literary Fund, a charity set up during the last decade of the century to aid destitute authors: "We have lost by a lodger and boarder, a considerable sum," Emily Clark, a contemporary novelist and poet, wrote the trustees of the Fund, "A note of hand given to our Baker by my mother for a bill due, will be presented for payment on the seventh of April next and if we do not pay it, will be the ruin of a house. Fifteen pounds would relieve our distress."[16]

As the Muis note, the petty shopkeeper was omnipresent in villages, towns, and cities throughout the century. As a consequence, the world of credit with its ever-present threat of prison for unpaid bills was directly in the experience of women. Elizabeth Somerville, widowed with two children and in hiding from her creditors, wrote the Fund for help with her debts, but omitted a return address, "for personal safety."[17] Emily Clark, still in difficulties six years after her first letter in 1811, claimed, "On the thirty first of December we have a bill of fifteen pounds to pay for bread, and at Christmas, taxes to the amount of six pounds, which makes me shudder to think of." The trustees sent her £5.[18] At the very lowest edge of solvency, Mary Matilda Bentham, diarist and poet, reported to the Fund that her rent was 5 shillings a week, but that she could get her room for 2 shillings a week by giving up the bed and sleeping on a mattress on the floor. Such disturbing tales were not, one assumes, the experience of all women, but they were certainly a part of the general imagination of an uncertain economic future.

Women authors of all ranks, not just the economically distressed, addressed the subject of women and money in their works. In the 1790s, however, the credit anxieties of the domestic budget – the usual material of real-life pleas to the Royal Literary Fund – became the regular subject of novels published by William Lane's Minerva Press, gothic tales characterized by Joseph Wiesenfarth in his study of gothic literature as caught between the confusions of gothic fantasy and the confusions of social order.[19] In Lane's Minerva novels, for which the publisher paid his authors notoriously little, we find a literature of consumption poised at the very edge of economic disaster, the "horrid" novels of Jane Austen's *Northanger Abbey*. Authors with claims to genteel status approached women's participation in the economy with less melodrama, but with their attention equally focused on women's economic liabilities. Frances Burney's heroine in *Camilla* (1796) has severe problems with credit, in fact almost as melodramatic as her sister heroines from the Minerva Press. In Austen's *Sense and Sensibility*, a novel conceived in the 1790s, Elinor Dashwood must actively monitor her mother's and sisters' expenses to keep the family free of debt. In *Pride and Prejudice*, also conceived in the 1790s, it is the threat of comparative poverty facing the Bennet women after Mr. Bennet's death that drives the plot. Charlotte Smith's string of novels, ten of them, offer an unmitigated series of economic disasters for genteel women who are long on claims to station, but short on funds.

Ten years later, still focused on women and money, women's novels move away from depictions of economic liability to entertain visions of economic empowerment. Among the Minerva writers, the emphasis turns to marking out social respectability for their heroines from the commercial ranks. Probity, honesty in all financial affairs, and a frank celebration of commercial life are the signs of the later Minerva novel. Didactic authors from the genteel ranks are more concerned to link the domestic budget to social action. Their novels feature useful suggestions for projects in the village that their heroines

can undertake for the deserving poor. And finally there are those
authors, like Austen, writing for the carriage trade, who offer a highly
specific economic vision for their own rank's favored place in society.
Jane Austen, as I discovered, most certainly does not represent the
print culture of all women. She responds to it, depends on it, and has
valuable stock holdings in it of her own, but she must share the larger
culture of women's literature with competing voices from different
levels in the middle ranks.

The circulating library supplies a paradigm for the organization of
women's literature. A seasoned borrower could take one look at the
books on the crowded tables of the library and tell the essentials at a
glance: a check for the date and title, a look at the author's name, or
failing that, a glance to see who the publisher might be, usually a
giveaway to the contents.[20] From such casual browsing, an observant
patron could be almost certain of what she held in her hand, the kind
of story she would find, the issues that would interest her, the
ideological tack the book would take, and, as a significant consideration, the social rank the book was intended to appeal to.
Genteel readers could be comfortable with something from one of the
established publishers – Longman, Hookham and Carpenter, the
Robinsons, Cadell, Johnson, or Noble. Readers from trade or from
the lesser professions, though they could find pleasure in the genteel
books, would discover that the Minerva Press addressed them
specifically and as a matter of policy. The women's magazines also
divided their readers by rank. The genteel reader might take home
La Belle Assemblée; the tradesman's daughter might be more likely to
choose the *Lady's Magazine*, but, again, both magazines could appeal,
like the novels, across the entire span of the middling ranks.[21]

The image of a conversation among women, from one book to
another, from one magazine to another, from one rank to another,
becomes clearer. Marilyn Butler and Gary Kelly some years ago
recognized the importance of this conversation in the fiction of the
period, but not with an eye turned to the wider print culture, the
"horrid" novels of Jane Austen's *Northanger Abbey*, for example, or
the fiction of the magazines.[22] Jane Spencer, Dale Spender, and Ann
Jones listen for the less frequently noticed voices, but over a wider
span of time and not with a focus on fiction as a function of rank or
publishing conditions.[23] In fact, from 1790 to 1820, there was a more
free-wheeling conversation in print among women than at any time
before or since. After the publishing industry began a rapid, market-

driven expansion around 1820, women's publications became far
more specialized, less responsive to the general conversation. In
short, the years immediately prior to this change in the book market
are optimum years for listening-in on women's concerns in fiction.

Money, like the weather, is the one topic on which every novel has
an opinion. Whatever the political argument, whatever the social
agenda, whatever the romantic entanglement in women's fiction,
women can be heard talking about money, the lack of it, how to
spend it, or how to get it.[24] The conversation shifts tone as decade by
decade new styles of heroines conspire to fit new ideologies of expense
to the middle-class woman's world. The single essential key to
consumption, however, as women's fiction always acknowledges, is
an adequate income. This study organizes its chapters around the
edges of that conversation.

The first two chapters examine the 1790s as a "marker" decade.
We now know that the concept of a "revolution" in the eighteenth-
century economy – industrial or consumer – is a dubious assumption.
Michael Fores' influential essay, "The Myth of a British Industrial
Revolution" (1981), argued that the so-called "industrial revolution
... turns out to be more a part of myth than historical reality."[25] And,
except for recent and much-qualified objections from Maxine Berg
and Pat Hudson,[26] economic historians tend to accept "evolution"
rather than "revolution" as the term best describing economic
change in the eighteenth century.[27] The question for the 1790s then
becomes: *why* was the perception of economic change so overwhelming in women's literature of these years when real change in
the economy was, as the evidence indicates, not as great as
contemporary outcry would indicate?

For women's literature, the answer may lie in the troubles that
circle around matters of credit. Certainly the gothic literature of the
1790s, both in novels and in short magazine fiction, concerns itself
with the pressing dangers to women from debt: harassment,
humiliation, confinement. Sometimes the "horror" of the pieces is
translated into less specific anxiety – loss, dispossession, forced
removal, isolation – depicted through lonely castles, remorseless
barons, blasted landscapes, and the like, but the action is inevitably
economic. Always at the center of the story there is the bereft,
penniless, and wandering woman, victim of an unforgiving economy.

Inflation, aggravated by an author's residence in London, may
also be part of the "gothic" economic dilemma. Emily Clark, forced

to live outside London for cheaper lodgings, wrote angrily to the Royal Literary Fund, "I have written another work... which I negociated with a bookseller to purchase... [W]ishing to take advantage of my distress being at a distance (East Grinstead) he has offered me a mere trifle, which it would be injurious for me to accept and which was never offered by any other bookseller."[28] Women situated in London and employed at the lower end of the publishing trade – with William Lane's Minerva Press, for example, the major publisher of gothic fiction – were exposed to the concentrated hazards of credit in an expensive city where all daily provisions had to come from the shops, often from the shops of those petty, equally hard-pressed shopkeepers, who, as the Muis explain, had to pay their suppliers promptly to stay in business and could not extend credit for long. Charlotte Smith found herself in receivership for petty debts in Storrington, where she had fled to escape the higher prices of London: "There is now an execution in my house at Storrington for £25 – & my books the only things I had been able to reserve, are seized for rent & will be sold."[29] There is no reason to disbelieve the testimonies of contemporaries about increased economic hard times, especially the sufferings of those people already at the edge of subsistence incomes, but a desire for luxury is certainly not the source of their complaints: "Their characters are irreproachable," the character witness for an applicant to the Royal Literary Fund reports, but "the encreased [*sic*] prices, of late years, of the necessaries of life has quite sunk down their Fortunes, & render'd them true objects of Charity & Commiseration."[30]

Even women authors more comfortably situated financially in the 1790s saw a bleak economic landscape before them. This seeming anomaly suggests a different, and, I think, a far more interesting explanation for the general anxiety to be found in women's fiction of the period, one that rests on our understanding of economic change in the eighteenth century as having evolved in a gradual process over a period of many years. The difference between "necessaries" and "luxuries," an ancient distinction, as John Sekora demonstrates in his study of the history of luxury,[31] had become by the end of the eighteenth century a distinction fixed in contemporary minds more or less as Adam Smith defined it:

By necessaries I understand, not only the commodities which are indispensably necessary for the support of life, but whatever the custom of the country renders it indecent for creditable people, even of the lowest order, to be without.[32]

Thinking in these terms, Charlotte Smith complained in a letter to a friend,

My house is indeed triste & what is worse, I have embarrassed myself in getting into it, by paying for pictures & having furniture still to pay for... I could not help it. My family is *such*, that a small house will not hold us – nor a small number of servants suffice. And I have the character of being expensive, when perhaps no Woman brought up as I was, was ever so *little* expensive.[33]

With the long, gradual evolution of a market economy, unfulfilled expectations of women of all ranks for "necessaries," depending on how they defined *their* necessaries, would be perceived as a severe economic threat. It would seem that the war, an increase in taxes, a general rise in prices, and periodic economic depressions must have acted upon each other as self-magnifiers of economic distress for everyone of the middling sort, no matter where situated, who looked simply to secure the "necessaries" of their lives. The heroine of Eliza Parsons' *The Castle of Wolfenbach*, published in 1793, for example, looks into her "Portmantua" to "take out some linens for the ensuing day," and bursts into tears at the sight of "the small quantity of necessaries she possessed; she cast a retrospection on her past calamities, they made her shudder; she looked forward to the future, all was dark and gloomy" (I, 16). Certainly there is little economic rejoicing to be found in women's fiction of any sort in the 1790s.

The marked improvement in the tone of response of women's fiction to the economy that emerged after the turn of the century fits the same pattern, paradoxically, of the earlier gothic response. If 1790s fiction met a perceived economic threat to the "necessaries" of life (Adam Smith's definition) with gothic protest, the new fiction of the next decades continued the focus on women and money, but with an altered code that supplied an answer to the economic crises of 1790s fiction through an aggressive new image for woman's economic role, this one employing the tropes of the domestic budget. As a matron in Margaret Cullen's *Home*, published in 1802, says firmly, "My expenses are regulated by my judgment, with very little regard to appearances," adding pointedly: "An important part of my economy is the paying ready money for every thing I purchase" (II,

29–30). Nancy Armstrong's powerful study, *Desire and Domestic Fiction*, brings this economic program of women's fiction into focus as a conscious political act.[34]

Unfortunately for today's reader of fiction written in the period between 1790 and 1820, prices and incomes as they are experienced variously, that is across the span of society's middle ranks, present an impenetrable puzzle. Without a guide, the cries of distress from middle-class fiction, and also from letters, diaries, guides to domestic economy, cookbooks, and newspapers, are lost. As a means of negotiating the uncharted distances between the world of contemporary reader experience and the coded world of the heroine, the first chapter of this study offers a "competence scale."

A "competence" is that amount of money that it takes to live "genteelly," a negotiable sum of course, but well enough established in the contemporary mind to be instantly recognizable. Readers could calculate in the wink of an eye what a given competence could buy in those specific comforts appropriate, "necessary," to a particular station in life. The competence scale, universally understood, settles even the most outrageous plots into a translatable, recognizable social perspective.

The decade of the 1790s, the subject of the first chapter, produced the most extravagant fiction of the period. The gothic tropes of the circulating library novels remain painfully attached to their writers' lives. Whether with romance, politics, or the patriarchy, the bottom line in novel after novel, story after story, rests in the amount of spendable income in the heroine's pocket at any given moment of her history. Credit, of the "petty" shopkeeping kind, haunts this fiction with no convincing knight in shining armor anywhere on the horizon. Authors may provide last chapters in which well-bred young men with landed estates and sensitive feelings appear to spirit the heroine away from her crumbling castle, but the next novel with the same birds of prey immediately takes its place on the tables of the circulating library. The terrors of a threatening economy are not to be dispelled so easily.

Chapter 3 shows how fictions of active economic engagement displace the 1790s fictions of loss. Duties of domestic spending grant the heroines of the new decade the keys to the kingdom. Maria Edgeworth's "The Purple Jar," for example, drives away the gothic shadows of consumption with the clear light of "use." Hannah More and Susan Ferrier reorganize nature itself: no more terrifying precipices and destroying gales, but neatly tended borders, paths swept clean by village boys, apple trees in the village gardens, woodbine and honeysuckle over the cottage door. Edgeworth, More, and Ferrier, in this respect, however, speak mainly to one part of the women's reading public, the genteel portion. Mary Meeke, Sarah Green, and Rachel Hunter, all Minerva novelists, turn their backs on the genteel economic resolutions of Edgeworth, Ferrier, and More for a vision that celebrates their urban heroines' origins in the ranks of commerce.

Jane Austen's place in this larger conversation of women thus becomes part of a general pattern, explored in chapter 4. Austen's social station as the unmarried daughter of a moderately well-beneficed clergyman living in the country puts her right in the center of a social group with particularly sensitive relations to consumption. David Spring calls it the "pseudo-gentry," a group living in the country – clergymen, upper professionals, officers in the army and navy, retired *rentiers*, great merchants – with social or kinship connections to the landed classes, and, most significantly, with strong aspirations to the style of life enjoyed by the latter, including, let it be noted, aspirations to a considerable share of their power.[35] Keenly aware of consumption's ability to convey social meaning, and, most important, to convey power itself, Jane Austen seems to us the most modern of her contemporaries. Recognizing the difference between her own station and the landed gentry, she deliberately takes possession of the meaning of positional goods for her own purposes. Every social rank in Austen's novels lays claims to material goods, but their rightful ownership is regularly submitted to the standard of Austen's pseudo-gentry values. The clarity of this mission never dims in Austen's works, from the earliest of her juvenilia to the last words of *Sanditon*. In this respect, Austen's position in fiction is no different from that of William Lane's Minerva authors. The significant difference is that in Austen's novels the first blessings of material culture go to her own rank.

Women's magazine fiction occupies chapter 5, as fiction and consumer desire meet in fateful embrace. The practice in the magazines of illustrating fiction with engraved illustrations brings the economic fears of contemporary women into a startlingly modern focus. Without illustrations, the magazines' tales are remarkably spare, even brutal, about the economic anxieties of middle-class women. But with an alluring plate attached to a tale, the tale and illustration combine to unite economic anxiety to the glamour of material goods. The illustrated tales of the magazines bring the reader an "image," in the modern advertiser's sense, an object on which to focus the spirit of desire. By coupling illustration to fiction, the early women's magazines eschew *life* to discover *lifestyle*.

The subject most briskly handed back and forth across the circulating library counter, however, is the highly troublesome one discussed in the penultimate chapter of this study, that of women's employment. In truth, fiction provided women with their only substantial public forum for canvassing the potential of employment – miserable working conditions, low pay, intolerable hours, and certain loss of station. Women's fiction confronts the unhappy prospects of employment with a Bakhtinian cacophony of voices: genteel fiction rejecting employment completely, didactic fiction embracing it with the fervor of the Christian martyrs, and Minerva fiction taking it on with stoicism and cold fury. This public discussion takes its winding course through universal agreement on employment's misery, but through contention and major partings of the way on the possibility of its success.

Authorship itself as employment, discussed in chapter 7, strikes closest to home. Novelists are reluctant indeed to introduce women as authors into their fictions. Patriarchal restrictions, urgent financial need, grave economic risk, and real personal danger – debtors' prison and the rest – make it the sorest and rarest of topics. The measure of women's experience in the writing profession emerges far more clearly in their letters, diaries, and, disastrously, in the records of the Royal Literary Fund than in their works. In fiction there is the very occasional example of the suffering woman author: Charlotte Smith, a highly respected author of the genteel camp, provides a much-harassed woman author in one of her novels; Amelia Beauclerc, from the Minerva end of the profession, presents a middling-rank novelist in one of her works, and Lady Morgan exhibits an aristocratic author in one of her Irish novels. Smith's unchecked rage at the conditions of the profession, her sense of personal and class betrayal, provoke a freedom of expression in print that makes both Lady Morgan's and Amelia Beauclerc's anxious concerns about the social respectability of writing seem at first glance little more than ladylike distress. In fact, Beauclerc's and Lady Morgan's fictional authors, like Smith's, must also calculate bread for their tables, but each heroine makes different calculations to match those "neces-

saries" that are specifically attached to her author's social pretensions.

In all, women's fiction of the late eighteenth and early nineteenth
centuries negotiates an unsteady balance between rank and gender as
it confronts the economy. That dilemma is the thread that runs
unsevered through countless four- and five-volume novels; it marks
the wandering trail that guides heroines through every crisis and
readers through the most convoluted of plots. W. H. Auden's well-
known verses about Jane Austen could serve for a generation of
women writers:

> It makes me most uncomfortable to see
> An English spinster of the middle class
> Describe the amorous effect of "brass",
> Reveal so frankly and with such sobriety
> The economic basis of society.[36]

Auden describes a generation of women novelists. When contemporary authors turn from sentimental convention to economic
injustice, to the fecklessness of men, to the vulgarity of the parvenu,
and to the courage of the single woman alone and struggling in a
hostile economy, their novels grow incandescent. Even if the heroine
herself remains frozen in sentimental convention, there is the odd
matron on the sidelines of life who holds a story in her breast with the
power to bring absolute economic clarity to the novel. Clichés and
formulas dissolve, the mists clear, and a discourse of women's
literature emerges that, 200 years after the fact, still retains enough
heat to ignite passion. Even Q. D. Leavis, who had nothing but
contempt for popular fiction, confessed that fiction in Austen's time,
even though "the circulating library conventions are in full possession
yet there is still something alive in the body of the book."[37]

This study attempts to resurrect the presence of that "something
alive" that Leavis felt, something I felt too as a child listening to
"The Purple Jar." That story continues to pack a punch because we
too live in a consumer world, much altered by mass consumption of
course, but little different in its joining of human passion to consumer
signs. The finer lines of rank and gender give women's fiction,
1790–1820, an identity that makes for a defining difference, but all
the more interesting for that. The period also marks a privileged
moment in publishing history for women – traditional practices and
new ones not yet separated – an opportunity for women to talk

among themselves and to weigh women's problems in a market economy. These writers felt their times to be touched by chance, promise, and palpable danger for women. In retrospect, it appears that they were absolutely right. Their fiction grapples with this reality in every sentence.

CHAPTER I

The general calamity: the want of money

Cecilia – Broke? – O Heaven, I am ruined! *Mrs. Sapient* – I, too, am greatly terrified! I know not but what I may be myself concerned in this transaction; & really the thought of losing one's money is extremely serious, for, as far as *I* have seen of the World, there's no living without it.

Frances Burney, "The Witlings" (1779)

Indeed, there is no living without money, as Frances Burney's Mrs. Sapient says, but for women jealously guarding their lady status, there is hardly any living with it either.[1] "All money transactions have some portion of distaste to me," confessed Burney.[2] Mary Wollstonecraft also remembered that the only time she had ever seen her perennially unhappy sister Everina in real "anguish," "had been on account of money or bodily fatigue."[3] Lady Diana Beauclerk, who fell on hard times in her later years, concluded ruefully, "I know nothing (nor ever did) about Money!"[4] Years later, when Burney as Madame D'Arblay, wife, mother, and respectable lady of letters, prepared her journals for publication, she painstakingly expunged passages that dealt with that one sore subject, money.[5] Before it gentility quakes: "The benevolent delicacy of Mrs. Harley was always uniform," writes Anna Maria Bennett in *The Beggar Girl* (1797): "She had tenaciously avoided all pecuniary subjects" (II, 127). The subject, nevertheless, raised its ugly head.

Economic inflation forced the issue. "Everything daily encreases in price in England," the novelist Charlotte Smith wrote a friend in 1794, "& I do believe there is no Country in the World, where one pays so much for accommodations so inferior."[6] Madame D'Arblay, trying to stretch her own small income, was just as anxious: "What the occasion of such universal dearth can be we can form no notion, & have no information," she told her father; "the price of *Bread* we can conceive from the bad Harvest, – but Meat – Butter – & *shoes*! –

The Brothers.

Plate 1. Mrs. Henry Ashton is evicted from her home.
From *The Lady's Magazine* (July 1795).

nay, all sort of nourriture or cloathing, seem to rise in the same proportion, & without any adequate cause."[7] People like the anonymous author of *Edward and Harriet; or The Happy Recovery* (1788) looked about and found distressing proof of "the general calamity, the want of money" (I, 114).[8]

Women found themselves vulnerable as economic beings, as authors now regularly noted in their novels that featured heroines with specifically economic lives: heroines barred from the possession of land (the period's single most important source of capital), or heroines with fixed incomes, usually in trusts, annuities, and stocks.[9] With no inheritance rights to land, for example, the Bennet women in *Pride and Prejudice* are destined at the death of Mr. Bennet to lose the Longbourn estate to Mr. Collins, the nearest male heir, and become dependent on the meager income to be derived from the interest on the £5,000 from their mother's "marriage articles." Even if a woman possessed a fortune in stocks, and in her own name as well, control of it would not be in her hands, but placed in the custody of male trustees. If her trustees were vigilant, honest, and active, her fortune would be given over to safe investments – trusts, annuities, rents, consols – which would pay her only a fixed, regular income, subject of course to the inroads of inflation. If the trustees were dishonest, or if they simply refused to act, a woman could be left with no recourse at all. Burney's heroine in *Cecilia* (1782) suffers all the problems of a stock-owning heiress. In real life, Charlotte Smith experienced major obstructions from her trustees: "Such has been the conduct of the Trustees," Smith complained bitterly in a letter describing her economic position, "that they have now robbed me of everything."[10] In Austen's *Persuasion* (1818), Anne Elliot's friend Mrs. Smith falls victim to the indolence of Mr. Elliot, the executor of her late husband's will, who refuses to pursue her rights to an income from her West Indian property. "Anne felt at some moments," writes Austen, "that no flagrant open crime could have been worse" (p. 210).

Married or unmarried, women were economically at risk.[11] In 1813, Jane Austen's near neighbors, the Harwoods, suffered an appalling fate, one that sixty years later Austen's niece Caroline still remembered in specific detail: "Old Mr. Harwood," she wrote in her memoirs, "had contracted debts, quite unsuspected by his family. He had borrowed and mortgaged so freely, that it seemed as if the estate itself could scarcely pay its own liabilities. There was nothing for his widow, and his sister's small portion had been left in

his hands, and had gone with the rest of the money, so that both ladies
were dependent on the heir."[12] Margaret Cullen succinctly sums up
the dilemma in her novel *Home* (1802): "Till women have the place
and weight which property confers, in vain may they appeal to
Justice" (IV, 218–19).

Women from the professional ranks and women from the ranks of
trade found themselves bound together in a particular economic
peril. Upon the family breadwinner's death, a catastrophic loss of
income inevitably faced female survivors.[13] Clara Reeve lists the
potential victims in her *Plans of Education* (1792): "the daughters of
indigent clergymen, of officers in the army and navy, of placemen of
all kinds, and, in short, of all whose incomes depend on their lives,
and who generally leave their children unprovided for" (pp. 138–39).
Appeals for rescue appeared every week in the advertisements of the
Bath Chronicle:

A Distressed Gentlewoman, The Wife of an Officer in his Majesty's Service,
having been left by her Husband with Six CHILDREN, for some time past in
a situation greatly to be pitied. (16 March 1800)

Mrs. Paul, the widow of the late Mr. Peter Paul, Treasurer of the Bath
Theatre ... once in possession of a competent, if not affluent fortune – but
the losses and chances attendant on a commercial life reduced an ample
fortune to a bare and scanty subsistence. (3 April 1800)

The Daughter of a Clergyman deceased, and the Widow of a respectable
member of society ... in consequence of her late husband's illness having
continued two years and a half, she was reduced to the necessity of parting
with every article of wearing apparel, to discharge debts incurred for
common necessaries. (17 April 1800)

To women it looked as if society was prepared to turn its back on
them without so much as a hesitating qualm. "Brothers generally
look on sisters as incumbrances [*sic*] on families," writes Reeve;
"more remote relations seldom trouble themselves about them:
without fortunes, without friends, how can they sustain – 'Th'
oppressor's wrong, the proud man's contumely'" (*Plans*, p. 122). A
beleaguered widow in Sarah Green's novel *The Fugitive, or Family
Incidents* (1814) finds herself overcharged for her late husband's burial
place and then dunned by the officiating clergyman for extra fees,
"some pounds," for the inconvenience of reading the burial service
at "twelve o'clock at noon" (I, 69–70). As a final outrage, she is
refused so much as a shilling of help by her own well-to-do father: "I

recollect, as I crossed a stile near one of his meadows, on Saturday, he had the cruelty to say, instead of assisting me, 'Ah! get over, Mrs. Southby, as well as you can, it may, perhaps not be the last difficulty you may have to go through'" (1, 129).

Inflation is the first topic of the day in an essay, "The Domestic Economy," in the *Universal Magazine* of March 1793: "If nothing happens in his own family to cause a demand for extraordinary expences," writes the author, the family provider "will reflect, that if *his* affairs are stationary, those of the world around him are in fluctuation, and that demands may be made from external circumstances, equally important with those included in his plan, but which he cannot honourably or conscientiously refuse." In 1800, Lady Diana Beauclerk wrote her daughter Mary, Countess Jenison of Walworth, who was then in Wertburg: "So you think living is cheap in England! alas! everybody except the enormous Estates like my Bro^r M.,Duke of Bed. &c. are ruin'd. My income will not pay half the small establishment of my family (even upon Paper), every article is raised to three times what it was when you were last in England, and our Great men (as you call them) don't care a straw about it!"[14]

Cries of increased prices in very much the same language had been heard earlier, in the 1760s, as well. John Sekora cites a "flood of sermons, pamphlets, and books" bemoaning "luxury" and the rise of prices.[15] Catharine Macaulay, in her *Address to the People of England … on the Present Important Crisis of Affairs* of 1775, adds her voice to the debate, decrying a declining economy, rising prices, and an oppressive burden of taxes. But Macaulay's *Address* belongs to the argument about "luxury" that Sekora analyzes in his study. It looks past women and their particular economic liabilities to join company with Mandeville, Swift, Shaftesbury, Hume, Smollett, and Adam Smith in a national discourse on "luxury."

The cause of contemporary anxiety in the 1790s is confirmed by present-day economic historians as a specific and truly extraordinary experience with inflation. Deane and Cole suggest that prices at the end of the century must have averaged "more than a third above those of the first decade of the century" and that at the peak of the Napoleonic Wars, "prices may have been double what they had been fifty years earlier."[16] John Burnett estimates that prices rose "from 50 to 100 percent between the middle of the century and the early 1790s."[17] Burnett supplies two different indices of commodity prices that contain figures that can hardly be read, even in today's inflation, without genuine dismay. One of them, an index compiled by E. H. Phelps Brown and Sheila V. Hopkins, establishes a base figure of 100 derived from the years 1451 to 1475; it reports a figure of 643 for the year 1760, an increase to 871 by 1790, and an astonishing increase in the year 1813 to a figure of 1881.[18] Burnett's other citation, "Indices of British Commodity Prices, 1790–1850," uses wholesale and import prices, but weights them to take into account retail consumer prices. The calculations are figured on a scale of 100 set at the monthly average of the years 1821 to 1825. In 1790, the figure stands at 89, but from this year onwards climbs sharply from year to year to peak in 1813 at a staggering figure of 168.9, almost double that of 1790.[19] As a character in a *Universal Magazine* tale of October 1795, exclaims, "The mutability of human affairs may convince us, that he who is born to riches is not always secure of their possession."[20] With another bad harvest in 1794, the price of grain soared – "the necessaries of life are not to be had at any price such as Butter, Milk, &c. &c," complained Charlotte Smith in a letter of that year.[21]

The tropes of melodrama supply a common language for novels and personal correspondence, as taxes to support the war are added to the burden. An agitated homeowner in Mary Ann Hanway's novel *Falconbridge Abbey* (1809) complains bitterly: "There are imposts that cannot be evaded by the man of small fortune, that deprive him of every decent, every accustomed comfort ... Does he not pay a tax on every article of food and raiment worn by himself or family; for the hut that covers them, the earth upon which they travel" – and, in an outraged reference to the window tax, "even for the first gift of the Almighty to his creatures? – who said – 'Let there be light, and there was light'" (I, 71–73). In real life, the same window tax, along with the new income tax, draws a like cry of anguish from Madame D'Arblay: "The new threefold assessment of taxes has terrified us rather seriously," she writes in 1797, adding that she and the General, "have this very Morning, decided upon parting with 4 of our new windows."[22]

On the other hand, there did seem to be money around – for others. Anyone who had capital to spend, however small the amount, could do well. "Great fortunes have been made from very small beginnings," observes John Trusler, a contemporary domestic economist, in *The Master's Last Best Gift, to His Apprentice* (1812): "I overheard two gentlemen conversing at Brighthelmstone. One said to the other, 'Do you remember our going up to London together, on the coach-top, about forty years ago? I believe I was the richest of the two, for I had half-a-crown in my pocket when I got there, and can now put my hand upon 100,000*l.*' 'Yes,' returned the other, 'I remember it well, but I am the richer now, for I can command 150,000*l.*'" "These men," Trusler concludes with impressive solemnity, "were grocers" (pp. 34–35).[23]

Sekora's traditional concept of "luxury" seemed oddly irrelevant.[24] The "children of farmers, artificers, all come into the world as gentry," Clara Reeve complains in *Plans of Education*: "They send them to the same schools with the first gentry in the county, and they fancy themselves their equal" (p. 61). "When the cost of a gown excels the countess's which it resembles in shape," Jane West writes in *Letters to a Young Lady* (1806), "the wearer feels an immense satisfaction, no matter though her dress be but a publication of her vulgar manners; elegance is, in her opinion, a saleable commodity; she has the draper's bill in her pocket... and she knows that she is better dressed than her ladyship by fifteen shillings a yard" (I, 148–49). Mrs. Elton's lace and pearls join a vigorous literary tradition.

But the possession of capital, as everyone recognized, was the key to the kingdom, and every rank yearned for its share with equal avidity. The young beginning tradesman, cautions John Trusler, should not be "in haste to be married, but wait his opportunity, a wife with money may as readily be obtained as one without, and be a young trader's fortune what it *may*, a little addition cannot but be desirous." A thousand pounds would be a highly satisfactory portion from the woman in question, Trusler advises, naming sums, "if the man have an equal sum of his own."[25] The aristocracy is no more delicate. Lord Sefton, in 1791, instructs his heir, Lord Molyneux, "not to look at less than 60,000... *Many* a great and rich banker would be glad of the offer to give his daughter that fortune for her advancement and dignity... or many a rich heiress to a large estate and of good family would also be glad of the offer."[26] Jane Austen hits the economic target dead center with Elizabeth Bennet's joking retort to Colonel Fitzwilliam's complaint of poverty in *Pride and Prejudice*: "And pray, what is the usual price of an Earl's younger son? Unless the elder brother is very sickly, I suppose you would not ask above fifty thousand pounds" (p. 184).[27]

The unstated joke, of course, is that Elizabeth cannot afford him. Women, as Austen well knew, were at a distinct disadvantage in the sweepstakes. As for the more pressing problem of inflation, Mary Berry, two decades after the worst of it seemed past, remembered the plight of the fixed annuitant with pity: "All those living on annuities or fixed salaries who had everything to purchase and nothing to sell, were, every succeeding year, deprived of some accustomed comfort. Instances of economy, unknown before in the classes adopting them, were professed and boasted of."[28]

John Trusler, writing in the midst of the turmoil in 1796, reported first hand: "The articles of living are ... increased in their price, so much so, that a man cannot live so well for 500*l.* a year, as he could then [three years ago] for 400*l.*"[29]

Both fiction and accounts from real life make much the same claim. The spectre of inflation called out for explanation. "We are *reducing* our expences, & way of life, in order to go on, in a manner you would laugh to see – though almost cry to hear!" Frances Burney writes her sister in 1798.[30] In fiction, Anna Maria Bennett pauses in the midst of her novel *Ellen, Countess of Castle Howell* (1794) to explain the phenomenon to her readers: "The family lived precisely in the same style, from generation to generation; the same number of domestics, the same mode of living, and the same rental from their farms; and having neglected to raise their tenants, equivalent to the advance of every necessary of life, these had grown into opulence, as their generous landlord had, insensibly, become involved in difficulties" (I, 9–10). Women's novels embraced the topic with the unflagging interest of survival.

The blessed competence

The amount of money that it takes to ride the social escalator becomes the central focus of economic concern in women's fiction. A competence is that amount of money, a kindly gentleman tells the heroine of Mary Ann Hanway's *Ellinor; or, The World As It Is* (1798), that "will enable you to live independant of your own exertions" (II, 320). A competence, writes Jane West in *The Gossip's Story* (1797), is "amongst the prime ingredients in the cup of human happiness" (II, 39–40). "O enviable state of retired competence," cries the heroine of *Modern Novel Writing* (1796), William Beckford's clever parody of women's fiction (I, 2). As Harriet Lee warns ominously in her novel *The Errors of Innocence* (1786), "Without an acquired or hereditary competence, man is subject by turns to insults and misfortunes, for which there is no alleviation but the merit of supporting them" (v, 167).

The competence sets the bottom line of gentility, increasing and decreasing with the pretensions of its possessor to rank and status. "What is competency to one, is not so to another," John Trusler warns.[31] Just how movable a feast it can be Austen demonstrates in *Sense and Sensibility*, when she has Marianne and Elinor Dashwood share their estimates of just what each sister thinks an adequate competence might be. Marianne names an annual income of "about eighteen hundred or two thousand a-year; not more than *that*," as her ideal. "*Two* thousand a-year!" replies Elinor, "*One* is my wealth!" (p. 91). Out of the scale of competences, Marianne chooses an income exactly appropriate to the minor gentry; Elinor selects an income just as specifically appropriate to David Spring's "pseudo-gentry," the income of a prosperous Anglican clergyman.[32] By the conclusion of the novel, each woman finds her desired competence – and station. But in that novel and in all her others, Austen alludes to a much wider scale of possible competences.

In contemporary women's fiction, the competence ledgers are kept meticulously neat, clean, and balanced. No matter what the scenery or the philosophy, the main plot or the subplots, the sound of adding and subtraction makes its way to the surface, the clinking and clanking of arithmetic as each sum finds its way into the projected competence that fate bears in its womb for the deserving heroine. "Every girl ought to possess a competent knowledge of arithmetic," advises Jane West: "It is also desirable that this knowledge be practical as well as theoretical; that she should understand the value of commodities, be able to calculate expenses, and to tell what a specific income should afford."[33]

Any lump sum is automatically calculated by the contemporary novel-reader for its annual, spendable income. A simple formula suffices: the amount of a lump sum inheritance multiplied by 5 percent, the annual yield a heroine can expect from the investment of that sum in the 5 percent government funds.[34] An heiress with an inheritance of £10,000, as any reader would know, would possess an income of £500 a year. An heiress like Miss Grey in *Sense and Sensibility*, with £50,000 as an inheritance, has an income of £2,500 a year.

Today, the mystery for us lies in the unfamiliar consumer value of the late-eighteenth-century pound. What style of life can a woman with £500 a year expect to lead? What kind of expectations does an income of £2,500 a year bring? What are the horrors of £50 a year? Women's fiction takes on a specifically didactic function for its readers, especially for young women with only beginning notions of incomes, as it explores for women from novel to novel the implications of consumable yearly incomes.[35] The yearly income is an obsessive motif in women's fiction at the turn of the eighteenth century. Women novelists of all ranks and political opinions join hands to calculate and confirm the specific spending power of different annual incomes. *Sense and Sensibility* simply extends and amends a familiar financial plot shared across the whole span of contemporary women's fiction. Not to know it is to miss half the action.

£25 a year

The income of the laboring poor brings the genteel competence scale into social perspective. A common laborer, writes Anna Laetitia Barbauld in *Evenings at Home* (*c.* 1793–96), has only 7 shillings a week, to which "if you add somewhat extraordinary for harvest work, this will not make it amount to four half crowns [10 shillings] on an average the year round" – about £25 a year. "For this ten shillings per week," she claims, "he will maintain himself, his wife, and half a dozen children, in food, lodging, clothes, and fuel."[36] The relentless good cheer that Hannah More's Mrs. Jones, in "The Way to Plenty," a tale in More's *Cheap Repository Tracts Published during the Year 1795*, devotes to the diet afforded by such a laborer's income (she estimates 7 or 8 shillings a week) gives an idea of its privations:

I am certain ... that if a shilling or two of the seven or eight was laid out for a bit of coarse beef, a sheep's head, or any such thing, it would be well bestowed. I would throw a couple of pound of this into the pot, with two or three handfuls of grey peas, an onion, and a little pepper. Then I would throw in cabbage, or turnip, and carrot; or any garden stuff that was most plenty; let it stew two or three hours, and it will make a dish fit for his Majesty. The working man should have the meat; the children don't want it, the soup will be thick and substantial, and requires no bread.[37]

In comparison, an impoverished curate, with seemingly little more, is far better off. He has station of a sort, a house and garden, and at £40 a year (a budget of 15 shillings a week), almost twice as much cash for commodities as his struggling neighbors, the laboring poor.[38]

£20 to £40 a year

However, the humble curate, with £20 to £40 per annum, resides by common agreement on the lowest margins of gentility. In women's fiction his status is mythic, binding the virtues of Baucis and Philemon to the agonies of the Christian martyrs. Such impoverished curates and rectors find themselves impaled on the horns of a genteel dilemma, as Anne Plumptre explains in *The Rector's Son* (1798): "Placed in a situation in which they are expected to sustain the rank of gentlemen, they have scarcely the means of procuring even the common necessaries of life, much less of obtaining those superfluities which are considered as essential appendages to that of rank." Even more galling, she continues, "they are cut off by their profession, from numberless ways of amending their circumstances, which might be resorted to in a different situation" (1, 1). "At the time when our history commences," she begins, "the Rev. Mr. Meadows had been for more than twenty years rector of the parish of Llanwelly in Denbighshire, with a salary of only forty pounds a year." Mr. Meadows has a wife, six children, and another on the way: "And he did support them – hear it, O ye sons and daughters of affluence!" Plumptre exclaims: "He did actually support a wife and six children with only forty pounds a year." Her prose rises to righteous astonishment: "Nay, what was still more extraordinary, he even contrived to spare something out of his slender pittance, for the relief of his still poorer neighbours" (1, 3–4). Her heroic rector's retirement in the country makes his economic survival possible, but even with his views of the landscape, "sublimely picturesque," Plumptre admits, "what was beauty to a man who could just but live" (1, 5).

Goldsmith's nostalgic curate, "to all the country dear, / And passing rich with forty pounds a year," retreats even farther into the mythic past as keen-eyed women writers address the matter of the competence. Eliza Parsons reflects bitterly on the great discrepancies in ecclesiastical livings in *The Voluntary Exile* (1795): "Mr. Mead... was curate to a small parish in Lincolnshire, and performed the whole duty within eight miles round, for the noble salary of thirty-five pounds a year, whilst the rector received three hundred for doing nothing." "But," she adds, "such instances are too common, to admit of particular observation" (1, 19).

In comparison to the laboring poor, as noted, the curate is well off indeed, but in the women's novel the curate's comparative prosperity lies under the sway of Newton's law: the ground appears more threatening to those who are falling *towards* it than to those who are rising above it.

£50 a year

The next marginal competence, £50 a year, leaves the realm of mythology to enter the calculations of economists and novelists as well. A notice in *The Times* of 22 April 1791 asks whether it is "morally possible" at a time "when butcher's meat is 6*d.* and 7*d.* a pound, [with] coals, candles, sugar ... at equally extortionate prices," for "the most frugal man" among the "clerks in the offices" ("in receipt of 48 to 50 pounds a year") "with the utmost care and economy, to support himself, a wife and a child, or children, on an income of only 2*s.* 9*d.* a day?"

In fiction, the heroine of Mary Hays' *Emma Courtney* (1796) possesses an income of £50 a year, that is, the income from a legacy of £1,000 left her by her mother, now invested in the government funds at 5 percent yearly interest. This sum "must now enable you to make your way in the world," her adviser tells her, "for the scanty pittance, that the interest of your fortune will produce, is, I doubt, insufficient for your support" (I, 50). The heroine's response: "I felt my heart die within me ... What could the interest of my little fortune afford? It would neither enable me to live alone, nor even to board in a family of any respectability" (I, 54).

If this pitiable wail seems far removed from the world of Jane Austen, it must be remembered that £50 is precisely the annual income left to each of the Dashwood women in *Sense and Sensibility* by their great-uncle, "a thousand pounds a-piece." Elizabeth Bennet and her sisters are even worse off: "I am well aware," says Mr. Collins, "that one thousand pounds in the 4 per cents. [£40 a year] which will not be yours till after your mother's decease, is all that you may ever be entitled to" (p. 106). Moreover, a real-life figure of £50 per annum percolates to the surface when Austen's father dies in 1805, and it is reported that Austen's sister Cassandra has a £50 a year income derived from a £1,000 legacy that she had invested in the 5 percent funds. Austen herself had no personal income at all.[39]

"It would appear a very ungracious task to attempt to exhibit a lower scale," James Luckcock writes in his *Hints for Practical Economy* (1834). Such an income, certainly not much more than this basic £50 a year, supports Mrs. Smith, Anne Elliot's invalid and impoverished school chum in *Persuasion*, who is "unable even to afford herself the comfort of a servant" (pp. 152–53). A tract written earlier, in the much less expensive year of 1767, recites the bitter details of life for a single man consigned to live in London on £50 a year:

I have driven him to the dirtiest and meanest parts of town to seek for a cheap lodging; I have cloathed him in the plainest and coarsest manner; I have scarcely allowed him to be clean enough for the place of his stated appearance... and yet, with all this economy and penury the wretch, at the year's end, has no more than twelve shillings and ninepence to lay by for sickness and old age.[40]

The passage closely suggests Mrs. Smith's predicament in Bath: "a noisy parlour, and a dark bed-room behind"; her anxiety over medical expenses – "the absolute necessity of having a regular nurse, and finances at that moment particularly unfit to meet any extraordinary expense" (p. 154); a bad part of town – "Westgate-buildings must have been rather surprised by the appearance of a carriage drawn up near its pavement!" (pp. 157–58).

£100 a year
A hundred pounds a year brings only small relief to the gentle-minded. Frances Burney's sister, hearing that she was about to marry General D'Arblay, a penniless French emigré, on the £100 a year pension given her by the Queen, writes in considerable agitation: "– – But – but – but – – You do not wish yourself *richer* you say! – Ah my Fanny! – but that wd be essentially requisite in such a union – your single £100. per ann – his – Alas! his *NOTHING* – How wd it be possible for you to live?... if in short £100 a year cd procure the necessary comforts of existence – but that – that alas I doubt."[41] "It grieves me," her father wrote the General, "that I cannot help fore-seeing much future uncomfortableness, mortification, & privation, from the narrowness of circumstances, to persons deserving of a better fate, and who are likely to condemn themselves to a perpetual struggle with penury to the end of their days."[42] The Rev. Thomas Archer, with an income of £85 a year in 1802, wrote the Royal Literary Fund for assistance, because the distance between his cures obliged him to keep a horse, making that income insufficient for his family of a wife and five children. Ten years later in 1812, having increased his income, he wrote again, but still in need: "My income (after deducting the expense of keeping a horse and payment of taxes) amounts to very little more than One Hundred Pounds." The Fund sent him £10 to help out.[43]

A £100 per annum income, however, according to contemporary domestic economists, could, with care, support a servant. "A *Widow* or other *unmarried Lady*, may keep a *Young Maid Servant*, at a low salary; say from 5 to 10 Guineas a year," Samuel and Sarah Adams suggest in *The Complete Servant* (1825, p. 5). This fits Miss Bates' circumstances in *Emma*, even to the detail of her unmarried state, except that Miss Bates has her mother to support as well as herself. Their one servant, Patty, cleans, cooks, and answers the door. Any additional expense arrives as a shock: "Oh!" cries Miss Bates upon hearing that the chimney needs sweeping, "Patty do not come with your bad news to me" (p. 236). Mrs. Jennings in *Sense and Sensibility* foresees the same hard-pressed future for Edward and Lucy on Edward's meager £100 yearly income: "I must see what I can give them towards furnishing their house. Two maids and two men indeed! – as I talked of t'other day. – No, no, they must get a stout girl of all works. – Betty's sister would never do for them *now*" (pp. 276–77).

£200 a year

With £200 the tone of contemporary witnesses shifts from martyrdom and heroic self-denial to one of grudging admission among some authors that such a competence might just achieve gentility. Depending on the social aspirations, £200 may be either good or bad. An elderly benefactor in Hanway's *Ellinor* (1798) presents the heroine with a £200 annuity: "This with your modest expectations," he tells her, "will enable you to live independent of your own exertions" (II, 320).

The "expectations" are no doubt "modest," since, for example, a tyrannical husband in Elizabeth Bonhote's *Olivia* (1787) imprisons his wife in a remote house deep in the country, telling her, "I will allow you two hundred pounds a year, and which will enable you to keep up the gardens, where you may wander like your first parent and lament your fall" (I, 279). A gentleman in Eliza Parsons' novel *The Voluntary Exile* (1795), "found himself, on summing up his effects, to be in the receipts of less than two hundred a year ... He now saw himself reduced to live on a very narrow income, and his heart bled for the distress his wife now suffered, and what she had yet to endure, when all the dreadful consequences of his neglect and inattention came to her knowledge" (I, 137–39). Charlotte Smith confirms the "prison" of a £200 competence in *Ethelinde* (1789). The mother of the hero of the novel retires to economical Grasmere when she is "reduced to less than two hundred a year." She lives completely alone, sees no company, and has no friends. Even so she manages to fly the flag of genteel breeding on £200 a year: "The whole cottage, for it was still merely a cottage, had about it a look of neatness and comfort, which convinced Ethelinde it belonged not to a labourer" (1, 58–59).

£300 a year

For Austen, £300 a year is not appreciably more comfortable in the scale of genteel expectations. In *Sense and Sensibility*, £300 a year will make Edward Ferrars "comfortable as a bachelor," says Colonel Brandon, but "it cannot enable him to marry" (p. 284). "The Colonel is a ninny," exclaims Mrs. Jennings, who reckons that her relation Lucy, the niece of a provincial schoolmaster, will be pleased to marry on that sum. Lucy, however, rejects marriage with Edward and his £300 a year (£100 of his own and £200 from the Delaford living) by setting her cap for his younger brother Robert, who has £1,000 a year. Nor are Edward and Elinor, "neither of them quite enough in love to think that three hundred and fifty pounds a year would supply them with the comforts of life," writes Austen (p. 369). The hero of Eliza Parsons' *Voluntary Exile* (1795) in a noble gesture gives his large fortune to charity, saving back only £300 a year for himself, not too little for a single man, as Austen and Parsons would agree, but only "comfortable as a bachelor."

£400 a year

A sum of £400 a year moves the heroine considerably closer to the prime ingredient in the cup of human happiness. In Parsons' *The Castle of Wolfenbach* (1793), friends of Matilda, the heroine, decide to settle a competence on her: "Four hundred a year, English money, paid her quarterly," says her benefactor, "will enable her to live genteelly, should she ever wish to separate from us, and will be a handsome provision for pocket expenses, if she does us the favor of continuing under our protection."[44]

John Trusler in *The Economist* (1774) claims that precisely £370 16s. a year would be needed to support a household with two servants (p. 14).[45] In *Mansfield Park*, Fanny Price's mother has just this number of servants in her Portsmouth household – and just the income to go with them. The rapidly calculating contemporary reader would understand that Mrs. Price probably came to her marriage with £7,000, the same amount Austen reports that her sister Lady Bertram brought to Sir Thomas. Invested in the 5 percent government funds, £7,000 would return the Price family £350 a year. Mr. Price's income as a half-pay naval officer would bring them about £45 a year, a familiar bit of public information, which together with the £350 a year income of the marriage portion would boost the family income to the sum needed to support two servants. As Fanny notes, her Aunt Norris could have managed such an establishment more respectably than her slatternly mother (p. 390).[46]

£500 a year

Five hundred pounds a year brings a general sigh of relief: a three-servant income, two women and a boy, and an occasional gardener are the expected perquisites.[47] In Mrs. Gomersall's *Eleonora* (*c.* 1789), we find that this income provides a comfortable, if restricted life: "Her house was small, but furnished with elegant neatness, she kept no carriage and only two female servants" (1, 46). The Dashwood women in Austen's *Sense and Sensibility* move to a cottage in Devonshire on £500 a year with "two maids and a man" (p. 26). When Austen's parents retire to Bath on this income, they, too, envision employing two maids and a man.[48] Susan Ferrier reports that a friend "Anne Walker has been here straight from her brother Frank's, where she has been spending some days with a bride and bridegroom – Miss Cornell and Mr. Knatchbull; she says he is very handsome, and has 500 *l* a year, so for a poor *plainish* miss it is no bad match."[49]

In Mary Pilkington's *Obedience Rewarded* (1797), £500 even has an uplifting moral tone: "At a beautiful village in Hampshire," she enthuses, "resided Mrs. Lascelles, the widow of an officer in the guards; who, with the moderate fortune of five hundred a year, contrived to perform more acts of real benevolence than is usually practised by those who are possessed of as many thousands" (p. 1). In *Minor Morals*, Charlotte Smith's Mrs. Belmour, a woman living on a similar sum in a "pleasant but small house near London," explains her way of life to her niece: "'Of what value,' she would say, 'my dear Sophy, is the preference which is given by vulgar minds to outward appearance? ... Poverty, and the want of the comforts and conveniences of life are real evils; but it is no evil to be without superfluities and luxuries'" (pp. 7–10).[50]

Jane Austen is not so sanguine, however, about the comforts of £500 a year: "Altogether, they will have five hundred a-year among them," begins Mrs. John Dashwood in *Sense and Sensibility* as she enumerates the luxuries her four female in-laws' meager new income will bring them: "And what on earth can four women want for more than that? – They will live so cheap! Their housekeeping will be nothing at all. They will have no carriage, no horses, and hardly any servants; they will keep no company, and can have no expences of any kind! Only conceive how comfortable they will be!" (p. 12). Austen's brother Henry, in explaining his widowed mother's and his two sisters' finances to his brother Frank, produces an unexpected echo of Fanny Dashwood:

So you see My Dear F., that with her own assured property, & Cassandra's, both producing about £210 per ann., She will be in the receipt of a clear £450 per Ann. – She will be very comfortable, & as a smaller establishment will be as agreeable to them, as it cannot but be feasible, I really think that My Mother & Sisters will be to the full as rich as ever. They will not only suffer no personal deprivation, but will be able to pay occasional visits of health and pleasure to their friends.[51]

This was Austen's fate in the great lottery of life, a competence of a little less than £500 a year.

£800 to £1,000 a year

At this level of income, servants cease to be the indicator of income and the carriage becomes the crucial sign of consumer prosperity. John Trusler, in *The Economist*, suggests that £800 a year would allow a gentleman to keep a carriage (p. 10). Samuel and Sarah Adams, in *The Complete Servant*, recommend a carriage as a prudent purchase only for incomes between £1,000 and £1,500 per annum (p. 6). When rumor has it that Mr. Perry, the apothecary in Austen's *Emma*, is setting up a carriage, his income and his social pretensions become the focus of village interest. Mr. Weston, who has himself recently bought a small estate and set up his own carriage, is cautious in accepting the story: "just what will happen, I have no doubt, some time or other; only a little premature" (p. 345). Robert Ferrars in *Sense and Sensibility* buys a carriage on the strength of the £1,000 per annum his mother promises him; Mrs. Dashwood in the same novel sensibly relinquishes her carriage when her income falls to only £500 a year (p. 26).[52]

A thousand pounds a year attracts the disapproving monitors of consumer "excess." "You will find not only equipages, but a show of fashion and change in them," claims a tract, *Letters Concerning the Present State of England* (1772): "You will see improvements in the house – rich furniture – a regular table – company. You will find journeys of amusement, expeditions to the capital or some spaw [*sic*]," just the kinds of consumer expense to appeal to Lucy and Robert Ferrars, the recipients of this handsome income.[53]

£4,000 to £5,000 a year, and up

The splendors of a house in the country and the season in town function as the yardstick for incomes above £4,000 to £5,000 a year, but with some significant movement on the scale. G. E. Mingay's tables are especially useful in understanding the variability of yearly incomes among the genteel ranks in the eighteenth century: gentlemen, according to Mingay, possessed a yearly income between £300 and £1,000; the squires, between £1,000 and £3,000 a year; the wealthy gentry, between £3,000 and £5,000 a year; and the great landlords, £5,000 to £50,000 a year, with £10,000 as the average yearly income for this group.[54] Throughout the nineteenth century, the rule of thumb for undertaking the expenses of the London season was an income of £10,000 a year. To spend more, according to contemporary wisdom, a man "must go into horse-racing or illegitimate pleasures."[55] F. M. L. Thompson suggests, however, that at the end of the eighteenth century it might perhaps take only half that amount.[56] In Jane Austen's *Mansfield Park*, Sir Thomas Bertram and Lady Bertram go to town on £7,000 a year. The Rushworths take a house in town on £12,000 a year, and Mary Crawford assumes that her brother Henry will take a house in town, though not so fine, on his fortune of £4,000 a year when he is married. Fanny Price sees nothing but ruin for Edmund Bertram and Mary Crawford if Mary insists on a house in town on their potential income of £1,700 a year, £700 from Thornton Lacey and £1,000 from the interest on Mary's £20,000 fortune. In *Pride and Prejudice*, Darcy maintains establishments in town and country on £10,000 a year, but Bingley takes a house for himself and his sisters in town on half that, though of course he has only a leased establishment to maintain in the country. Sir Walter Elliot and his daughter Elizabeth go to town in *Persuasion* until they no longer can, their loss of the London season indicating the precise extent of their financial difficulties. The

John Dashwoods, by contrast, just at the beginning of their new consumer show in *Sense and Sensibility*, celebrate their rise to fortune by making the trip to town for the first time, Mrs. Ferrars, with her "noble spirit," John confesses, giving Fanny an extra £200 to help with unexpected expenses (pp. 114–15).

The economic vulnerability of female characters in women's fiction throws a baleful light indeed on the John Dashwoods' gloating new prosperity. For most middle-class readers and writers, an independent competence might as well be on the other side of the moon. "The power of gold," writes Mary Ann Hanway in *Falconbridge Abbey* (1809), "all-powerful gold, tempting metal, its influence is incalculable; for its possession, wives have been widowed, children have become fatherless, friends betrayed, and countries desolated!" (I, 19). No women writers of the 1790s seriously challenge Hanway's despairing assertion.

The drive to tell the unhappy story, to tell it again and again, characterizes women's fiction of the decade. The heroine of Charlotte Smith's *Celestina* (1791) finds herself sharing a coach bound for Scotland with an older woman, Mrs. Elphinstone, who like the heroine herself is fleeing an economically hostile England in search of a cheaper place to live. Mrs. Elphinstone introduces herself to the lovely stranger by offering to relate her own tale of woe:

She waited therefore a fit opportunity the second day of their journey to drop something of her family; and seeing that Celestina wished to know more, she said, smiling, – "It is something like the personages with whom we are presented in old romances, and who meet in forests and among rocks and recount their adventures; but do you know, my dear Miss De Mornay, that I feel very much disposed to enact such a personage, and though it is but a painful subject, to relate to you my past life?"

"And do you know, dear Madam," replied Celestina, "that no wandering lady in romance had ever more inclination to lose her own reflections in listening to the history of some friend who has by chance met her, lost in the thorny labyrinth of uneasy thoughts, than I have to listen to you."

"Well, then," rejoined Mrs. Elphinstone, "you shall hear all that has befallen me, "even from my girlish days." (II, 247–48)

And so the tale begins.

Plate 2. "Julia, or the Convent of St. Claire," from *The Warrior's Return,
And Other Poems* (1808), by Amelia Opie.

Yes... be a nun's vocation mine,
  So I my brother's bliss improve;
His be their wealth," sweet Julia cried,
  So I may boast my parent's love!

CHAPTER 2

Gothic economics: the 1790s

·

Alas! I have *no* certainties; sudden accidents, or sickness, might deprive me of all, and I may here perish from want. Yes, you have opened my eyes; I see I must go into this dreaded world, or perhaps die a miserable death.

Eliza Parsons, Lucy (1794)

The economic winds that blow through women's fiction in the 1790s, sometimes in raging gusts and sometimes with the softer waftings of summers gone, unite Jane Austen with lesser-known authors in an unsettling sisterhood of loss. Ideologies of rank and station retreat precipitately in the woman's novel before the terrors of the economy.[1] "Young, beautiful, indigent, and friendless," writes Charlotte Smith, speaking for a generation of genteel heroines in her novel *Ethelinde* (1789), "the world was to her only as a vast wilderness, where perils of many kinds awaited her" (v, 38).[2]

Anna Maria Bennett strikes the familiar note for Minerva Press readers in *The Beggar Girl* (1797):

From such a state of happy security, to be at her age at once sunk from affluence to poverty, without one natural friend, was enough to shake the strongest mind. (II, 127)

Charlotte Lennox, the much-praised senior novelist fêted by Samuel Johnson in her youth and admired by Jane Austen, swells the chorus of lamentation in her novel *Euphemia* (1790):

What a reverse, in the space of a few months! An orphan! your inheritance lost! married! and, in consequence doomed to waste your days in America! I cannot bear to think of it! (I, 5)

Jane Austen contributes her voice in *Sense and Sensibility*, published in 1811, but conceived in the late 1790s:

He had left the girl whose youth and innocence he had seduced, in a situation of the utmost distress, with no creditable home, no help, no friends, ignorant of his address! He had left her promising to return; he neither returned, nor wrote, nor relieved her. (p. 209)

Finally, Ann Radcliffe, the best known of the gothic writers, in the first sentence of *The Romance of the Forest* (1791),[3] captures the abiding anxiety of all women's fiction during the 1790s:

When once sordid interest seizes the heart, it freezes up the source of every warm and liberal feeling. (p. 1)

Gothic terror in women's fiction is unremittingly economic. Radcliffe's villain in *The Castles of Athlin and Dunbayne* (1789)[4] threatens the mother of the heroine with a ruin she can calculate in pounds sterling: "I come, madam ... to inform you, that you quit not this castle. The estates which you call yours, are mine; and think not that I shall neglect to prosecute my claim." "Whichever way she looked," Radcliffe observes, "destruction closed the view" (p. 151).[5] Emily St. Aubert, the heroine of Radcliffe's *The Mysteries of Udolpho* (1794), languishes in Montoni's castle until she receives an inheritance from her aunt. Then and only then, with her money tucked safely in her pocket, is she free to leave.[6] Ellena, the impoverished heroine of Radcliffe's *The Italian* (1797), is pursued by Schedoni, the murderous emissary of the hero's proud mother, solely because she is poor: "'Alas!' said she, 'I have no longer a home, a circle to smile welcomes upon me! I have no longer even one friend to support, to rescue me! I – a miserable wanderer on a distant shore!'"[7]

The past: it was better because, as Madame de Genlis explains in *Alphonso; or The Natural Son* (1809), "moderation existed in prosperity," and, she adds pointedly, "respect always attended misfortune" (III, 161). The present? Elizabeth Gooch in *The Wanderings of the Imagination* (1796) knows it too well: "Money, and its concomitant, *interest*, bear all before them" (I, 9–11).[8] The future? As heroines and their authors looked about, they could only conclude with a newly impoverished woman in Anna Maria Bennett's novel *Vicissitudes Abroad* (1806): "Mercy on me! I do believe the old one is let loose in this world" (V, 209–10).

Rising prices and shrinking incomes regularly send novelists to a happy mythic past to imagine an economy in which women could be secure. "In the good old times of our forefathers, the farms were

portioned out in small partitions, equal to the wants, and sufficient
for the decent comforts of life!" exclaims Mary Ann Hanway in
Falconbridge Abbey (1809). "No dreams of rackrents from a needy
master, disturbed their peaceful slumbers!" In this imagined world,
Everywoman sleeps undisturbed, untroubled by money, and assured
of her useful place in the economic scheme: "The daughters were a
cheerful, blooming, blushing race, that rose with the lark, and went
to rest with the lamb! They assisted their fathers in the hayfield, and
their mother in the dairy!" Pocket-money appears when it should:
"With a basket filled with the butter they had helped to churn, and
the chickens they had reared, they trotted upon Dobbin to the next
market town, and, with the money they procured, brought back, in
return, those articles of comfort, not to be procured from the village
shop" (I, 65–66).

As for the present, women writers of the 1790s look about their
rapaciously money-oriented society to find their worst nightmare
realized, that theirs was indeed a society in which a woman without
access to cash might have no place at all. "The golden age in all its
primitive simplicity is, alas! no where to be found but in the pastoral
eclogues of Pope and Gay," laments Hanway in *Andrew Stuart* (I,
181). When a character in Jane Timbury's *The Philanthropic Rambler*
(1790) learns that a worthy widowed gentlewoman of the neighborhood is about to be evicted from her lodgings because she is
unable to pay her last quarter's rent, he asks a neighbor lady, "Who
is her landlord, pray?" The indignant neighbor replies from her own
fear of displacement: "Why an upstart fellow, that lives just by; he
was a journeyman bricklayer but a few years ago, a relation dying
and leaving him a legacy, he bought a parcel of old houses and
patched them up" (pp. 88–90).

The specter of lessened expectations haunts women's fiction. No
woman is immune from the chances of a diminished life. "Many of
the servants in genteel families," writes Elizabeth Bonhote in *The
Parental Monitor* (1788), "have been reduced, perhaps, to their
humiliating situations by the imprudence of their parents, or by
many other unavoidable misfortunes, whose education may have
been as liberal as theirs whom a reverse of fortune has reduced them
to serve." "So uncertain is every thing on earth," she adds darkly,
"it may one day be our turn to submit" (II, 160–61). Mrs. Gomersall's
heroine in *Eleonora* (c. 1789) contemplates the miserable fate of her
once-proud stepmother: "Alas! poor woman! she little thought how

soon the haughtiness of her temper was to be subdued by the most humiliating stroke of fortune; for in something less than five years after this, my father became a bankrupt" (1, 7–9). "Ah! poor girl!" exclaims a character in the anonymous *Rosemary Lodge; or Domestic Vicissitudes* (c. 1800), "Ladies, as well as gentlemen, are obliged to buffet with the storm" (p. 99).

The key to a woman's survival is the possession of a spendable income. Clara Reeve provides a traditional listing of the ranks of society in her *Plans of Education* (1792), but her list defines the ranks, significantly, not only by their traditional placement, but by the order of their spendable incomes. Amongst the nobility, writes Reeve, there is both an *old* and a *new* nobility, "which," she adds, "the old families well understand." Second in line, she names "the old families of wealth and consequence ... whose families are older, and their fortunes superior to many of the nobility." Third, there are the *nouveau riche*, that spurious lot "who have acquired great wealth by any profession or calling, and whose wealth however gained, stands in lieu of birth, merit, and accomplishments." Fourth, and beneath the vulgarians, she finds the eminently respectable "inferior gentry, who can only count hundreds, where the above classes number thousands a year." In the inferior gentry, she insists, "every real blessing and comfort of life is to be found, and those who know how to enjoy them, and with virtue and moderation, are the wisest and happiest of mankind." Danger, however, lurks in even this blessed rank: consumerism, the smiling villain, lies in wait to prey on the unsuspecting middling way – "a canker-worm which too frequently destroys their fortunes and their happiness; a foolish ambition to imitate their superiors, in manners, in vanity, in expence." Fifth, she continues, there are "the men of genteel professions, law, physic, and divinity; to these may be added, those employed in the public offices under government, and the officers of the army and navy," her own class and Jane Austen's as well. "In this class," she comments, "I would also include all merchants of eminence." Below this group yawns the great divide that separates gentility and "trade." In that distinctly ungenteel group, her sixth in the ranking, she locates "retail traders, artificers, and mechanics; and the farmer who rents his lands, and is a more useful member of society," she emphasizes piously, "than any of the rest; – he likewise is the most respectable, as long as he keeps within his degree and calling" – that is, so long as he keeps to Reeve's notion of his proper consumer status: "When he steps over it," she warns, "he becomes ridiculous and contemptible in the eyes of his superiors, and lays a foundation of misery and ruin for himself."[9] Finally, in the large basket at the bottom, in her seventh group, she heaps "the lowest mechanics and artizens [*sic*], and the whole peasantry of the land": "the strength and sinews of the nation," she maintains, though with this caveat: "Every check should be laid upon their attempts to imitate the vanities and follies of the higher orders" (pp. 64–71).

However, as Patrick Colquhoun's tables for the "Distribution of the National Income" (1803) reveal, Reeve's closely defined structure has little to do with the economic world in which she lived. A radical change in accepted notions of luxury had taken place in the last quarter of the century.[10] In Colquhoun's tables, wives and daughters of tailors and shopkeepers, distinctly *not* genteel in Reeve's system, share the same income range of £150 a year with the conditionally genteel wives and daughters of lesser professionals, that is, the holders of minor civil offices, the lesser clergy, and the families of poorer officers in the army and navy. If the lowest income that could support a subscription to a circulating library hovers around £100 to £150 a year, as contemporary economists Trusler and Luckcock estimate, then the virus of consumer desire could be carried by novels into any household in the kingdom with that income or higher.[11] At higher incomes, from £300 to £800 a year, merchants, manufacturers, warehousemen, shipbuilders, shipowners, surveyors, and engineers rub elbows with traditionally genteel professionals – successful attorneys, holders of higher civil offices, and members of the higher clergy.

Where to place the heroine of a novel in Reeve's seven-fold universe of spendable incomes becomes a considerable point for women writers. Reeve, with due respect for the first and second orders (nobility and old families), and bitter contempt for the third (the *nouveau riche*), finds the center of her social universe in the fourth order, "the happiest of mankind," the inferior gentry. Jane Austen, distinctly different, negotiates her happy endings somewhere between Reeve's second order of "old families" (Darcy Fitzwilliam's station in *Pride and Prejudice*) and the fifth order, the place of her own family, in the genteel professions of the clergy and the navy (Catherine Morland's, Elinor Dashwood's, Fanny Price's, and Anne Elliot's fates). In turn, Charlotte Smith finds happy homes for her heroes and heroines on a scale that runs from the sentimentalized yeomanry of

Clara Reeve's sixth category to Reeve's "old families," with telling omissions along the way, especially among lawyers and the nobility. Jane Austen mocks this in *Northanger Abbey*, probably in reference to Smith's novels in particular, by refusing to give a history of Mrs. Thorpe, "in which the worthlessness of lords and attornies might be set forth, and conversations, which had passed twenty years before, be minutely repeated" (p. 34). In sharp contrast to the others, Rachel Hunter, a Minerva writer, locates her notion of a "happy mediocrity" exclusively in commerce, that is, among Reeve's prosperous "merchants of eminence," barely tolerating the gentry and any class above it.

The correspondences, however, that exist between the social orders of the novel and those of social reality hang by ideological threads far more complexly woven than any of those in Clara Reeve's scheme. In women's fiction, the heroine's final resting place, her heaven on earth, becomes a delicately spun web indeed, composed in part from the real world of spendable incomes, of shop windows and household budgets, but also from powerful ideologies of gender and station enshrined amongst the author's treasured notions of what *ought to be*.

Minerva gothic: Anna Maria Mackenzie, Elizabeth Bonhote, Anna Maria Bennett, and Eliza Parsons

The economy throws its fitful light into the dark castles and gloomy grottoes of the gothic novel. By the middle of the 1790s, the relationship between the heightened world of fiction and contemporary economic life had become an object of self-conscious parody. Anna Maria Mackenzie marks the moment in her introduction to *Mysteries Elucidated* (1795) where the heroine of a modern romance, she claims, "quietly consents to enter the same road, substituting *cross guardians* for *cruel dragons* – travelling chaises for *flying chariots*" (1, vi–vii).[12] Neither she nor Eliza Parsons, one of the most prolific writers for Lane's Minerva Press, considered that as a gothic writer she was out of the main tradition of women's fiction. Mackenzie claims sisterhood with Frances Burney in the "Introduction" to *Mysteries Elucidated*, as well as with Parsons and Anna Maria Bennett, both Minerva writers. Eliza Parsons asks for indulgence in the "Preface" to her novel *The History of Miss Meredith* (1790), for writing "after a BURNEY, a SMITH, a REEVE, a BENNET, and many other excellent female novelists," with whom she obviously considered herself fit and equal company.[13]

For these writers, contemporary economic life and gothic imagery seemed not an odd combination, but closely related indeed. Elizabeth Bonhote, another Minerva writer, looks about the neighborhood of her own home near the ruins of Bungay Castle to observe in the "Preface" to *Bungay Castle* (1796) that under the castle's broken walls "cottages are now built, and inhabited by many poor families, and those very walls, which perhaps sheltered royalty, are now the supporters of miserable hovels. Such are the awful effects of time," she concludes, "and the unaccountable revolutions it produces!" (I, xi–xii).[14] When the father of Rosaline, Bonhote's modern heroine, insists that Rosaline marry a rich, but unwelcome, suitor – her consent will be to the advantage of her brothers and her sister – he addresses her in the gothic mode: "Rosaline (cried he, striking his clenched fist on the table, and looking with the wildness of a maniac) ... What business can a girl of your age have to like or dislike but as your parents shall direct?" (I, 230). A gothic metaphor also falls ready to hand in Mary Ann Hanway's *Ellinor; or, the World as It Is* (1798) to describe the analogous predicament of contemporary women: "Restrained and trammelled by laws and customs, women are already slaves to man; no privilege is left for them, but that of choosing their own prison and jailor" (II, 130–31).

In Minerva gothic, it is the economy, as it is represented by unpredictable, feckless, improvident, destructive, and tyrannical males, that provides the active source of terror for women. Lucy Blandford in Bonhote's *Bungay Castle* meets the economy's destructive force in her suitor, Narford, who fritters away his fortune in expensive pleasures. Her parents forbid the marriage, with good reason, but Lucy's health wastes away in repining and she dies. At her graveside, the guilty Narford goes mad, throwing himself onto her coffin, protesting at the "unfairness" of his loss: "Avaunt, deceiver! (cried the enraged maniac.) – I tell you that Lucy was unfairly robbed of life, – stolen from my arms, and forced into this place, where I will watch by her and protect her from farther violence." Bonhote, with clearer vision, keeps the finger of blame firmly on Narford, where she insists it belongs: "– Go on, I say, – bury me deep and sure!" cries the guilty wretch, "I wish to become a worm, that I may crawl to the side of Lucy. – She will own her poor distracted Narford, even in that most loathsome and degraded form" (II, 26–27).

Bonhote's coffin-and-loss motif strikes a sympathetic chord in most women's fiction of the 1790s. Alicia, the penniless heroine of Agnes Musgrave's *The Solemn Injunction* (1798), interrupts the funeral of her father: "'Oh! give me way! I will not be held!' (and a young and beauteous maiden, in all the wild delirium of grief, sprung forward and leaped into the grave) 'ah! cover me, hide me, fatherless, motherless, friendless!' she exclaimed, as she sunk in a strong convulsive fit on the coffin." She is removed from the affecting scene by a handsome stranger and "by Mr. Hammond, the curate," who take her into "the parsonage, which was near at hand" (I, 2–3). The comfortable hearth of a prosperous, modern English parsonage contrasts bitterly with the gothic grave of the heroine's lost hopes. The heroine of Eliza Parsons' *The Mysterious Warning* (1796) joins the symbolic rush to the grave:[15] "'Yes, I *was* called Louisa Hautweitzer, but *now* I am *nobody*,'" cries Parsons' distraught heroine as she bends over her father's corpse. "'*There*,' putting her hand to her father's cheek, 'there is the author of *my being*, and *I* am a wretch without a name, a home, or a parent. Pray, pray, afford us one small spot of earth, bury us together!' She threw her head down on the face of the deceased, with sighs that seemed to burst her heart-strings." An old school chum arrives with her wealthy father just at the moment of the heroine's last passionate outburst: "Miss d'Allenberg took her hand, and addressing her father, 'My dear Sir, this young Lady is an old school-fellow of mine, good, amiable, and of genteel birth, save her, pray save her from despair and death'" (pp. 171–72).

Anna Maria Bennett, one of Lane's best-known authors, finds gothic terror in the heart of the modern city.[16] As a countrywoman exclaims of the heroine in Bennett's *The Beggar Girl and Her Benefactors* (1797), "Lord have mercy upon me, what will such a pretty creature do in Lunnon without money!" (IV, 23). Bennett answers the question explicitly in *Vicissitudes Abroad* (1806). In this novel, the heroine unsuspectingly marries a "professed gamester" who abandons her in London.[17] Alone and without money, she finds that she cannot pay for her cab: "The coachman now demanded his fare," she recalls, "but it was impossible to make me understand either that or the coarse allusions to 'shabby genteel,' 'scum of the earth.'" When a crowd gathers and she is taken for a prostitute, she goes mad and is delivered, finally, to a charity hospital, Bennett's apt image for women's predicament in the economy:

I fell into a deep sleep, in which I continued five hours, and awoke perfectly sensible, though weaker than a newborn infant ... It is impossible to conceive my astonishment, when I beheld the vulgar and pallid faces that occupied the various beds in a room to which I could see no end, and when, after trying in vain to discover one feature, or distinguish one sound of voice to which my heart was familiar, I found myself literally in a new world, among people as strange in manner as in face; and too weak to articulate, could only mentally ask myself, what I had done to deserve being condemned to a residence in such a place, among such companions. (I, 108)

Bennett has no answer. The final insult: the heroine's doctor offers to let her pay for her medical care by becoming his mistress.

Minerva writers, in sharp distinction from Austen and the genteel novelists, examine those economic threats that lie in wait for heroines drawn from the lower ranks of the middle class, from the families of merchants, tradesmen, and the lesser professions.[18] For Eliza Parsons, one of the most eloquent spokespersons for these ranks, the shared experiences of women rise directly from their common struggles with a hostile economy. She takes the opportunity in her last novel, *Murray House* (1804), to rebuke Radcliffe, her greater rival in gothic fiction, implicitly for what she perceives as Radcliffe's inadequate account of the miseries of women's economic isolation: "I find nothing in this castle, in these sublime and picturesque views," cries Parsons' suffering heroine, whose adulterous and spendthrift husband has sent her to live in a crumbling Scottish castle, "to compensate for the loss of society, the deprivation of liberty. – Prospects, however grand and beautiful, cease to interest when the novelty is over" (II, 263). Ann Radcliffe speaks to a readership with different experience altogether, as does Jane Austen. It is no coincidence that in *Northanger Abbey* where Radcliffe is praised by Henry Tilney, Austen's readers find two of Parsons' novels, *The Castle of Wolfenbach* (1793) and *The Mysterious Warning* (1796), on Isabella Thorpe's list of "horrid novels."

Eliza Parsons knew financial anxiety and poverty first hand. After the disastrous fire that destroyed her husband's turpentine warehouse, she applied for aid to the Royal Literary Fund: "I was compelled by dire necessity to become an Author," she wrote the trustees, "and in the course of 12 years have written 65 vols of Novels, under every disadvantage of Sickness, Indigence, never ceasing Anxiety and as many repeated misfortunes as human sufference could well support."[19] Parsons' dark vision of women's economic struggle runs the plots of all her novels. A sampling reveals the steadily deepening shadow in her own life. The plot of *The History of Miss Meredith* (1790), her first novel, circles around the cunning attempts of men to cheat women of their money, some attempts successful, some foiled by prudent legal arrangements. The heroine of the novel, at her father's insistence, marries a man who dissipates her entire fortune, "every shilling," claims Parsons, and even though he dies in remorse, "He thrust himself under the bed clothes, where he lay panting and groaning most shockingly" (II, 141), Parsons is clear about the bottom line: the money is lost forever (II, 141). In *The Castle of Wolfenbach* (1793),[20] Parsons' impoverished heroine arrives in England from abroad as "a poor dependent [*sic*], without friends or family" (p. 60). At first she finds much to admire, especially "the great encouragement given to all manufactories," but she is perplexed by the paradox of a bustling economy and the general poverty she sees around her: "there ought not to be any poor, that is, I mean beggars, in England ... If proper management was observed, none need complain of cold or hunger; yet in my life I never saw so many painful and disgusting objects as there are in the streets of London" (p. 52). The heroine of *Lucy* (1794), Parsons' next novel, is driven from her late parents' home by the new heir. She takes refuge with an impoverished elderly couple who have found their own miserable shelter in a deserted castle surrounded by "birds of prey." Echoes of Parsons' distressed letter to the Royal Literary Fund are heard clearly in her description of the old couple's terror: "They had suffered every calamity that could render life hateful, had out-lived every hope, and survived every thing that was dear to them; yet, when those tremendous storms gave the alarm to terror, frighted nature revolted at death in so horrid a form, and they cast their eyes around in vain to look for safety, for where could they fly to, without money, without friends, worn down by misfortune and misery, equally incapable of seeking or procuring another asylum, or their daily bread?" (I, 7–8).

Gothic terror is never far from economic anxiety in any of Parsons' novels, but in *The Voluntary Exile* (1795) where the novel's economic trials rise specifically from the embers of Parsons' own financial ruin, she makes the connection painfully autobiographical. The heroine's husband bursts into his wife's parlor unannounced: "'Oh! Eliza, my dear wife! all is over, we can suffer no more.—No!' exclaimed he, with a wildness in his manner, that terrified every one; 'no, where every hope is extinct, all is fixed despair.'" His warehouse, he tells the assembled group, has just burned to the ground and all is lost. Not only that, he has neglected to pay for the insurance that could have saved the family from utter catastrophe:

The whole was a heap of ruins, not one valuable was saved from the devouring flames; and what compleated the misfortune was, that no part of the property lost, had been insured ... He had even received notice from the office some months previous to this event, but unhappily it was at a time when his mind was occupied ... and he either forgot, or neglected to pay the insurance, consequently all was lost; he had no claims, no resources ... He now saw himself reduced to live on a very narrow income, and his heart bled for the distress his wife now suffered, and what she had yet to endure, when all the dreadful consequences of his neglect and inattention came to her knowledge. (I, 137–39)

The Voluntary Exile might well be called "Business Gothic." Its catastrophes are remorseless, violent, and always commercial. The frequent and predictable stories of financial disaster in the novel furnish a thematic highway that rolls remorselessly across the hills and dales of the perfunctory main plot. "Yes," begins one of the many sad inset stories in *The Voluntary Exile*, "a better woman never lived, nor one who has experienced more trouble ... Mr. Franklyn, Sir, was a very respectable merchant, his wife a gentlewoman, and esteemed by every one." The unfortunate Mrs. Franklyn's life thus unfolds in a series of calamities that bring her to her present wretched situation: her husband loses his business, the victim of dishonest partners; her son drowns on a commercial voyage to Holland; her husband falls "into a terrible melancholy, loss of rest and appetite, and soon followed his son to the grave," and the miserable, bereft Mrs. Franklyn lives to eke out an impoverished existence, as Parsons notes with specific detail, on an income of £150 a year (II, 176–77).

Parsons' economy is middle-class gothic in contemporary dress. Families plunge overnight from great wealth to utter poverty; brothers cheat sisters; a mother robs her son. When the heroine of *The Voluntary Exile* discovers that her widowed mother has run through their entire shared inheritance, "Never was astonishment equal to what poor Eliza felt; in one short twelvemonth – was it *possible* to have expended all their joint property? unable to speak, she grasped her mother's hand, and looked unutterable things." "I see your surprise," replies the unrepentant mother, "and I will be explicit.

The paltry income, and the trifling sums that accrued to me by the death of your father, were too insufficient to support me like a gentlewoman ... I could not give up those elegancies I had been so long accustomed to" (I, 68–69). The mother elopes with her youngest daughter's beau in the cavalier style of Jane Austen's *Lady Susan* (also a 1790s piece), but with more spectacular results: "Great God, never shall I forget the dreadful moment, the horrid sight!" remembers the girl's brother who witnesses his sister's consequent suicide: "That instant as we entered into the court, a window above burst open, and our unhappy sister precipitated herself from it, fell with violence on the pavement, and we were sprinkled with her blood and brains!" (II, 83).

In spite of Parsons' pious insistence in her last novel, *Murray House* (1804), that Anna Sydney, the heroine, must, as the whole duty of woman, obey the demands of her feckless father and her philandering husband, she draws a devastating picture of a male-controlled economy. Parsons' only recourse is to exact revenge on the men responsible through the most appalling physical tortures. When the mortally injured Sir John, Anna's husband, is told that his legs must be amputated (crushed in a coach accident with his mistress), Parsons reports with satisfaction, "The wretched sufferer groaned most dreadfully." In his last hours, "between paroxysms of pain which seemed greatly to encrease [*sic*]," he alters his will in Anna's favor, finally falling "into a gloomy reverie, only broken," she notes, "by groans and painful exclamations ... his eyes were turned to Heaven, his hands clasped, and his features distorted." "Violent convulsions" mark his end (III, 202–13). As for Anna's father, the old man who sets her disastrous marriage in motion through his gambling losses, he too suffers the torments of the damned. "'Oh! Anna!'" he cries out during his death agonies, "'A gamester *is* and *must be a villain*! – regardless of the misery he entails upon innocent families, the ruin of domestic happiness ... Here is the sting of death!' As my dear unhappy father uttered the last word, he fell into strong convulsive spasms" (I, 187).

The Minerva writers had the formula perfected. Any reader who picked up a Minerva novel knew before turning the first page just what a gothic castle meant and what sort of economic treacheries would be likely to lead the heroine into one. The journey to the castle might be varied by scenery and sentiment, but it was essentially the same sorry path through economic loss and exploitation in every novel. If Lane's Minerva novels gave their readers toy castles, they were toy castles with real locks.

The notion of "genteel poverty," the kind of deprivation that buttresses Bourdieu's theory of "the sacred sphere of culture" and supports Elinor Dashwood's spirits in *Sense and Sensibility*, has no place in Eliza Parsons' novels.[21] The prospect of missing the consumer feast demands from the Minerva heroine stoic courage of a high order indeed: "I always found pleasure in affluence, and consequently *do* regret the loss of our fortune," admits the heroine of Parsons' novel *The Miser and His Family* (1800). "I am no heroine," she continues, "but reason, and pride also, assist me to *bear* with fortitude, that I may not drive our few friends from us, nor pain my father by the melancholy of my looks." "You are *more than a heroine!*" returns Parsons' hero, "in an extacy [*sic*]" – "You are above *affecting* that stoicism of soul which soars beyond the love of riches, that pretends to regard poverty as no evil ... No, charming Emily, you acknowledge your feelings, but you nobly struggle against them to perform the duties of a daughter, and give a glorious example to your sex" (IV, 161). You, too, as the Minerva novel reminds its Gentle Reader, may pass this way.

Genteel gothic: Charlotte Smith and the banished woman

Like Eliza Parsons, Charlotte Smith writes with first-hand experience of straitened circumstances, of her own miserable struggle as the primary breadwinner of a large family. Unlike Parsons, she examines the burden as it falls on the shoulders of women of genteel station where there is an added and urgent task. The struggle to hold on to station despite economic vicissitude drives a series of ten Smith novels, each one inevitably featuring an impoverished and struggling, but adamantly genteel, heroine.

Contemporaries knew to expect nothing but gloom from Charlotte Smith, who made no attempt to hide the autobiographical nature of her work, turning her life into public property through a string of deeply personal novels that appeared almost yearly throughout the 1790s. In the "Preface" to *Desmond* (1792), she candidly admits "that the circumstances which have compelled me to write, have introduced me to those scenes of life, and those varieties of character which should otherwise never have been seen: Tho' alas! it is from thence, that I am too well enabled to describe from *immediate* observation, 'The proud man's contumely, th' oppressors wrong; / The laws delay, the insolence of office'" (I, iii–iv).

It was not to everyone's taste: "An indefatigable authoress, and very unfortunate woman, whose works," writes the reviewer for *La Belle Assemblée* (November 1806), "seem to partake of the gloomy colour of her destiny, and display a certain habitual discontent, which impairs her talents, and prevents their being sufficiently diversified." Nevertheless, Smith's power lies in her unflagging memory of private wrongs. A whiff of paranoia wafts up from the abyss as each social institution turns its malevolent influence against the heroine, and as each rank conspires to withhold its blessings from her. Smith's ten novels, her poems, her one play, even her children's stories, all burn with the anger of a woman "banished" from the rights and privileges of the society she claims as her own.

In the accents of one of her own heroines, she calls herself, "a wanderer upon Earth."[22] "When I fell from the situation of high affluence," she writes her confidante Sarah Farr Rose,

to that of being obliged to wander as I could, round the world & on 70£ a year and support eight children, I had advice given me by persons who had before fed me only with flattery, and I underwent insult & persecution from the proud & the profligate: the purse proud Tradesman and the rapacious Attorney ... all were like the birds of ill omen, that surround a dying animal, ready to pluck me limb from limb.[23]

Contemporary lawyers, she suggests in the *The Young Philosopher* (1798), supply a thoroughly satisfactory substitute for the conventional "giants, necromancers, and ogres of ancient romance": "Men whose profession empowers them to perpetrate, and whose inclination generally prompts them to the perpetration of wickedness" (II, vii). "Robespierre and his agents are not more destructive and more cruel than English lawyers" (IV, 741), claims a character in *Marchmont* (1796).

Charlotte Smith had reason to complain. Born to the expectations of a comfortable life among wealthy merchants and gentry, she was married at the age of fifteen, "sold," she called it, to the second son of a rich East India merchant (he was twenty-one) in order to clear the house for her widower father's new wife. Smith's husband, Benjamin Smith, was an unmitigated catastrophe: an uncaring father, a wife-beater, an adulterer, a wastrel, a spendthrift, and a gambler. Mr. Smith's own father, recognizing the sterling insignificance of his son's character, adjusted his will to leave his grandchildren inheritances independent of Benjamin's control. The will, however, proved deeply faulty, producing thirty years of litigation in which Benjamin took what he could for himself (all the interest whenever possible), leaving his children totally unprovided for, and his wife, Charlotte Smith, involved in a lifelong struggle to meet her and her children's expectations of genteel station. Her continual litigation over her father-in-law's will, along with severe and repeated bouts with rheumatism, and, of course, the unremitting pressure to write novels in order to support herself and the children, kept Smith in a state of day-to-day desperation.[24]

In her life and in her novels, Charlotte Smith confronts the near-insurmountable task of imagining a place for the genteel but poor heroine in a competitive economy, a dilemma that other gentry-oriented novelists of the 1790s, Burney, Edgeworth, and Austen, found equally troublesome. Smith's chain of novels – *Emmeline* (1788), *Ethelinde* (1789), *Celestina* (1791), *Desmond* (1792), *The Old Manor House* (1793), *The Wanderings of Warwick* (1794), *The Banished Man* (1794), *Montalbert* (1795), *Marchmont* (1796), and *The Young Philosopher* (1798) – exhibit repeatedly an unresolved mix of sentimental suffering and ruthless financial chicanery: a serial narrative of good folk whose hands are tied, and wicked folk whose hands should be. Virtuous characters make their passive way through her novels as an androgynous, melancholy class whose disaster-prone histories exist only to expose the malevolence of proud aristocrats, ambitious gentry, corrupt merchants, miserly bankers, dishonest lawyers, gouging priests, self-seeking physicians, and dunning tradesmen. These are the gothic vultures and harpies who take over the action of the novel and make the heroine's life a misery.

At the center of the storm stands the isolated woman, the heroine, or, more often in Smith's novels, an unhappy, married older woman, "banished" from society. The younger heroine is "banished" too, in the capacity of an orphan, but the older married woman is "banished" solely through her economic state as a legal nonentity.[25] Benjamin Smith could slip into England from Scotland, where he was in hiding from his creditors, collect the interest on his wife's estate, his rightful due by law, and extract what of her earnings he could get from her publishers (also legally his) – all with no hope of legal redress for his wife. The widowed heroine of Smith's stage comedy

What Is She? (1799) announces in settled despair that she is "going away." When asked where, she replies, "Alas! Sir, I can scarcely tell. If possible, where I shall be no longer liable to the persecution of men" (Act v).

Smith calculates sympathy in her novels in the coin of financial suffering, extending it in plenty to those older women of her novels, wanderers all, who experience only slightly altered versions of Smith's own personal trials: Mrs. Stafford in *Emmeline* (1788), Mrs. Montgomery in *Ethelinde* (1789), Mrs. Elphinstone in *Celestina* (1791), Mrs. Verney in *Desmond* (1792), Mrs. Denzil in *The Banished Man* (1794), and Mrs. Glenmorris in *The Young Philosopher* (1798).

These wanderers of the earth, its banished women, take over Charlotte Smith's imagination. Her well-known political sympathies, liberal, are set aside for female wanderers of whatever political persuasion.[26] In *The Young Philosopher* (1798), for example, she expresses admiration for the late Mary Wollstonecraft, but in her long poem *The Emigrants* (1793), she finds sympathy for the imprisoned Marie Antoinette: "Ah! who knows, / From sad experience, more than I to feel / For thy desponding spirit, as it sinks / Beneath procrastinated fears for those / More dear to thee than life! ... Whate'er thy errors were, / Be they no more remember'd ... More than enough / Thou hast endur'd" (pp. 49–50).

Plots for her novels often seem little more than a laborious necessity. As the speaking "Author" in *The Banished Man*, she announces, "it is time to resign the field of fiction before there remains for me only the gleanings, or before I am compelled by the caprice of fashion to go for materials for my novels ... to children's story books ... or a dismal tale of a haunted house, shewing how the inhabitants were forced to leave the same by reason of a bloody and barbarous murder committed there twenty years before." Characters tire her as well: "I have no pleasure in drawing figures which interest me no more than the allegoric figures of Spenser" (II, x–xii). Settings are of scarcely more interest: "Be not alarmed, gentle reader," she interrupts a description in *The Banished Man*, "though seven castles have been talked of in a preface, thou shalt not be compelled to enter on another at this late period of the story." She begs off writing yet another house description by suggesting that "the little printed book sold by the housekeeper, Mrs. Empson, will give a perfect idea of it all" (IV, 174–75).

What informs Charlotte Smith's novels with genuine power is her anger, her blazing fury at women's "exile," as she repeatedly calls it, from social and economic power, the two conditions of women's existence that are hardly separable in her mind. The feelings produced by this insight into women's economic reality overwhelm and sink Smith's plots. The narrative – the oppression of the hero and heroine, together with the interpolated tales of her long-suffering married women – moves forward on a wave of unresisted moral outrage. Rank by rank, society lines up against the welfare of unprovided women.

In her first novel, *Emmeline, The Orphan of the Castle* (1788), it is aristocrats and bankers who combine against the heroine.[27] The gloomy Lord Montreville exiles his niece Emmeline, his dead elder brother's daughter, illegitimate, or so it is handed out, to a neglected family property in the country. Thus banished, she receives infrequent and grudgingly meager gifts of cash for her support. When Montreville's passionate son Delamere falls in love with Emmeline – "He stamped about the room, [and] dashed his head against the wainscot" (p. 64) – Lord Montreville, in order to get Emmeline out of the picture, demands that she marry a miserly banker named Rochely: "In the inferior ranks of life, his money had procured him many conquests," writes Smith, "tho' he was by no means lavish of it; and much of the early part of his time had been passed in low amours; which did not, however, impede his progress to the great wealth he possessed" (p. 80).

When Emmeline objects, Lord Montreville terrorizes her with the ultimate Charlotte Smith threat: total loss of income. "If you absurdly refuse an offer so infinitely above your expectations," he says menacingly, "I shall consider myself as having more than done my duty in putting it in your way; and that your folly and imprudence dissolve all obligation on my part" (p. 123). Her wealthy female cousins taunt her with the same threat: "If you do not marry this rich city-man, what do you think is to become of you?" (pp. 133–34).[28] Emmeline refuses to *sell* "her person and her happiness for a subsistence," writes Smith, but only after striking a deal: a signed document in which (1) she promises Montreville that she will never marry Delamere *without his permission*, and (2) an agreement for permanent financial support from Montreville, the indispensable clause that addresses Smith's abiding attention to women's lack of money.

The marriage difficulty waits to be resolved by the death of the giddy Delamere, who falls in a duel, but not until after it is discovered that Emmeline is not the illegitimate daughter of the elder brother after all, but is the legal heiress to all the Mowbray fortune that the wicked Lord Montreville has dishonestly sequestered, knowing all the time that Emmeline was the legitimate daughter and heiress of his elder brother. Emmeline thus becomes a very desirable partner indeed for his son Delamere. Smith luxuriates in the exchange of economic power. Lord Westhaven, one of Emmeline's earliest protectors, can "hardly contain his indignation" as he reflects on the altered situation: "knowing that to her whom he [Lord Montreville] thus insulted with the distant offer of fifty or an hundred pounds, he really was accountable for the income of an estate of four thousand five hundred a year, for near nineteen years, and that he still withheld that estate from her" (p. 374). Lord Montreville is, moreover, most satisfyingly in debt to his former victim, his niece Emmeline, for at least £85,000 cash, not including the substantial interest on that sum, plus an estate producing £4,500 spendable income a year – all in all, an enormous fortune for a much-abused heiress.

Smith's revenge is sweet, but empty. The frustrations of Emmeline's economic marginality remain unresolved. First, only the lucky arrival of the author with some newfound papers removes the barrier that stands between the heroine and a likely future of settled poverty. Second, Emmeline's marriage to "the most generous and most amiable of men" in which she finds a happiness just short of "that heaven, where only she can enjoy more perfect and lasting felicity" is egregious indulgence of the wishful imagination (p. 527). The hero and heroine retire to the never-never land of an estate in the country, still at odds with all the rest of the corrupt materialist society of the novel.

The rest of Charlotte Smith's ten novels thrum the same chord: there is not a single place in the world that Smith can imagine, "middling" or otherwise, in which the heroine is not at the mercy of a ruthless system that bars women from all effective economic power. In her next novel, *Ethelinde, or the Recluse of the Lake* (1789), aristocracy, gentry, and trade line up against the heroine. First, the aristocracy:

Lord Danesforte inherited from his ancestors an immense fortune; and was one of those who seem, by the consent of their cotemporaries [*sic*], to be the acknowledged leaders of fashion, and arbiters of taste. His horses, his mistresses, his dinners, were the theme of the day; and had for some years made a conscious figure in those fleeting annals, which give, in the eyes of trifling imbecility, a temporary consequence to dissipation and vice. (II, 193)[29]

Next, the commercial ranks:

The sordid soul of the money-loving trader, never more evidently appeared than in the behaviour of Mr. Ludford towards his newly made acquaintance, whom he treated with fatiguing and fawning civility. (V, 143)

Finally, the gentry, in the person of her own feckless father:

My child – thy father, thy brother, have undone thee!—Ethelinde is a beggar! (III, 57–58)

Her father and her equally irresponsible brother have bankrupted the family by their gambling debts and extravagant spending.

Ethelinde thus falls dependent on the ungracious charity of two opposed sets of relatives from, respectively, the merchant and the aristocratic sides of her family. A vague possibility of rescue appears in the genteel figure of Sir Edward Newenden, the husband of one of Ethelinde's wealthy merchant cousins, but Sir Edward is one of those "horizon-figures" described by Fredric Jameson in *The Political Unconscious*: "He blocks out a place which is not that of empirical history but of a possible alternate one" that is merely "ideal."[30] Sir Edward, secretly in love with Ethelinde and thoroughly aware of her misery, is also wealthy enough to offer help even without recourse to the great merchant fortune of his wife, but he must remain inactive: his wife is jealous of Ethelinde.

The last volume of *Ethelinde* produces solid rescue for the hero and heroine in the figure of a Mr. Harcourt, the hero's wealthy merchant uncle, who arrives from Jamaica with a large fortune and the news that his only son is recently dead. Mr. Harcourt's merchant taint is washed away by his suffering, a never-failing source of respectability in Smith's novels, his spirits ruined by the loss of his son, his heart now open to communion with a sympathetic soul. He too is a wanderer: "I have suffered so much – my nerves are so shaken," he tells Ethelinde, "that they intrude upon me in spite of myself. I have been long a lonely and unhappy wanderer, and have fancied myself a being to whom nobody would attend but through mercenary motives, nobody listen, but in hopes of some advantages from the calamities I deplored, and now ... I have found in your gentle pity," he tells her, "a balm for my wounded spirit" (V, 146).

The "balm" that Ethelinde offers him is more problematic than the poor suffering wanderer imagines: "The emotion of Ethelinde now exceeded all description; to find, that if Montgomery had remained a few weeks only in England, the arrival of his uncle would have rendered his voyage [to India] unnecessary; to reflect on all the sufferings which a little patience would have spared them... Harcourt imagined that she was merely affected by pity for him" (v, 122–23). Ethelinde's offered "balm" consists of equal parts "wounded spirit" and financial disappointment. It is also ironic to reflect that Mr. Harcourt's condition, his nerves so dreadfully shaken by distress over the exploitation of slave labor on his Jamaican plantations (a favorite Smith cause), do not suggest to the hero and heroine for a moment that there is any impropriety in accepting his enormous slave-based fortune.

In her darkest moments, Smith can envision the middle-class woman as no more than one more vendible commodity in an already overcrowded market. In *Desmond* (1792), Mr. Verney, the husband of Geraldine Waverley, the heroine, literally *sells* his wife to the Duc de Romagnecourt to pay his gambling debts (II, 66). With less melodrama, Smith's heroine in *Montalbert* (1795) resists her mother's insistence that she attend an assembly in provincial Chichester: "'Gracious Heaven!' (exclaimed Rosalie, as soon as her mother had left her), 'I am thus to be dressed up, and offered like an animal to sale; and my mother seems to think it a matter of course'" (I, 75). Mr. Lessington, her supposed father, a gourmandizing clergyman, speaks sternly to her: "Do you consider, girl, that you have no fortune? That a clergyman's income dies with him? That it is your business to endeavour to procure an establishment, instead of affecting these fine romantic airs?" (I, 57). Rosalie rejects the clergyman's advice in order to marry Montalbert, her aristocratic but impoverished lover: "Oh! Montalbert, how different are your manners from those of the people I am condemned to live among!" (I, 75), she cries.

The aristocratic Montalbert's poor financial sense and "different manners," however, nearly ruin her life. Even with rescue at hand through the generous intentions of a wealthy merchant relative, a Mr. Ormsby, the aristocratic Montalbert pines with grief at the disgrace of such tainted help: "he found himself and his son now almost entirely dependent on Mr. Ormsby, who, though related to him by blood, the notions he had acquired among foreign nobility taught him to consider as a merchant and an adventurer for gain."

On the other side, Mr. Ormsby has his own hurt feelings: "[He] had been so long used to the most perfect obedience to his will from every body about him, that he was hurt at the little submission which Montalbert shewed to his wishes, when he expressed an intention of making a considerable purchase, and placing Rosalie as mistress of his house and fortune" (III, 313–14). If men are not knaves, they are fools. The aristocratic Montalbert cannot appreciate the merchant Ormsby's generosity; Ormsby cannot understand the niceties of Montalbert's aristocratic feelings. The heroine, as usual, remains "banished" from economic security even though both aristocrat and merchant, sentimental and well disposed, wish to accommodate her with a settlement.

In Smith's best-known work, *The Old Manor House* (1793), the heroine falls victim to an unholy collusion between a petty aristocrat, Mrs. Rayland, and Mrs. Rayland's companion, a tradesman's daughter, Mrs. Lennard.[31] Although the hero and the heroine suffer the usual economic privations at the usual hands, *The Old Manor House* includes a condemnation of the professional ranks far more sweeping and explicit than in any of Smith's earlier novels. Grasping clergymen, dishonest lawyers, greedy physicians receive Smith's steady fire of anger and contempt. Carr, a young lawyer and friend of Orlando, the hero of *The Old Manor House*, searches to defend his profession, but must admit, finally, that the law is just as bad, no *worse* than any of the others:

But, my friend, not to be too hard upon *us*, do reflect on the practices of other professions. The little, smirking fellow, with so smiling an aspect, and so well-powdered a head, whom you see pass in his chariot, administers to his patient the medicine a physician orders, though he knows they are more likely to kill than cure; and, in his account at night, thinks not of the tears of a family whom he has seen in the greatest distress, but of the bill he shall have for medicines and attendance.

"Do, dear Carr," cries Orlando, "finish your catalogue of human crimes, unless you have a mind to make me go home and hang myself" (p. 501).

Life in England is an economic horror for Charlotte Smith's women: "To tell you the truth, my dear friend," comments a character in *The Young Philosopher* (1798), "were it not for you England would be utterly intolerable to me. – I never recollect a moment's uneasiness till I came to England, and since I have been here I am sure I have felt a great deal, and a great deal more than I

have owned" (II, 262). Mrs. Denzil, the much-harassed author, and
Smith's spokesperson in *The Banished Man* (1794), compares her
hard-pressed life in England to the unhappy fate of French political
refugees and finds her fall from prosperity to be equally catastrophic:
"*I* have, perhaps felt more for these unfortunate victims of political
fury, than those who have not known by experience what it is to fall
from affluence to indigence... It naturally awakens all one's sympathies" (III, 180–81). Her hero in *Marchmont* (1796), threatened
with debtors' prison, draws a similar parallel: "And whether I am to
pass my life in the Fleet, or the Abbaye," he proclaims, "whether I
am to exist under the tyranny of Robespierre, or a victim to the
chicanery of Vampyre [a lawyer], seems to me a matter so
immaterial, that it ought not to induce me to cross the water to
embrace the one, or escape the other" (II, 163).

The poles of Smith's economic world remain obdurately un-
compromising for economically distressed, genteel aspirants to
station. The wished-for resolution – "Rosalie represented to her
father, that, beyond a certain point, fortune contributed nothing to
real happiness" (III, 321) – hovers in the unreachable distance:
"Alas! it is not a palace I wish for to place her in," explains
D'Alonville, the hero of *The Banished Man* (1794), "but some quiet
asylum where she might watch the declining health of her mother,
nor dread such alarms and inconveniencies as she has already
undergone" (IV, 184–85).

It scarcely overstates Smith's bitterness to recognize that in her
novels, genteel women of limited means have no effective status in
society at all. Ironically, her Banished Woman is exactly one of the
"allegoric personages," "like Spenser's," that she claims to eschew;
Everywoman herself, dressed in a good, if worn, gown, lost in an
economic "desart" that lies between the camps of feudal privilege
and those of commercial rapacity, unwelcome in both and suited for
neither.

Revisionist gothic: Jane Austen

Jane Austen mocks such economic wanderers mercilessly in her
juvenile works of the 1790s and again at the end of her career in her
"Plan of a Novel" (*c.* 1816), where the heroine and her father,
"hunted out of civilized Society, denied the poor Shelter of the
humblest Cottage, they are compelled to retreat into Kamschatka"
(*MW*, 430). Nevertheless, the persistent mockery only confirms the

power of the convention.[32] Undiluted, two such melodramatic
wanderers appear in *Sense and Sensibility*: Eliza Williams, Colonel
Brandon's youthful love, sold into marriage for her fortune, seduced,
abandoned, and turned prostitute; next, Eliza's unfortunate daughter of the same name, seduced, abandoned, and left penniless, this
time by Marianne Dashwood's own lover, Willoughby. "All Willoughby's difficulties have arisen from the first offence against virtue,
in his behaviour to Eliza Williams," says Elinor Dashwood (p. 352).
In *Persuasion*, Anne Elliot's friend Mrs. Smith is left destitute by an
improvident husband, Jane Fairfax very nearly sets out on the
wanderer's path in *Emma*, and Emma Watson, the heroine of Austen's
unfinished novel *The Watsons*, seems destined to join the exiled tribe
of distressed gentlewomen with every appropriate disadvantage:
raised by her aunt and uncle with the expectations of an heiress,

from being the first object of Hope & Solicitude of an Uncle who had formed
her mind with the care of a Parent, & of Tenderness to an Aunt whose
amiable temper had delighted to give her every indulgence, from being the
Life & Spirit of a House, where all had been comfort & Elegance, & the
expected Heiress of an easy Independance, she was become of importance to
no one, a burden on those, whose affection she c^d not expect, an addition in
an House, already overstocked, surrounded by inferior minds with little
chance of domestic comfort, & as little hope of future support. (*MW*,
361–62)

Finally, Clara Brereton in *Sanditon*, Austen's last, unfinished piece,
seems destined to fill the role again, "more helpless & more pitiable
of course than any – a dependant on Poverty – an additional Burthen
on an encumbered Circle – & one, who had been so low in every
worldly view, as with all her natural endowments & powers, to have
been preparing for a situation little better than a Nursery Maid"
(*MW*, 379). Charlotte Heywood, the probable heroine of *Sanditon*,
"c^d not separate the idea of a complete Heroine from Clara Brereton
... Such Poverty & Dependance joined to such Beauty & Merit,
seemed to leave no choice in the matter" (*MW*, 391). Austen may be
about to turn the tables on the convention, but that is impossible to
determine. Whether or not she would have done so hardly matters.
Banished Woman lives! The convention is irrepressible.

Austen's early novels partake of the economic turmoil of the 1790s
with an unselfconscious acceptance of its baleful promise for women.[33]
The chilling economic winds that blow through *Sense and Sensibility*,
Pride and Prejudice, and even around the modern windows of *Northanger*

Abbey confirm Austen's participation in the novelistic conversation of Eliza Parsons and Charlotte Smith.[34]

Sense and Sensibility retains the desolation of the 1790s vision intact. Elinor and Marianne are not the certified wanderers of Smith and Parsons, but they are subject to the same grim economic conditions: sudden loss, unpredictable gain, ingratitude, treachery, and a world peopled by mean-spirited characters from every rank.[35] Disparities between the spendable incomes of *Sense and Sensibility* are staggering: a mere £500 a year for the four Dashwood women in pointed contrast to two immense fortunes and a landed estate for the John Dashwoods; £1,000 a year for Robert Ferrars, and only £100 a year for his brother Edward.[36] As for family ties, they mean nothing to the John Dashwoods, and worse than nothing to tyrannical old Mrs. Ferrars, who in a moment of spite, disinherits the worthy elder son to leave her fortune to her spendthrift younger son. Although kindly Mrs. Jennings and bluff, generous Sir John Middleton represent the old nostalgic economy that gives an ear to women's economic needs, Constantia wine is a poor remedy for Marianne's loss of Willoughby, and gifts of game and the newspaper cannot restore the Dashwood women to their former station. Even Colonel Brandon's presentation of a £200-a-year living to Edward Ferrars, though a noble gesture, cannot match the loss of his expected £1,000-a-year inheritance. In fact, typical of the economic action of *Sense and Sensibility*, Colonel Brandon's surprising gift of a church living to Edward is as arbitrary as Mrs. Ferrars' disinheritance of him, and as John Dashwood notes, not nearly so natural as her motherly revenge (pp. 294–95).[37]

Although comic rather than distressed, the world of *Pride and Prejudice*, also conceived in the 1790s, operates on the same principle of sudden-death economics as does the gloomier world of *Sense and Sensibility*.[38] Mr. Bingley arrives on the scene with no warning, with a rumored £4,000 or £5,000 a year, then disappears over the horizon (just as Edward Ferrars, Willoughby, and Colonel Brandon do in the multiple disappearings of *Sense and Sensibility*) and returns just as suddenly, this time with his fortune and an offer of marriage for one of the Bennet girls. Mr. Collins arrives, unexpectedly, also looking to marry one of the Bennet girls, it hardly matters which, as an imagined duty of his inheritance. The money to save Lydia Bennet from infamy appears mysteriously and unexpectedly – we never know the amount. Darcy's marriage proposal to Elizabeth, together with his £10,000-a-year income, drops like a thunderbolt on

Longbourn: "I shall go distracted" (p. 378), cries Mrs. Bennet. And, as in *Sense and Sensibility*, the large incomes dwarf the small ones. Jane and Elizabeth Bennet's pathetically small inheritances, £1,000 each, can hardly match Miss King's "only" £10,000, or Miss Bingley's £20,000, or Georgiana Darcy's £30,000. The inevitable loss of Longbourn by entail – a disastrous fall from fortune completely without remedy – echoes the Dashwood women's predicament, but even more desperately. The raw truth in Mr. Collins' remark to Elizabeth exposes a painful kinship for any reader with an equally modest marriage portion of her own: "Your portion is unhappily so small that it will in all likelihood undo the effects of your loveliness and amiable qualifications" (p. 108).[39]

Northanger Abbey, written between 1798 and 1799, advances a determinedly sunny corrective to the "horrid" fiction of the circulating library, yet, paradoxically, it shares the same economic assumptions with the objects of its derision.[40] The most violent act of the novel, General Tilney's Montoni-like ejection of Catherine Morland from the Abbey, is as arbitrary an exile as any held in store for the Dashwood or the Bennet women. If the General cannot prevent Catherine and Henry's marriage, he can certainly delay it indefinitely. His tyrannic authority over his daughter is secure from challenge. Austen refrains from making General Tilney a dangerous threat to her heroine, but she does provide Catherine with one very practical glimpse of economic distress. As Eleanor Tilney and Catherine wait for the coach that will remove Catherine from the Abbey, Eleanor suddenly remembers to ask Catherine if she has "money enough for the expenses of her journey." Catherine is horrified to remember that she does not, and Eleanor speedily lends her £5, but, "the distress in which she must have been thereby involved filling the minds of both, scarcely another word was said by either during the time of their remaining together" (p. 229). The specter of another female wanderer, however much diminished in proportion through the small amount of cash and the ready loan, leaves both women shocked and speechless. Catherine Morland may have less immediate cause for alarm than any one of Smith's banished women, but her own economic marginality originates in a common vision of the economy.

Rich or poor in the 1790s, no heroine can rest secure in her fortune prior to the last page of the novel. Jane Austen, Charlotte Smith,

Frances Burney, Eliza Parsons, and Anna Maria Bennett, among many others, remain acutely aware of the economic perils that threaten their heroines in their progress to their destined "heaven on earth" in the concluding volume.

Clara Reeve's novel *The School for Widows* (1791) presents the economic dilemma of the 1790s with emblematic clarity. Two old boarding school chums, Mrs. Strictland, the widow of a miser, and Mrs. Darnford, the widow of a spendthrift, write each other from opposite ends of the troubled economic cosmos. "After being the slave and prisoner of a tyrant for ten years," the newly released Mrs. Strickland confesses, "I feel as does the captive just delivered from his chains. It would be folly, it would be sinful, in me, to affect the part of a disconsolate widow" (I, 12). Of Mrs. Darnford, the suffering spendthrift's widow: "She was married to a Mr. Darnford, who was said to be a man of good fortune; but he ran through it all in a few years, and then died. All that remained of his estate was entailed on the next male heir of the name; and the widow was left without any provision, and obliged to go out as governess to some young ladies" (I, 13).

From novel to novel in the 1790s, spending money or *not* spending money, as Mrs. Strickland's and Mrs. Darnford's unhappy letters suggest, is an equal anxiety. Clara Reeve's pathetic desire to turn back the clock to a mythical, happier time, a dream shared by a decade of women novelists, appears comically out of touch. "The revival of sumptuary laws is devoutly to be wished, but not greatly to be hoped for," Reeve concludes sadly in her *Plans of Education* (1792): "I acknowledge that many difficulties lie in the way" (p. 74). Instead, novelists must readjust the economic fictions of their plots to transfer money into women's pockets. The gothic gloom of the 1790s disperses only when, during the next two decades, women's fiction systematically lays claim to an economic frontier of its own: the domestic budget.

CHAPTER 3

The gifts of heaven: consumer power, 1800–1820

Let no young woman hereafter rest satisfied in ignorance of *domestic economy*; and let no mother deceive herself by believing that it is kindness to exempt her girls from the exertions required in gaining a practical knowledge of this most valuable attainment.

La Belle Assemblée (April 1813)

After 1800, money finds a far less anxious place in the women's novel. Women's fiction abandons, bit by bit, its narrative of economic victimization to embrace a narrative of economic empowerment, a fictional world in which women assertively participate in the economy as managers of the domestic budget. Such an idea was not a new one, nor was the practice, as recent scholarship has shown.[1] For a century, conduct books for women had been encouraging women to practice "economy," a piece of advice that was probably no more than the confirmation of an already existent state of affairs.[2] But in fiction, at least, the exhortations suffered the fate of most good advice until near the end of the century, when women's fiction actively embraced the idea as an image: the middle-class woman as manager of the domestic budget.[3] Readers of Jane Austen will recognize the difference in economic emphasis immediately: the contrast between the relatively passive voice of the Dashwood women in *Sense and Sensibility* and the assertive, outspoken words of Anne Elliot, Lady Russell, and Mrs. Croft in *Persuasion*.

Jane Austen was not alone in exploring an active place for women in the economic landscape. Fiction in the popular *Lady's Magazine*, a monthly production ever sensitive to the tastes of its readers, displays a year-by-year record of woman's empowerment through her management of the domestic budget. The graph "Plot frequencies in the *Lady's Magazine*, 1793–1815," traces five common plots in the magazine, their waxing and waning, over a twenty-year span. The

Plate 3. The youthful heroine and her aunt visit a cottage of the deserving poor. From *The Calendar; or Monthly Recreations* (1807), by Mary Pilkington.

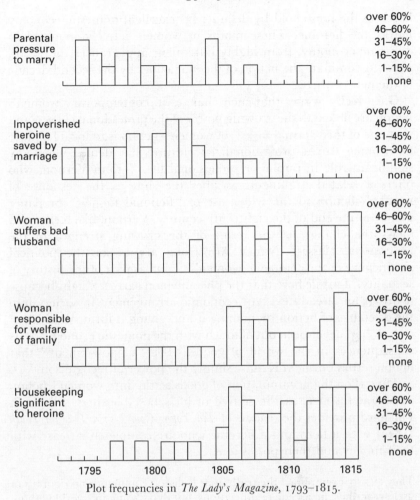

Plot frequencies in *The Lady's Magazine*, 1793–1815.

stories in which women get money passively, that is, exclusively through the providential appearance of an eligible suitor, monopolize the columns of the magazine during the 1790s and into the first years of the new century. Parents in such stories insist, sometimes tyrannically, that their daughters marry fortunes, but oftentimes, as the authors admit, because the romanticizing heroines have need of parental guidance. In either case, the heroine remains excluded from anything more than passive participation in the economy. As these two plots drop in frequency, three plots with a rather different focus begin to rise: (1) women suffer bad husbands; (2) women become heads of the household by default; (3) excellent domestic economy marks the heroine. These motifs of women actively involved in domestic economy, from highly infrequent appearances the 1790s, come to dominate the fiction of the magazines by the second decade of the new century.

Gary Kelly argues that such changes in contemporary women's fiction are linked to the growing power of the professional classes, and that one of the "formal tasks" of women's fiction is to locate a place for women "in a professionalized culture that denies them any significant role in public or professional life."[4] John Vernon, who offers a related argument, ascribes the shift as the response of women's fiction to the wider use of "fictional money" or paper money at the end of the eighteenth century. Vernon, like Kelly, also views the change as the result of the growing strength of the professional classes.[5] Nancy Armstrong argues for the political significance of the change in women's fiction as part of the history of sexuality.[6] I argue here that the phenomenon carries weight because it brings an already existent economic arrangement in society into the discourse of fiction by naming it and giving it form. Women, of course, had never been out of touch with the domestic economy or its consequences in the world of goods.[7] The "empowerment" that fiction settles on them is quite simply the power of recognition.

After 1800 the accumulation of goods settles into women's fiction as a grateful fact, as the source of life's best blessings. Elizabeth Pinchard provides the readers of *The Young Countess: a Tale for Youth* (1820) with a hero and a heroine who are completely at ease with their money and their possessions:

They clearly exemplified the truth, that Religion commands no rigorous or useless sacrifice, no ascetic renunciations, but that "using the world without abusing it," the gifts of heaven, although they come in the tempting form of wealth or station, may be so applied as to become a blessing instead of a snare; and so enjoyed, as to be perfectly compatible with a life of virtue, and promote, rather than endanger, the highest views of a Christian. (pp. 213–14)[8]

Jane Austen recognizes the limitations of the consumer contract in *Northanger Abbey* when she has the comically repulsive John Thorpe accept literally the words of Goethe's Faust: "If I can buy myself six steeds, / Then aren't all their powers mine?"[9] "Do but look at my horse," Thorpe boasts to Catherine Morland: "Did you ever see an animal so made for speed in your life?... What do you think of my gig?" (p. 46). At the same time, Austen also acknowledges the irresistible temptations of the consumer show. When Elizabeth Bennet's thoroughly admirable aunt, Mrs. Gardiner in *Pride and Prejudice*, first understands the possibility of her niece becoming Mrs. Darcy, she teases Elizabeth with the consumer privileges of her prospective station: "A low phaeton, with a nice little pair of ponies, would be the very thing" (p. 325). Elizabeth confirms her engagement to Darcy in the same currency: "Your idea of the ponies is delightful," she writes her aunt, "We will go around the Park every day" (p. 382).

After 1800, the mixture of ranks that had horrified Anna Maria Mackenzie two decades earlier in *The Gamester* (1786) – "The lord, the gentleman, the cit, and – dreadful addition! – the swindler, are all upon the same footing, while full purses declare their ability to fill the set" (I, 41) – now appears to women novelists, in greater and lesser degrees, in a much more promising light. Traditional distinctions of rank are no longer operable under traditional rules. Mr. Stewart, the father of Elizabeth Hamilton's heroine in *The Cottagers of Glenburnie* (1808), embraces the cross-rank marriage of his daughter to the son of a shoemaker with positive enthusiasm: "They are in every respect upon a footing," cries the delighted Mr. Stewart, the principal landowner of the neighborhood. "If his father is an honest tradesman, what is her father but an honest farmer. Believe me, I am quite relieved ... If he has sense to apply to business, I shall put him in the way of doing it, and all may yet be well" (pp. 339–40). Anne Plumptre's novel *The History of Myself and My Friend* (1813) features a hero who has a "worthy blacksmith" for a father, and Anna Maria Porter's *Honor O'Hara* (1826) elevates a yeoman's daughter to the position of social arbiter for an entire neighborhood. The parlor of Porter's Mrs. Preston provides the women's novel with a more democratic vision of society: "As the eccentric clever Dr. Preston's wife, and since as his widow, she visited, and was visited by all, except the nobility of the county; her house, consequently, was the neutral ground upon which both parties met, and met amicably" (I, 46–47). It's a position that Austen's Mrs. Elton, "Insufferable woman!" aspires to, as local social director and Lady Bountiful, but one in point of fact that Emma Woodhouse actually occupies, though certainly not with the ideological fervor embraced by Mrs. Elton or by Anna Maria Porter's clever Dr. Preston's wife. But, as Mrs. Elton tells Emma with comic accuracy, "If *we* exert ourselves, I think we shall not be long in want of allies" (p. 277).

Objects undergo a profound reassessment of meaning in a world of domestic spending directed by women. Before 1800, for example, cottages in novels generally belong only to women in "unhappy circumstances": "'A cottage life, my love,' resumed Mr. Dudley," in Jane West's *A Gossip's Story* (1797), "'is not so pleasant in reality as in theory...To them who have been accustomed to the elegant enjoyments of life, it presents evils that patience and fortitude may teach us to support; but which are doubtless evils'" (1, 190). Little more than fifteen years later, nothing can exceed the pleasures of the heroine's cottage: "The parsonage was a low irregular building, and evidently ancient," writes Elizabeth Pinchard in *The Ward of Delamere* (1815); "its walls, however, were neatly whitened, and around its old fashioned porch and casements were entwined many creeping plants, such as jasmine, honeysuckles, &c." (pp. 117–18).

Even "the vegetable part of creation," as Susan Ferrier terms it, alters beyond recognition. Gardens in the 1790s, when they can be found at all, are insubstantial fictions, at best convenient retreats for concealing poverty or for giving the hero and heroine some privacy. With such minimal expectations, Mr. Harwood, a gentleman in Jane West's *The Church of Saint Siffrid* (1798), retires to remote Wales where he spends his daytime hours, "strolling on the banks of a romantic river, or in the thick shade listened to the murmuring of its cascades" (1, 7).

Ten years later, Mrs. Mason in Elizabeth Hamilton's *The Cottagers of Glenburnie* (1808), retires to an equally remote spot in Scotland, but for an altogether different garden experience. When she arrives at her new home, Mrs. Mason discovers the inhabitants of the local village living in feckless squalor. She sets about the task of their improvement with a vigorous program of corrective gardening:

By the time the Earl of Longlands came to take possession of Hill Castle, when he, accompanied by his two sisters, came to visit Mrs. Mason at Glenburnie, the village presented such a picture of neatness and comfort, as excelled all that in the course of their travels they had seen. The carts, which used formerly to be stuck up on end before every door, were now placed in wattled sheds attached to the gable end of the dwelling, and which were rendered ornamental from their coverings of honey-suckle or ivy. The bright and clear glass of the windows was seen to advantage peeping through the foliage of the rose trees, and other flowering shrubs, that were trimly nailed against the walls. The gardens on the other side were kept with equal care. There the pot-herb flourished. There the goodly rows of bee-hives evinced the effects of the additional nourishment afforded their inhabitants, and shewed that the flowers were of other use besides regaling the sight and smell. (pp. 397–98)

A semiotic earth-shift in the meaning of consumer signs rearranges the view. The worthy Mrs. Mason's picturesque cottage in Scotland snatches consumer triumph from economic retreat. Mrs. Mason's cottage and village, packaged so attractively together, become a desirable object because of "*the idea of the relation*": the social concept is "consumed" through the mediation of its sign.[10] Mrs. Mason acquires a freehold on the landscape from her exertions in the domestic economy. From her neat and empowering cottage, she sallies forth to challenge the universe.[11] Hamilton's tidy village marks an economic and social landscape for women just as surely as the comfortable parlor of Porter's "frankly social" Mrs. Preston in *Honor O'Hara* (1826), or the clear consciences of Pinchard's happy couple in *The Young Countess* (1820).

The furnishings of the hero's home in Mary Brunton's novel *Self Control* (1810) display the principles of domestic expense on a grander scale. Laura, the heroine of the novel, expects to find Norwood, the hero's ancestral estate, "dull with baronial magnificence," but she finds instead a house filled with the most up-to-date comforts. Norwood is a snug "retreat" where drafty rooms and baronial pomp yield to good fires and plentiful carpeting:

She saw nothing of the gloomy splendour which she had fancied; everything breathed comfort and repose. The furniture, though not without magnificence, was unadorned and substantial, grandeur holding the second place to usefulness. The marble hall through which she had entered, was almost covered with matting. In the spacious room in which she was sitting, the little Turkey carpet of our forefathers had given place to one of homelier grain but far larger dimensions. The apartment was liberally stored with couches, footstools, and elbow chairs. A harp occupied one window, and a piano-forte stood near it; many books were scattered about, in bindings which shewed they were not meant for ornament: and in the chimney blazed a fire which would have done credit to the days of Elizabeth. (II, 201–03)

De Courcy, the hero owner, provides everything a heroine could want: a satisfying dinner, "plain, neat, and substantial," a harp, a piano-forte, couches and footstools, a library furnished with all the appropriate devices of self-education, "globes, astronomical instruments, and cabinets of minerals and coins," and, in addition, a "smaller room which opened from it, used as De Courcy's laboratory ...filled with chemical and mechanical apparatus." Idealized consumption restructures the world: "Comfort, neatness, and peace reigned everywhere, and Norwood seemed a fit retreat for literary leisure and easy hospitality" (II, 201–03). Laura enthusiastically embraces Norwood's image of domestic order as she engages the housekeeper, Mrs. Dawkins, "in a dissertation on the various branches of household economy, and to the eternal degradation of her character as a heroine, actually listened with interest to the means of improving the cleanliness, beauty, and comfort of her dwelling" (I, 220). Religion spreads its angel wings over the prosperous display as well. Laura, like Fanny Price in *Mansfield Park*, rejoices to hear that De Courcy requires the servants at Norwood to attend regular evening prayers with the family.

The household budget: Jane West, Hannah More, Maria Edgeworth, Margaret Cullen, Mary Ann Hanway, Rachel Hunter

In the budget-oriented universe of women's fiction, heroines are prudent consumers. As Jane West urges in *Letters to a Young Lady* (1806), the trials of the great economy should stir women of every rank to action: "If we are deprived of our wedded partners," she warns, "the sole management of our fortunes, or perhaps the active superintendence of the business which supports our families, devolves upon us."[12] To avoid being made "the dupes of knaves, or the tools of parasites," women of the middling ranks should prepare themselves for the trial:

We should provide for this early in life, by gaining such knowledge of money transactions as will preserve us from imposition: few acquirements are more useful to females; and the increasing intricacy of public imposts and legal securities renders it daily more requisite. (I, 53)

Arithmetic, "the first tool," she writes, must be practiced from infancy.[13] Women must know the comparative incomes of "different trades and occupations," not only as "an admirable assistant to domestic management," which is the first call, of course, but as "an intelligent guide to benevolence" as well (III, 259–60).[14] A gentleman in Hannah More's *Coelebs In Search of a Wife* (1809) lays out the governing principle of female domestic economy with clarity: "'A discreet woman,' said Mr. Stanley, 'adjusts her expenses to her revenues. Every thing knows its time, and every person his place. She will live within her income be it large or small; if large, she will not be luxurious, if small she will not be mean. Proportion and propriety are among the best secrets of domestic wisdom,'" he concludes, "'and there is no surer test both of integrity and judgment, than a well proportioned expenditure'" (II, 172).

Maria Edgeworth's story "The Good Aunt" in *Moral Tales for Young People* (1801) presents a salutary widow managing her business affairs on her own. Mrs. Howard's most pressing problem is an estate in the West Indies. She desires to sell the estate, since "she did not particularly wish to be the proprietor of slaves," but she fears that she will sustain a considerable loss in the sale. Mrs. Howard "was neither one of those ladies," insists Edgeworth, "who, jealous of their freewill, would rather *act for themselves*, that is to say, follow their own whims in matters of business, than consult men, who possess the requisite information; nor was she so ignorant of business, or so indolent, as to be at the mercy of any designing agent or attorney." She reviews, she asks, then she acts: "After consulting proper persons and after exerting a just proportion of her own judgment, she concluded her bargain" (II, 14–15). However, before signing the final papers, Mrs. Howard "stipulated for the liberty and *provision grounds* of some old negroes upon her plantation." The admirable widow pursues her retrenchments with energy: she sells her Portman Square property, her jewelry, her personal effects, and by moving into a house near Westminster School where she receives schoolboys as boarders, she is able to send her son to Westminster School for a gentleman's education. Such excellent management speaks for itself, but it comes from a lifetime of good arithmetic: "She had never in affluence disdained economy," Edgeworth claims; "She had no debts: not a single tradesman was a sufferer by her loss. She had always lived within her annual income, and though her generous disposition had prevented her from hoarding money, she had a small sum in the funds, which she had prudently reserved for unforeseen exigence" (II, 18).

The heroine of Margaret Cullen's *Home* (1802) gilds her management of a "moderate fortune" of £1,000 a year with substantial contributions to charity: "She superintended all her affairs herself, and regulated her expenses with the strictest economy," claims Cullen: "It was benevolence reserving to itself the power of doing good" (I, 19–21). The secret of her success? "The first is my being in a great measure my own steward," the heroine confides, "and where I require assistance, I employ persons on whose understanding and fidelity I have strong reason to rely" (II, 29–31).

Quite simply, the woman's novel of the 1790s stated the problem: women had no legal economic power. In response, women's fiction of the following decades redirected the program. When Harriet Ancram's father loses the family fortune in Mary Ann Hanway's *Christabelle, the Maid of Rouen* (1814) – the most timeworn of 1790s plots – Miss Ancram takes shelter in a French nunnery, again a hoary metaphor in women's fiction for the deprived state of single women:[15] "torn at once from all those enjoyments, condemned to reflect upon her deprivations, immured within the solemn sanctuary of a cloister, whose impervious gloom no cheerful ray of mirth ever penetrated, to break the dull uniformity that marked each revolving day" (I, 51). But Harriet Ancram's dilemma of 1814 is given a surprisingly different perspective: not the undifferentiated economic terror of 1790s heroines, but the more manageable problem of passing the tedium of leisure time spent in reduced circumstances. "To enable her to banish these thick-coming fancies," Harriet commences a program of determined self-improvement, but instead of pursuing the "Haut ton" avocations taught her in her boarding school, such as landscape painting, "rattling" the piano keys, or singing to her harp – all traditional accomplishments associated with aristocratic leisure – she finds solace in books and in "lively conversation" with Christabelle, the titular heroine, confined to the same convent. Fortunately, Miss Ancram's father, before leaving for St. Domingo, consigns to his daughter a library "composed of the best authors [which] ... expanded her imagination, and amended her heart by the knowledge they inculcated, and the lessons of wisdom they conveyed" (I, 53–54). A life of limited consumption becomes a life of spirited self-improvement. The two women study together: "Together they trod the delightful paths of science," and, as a result, at no great outlay of funds, "ennui was banished from their breasts; sportive mirth kept not her court in the sombre confines of their dreary abode; though not buoyant in spirit they were neither querulous, nor miserable" (I, 60), an upbeat message for all readers of limited means, but genteel aspirations.

Rachel Hunter, a staunchly middle-class author from a commercial background, suggests in her novels that, in truth, women, not men, are the *natural* managers of the family budget. Hunter's tradesman-rank heroines invariably exercise more skill in domestic economy than their gentry-rank husbands.[16] A widow in Hunter's *Family Annals* (1808), Mrs. Urban, moves from London to Twickenham to live in suburban retirement on £500 a year. Her modest competence, an income secured to her in her own right through trustees, is all that remains from the expensive lifestyle of her late husband. When Hunter's widow learns of her husband's outstanding debts to shopkeepers and tradesmen in London for personal "domestic expenditure," she sacrifices her own comforts and her children's to set the financial books straight, even though, as Hunter notes pointedly, she is not obliged by law to do so: "She gave up her peaceful retreat at Twickenham, and, reserving 150 *l.* per ann. she satisfied, with the residue of her children's fortune, the claims of those creditors who had suffered by supplying their father with the articles of his private and domestic expenditure" (II, 9).

Hunter, to emphasize her point – that domestic budgets are best left in women's hands – supplies the salutary examples of two other families in this novel rescued by right-thinking women from the disastrous effects of male domestic mismanagement. In her first example, old Mr. Skinnerley, a successful great merchant and the best of men, designs a will to protect his grandchildren from their fashionable father's spendthrift ways: "It appeared as though Mr. Skinnerley, in the disposition of his fortune, which amounted to nearly a hundred thousand pounds, had been actuated by one sole object; namely, securing to his grand-daughters an independence and freedom from their father's authority and control" (I, 56). And for her second example, Hunter supplies Madame Picute, the former servant and humble friend of the heroine: Madame Picute assumes responsibility for the sole management of both her own and her husband's united incomes. She and her husband live "genteely" [*sic*] in retirement, writes Hunter, and "drive a whisky," their one consumer extravagance, "for the sole purpose of benefitting her husband's health" (VI, 178).

In Hunter's novels, it is always women, not men, who insist on fair dealing in money matters. When Selina Graves, a woman of humble birth in Hunter's *The Schoolmistress* (1811), discovers that her socially ambitious husband, Mr. Vernley, has incurred expenses through his

position at court "incompatible with their limited income" of £800
a year, she immediately moves herself and the children into
inexpensive lodgings in the country. Her husband, "a slave to
fashion," stays in town to live in the "humiliating" position of a
hanger-on at court (I, 19–21). Commercial honesty, domestic
economy, and good arithmetic establish the moral high ground for
Hunter's fiction.

Gentrifying the economy: Hannah More and Susan Ferrier

Hannah More's novel *Coelebs In Search of a Wife* (1809) typifies the
double-sided response of genteel fiction to the domestic budget. On
one side of the ledger, consumer desire is an abomination and a
plague, a danger to the welfare of women of all ranks and ages. On
the other, it is a glorious opportunity for women, an open door for
them to step into the mainstream of economic life.

On the debit side, the side of "excess," it destroys the mind: "I
believe," says the traditional Sir John in More's *Coelebs*,

> that an overflowing commerce, and the excessive opulence it has introduced,
> though favourable to all the splendours of art, and mechanic ingenuity, yet
> have lowered the standard of taste, and debilitated the mental energies.
> They are advantageous to luxury, but fatal to intellect. It has added to the
> brilliancy of the drawing-room itself, but deducted from that of the
> inhabitant. It has given a perfection to our mirrors, our candelabras, our
> gilding, our inlaying, and our sculpture, but it has communicated a torpor
> to the imagination, and enervated our intellectual vigour. (II, 153–54)

On the credit side, however, commerce in goods brings women both
power and influence. More's young heroine in the same novel,
Lucilla Stanley, keeps a little school and establishes an orchard on
her family's estate for the benefit of the neighboring poor:

> When there is a wedding among the older servants, or when any good girl
> out of her school marries, she presents their little empty garden with a dozen
> young apple trees, and a few trees of the other sorts, never forgetting to
> embellish their little court with roses and honeysuckles. These last she
> transplants from the shrubbery, not to fill up the *village garden* as it is called,
> with any thing that is of no positive use. (II, 50)[17]

A visiting stranger notes and appreciates Lucilla's managing hand in
the village economy: "I now recollected that I had been pleased with
observing so many young orchards and flourishing cottage gardens in
the village; little did I suspect the fair hand which could thus in a very

few years diffuse an air of smiling comfort around these humble habitations, and embellish poverty itself." This charity is no mere passing fancy for Lucilla. "She makes, they told me," the admiring gentleman reports, "her periodical visits of inspection to see that neatness and order do not degenerate" (II, 52).

Such gardens are planted by heroines in all three kingdoms: More's Lucilla shoulders the responsibility for English cottagers; Mrs. Mason, in Elizabeth Hamilton's *The Cottagers of Glenburnie* (1808), watches over them in Scotland; and Lady Clancare, in Sydney Morgan's *Florence Macarthy* (1818), takes charge of the Irish. "When I am not writing," Lady Clancare explains, "I am planting potatoes, or presiding over turf bogs; or I am seated with my [spinning] wheel in a barn, in the midst of would-be loitering, lounging, lazy matrons of Clotnotty-joy; and when [my] wheel goes round, every wheel in the parish turns with it" (pp. 269–70).

These gardens are economic pictures suitable for framing. In fact, the "roses and honeysuckles" over the doors of Lucilla's cottages in *Coelebs* match the "honeysuckle and ivy" over the doors of Mrs. Mason's cottages in *The Cottagers of Glenburnie*. Each picture demands the same brush-strokes, highlights, sunshine, flowers, and the same female managing hand. Moreover, such a picture can be created, so goes the claim, by any woman with moderate means, enough energy, and the right moral principles. As Mrs. Cockle's *Important Studies For the Female Sex* (1809) insists, it is not only the pleasure, but the positive duty of gentlewomen who reside in the country to transform the cottages of the neighboring poor into "the residence of neatness, good management, happy faces, and more happy hearts." The reward will come of itself, she counsels her readers, in "contemplating this picture of your own creation" (pp. 77–78).

Susan Ferrier's admirable Mrs. Douglas in *Marriage* (1818)[18] imposes just such a picture on the landscape of Scotland. Mrs. Douglas, an Englishwoman, lives with her Scots husband on a small farm in the Highlands of Scotland. When her husband's younger brother, reared fashionably in London, and his flighty aristocratic wife, Lady Juliana, pay their northern relatives a visit, Mrs. Douglas takes her brother-in-law on a walking tour of her little estate:

[He] was again in raptures at the new beauties this walk presented, and at the high order and neatness in which the grounds were kept.

"This must be a very expensive place of yours, though," said he, addressing his sister-in-law, "there is so much garden and shrubbery, and such a number of rustic bridges, bowers, and so forth: it must require half a dozen men to keep it in any order."

Mrs. Douglas finds a modest reply, but she leaves no room to doubt that her garden does indeed offer an example of right-thinking economic management that the nation itself could profit from heeding. With a graceful nod to her husband's limited income, she proceeds to give her brother-in-law a short lecture on the management of a small estate, along with a few well-chosen remarks on the duties of the local gentry towards a disruptive laboring population:

"Such an establishment would very ill accord with our moderate means," replied she; "we do not pretend to one regular gardener; and had our little embellishments been productive of much expense, or tending solely to my gratification, I should never have suggested them. When we first took possession of this spot it was a perfect wilderness, with a dirty farm-house on it; nothing but mud about the doors; nothing but wood and briers and brambles beyond it; and the village presented a still more melancholy scene of rank luxuriance, in its swarms of dirty idle girls and mischievous boys."

To solve the social problem on her own doorstep, Mrs. Douglas projects an ambitious vision of woman's power beyond the drawing-room door, and she clears a path for other women to join her:[19] "I have generally found that wherever an evil exists the remedy is not far off," she proclaims,

"and in this case it was strikingly obvious. It was only engaging these ill-directed children by trifling rewards to apply their lively energies in improving instead of destroying the works of nature, as had formerly been their zealous practice."

In the coldframe of Ferrier's imagination, the great economy flourishes with generous applications of moral grit. She uproots the unruly fictional economy that had terrorized heroines during the 1790s to replace it with a healthier, more productive social planting:

"In a short time the change on the moral as well as the vegetable part of creation became very preceptible [*sic*]: the children grew industrious and peaceable; and instead of destroying trees, robbing nests, and worrying cats, the bigger boys, under Douglas's direction, constructed these wooden bridges and seats, or cut out and gravelled the little winding paths that we had previously marked out. The task of keeping everything in order is now easy, as you may believe, when I tell you the whole of our pleasure-grounds, as you are pleased to term them, receive no other attention than what is bestowed by children under twelve years of age." (pp. 127–28)

Picturesque gardening becomes the telltale signature of the genteel novelist's hand in the economy. Ferrier, More, Hamilton, and other earnest instructors insist upon it so effectively, in fact, that by the third decade of the new century, their dynamic image hardens into the familiar cast-iron plant of female respectability, the calendar art of a nostalgic conservatism. The landscape of Anna Maria Porter's *Honor O'Hara* of 1826, for example, with its plot set in an earlier 1808, has lost the flourishing moral vigor of More's, Ferrier's, and Hamilton's social landscapes. The heroine does her duty to the village of course: "Honoria," writes Porter, "frequently created wants for herself, only that she might employ a poor neighbour, and so, make him earn the shilling which she would otherwise have given" (1, 31), but we hear nothing of the villagers themselves or the bustle of Honoria going about their business. The heroine views the scene from afar:

The view seen from this favourite window was, in reality, charming of itself: it consisted of a range of romantic hills, backed by the lofty Cheviots; discovering in their recesses, little glens, where wreaths of smoke and cheerful sounds rising above the tufted trees, told of cottages and contented labour. (1, 16–17)

Porter's landscape is, of course, a generation and a universe removed from Charlotte Smith's "lone Cottage, deep embower'd / In the green woods" in *The Emigrants* of 1793, but her conception of a distant view of the landscape is even more decisively removed from the humble conflicts of Hamilton's villagers in *The Cottagers of Glenburnie* (1808), or from Mrs. Douglas's determined efforts among the children of Scottish peasants.[20]

The landscape of genteel fiction in its most flourishing state depicts an economy in which all women of the middle class can assume the role of domestic manager. More's *Coelebs* and Ferrier's *Marriage* target landholders, but Hamilton in her *Cottagers of Glenburnie* (1808) and More herself, in her *Cheap Repository Tracts; Entertaining, Moral, and Religious* (1812), extend the possibility of women's action to the lower ranks of the middle class as well. More's energetic middle-class matron, Mrs. Jones, a merchant's widow now living modestly in the country on a limited income, employs her firsthand experience of domestic economics to change the spending patterns of her poorer neighbors.[21] In "The Cottage Cook, or *Mrs. Jones's Cheap Dishes. Shewing the way to do Much Good with Little Money*," Mrs. Jones persuades local housewives to brew their own beer in order to keep their husbands from siphoning off the family's income at the local alehouse. Mrs. Jones' improvements, like those of the genteel women of *Coelebs* and *Marriage*, impose on the social landscape an equally gratifying picture of the domestic budget well managed:

Mrs. Jones, in her evening walks, had the pleasure to see many an honest man drinking his wholesome cup of beer by his own fire side, his rosy children playing about his knees, his clean cheerful wife singing her youngest baby to sleep, rocking the cradle with her foot, while with her hands she was making a dumplin [*sic*] for her kind husband's supper.[22]

Although the authors generally confine themselves to the country – "I have often regretted the difficulty of discovering in London DESERVING objects of charity," says Mrs. Cockle – they find considerable scope in their rural walks for the economic empowerment of women. In the well-managed precincts of the didactic novel, "Vice and deception," as Mrs. Cockle asserts, "have no hiding place" (p. 69).

Heroicizing commerce: Mary Meeke and Sarah Green

Minerva novels, by reputation and in fact, as Jan Fergus' recent research into booksellers' records suggests, found their most enthusiastic readership among the ranks of the lower middle class, especially among the students at middle-class boarding schools.[23] Indeed, Lane developed his circulating libraries to attract this particular audience of upwardly aspiring readers, drawing on the expansion of boarding schools in the last quarter of the eighteenth century, both for girls and boys, as a prime market for the Minerva readership. The schools touched a live nerve in the prudent economy of middle-class spending. Among the standard "accomplishments" for women included in the advertisements for schools in rural Hampshire, at least eight schools promised arithmetic to their female pupils, and five claimed to teach them merchant accounts.[24] In fact Sarah Green, one of Lane's authors, specifically addresses her *Mental Improvement for a Young Lady, on Her Entrance into the World* (1793) to "the Superiors of the Various Seminaries for Female Education," and to their students, "to those who, from your hands, launch into the gay scenes of a polite metropolis, or whose lot is cast for the domestic scenes of elegant retirement" (xvii).

For the most part, however, women's novels, with the exception of Lane's Minerva products, have little good to say about boarding schools. In Austen's *Sense and Sensibility*, the "landscape in coloured silks" that graces Charlotte Palmer's old bedroom is Austen's wry "proof of her having spent seven years at a great school in town to some effect" (pp. 160). Jane West is less amused: Kitty Muggleton in *The Infidel Father* (1802) exchanges "her domestic employments" on the farm "for learning bad French, executing miserable drawings, and squalling out of all time and tune ... and this with the view of receiving a good education" (1, 23–24). The class dislocations implicit in the expanding readership inspire West's genuine hostility. From Lane's perspective as a businessman, however, boarding schools held the potential for considerable profit. Mary Mitford records that as a young girl she borrowed twenty-two titles from her local circulating library in only one month (in 1804), most of them with Minerva-style titles.[25]

Only the Minerva Press consistently defends its boarding-school patrons. Isabella Kelly, a Minerva author, finds comfort for her boarding-school readers in her novel *The Ruins of Avondale Priory* (1796). When Kelly's heroine must leave her school for the humble fireside of lesser mortals at home, she adapts to the change with the gracious poise of her genteel education:

For a little time the dignity of Miss Barry's appearance, with the superiority of her manners, awed her humble friends to silence and ceremonious distance, their respect being tinctured with fear, they conversed with timidity, and shrunk from her attempted freedom until the smiles of complacency beaming on her beautiful countenance, and a winning affability which distinguished every word and action encouraged their familiarity; dispelled the idea of superior advantages, and soon established a mutual harmony and contentment; they treated her with deference and attention, without ceremony, and she endeared herself so much to them by many kind offices, they soon considered her as being necessary to their happiness and welfare. She assisted and directed Agnes in several domestic matters, taught the elder children to read and work, and from the refuse of her own wardrobe decently attired the little ones ... In secret [she] breathed the sigh of melancholy remembrance. (1, 16–17)

It is Kitty's "sigh of melancholy remembrance" that reveals the source of Minerva fiction's most powerful attraction. The aspirations of shopkeepers' daughters require the enlivening ministrations of novelists just as urgently as the more genteel readers of Jane Austen's novels. The lower middle-class heroines, so often mocked and derided in genteel fiction – Polly and Biddy Branghton, Harriet Smith, Augusta Hawkins, Nancy and Lucy Steele, and Isabella Thorpe – find shelter and welcome in the novels of William Lane's Minerva Press. In proof of the considerable economic power of these readers, Lane left at his death a personal estate from his publishing business of £17,500, the solid tribute of a grateful reading public.[26]

This division of heroines by rank reflects an operating division of the reading public itself, one exploited successfully by Lane and later by his successor A. K. Newman.[27] Mary Meeke, one of the most popular of the generation of the Minerva writers after 1800, explains the influence of Lane's commercial judgment in her novel *Midnight Weddings* (1802). When the imagination of an aspiring author falters for want of a story, writes Meeke,

she must... consult the taste of her publisher. Indeed to secure their approbation is rather the general aim; for should you fail of meeting with a purchaser, that labour you hope will immortalize you is absolutely lost; a most mortifying circumstance in every sense of the word; and the gentlemen or ladies who sit in judgment upon the fine spun webs from the prolific brows of female authors, are very competent to decide upon the taste of the public. (1, 4)

The commercial success of Lane's Minerva Press scandalized contemporaries. "From the quantity of trash that has issued from Leadenhall Street," one observed, "it has been justly remarked that, instead of Minerva, a goose should have been the designation of its far-famed press."[28]

In truth, Lane's best writers, Anna Maria Bennett, Sarah Green, Mary Meeke, Regina Maria Roche, Eliza Parsons, Mary Ann Hanway, Mary Charlton, and Rachel Hunter, were not silly geese at all, but writers keenly aware of the social and economic realities faced by Lane's major customers, women readers from the lower middle class. Their "happy mediocrity," the Promised Land of novels designed for these customers, lies well outside the genteel landed ranks favored by Austen, Radcliffe, and Burney, and more towards the solid consumer comforts in the power of great City fortunes. "Although not a Trevanion," declaims Mr. Mordant, a great merchant in Anna Maria Bennett's *Anna; or Memoirs of a Welch Heiress* (1785),

I am a proud Briton; Lady Cecilia Edwin cannot be more anxious to preserve the honour of her noble blood, more tenacious of its dignity, or value it higher, than I do the title of British Merchant. Inflexible integrity, industry without parsimony, hospitality without extravagance, a noble confidence in the spirit of commerce, and above all, rectitude of heart and probity in dealings, are the marks which always should, and in general do, distinguish our respectable body. (IV, 50)

When Sarah Green's hero in *The Reformist!!! A Serio-Comic Political Novel* (1810) expresses outrage at the expenses of "the extravagant family of the king," a public-spirited gentleman stops him on the spot to offer a lively defense of tradesmen and commerce: "Oh fie, Sir!... this language is unbecoming a loyal subject. Princes are the support of the state; and many a tradesman in this great capital is established and enriched by this means, even if princes and nobles... are slow in their payments; for their name alone (such is the weakness of mankind in general) will bring him customers" (I, 191–92).[29] A character in Parsons' "horrid" novel, *The Castle of Wolfenbach* (1793), asserts staunchly, "I consider the English as the happiest people under the sun... Their merchants are rich and respectable, the first nobility do not disdain an alliance with them, they are considered the supporters of the kingdom."[30]

Mary Meeke, one of Lane's most prolific authors, attracted the favorable, if jocular, attention of Macaulay. "My tastes are, I fear, incurably vulgar," Macaulay wrote his sister, Lady Trevelyan, "as you may perceive by my fondness for Mrs. Meeke's novels." The plots, "which he all but knew by heart," according to Lady Trevelyan, who did not share her brother's taste, "were one just like another, turning on the fortunes of some young man of a very low rank of life who eventually proves to be the son of a Duke."[31] She does not exaggerate. The last pages of Meeke's *There is a Secret, Find It Out!* (1808) conclude just as Lady Trevelyan complains, with the revelation that Meeke's low-born, virtuous hero is of noble blood on his father's side, and, in addition, on the maternal side he has a great merchant grandfather whose wealth competes easily with that of his aristocratic grandfather. The best of two worlds combine in a satisfying recipe for unlimited consumer gratification.

Meeke's novel *Conscience* (1814) produces a programmatic defense of the commercial ranks as Arthur, the new-found Duke of Avon (known as James Treton in his days of struggle), reflects with pride upon the display of goods he encounters at a meeting of his two families, merchant and aristocratic: "A sumptuous dinner gave a turn to the discourse, and Arthur was convinced that British merchants and bankers fully vie with the nobility in point of luxurious living" (1, 280–81). In return for admittance into the aristocracy, the "low born" hero conveys Meeke's middle-class virtues of honesty, generosity, and loyalty into the higher ranks: "I think that a mind prepared as yours is by good nature, modesty, affability, and a kind concern for others," Arthur's titled uncle tells him, "is capable of the highest lustre of elegance, which you will attain with as much ease as you learnt your first language, merely by associating with graceful, well-informed people of both sexes ... and I can only say," he adds, referring to the hero's former humble profession as assistant to a surgeon-apothecary and accoucheur, "I wish I was half as much respected and beloved as you are in the neighbourhood of Ratcliffe Highway" (1, 142–43). Any middle-class woman with a Mary Meeke novel tucked under her arm could leave the library assured that the values of her class were safely represented within its covers.

Meeke adjusts the ranks of society in her novels with the exactness of an accountant, but always, finally, in favor of the commercial middle class. In *The Spanish Campaign* (1815), she presents a virtuous Jewish merchant (Jewish merchants have patriotically financed the war, says Meeke), a Mr. Levi, whose granddaughter, Donna Victoria, marries the hero, Charles Franklin. When Donna Victoria is killed in a carriage accident, she leaves her entire Spanish fortune to Franklin, which he invests in the British funds. With his resultant wealth, he revives an old family title to become "Lord Mowbray." Free to marry again, he weds an Englishwoman drawn, significantly for Meeke, from the respectable lower middle class, not from the gentry or aristocracy.

In all her novels, Meeke pieces together an energetic and frankly money-conscious society drawing from the aristocracy, from the great merchants, and from those representatives of trade and the lesser professions who loyally assist the "low born" hero during his evil days. Her villains are drawn from the highest and lowest extremes of her economic spectrum. At the top, there is the aristocratic father, uncle, or grandfather who hides the identity of the hero, usually because he is ashamed of the hero's mother's "base" origins in trade or the lower professions. At the bottom, there are dishonest, unworthy tradespeople who cooperate with the aristocrat's nefarious scheme. It takes a Great Merchant, an uncle or a grandfather on the mother's side, always generous and good, to expose the tyrannical collusion of proud aristocracy and conniving trade. In short, the central economic drama in Meeke's novels lies unashamedly in the great economy, not in the gentrified, domestic economies of Austen and Burney. Her novels depict a stable, thriving economy founded on commerce, in which Great Merchants monitor and correct the vices inherent in all the other orders of society: the temptations to pride in the aristocracy, fecklessness in the gentry, and graft and greed in tradesmen and petty professionals.

Sarah Green, also a Minerva author, but with a different perspective, emphasizes the respectability of incomes and budgets at the lowest level of the middle class. In an early work, *Mental Improvements* (1793), she advises her young readers to think twice before rejecting suitors from the lesser professions: "Without studying the graces, never indulge yourself, my dear niece," she writes, "in disliking this man because he is a soldier, another because he is a sailor, another because he is a lawyer, for be assured there are very honest, worthy men amongst them all, even of the latter description" (p. 24). As for her middle-class culture's enthusiasm for consumer luxuries, she advises the "niece" to adapt herself obligingly to such common conversations: "If they delight in the topic of fashion, know how to discuss the important subject of a new-fashioned bonnet, or fan," she counsels, and referring to the regular fashion features of the women's magazines, she reminds her niece to "remember the birthday suit that was most admired" (p. 29).

In Green's *The Reformist*!!!, the commerce itself, as it does for Meeke, becomes the focus of the narrative. Percival Ellingford, the naive hero of *The Reformist*!!!, courts ruin when he turns his manor into a charity hospital for the poor, who promptly cheat him of his fortune. The lesson the misguided Percival must learn, insists Green, is that prosperity comes only through making the wheels of commerce go round: the poor must work for their living and trust to the economy to pull them through. A neighboring landowner shows Percival the correct way to go about helping the poor:

The most judicious of these his charities, was the setting up of the widow of an innkeeper again in business, whose late husband had formerly been a faithful servant to old Lord Bentley; and when the present Lord sojourned at the house, he had the satisfaction of doing *real* good, by relieving only those persons which the landlady pointed out to him, and whose honest industry, struggling against repeated hardships, made them *true* objects of charity. (I, 150–51)

When severe economic depression strikes England in 1811, Green's fictions take it up. In her historical romance *The Royal Exile* (1811), D'Avenant, the hero, peers into the economic abyss to review its social consequences:

[He] had in a few months, experienced all the difficulties of poverty, and it rendered his mind reflective and feelingly alive to the wants of his fellow creatures. "Oh! could I but regain," he would often say to himself, "the rich possessions of my ancestors, and my paternal fortunes, how many, who are now hungry, miserable, and naked, should bless the bounty of Edward! But now the keen sufferings of my indigent fellow labourers are added to all the pangs I endure on my own account." (II, 150–51)

Even the king, Henry VIII, the royal "exile" of the title, experiences the same hardships of economic depression as his subjects: "Used to the luxuries and delicacies of life, and now keenly enduring their privation, Henry joyfully took the proferred good," "a basket of some excellent viands, and a bottle of wine ... Pride, and false dignity of feeling, soon get extinct in that mind, which experiences only the accumulated ills of severe poverty and distress" (II, 149).

The mood of Green's next novel, *The Fugitive* (1814), rebounds with the restored national economy, but also registers an admission that chance and fate are part of the economy as well. Green sends Emma Southby, her delightfully plucky heroine, to do battle with the economy. Emma never succumbs to its hardships, but presses on from one difficulty to the next with grit, determination, and cheerful common sense. Like Burney's heroine in *The Wanderer*, also published in 1814, Emma repeatedly attempts to secure employment, but, unlike Burney's genteel Juliet, Green's middle-class Emma succeeds in finding it. After a series of poor jobs – as a governess bilked of her earnings, as a companion to a bad-tempered gentlewoman, as a sempstress of plain work, and finally (successfully) as an embroiderer for a merchant with a large warehouse – Emma finds a satisfying measure of personal happiness: "In the mean time she went on with her embroidery, continued to give satisfaction, and she cheerfully ate the bread of industry, and would have been comparatively happy, as far as related to herself, had not the sorrows and indigence of her elder brother pressed heavily on her feeling heart" (III, 218). Unlike his successful sister, the brother fails in the battle to make a living (he is a writer), thus forcing his frail young wife to take in laundry to supplement the family income. Emma, however, manages to remain respectable in London as a single woman living on her own. Sent to the wrong end of town by a prankster when she asks for direction, cheated by a dishonest shopkeeper, suspected of prostitution by landladies, she survives, and even learns to use the pawnbrokers' shops for emergency funds. Before Green will allow untold riches to descend on Emma as the newly discovered *Lady* Emma Southby, with the title and a fortune in her own right, she insists that her middle-class Emma must earn a personal independence through the labor of her own hands.

Green's last novel, *Who Is the Bridegroom? Or, Nuptial Discoveries* (1822), affirms an economic program in which women across the social ranks are enabled to succeed in the great economy through mutual support of one another. The novel starts with one heroine, but ends with three: "Though Sophia is our ostensible heroine," Green explains at the conclusion, "yet the story may boast of two more, who well deserve the title" (III, 261–62). The figure of the "masculine woman," Lady Diana Wentworth, deprecated by the author at the beginning of the novel, grows by the last volume into a staunch and successful defender of women's rights. The heroine's elder sister, Eliza, who begins the novel as a stereotypical termagant, ends as the supportive defender of her younger sister's reputation against scandal. The heroine's mother, Lady Ashton, starts as a version of Mrs. Malaprop, but ends as a generous, loving, loyal mother. When she learns that her two genteel daughters face exclusion from society because of an unfounded, malicious scandal, she stands by them, pocketbook in hand:

"Oh dear!" said lady Ashton, "here's a pretty *kittle* of fish; and all along with that *preverse* young puss, and be hanged to her, God forgive me! But, however, I'm your mother still – so don't go for to make yourselves uneasy. Though I once worked for my bread myself [as a dairymaid], don't think that the daughters of sir Edward Ashton, to whom I owe all my riches, shall ever do the like of that! No, no, your poor mother, as prided herself so in her *vartuous* girls, and who never thought to see this day in her *inclining* years, she'll go with you, and share your *solintary* lot. Ah, lack-a-daisy me! no husbands now for my daughters – all's over; nothing but scandal talked everywhere about them, and their characters blasted by envy and *moll-violence*." (II, 74)

And when the Earl of Pyrwater, the marquis of Rainsbury's uncle, registers offense at the prospect of his nephew's marrying the younger daughter of the low-born and illiterate Lady Ashton – "How should

I feel at the idea of the marquis of Rainsbury calling such a being his mother-in-law!" – Green's admirable "masculine" woman, Lady Diana, answers him briskly: "Oh fie, my lord!" she says, "every one knows she is a good woman" (III, 170).

Sarah Green resolves the conundrum of rank very much as Meeke does, by reworking the semiotics of gender and station. Aristocratic virtues become bywords for candor and honesty as represented by the outspoken Lady Diana. Gentry values become the principles of honor and truth represented by the two genteel, falsely accused sisters. Commercial virtues appear with Lady Ashton, who is frank, loyal, and generous in all her financial dealings. Like Meeke, Sarah Green creates an economic foundation in fiction for the aspiring lower ranks of the middle class, and like Meeke, she defines their place socially upwards. With generous applications of cash from Lady Ashton, Green brings the gentry and the aristocracy into the economic world of an idealized commercial class.

Rachel Hunter, yet another Minerva writer to address the economy directly, shows a more rigorous sympathy with the lower ranks of the middle class than either Green or Meeke. Hunter denies the gentry and aristocracy any power whatsoever, symbolic or otherwise, to confer respectability on her lower-ranked heroes and heroines.[32] Rather than raising the social station of her heroes in the concluding pages by marriage or the discovery of inherited rank, which is the usual practice of Mary Meeke and Sarah Green, Hunter concludes her novels by providing modest positions for her heroes as merchants, clergymen, or barristers. Her sturdy middle-class loyalties earned her the ridicule of Jane Austen and her niece, Anna: "Jane Austen begs her best Thanks may be conveyed to Mrs Hunter of Norwich," Austen mockingly writes Anna, "for... the spirited sketches... Miss J. A.'s tears have flowed over each sweet sketch in such a way as would do Mrs Hs heart good to see, & if Mrs H. could understand all Miss Austen's interest in the subject she would certainly have the kindness to publish at least four volumes more about the Flint family" (*Letters*, 406–07).[33] A cast of worthy merchants and honest professional men appear in Hunter's *Family Annals* (1808), one of her typical productions, with such solid and worthy middle-class names as Brown, Hearne, Skinnerley, Mitchell, and Adams. Spendthrift gentlemen and villainous aristocrats in the novel bear the ostentatiously genteel names of Beverley and Wentworth.

Even with their differences, however, the task remains the same for Jane Austen and Rachel Hunter: the ordering of society by rank and budget. Women novelists may differ in evaluating the contributions of each rank to the economic whole, but the general terrain remains the same. This is nowhere more apparent than in the common agreement among women novelists that Great Merchants are admirable, but petty tradesmen need not apply. It is a telling paradox that Lane's intensely commerce-oriented writers reject the social ambitions of "upstart tradesmen" with even greater vigor than genteel authors like Austen or Burney.

Mary Meeke, Lane's most eloquent defender of Great Merchants, is also his fiercest opponent of petty shopkeepers. While Great Merchants represent an economically stable society for Meeke, petty shopkeepers represent just the opposite. "To have heard them talk," Meeke writes of a shopkeeper's family in *The Veiled Protectress* (1810), "a stranger would have supposed the gentleman had been at least a merchant, when the fact was, they had kept a jewellery and toy-shop at Southampton" (I, 52–53). The petty shopkeeper becomes the universal scapegoat in women's fiction.

Although Meeke's novel *There is a Secret, Find It Out!* (1808) abounds with lost heiresses and melodramatic villainy, it also contains the wry and knowing tale of two wily tradespeople, Mr. and Mrs. Wheeler, who have "wheeled" their way into a great deal of money, first by petty avarice, then by major treacheries. The Wheelers begin in the novel as figures of low comedy in the tradition of Fielding's Mrs. Slipslop, but by "Volume IV," they have become thoroughly reprehensible and corrupt. In ungrateful return to a genteel family who gave them protection in their early days, the Wheelers conspire to betray the very people who helped them rise. Meeke metes out rewards and punishments at the conclusion of her novel with wonderfully appropriate justice by forcing the villainous Wheelers back to their origins in low trade: "Mrs. Wheeler took a small chandler's and green-grocer's shop; but as she also took to drinking, her trade soon fell off, and, after going on from bad to worse, during the ensuing ten months, she, in an unfortunate moment, having made too free with her favourite liquor, slipped down her cellar stairs and broke her leg, and being conveyed to an hospital, she there ended her miserable career" (IV, 377). This is precisely the horrendous fate, even to the stairs, that Richardson reserves for the sexual treachery of Clarissa's Mrs. Sinclair, not an insignificant measure of economic priorities in women's fiction. The upstart Wheeler son, a vicious youth who tormented the hero as a child, concludes the novel as a scavenger in a "dust-yard" in the "vicinity of Gray's-inn-lane," as Meeke notes with pleased exactness, where it was "his place," she writes, "to keep an eye over the men, to precede the cinder-sifters, in turning over the dust when brought in, and to keep an account of the pigs who basked upon the fragrant heaps." The hero, now appearing in society as the new-found Lord Caerleon, drives through "Gray's-inn-lane" with his wife Lady Caerleon just as the young Wheeler appears in his dust-yard, "raking a dust-heap, and fighting with the surrounding pigs." The Wheeler youth, standing in this unsavory situation "without a hat" – a detail offered with special satisfaction – is "instantly recognized by Lord Caerleon," writes Meeke, "who as instantly turned his head, and soon dashed off, convinced that Heaven was just in its decrees" (IV, 375–76).

In effect, Minerva novelists wield a double-edged sword: one side of the blade for promoting the dignity of commercial station, the other for exacting revenge on "upstart wealth"; that is, one side for stabilizing economic life as it *should* be, the other for exposing it as it really is. Women's dress and deportment most often supply the occasion. The new rich Miss Rufford in Matilda Fitz John's *Joan*!!! (1796) attends a ball where she "sidled and shuffled through the figure, with the ease of a fettered ass" (I, 67). Mary Cayenne, a rich Jamaican heiress in Mary Ann Hanway's *Ellinor* (1798), "blended in her appearance all the fat and vulgarity of her mother, with the avarice and low cunning of her father" (I, 16–17). A kept mistress in Mary Ann Hanway's *Andrew Stuart* (1800), "taken from her natural element...floundered from side to side of the satin sofas, like a grampus left by the retiring ocean on the shores of Greenland" (I, 109).

The boarding-school miss with a subscription to a circulating library – possibly a tradesman's daughter herself – lives with the economic paradox willingly. It's a small enough price to pay. Though she may never achieve great wealth herself, her manners and cultivated sensibility can reach and exceed its proper requirements, exactly as the novels from the library promise. Her sole task is to avoid "proof of vulgarity." And that is guaranteed by possession of the very novel she holds in her hands.

The accomplishment of women novelists of all stripes lies in their success in making the novel the sounding-board for the discussion of women in the economy. Women's fiction captures the economy for women not only by assigning women the supervision of domestic spending in their novels, but by seizing a format for talking about the economy. Women's novels renegotiate the meaning of economic life for women, removing consumer spending from its traditional association with excess and disorder, old-style aristocratic vices, by consigning it to the supervision of sensible, respectable women from the ranks, high to low, of the middle class. In one sense, the effort to empower women economically comprises a single movement: a concentrated effort to codify a position of economic responsibility for women, a redefining of gender roles, and a thoroughgoing condemnation of those economic traditions that enfeeble women. In another account, the developments in fiction divide women's fiction along the lines of rank and station, where hearty contempt gets traded regularly by novelists across the tables of the circulating library. But this is classic consumer territory, the perfect paradigm of the economy they promote: novel readers can exercise the delightful empowerment of consumer choice, of wise management of the budget, by combing the tables of the library for the particular novels that shore up the claims of their own ranks.

The most startling aspect of the conversation among novels, however, lies in its scope and vigor. As Henry Tilney boasts in Austen's *Northanger Abbey*, "I myself have read hundreds and hundreds" (p. 107). Austen deliberately separates herself in *Northanger Abbey*, together with her admired Burney and Edgeworth, from the company of other women writers, but she also falls into a familiar Derridean bind: she is caught in "a certain relationship, unperceived by the writer, between what [she] commands and what [she] does not command of the patterns of the language that [she] uses."[34] The heartiness of Austen's laughter at didactic novelists like West, Brunton, Hunter, and More as too earnest and, of course, too middle class, or her contempt for Minerva Press writers as extravagant and, again, foolishly middle class (Isabella Thorpe's "horrid" novels) only serves to emphasize her complicity in the ongoing conversation. Austen's most surprising triumph may be, in fact, the preeminent place in posterity that she achieves for her own social rank through her incisive contributions to the very fray that she rejects, which is the subject of the next chapter.

Plate 4. Wedgwood & Byerley, York Street, St James's Square, from
Rudolph Ackermann, *The Repository of Arts, Literature, Fashions* (1809).

I believe I have done all my commissions, except Wedgwood.
Jane Austen, *Letters* (18 *April* 1811).

CHAPTER 4

Shopping for signs: Jane Austen and the pseudo-gentry

Taken one at a time, needs are *nothing*.
Jean Baudrillard, "Consumer Society" (1970)

"Now I will give you the history of Mary's veil, in the purchase of which I have so considerably involved you," Jane Austen writes her sister Cassandra: "I thought myself lucky in getting a black lace one for sixteen shillings. I hope half that sum will not greatly exceed what you had intended to offer upon the altar of sister-in-law affection" (*Letters*, 69). A gift, a sister-in-law, and an unexpected expense. To those of us with experience in these matters it sounds familiar and potentially ominous, but to unravel the "history of Mary's veil" is no simple task. Our days of easy credit and an unimaginable river of free-flowing capital can hardly be compared to the material culture of the late eighteenth century. Today, for example, anyone with a bank loan and a steady job can own a Jaguar. Not so in Austen's day for a barouche-landau. Still, Jane Austen's invocation of the minor deity of gift-giving sets up a sympathetic vibration in us that, if distant, is close enough to prompt a new pass through the Austen wares.

In sharp distinction to the mass consumerism of today, Austen and her contemporaries approach consumption through the much narrower gates of rank and custom. The historian David Spring describes Jane Austen's social rank as neither aristocracy nor gentry, but a third group he calls "pseudo-gentry."[1] These are the non-landed rural elite, those families who do not draw their income from the land, but live in the country and are strongly tied by culture and connections to country life: "first and foremost the Anglican clergy; second, other professions like the law – preferably barristers rather than solicitors – and the fighting services; and last, the rentiers recently or long retired from business." They are "pseudo-gentry" because, unlike the gentry, their income and status do not derive from the ownership of land.² They are, however, "gentry of a sort," Spring emphasizes with keen insight, "primarily because they sought strenuously to be taken for gentry."³ The distinction in rank is crucial: it is the condition that brings meaning to consumer life in Austen's fiction.⁴ The goods that fill Austen's letters and novels are only "the visible tip of the iceberg" of the social process that defines her group. Spending, like the hallmark on silver, marks Jane Austen's ambitious class as nothing else does.⁵ This formidable power to classify complex social and cultural relations makes the act of consumption in Austen's novels nothing less, as Bourdieu claims, than "obligatory" and "a ruthless call to order."⁶

Austen's wry genuflection to "the altar of sister-in-law affection" confirms the point, her ironic rendering of the consumer code completely unable to extract her from its "ruthless" order. The mere acknowledgment that others believe in the system sweeps her and her sister into its grasp.⁷ The implicit and revealing conflict in the history of Mary's veil lies somewhere between Jane Austen's resisting purse-strings and the ordering language of consumption. In the contest between the two, the identifying mark of pseudo-gentry culture inscribes itself directly onto the gift.

Austen's personal letters guilelessly expose the seam in the seamless coat of her rank's self-promotion.⁸ One must not overreach one's place, yet one must not settle for any *thing* less than the very sign that will confirm that place. Buying furniture: Austen attends a musical evening at her brother Henry's London house, but the new furnishings have not arrived – "A glass for the Mantlepiece was lent, by the Man who is making their own" (p. 273). Tableware is chosen for Edward, the gentry brother: "We then went to Wedgwoods where my Bʳ & Fanny chose a Dinner Set. – I beleive [*sic*] the pattern is a small-Lozenge in purple, between Lines of narrow Gold; – & it is to have the Crest," she notes with care, the all-important sign of his new status as heir to a great landed estate (p. 328). She, the pseudo-gentry sister, rides about London in the gentry brother's luxurious barouche: "I liked my solitary elegance very much, & was ready to laugh all the time, at my being where I was. – I could not but feel that I had naturally small right to be parading about London in a Barouche" (pp. 312–13).⁹

Paradoxically, material goods provide Austen with a language for her most intimate feelings as well.¹⁰ She reports a morning of special pleasure in Canterbury with Edward: "We paid no other visits –

only walked about snugly together & shopped" (p. 365). For Austen, who really longs for a letter from her sister Cassandra, the plaintive and homely, "You know how interesting the purchase of a spongecake is to me," speaks a heartfelt affection (p. 191). "I long to know whether you are buying stockings or what you are doing," she writes (pp. 362–63). And she reports a "great many pretty Caps in the Windows of Cranbourn Alley," but it is not the caps that are on her mind: "I hope when you come, we shall both be tempted" (p. 384).[11]

Austen's letters to Cassandra might be construed, quite plausibly, as an epistolary history of things, too many things for some readers.[12] But there is also the more potent implied narrative that winds its way through the letters and the purchases: the history of how a single and not very well-provided woman, the daughter of a clergyman, stakes her claim to station in a social group that sets its boundaries largely through the signifying power of the things it can afford to buy.[13] There is no overestimating the significance of material possessions in pseudo-gentry life.

From the beginning of her writing career, the fledgling author knows her subject. The very first letter of "Volume The First" recounts the following adventure: "DEAR CHARLOTTE / I should be obliged to you, if you would buy me, during your stay with Mrs Williamson, a new & fashionable Bonnet, to suit the complexion of your E. FALKNOR. Charlotte, whose character was a willingness to oblige every one," writes the young Jane Austen, "when she returned into the Country, brought her Freind the wished-for Bonnet, & so ended this little adventure, much to the satisfaction of all parties" (*MW*, 4–5).[14]

Although gratifying as a family joke, consumer desire does not transfer into fiction with the same transparency that it possesses within the family circle. "Catharine," one of Austen's last juvenile works, illustrates the problem. Isabella Stanley, a young friend and house guest of the heroine, receives a letter: "You received a Letter from Augusta Barlow to day, did you not my Love?" Isabella's mother asks. "She writes remarkably well I know." "Oh! Yes Ma'am, the most delightful Letter you ever heard of," replies Isabella. "She sends me a long account of the new Regency walking dress Lady Susan has given her, and it is so beautiful that I am quite dieing with envy for it." Mrs. Stanley asks for specific information about the travel arrangements of the Barlow family, to which

Isabella replies: "She says nothing indeed except about the Regency." Catharine, the heroine, is not satisfied: "She *must* write well thought Kitty, to make a long Letter upon a Bonnet & Pelisse" (*MW*, 211). Later, when Catharine gets her own letters from Isabella, Isabella's "letters seldom contained any Intelligence except a description of some new Article of Dress" (*MW*, 240). The same consumer goods that supply ready grist for the mill in Austen's letters to Cassandra speak a different language in fiction. In fiction, ordinary objects of desire parade inevitably as images of excess and self-absorption.

Lady Susan, the most extended of Austen's juvenile pieces, avoids the unwanted inference of luxury by confining consumption to those social ranks, the aristocracy and the upper gentry, where material goods display themselves more quietly than in pseudo-gentry houses. Lady Susan sizes up the house of her gentry relations only in the most general terms: "The house is a good one, the Furniture fashionable, & everything announces plenty & elegance" (*MW*, 250). Austen's own rank waits to assert its special perspective on material culture in the author's comic afterword. "For myself," the young pseudo-gentry author concludes, "I confess that *I* can pity only Miss Manwaring, who coming to Town & putting herself to an expence in Cloathes, which impoverished her for two years, on purpose to secure him, was defrauded of her due by a Woman ten years older than herself" (*MW*, 313).

The conflict between acceptable and unacceptable consumption throws the universe of Austen's early novels into a Manichaean dualism of consumer anxiety.[15] Whether or not, as Tony Tanner insists, the consumer-mad General Tilney in *Northanger Abbey* is a modern Montoni, Tanner's general point must be gratefully conceded.[16] Squire Western is dead, General Tilney lives, long live the Thorpes as well.[17] Austen's heroine, Catherine Morland, gets squeezed between two groups of obsessed consumers, the General at the top of the scale and the Thorpes at the bottom.[18] Catherine joins the hapless Emilys and Louisas of the 1790s gothic novel as yet another innocent victim of the same economy she reads about in *The Mysteries of Udolpho*.

General Tilney and the Thorpes are definitely not the simple "emulative consumers" of Fielding, like Mrs. Slipslop or Black George, who function as lamentable examples of greed or excess in the lower ranks. On the contrary, consumers of the Tilney and

Thorpe variety follow a different code of acquisition entirely. The insatiability of their desire issues from an imaginative act, the illusory sense of control over the object's meaning. Traditional old-style hedonists want control over the *objects*; the modern consumer wants control over the *meaning* of the objects. Modern consumer pleasures derive, according to present-day consumer theorists, not from possession of the object, but from the ever-illusory promise of owning the meaning of the object.[19] Failure, as all agree, is inevitable.

Indeed, General Tilney is driven to supply Austen's naive heroine with the approved meaning of his possessions as he takes her through the Abbey: "all the minuteness of praise, all praise that had much meaning, was supplied by the General" (p. 182). Even the breakfast china receives his exegetical attention: the General, "thought it right to encourage the manufacture of his country, and for his part, to his uncritical palate, the tea was as well flavoured from the clay of Staffordshire, as from that of Dresden or Sève" (p. 175). John Thorpe finds that he too must direct Catherine's attention to the authorized version of his possessions: "Curricle-hung you see; seat, trunk, sword-case, splashing-board, lamps, silver moulding, all you see complete; the iron-work as good as new, or better" (p. 45).[20]

When Catherine receives Isabella's infamous letter from Bath, she expects a Jane-and-Cassandra type of letter, one between sisters, "and especially was she anxious to be assured of Isabella's having matched some fine netting-cotton, on which she had left her intent" (p. 201), but, of course, the duties of friendship that reside in netting-cotton go neglected by Isabella in the dry wind of her consumer desire: "The spring fashions are partly down; and the hats the most frightful you can imagine... Anne Mitchell had tried to put on a turban like mine, as I wore it the week before the Concert, but made wretched work of it." Her offer to Catherine of a tradesman-like exchange of suitors, John Morland for Frederick Tilney, caps the joke: "Pray explain every thing to his satisfaction," she instructs Catherine (pp. 216–17).[21]

In *Sense and Sensibility*, the traditional, comforting way to consider consumption is represented by Mrs. Jennings, Sir John Middleton, and Colonel Brandon, but unfortunately it is the order of a lost world. Elinor Dashwood, through a rather different spending program, reinforces the values appropriate to her own reduced station. Although connected to the landed gentry by blood, the Dashwood women, like Austen herself, have no real claim upon its resources, taking their seat in the same fragile boat with other pseudo-gentry women whose livelihood depends upon the life or savings of the male head of family. In the moral economics of this novel, represented by Elinor most particularly, affordable material comforts operate in a dialectical relationship with extravagant display. The Steele sisters at the bottom of the social scale and the John Dashwoods at the top energetically embrace display; the Dashwood women, through necessity and Elinor's right-thinking management of the domestic budget, choose affordable comfort.

When the traditional economy of inherited estates slams the door on the Dashwood women, the economy of competitive consumption sets the door swinging in equally arbitrary and dangerous ways. Lucy Steele is the perfect representative of this order: "The whole of Lucy's behaviour in the affair, and the prosperity which crowned it, may be held forth as a most encouraging instance of what an earnest, an unceasing attention to self-interest, however its progress may be apparently obstructed, will do in securing every advantage of fortune, with no other sacrifice than that of time and conscience" (p. 376). The prudent way of the pseudo-gentry, that is to say, of the Dashwood women and Edward Ferrars (a parson-to-be), becomes ever more vulnerable. Material objects turn into weapons to be used against them.

Robert Ferrars, having usurped his brother Edward's fortune, laughs "most immoderately" at Edward's impending poverty: "The idea of Edward's being a clergyman, and living in a small parsonage-house, diverted him beyond measure" (p. 298). Mrs. John Dashwood, if she could, would thrust her Dashwood kinswomen even further down the social scale by laying claim to the china, linens, and plate that they inherit from the Norland estate: "a great deal too handsome, in my opinion, for any place *they* can afford to live in," she tells her husband (p. 13).

Fashion drives Lucy Steele, Mrs. Ferrars, Mrs. John Dashwood, and in lesser ways Mrs. Palmer, Nancy Steele, and Lady Middleton, to mindless obsession. If a seat in parliament is not immediately possible for her brother Edward, Mrs. John Dashwood's ambition would be "quieted" by seeing him "driving a barouche" (p. 16). "I always preferred the church, as I still do," Edward tells Elinor's mother, "But that was not smart enough for my family" (p. 102). "Smart" characterizes the Steele girls at their first appearance (p. 119). Lucy has a "smartness of air" (p. 120). Nancy is happy to have as many beaux about as possible, "provided they dress smart and behave civil" (p. 123). Miss Grey, reports Mrs. Jennings, is "a smart, stilish girl they say, but not handsome" (p. 194).

In contrast, Elinor and Marianne are never "smart." Elinor has "a delicate complexion, regular features, and a remarkably pretty figure. Marianne was still handsomer... her smile was sweet and attractive, and in her eyes, which were very dark, there was a life, a spirit, an eagerness which could hardly be seen without delight" (p. 46). Nature's own sweet assets devolve on the Dashwood women of *Sense and Sensibility* with no price-tag attached. We know nothing at all of their clothing.

The Steele girls, however, are born to shop. In a satisfying stroke, Austen has Mrs. Jennings pick them up on a shopping trip to Exeter. "Nothing," writes Austen, escapes Nancy Steele's "minute observation and general curiosity ... She was never easy till she knew the price of every part of Marianne's dress; could have guessed the number of her gowns altogether with better judgment than Marianne herself, and was not without hopes of finding out before they parted, how much her washing cost per week, and how much she had every year to spend upon herself" (p. 249). Mrs. Palmer, at the gentry end of the scale, shops with equal idiocy: "Mrs. Palmer, whose eye was caught by every thing pretty, expensive, or new; who was wild to buy all, could determine on none, and dawdled away her time in rapture and indecision" (p. 165). Elinor Dashwood, however, does not "shop." Elinor visits Mr. Gray's in Sackville-street where she carries on "a negociation for the exchange of a few old-fashioned jewels of her mother." The choice of the word "negociation" is a deliberate distinction (p. 220).

Elinor does, however, see two genuine shoppers there, both of them men. Women are the silly shoppers of the novel, but they are small fry indeed in comparison to the men. Robert Ferrars stands at the counter "deciding on all the different horrors of the different toothpick-cases presented to his inspection," and John Dashwood arrives to bespeak a seal for Fanny, a mandatory item of display for rising country mice on their first *at home* visit to Mayfair. John has not called on his sisters sooner, he explains to Elinor, though the family has been in town for two days, because of urgent demands: the task of taking his son, the ever-fortunate Harry, to see "the wild beasts at Exeter Exchange," and the absolute necessity of getting to Mr. Gray's for Fanny's seal. Foolish and idle, wasteful and selfish, the men of this novel, Willoughby, John Dashwood, Mr. Palmer, Robert Ferrars, and Colonel Brandon's elder brother, are all destructive consumers.

By far the worst offender, of course, is Willoughby. Almost from his first appearance, Austen makes excess his major trait of character: "His estate had been rated by Sir John at about six or seven hundred a year; but he lived at an expense to which that income could hardly be equal, and he had himself often complained of his poverty" (p. 71). Mrs. Jennings bustles in with the news of his engagement to Miss Grey: "Fifty thousand pounds! and by all accounts it wo'nt come before it's wanted; for they say he is all to pieces. No wonder! dashing about with his curricle and hunters!" (p. 194). Willoughby repeatedly admits his weakness: "My fortune was never large, and I had always been expensive, always in the habit of associating with people of better income than myself. Every year since my coming of age, or even before, I believe, had added to my debts...my circumstances were so greatly embarrassed ... it was all insufficient to outweigh that dread of poverty, or get the better of those false ideas of the necessity of riches, which I was naturally inclined to feel, and expensive society had increased" (pp. 320, 321, 323). Elinor has the last pseudo-gentry word on right principles of expense: "Had you married," she tells Marianne, "you must have been always poor. His expensiveness is acknowledged even by himself, and his whole conduct declares that self-denial is a word hardly understood by him" (p. 350).

Austen creates no effective system for opposing the consumer madness of *Sense and Sensibility*. Sir John Middleton, with all his good will, is simply a hearty, bumpkin squire updated with picnics and cold collations. Mrs. Jennings, motherly, kind, and generous, is no match for Lucy Steele, and the character of Colonel Brandon remains sentimental invention pure and simple. John Dashwood readily takes the modern measure of the Colonel's gift to Edward: "Well, this is very astonishing! – no relationship! – no connection between them! – and now that livings fetch such a price! – what was the value of this?...It is truly astonishing!...What could be the Colonel's motive?" (pp. 294–95). When Marianne Dashwood converts her fate to gothic melodrama when she receives Willoughby's final letter – "Nothing but the blackest art employed against me can have done it" (pp. 188–89) – she is right, but not in the way she thinks.

Pride and Prejudice in its turn presents right-thinking consumption brilliantly illuminated against a backdrop of outrageous extravagance. Among the abusers, Lydia, Kitty, and Mrs. Bennet show the flag for the lesser gentry; Mr. Collins does it for the pseudo-gentry; the Bingley sisters, "in the habit of spending more than they ought" (p. 15), do it for the parvenus, and Lady Catherine de Bourgh takes responsibility for the aristocrats. Elizabeth, Darcy, and the Gardiners supply examples of the *correct* way of dealing with the act of consumption. As Bourdieu suggests, such a careful arrangement of ranks is no minor affair, but a means of legitimating power: "That is why manners, especially the manner of relationship to legitimate culture, are the stake in a permanent struggle. There can be no neutral statement in these matters."[22]

Austen repeats the consumer comedy she explored in *Northanger Abbey* by giving the Thorpes, Lucy Steele, Willoughby, and the John Dashwoods another run of life in Mrs. Bennet, Lydia, Wickham, and the Bingley sisters. The difference in *Pride and Prejudice*, however, is that the hero and heroine, and their thinking friends, consciously address the unsteady relationship between station and spending. "If they had uncles enough to fill *all* Cheapside," Bingley says handsomely of Elizabeth and Jane, "it would not make them one jot less agreeable." "But it must very materially lessen their chance of marrying men of any consideration in the world," replies the matter-of-fact hero (p. 37). "A man in distressed circumstances," says Elizabeth, equally matter-of-fact, "has not time for all those elegant decorums which other people may observe" (p. 153).

Consumption appears in *Sense and Sensibility* negatively, through the losses it represents, but it strides into *Pride and Prejudice* with a cheerful, vulgar bustle. Austen shifts her attention from the *loss* represented by acquisition to the *power* invested in material items that convey meaning. That is to say, she directly confronts in this novel the pseudo-gentry's lifeline to station. Mr. Collins reveals his rank's strategy in shameful nakedness as he dwells covetously on the material belongings of the landed classes.[23] Thoughts of Lady Catherine's *things* give such flight to his narrative skills at the Philips' house in Meryton that, "when Mrs. Philips understood from him what Rosings was, and who was its proprietor, when she had listened to the description of only one of Lady Catherine's drawing-rooms, and found that the chimney-piece alone had cost eight hundred pounds, she felt all the force of the compliment, and would hardly have resented a comparison with the housekeeper's room" (p. 75).

His love of fine things, however, does not restrict itself to Lady
Catherine's possessions alone, as Mrs. Bennet finds to her dismay on
his visit to Longbourn: "The hall, the dining-room, and all its furniture were examined and praised; and his commendation of every
thing would have touched Mrs. Bennet's heart, but for the mortifying
supposition of his viewing it all as his own future property" (p. 65).
Marriage for Mr. Collins is simply an array of new possessions. As he
shows Elizabeth around his "humble abode" at Hunsford, he calls
upon her to "admire every article of furniture in the room, from the
sideboard to the fender," so much so that "she could not help
fancying that in displaying the good proportion of the room, its
aspect and its furniture, he addressed himself particularly to her, as if
wishing to make her feel what she had lost in refusing him" (p. 156).

Lady Catherine de Bourgh, the daughter of an earl, joins the farce
at Rosings. The praise lavished on every dish by Mr. Collins and Sir
William Lucas is so fulsome that "Elizabeth wondered Lady
Catherine could bear [it]." On the contrary, "Lady Catherine
seemed gratified by their excessive admiration, and gave most
gracious smiles, especially when any dish on the table proved a
novelty to them" (p. 163). She enters the competition with spirit as
she asks Elizabeth "what carriage her father kept" (p. 164); she
marvels at Elizabeth's Uncle Gardiner keeping a manservant (p.
212), and she stops herself only just in time to prevent an unseemly
comparison of pianofortes: "Our instrument is a capital one,
probably superior to—You shall try it some day," she tells Elizabeth
(p. 164).

Among the right-thinking characters, gift-giving consciously
detaches consumption from the competitive economy. "In the next
room," says Mrs. Reynolds, "is a new instrument just come down for
[Miss Darcy] – a present from my master," she adds (p. 248).
Elizabeth's response to the gift typifies the naturalizing program:
"'He is certainly a good brother,' said Elizabeth, as she walked
towards one of the windows." Mrs. Reynolds glosses the text: "'And
this is always the way with him,' she added. – 'Whatever can give his
sister any pleasure, is sure to be done in a moment. There is nothing
he would not do for her'" (p. 250). Darcy's offer of fishing-tackle to
accommodate Mr. Gardiner's pleasure is a personal attention that
incorporates both nature and material possessions in a single,
signifying act, a proposed gift that surprises Elizabeth all the more for
the clarity of its social message (p. 255).[24]

Consumer jocularity provides the genteel characters of the novel with a self-conscious strategy for defusing the raw power of Darcy's great wealth.[25] The nearest that Mrs. Gardiner, the pseudo-gentry aunt, will allow herself to approach Darcy's relationship with Elizabeth, for example, is to allude playfully to its consumer potential: "a low phaeton" and "a nice little pair of ponies" stand in for Elizabeth's potential match with Darcy's fortune (p. 325). Elizabeth performs the same maneuver of playfulness when she thanks Darcy for saving Lydia: "Mr. Darcy, I am a very selfish creature," she begins, "and, for the sake of giving relief to my own feelings, care not how much I may be wounding yours. I can no longer help thanking you for your unexampled kindness to my poor sister." "Kindness," not "money," is the proper line to take, but Darcy's straightforward reply sets the gift in its inevitable context of exchange: "If you *will* thank me ... let it be for yourself alone. That the wish of giving happiness to you, might add force to the other inducements which led me on, I shall not attempt to deny." The lapse of time is all that interposes, according to sociologists, between calling a gift by a stronger name.[26] Elizabeth is rendered speechless by its implication, "too much embarrassed to say a word" (p. 366).

If Charlotte Lucas' defection from right-thinking in *Pride and Prejudice* is a glancing reminder in that novel of the desperation that characterizes women's fiction in the 1790s, Jane Austen's unfinished novel *The Watsons*, dated around 1804–05, presents the pseudo-gentry woman's darkest social nightmare. In *The Watsons*, the Watson family falls into utter moral collapse under the pressures of competitive consumption.

The story opens with Emma Watson, the heroine, reduced to comparative poverty in a typical 1790s-style dislocation. A wealthy aunt has raised Emma with the expectation of a handsome fortune, but when the aunt remarries, the niece is sent home penniless to live in a modest country vicarage with a dying father and three unmarried sisters. The kinship ties of the Dashwoods, Bennets, and Tilneys undergo their economic rubs and irritations, but in the Watson family, money stretches the ties of kinship considerably past the breaking-point. "What a blow it must have been upon you!" says Emma's brutally tactless brother Robert Watson, greeting her on her return home, "To find yourself, instead of heiress of 8 or 9000 £, sent back a weight upon your family, without a sixpence" (*MW*, 352).

Consumer expense literally maps the neighborhood. The "Town

of D." in *The Watsons* marks its borders by the material signs of wealth. The Edwards live at one end of the town, prosperous retired rentiers, while the Tomlinsons, newly rich bankers, settle at the other end, and between them the local trade life of the town, including a milliner's shop and the White Hart Inn where the gentry, the pseudo-gentry, and even the aristocratic Osbornes, meet for the local assemblies. Positional goods define relations: "The Edward's [*sic*] were people of fortune who lived in the Town & kept their coach; the Watsons inhabited a village about 3 miles distant, were poor & had no close carriage" (pp. 314–15). Elizabeth introduces her younger sister to the Edwards' provincial splendor with obvious appreciation of its social meaning: "The door will be opened," she announces as she and Emma arrive on a visit, "by a Man in Livery with a powder'd head, I can tell you" (p. 322).

Relations between the ranks are distinctly hostile in the fragment, with tense divisions drawn along the strict lines of the culture of consumption. "The Great Folk" reside at Osborne Castle, where, Mr. Edwards remarks to his wife, "they are but just rising from dinner at midnight." "The Osbornes are to be no rule for us," she replies firmly (p. 325). Emma's father is "far from being delighted" when Lord Osborne and his sycophant Tom Musgrave call at the vicarage: "Phoo! Phoo! – What occasion could there be for Ld O.'s coming. I have lived here 14 years without being noticed by any of the family. It is some foolery of that idle fellow T. Musgrave." Pleading ill health, he tells his daughters, "I cannot return the visit. – *I* would not if I could" (p. 348).

Finally, another group, the London suburbanite, appears with Emma's brother Robert Watson and his wife Jane.[27] These two egregious shoppers are competitive materialists through and through: "Robert Watson was an Attorney at Croydon, in a good way of Business; very well satisfied with himself for the same, & for having married the only daughter of the Attorney to whom he had been Clerk, with a fortune of six thousand pounds. – *Mrs* Robt was not less pleased with herself for having had that six thousand pounds, & for being now in possession of a very smart house in Croydon, where she gave genteel parties, & wore fine cloathes" (pp. 348–49). Jane Watson's newish, London standards are the sum of her character: "I had seven Tables last week in my Drawingroom," she announces upon meeting Emma: "Are you fond of the Country?" The gauge of her superiority to Emma turns on Emma's fall in the consumer race: "the loss of the Aunt's fortune was uppermost in her mind, at the moment of meeting; – & she cd. not but feel how much better it was to be the daughter of a gentleman of property in Croydon, than the neice of an old woman who threw herself away on an Irish Captain" (p. 349).

The potential of such a rank-conscious world, with all its consequent confusions of money and place, is codified in material possessions. When Lord Osborne and Tom Musgrave interrupt the Watsons' unfashionably early and meager dinner with an un-announced social call, Emma must draw some fine lines indeed. Nanny has just come into the parlor with "the Tray & Knife-case": "No visitors would have been welcome at such a moment; but such visitors as these – such a one as Ld Osborne at least, a nobleman & a stranger, was really distressing." Emma "felt all the inconsistency of such an acquaintance with the very humble stile in which they were obliged to live; & having in her Aunt's family been used to many of the Elegancies of Life, was fully sensible of all that must be open to the ridicule of Richer people in her present home." Elizabeth, the older sister, is saved distress only by her less sophisticated knowledge of the meaning of material goods: "her simpler Mind, or juster reason saved her from such mortification – & tho' shrinking under a general sense of Inferiority, she felt no particular Shame" (pp. 344–45).

The Watsons was to conclude in the triumph of the pseudo-gentry at its domestic best. Emma Watson, Austen told Cassandra, "was to decline an offer of marriage from Lord Osborne, and much of the interest of the tale was to arise from Lady Osborne's love for Mr. Howard, and his counter affection for Emma, whom he was finally to marry" (p. 363). In effect, the pseudo-gentry hero, the valued clergyman companion of aristocrats, refuses an aristocratic alliance in order to marry a clergyman's daughter, educated to a "stile of life" beyond her father's poor parlor, of course, but loyal to her pseudo-gentry station and to its principled notions of consumption.

Nevertheless, the vision remains a dark one. *The Watsons* under-scores the most pressing economic issue for women in the 1790s – the fear of being without money. In *The Watsons*, Emma Watson is twice disinherited: once gentry-style through the loss of the inheritance from her aunt, and second, pseudo-gentry style, through the death of her clergyman father and the consequent loss of his small income. Ranks harden up, competitive spending hastens the constriction, and the family structures that should support women crumble under the pressure. *The Watsons* fails to show the way out of despair, but the fragment does suggest Austen's shift, with the rest of women's fiction, to a focus on the social consequences of consumption.

In *Mansfield Park* (1814) the shift is complete. The social bomb ticking away in the act of consumption becomes central to the conflicts of the novel. Consumer desire fuels the moral action of *Mansfield Park*, and sexual desire is inextricably intertwined in the struggle. Without lessening the moral gravity of *Mansfield Park* in the slightest, its action may be read as an extended tale of disastrous consumer decisions.[28]

On one side, Austen treats consumption in this novel as dangerously invasive, like an "infection," which is exactly what Tom Bertram calls it when he confronts his father's disapproval of his alterations of the billiard room. On the other hand, consumption appears in the novel as a source of useful goods, a system to be tapped, with suitable constraints and cautions, for happiness. Austen's dialectic in *Mansfield Park* operates between these two conceptions. It is all right, nay admirable, that Fanny Price taps the system for a silver knife for her sister and a ticket to a lending library, but it is not all right to have the Crawfords, two high-flying London consumers, move into the Mansfield Parsonage next door. That is too close for safety. They bring with them an aristocratic taste for luxury that they have imbibed in London; the Bertram family, country gentry grown torpid, have lost touch with the principles of a proper expense; Fanny Price, their cousin from the pseudo-gentry, sets them all straight.

Obsession for material possessions drives the plot. The most obvious victims, Mary Crawford, Mrs. Norris, Henry Crawford, and Maria Bertram, are caught fast in their individual rounds of unattainable desires, but they are not alone: the temptations of consumption overtake and invade the lives of all the novel's characters.[29] There is the foot-in-the-door ploy: "Yes, the expense of such an undertaking would be prodigious!" replies Tom, with heavy irony, to Edward's objection to the theater on grounds of expense: "Perhaps it might cost a whole twenty pounds" (p. 127). Tom's predictions, of course, fall well short of the rising costs of the theatre, and, it might be noted parenthetically, that Tom's casual sum of £20 equals Jane Austen's clothing budget for an entire year.[30] Edmund's imagination succumbs willy-nilly to the alluring blandishments of the shop-window display arranged for him at the Grant's parsonage: "A young woman, pretty, lively, with a harp as elegant as herself;

and both placed near a window, cut down to the ground, and opening on a little lawn, surrounded by shrubs in the rich foliage of summer, was enough to catch any man's heart" (p. 65). The scene is an illustration straight from the pages of the women's journals (see plate 25, "Female Accomplishments", p. 160), and it serves its purpose: "Without studying the business, however, or knowing what he was about, Edmund was beginning at the end of a week of such intercourse, to be a good deal in love" (p. 65).

Mary is a devoted consumer, in every sense. "A large income is the best recipe for happiness I ever heard of," she announces to Edmund. "You intend to be very rich," he asks. "To be sure," says Mary, "Do not you? – Do not we all?" Edmund answers soberly, "My intentions are only not to be poor," an assertion that Mary rejects with faintly disguised contempt: "By moderation and economy, and bringing down your wants to your income, and all that," she replies, dismissing in one statement the pseudo-gentry's first principle of domestic economy. "Be honest and poor, by all means," she taunts him. "I do not much think I shall even respect you. I have a much greater respect for those that are honest and rich" (p. 213).

Mary and Henry Crawford in their pursuits of material possessions ride perilously close to pathology – which for Austen is social pathology. Mary's reply to Edmund's probing question, "You intend to be very rich," makes the point: "Do not we all?" (p. 213).[31] Finally, Mary is herself consumed by her own obsession, swallowed-up as a marketable item consigned to the shelf in London to be taken, or perhaps not, by one of "the dashing representatives, or idle heir apparents, who were at the command of her beauty, and her 20,000 *l.*" (p. 469). Austen ostensibly gives Mary a moral choice, to eschew the market for love, and for the reasonable competence of a very good clergyman's income, but the "choice" for Mary remains stubbornly and narrowly a consumer's choice, that is to say, no choice at all. The system she subscribes to is inexorable.

Fanny, quite the opposite, spends her energies avoiding, or trying to avoid, any participation in the market at all.[32] Complications, however, descend on her unavoidably, as gifts from Tom, Edmund, Mary Crawford, Henry Crawford, and Sir Thomas – puzzling, dangerous, and always carrying some implicit, but uncertain demand for repayment. If Mary's notions of consumption are associated with the marketplace, Fanny's notions insist that consumption really

begins after the purchase, when the item is at home and in use. For
Fanny Price and for Jane Austen, "goods make and maintain social
relationships," goods are for communication.[33] In *Mansfield Park*,
however, they almost invariably come to Fanny with mean-spirited
messages. Gifts sent to Fanny, rather than celebrating the whole of
the consumer feast by the presentation of a symbolic part of it,
represent considerably less than the whole.[34] Maria and Julia "make
her a generous present of some of their least valued toys, and leave her
to herself" (p. 14); Tom gives her "very pretty presents, and laughed
at her" (p. 18); "Sir Thomas, who had done so much for her and her
brothers ... would he only have smiled upon her and called her 'my
dear Fanny'" (p. 33). Such gifts articulate the program announced
by Sir Thomas Bertram as the condition of receiving her into the
family: "I ... would on no account, authorize in my girls the smallest
degree of arrogance towards their relation; but still they cannot be
equals" (p. 11).

Fanny understands it well: goods "are most definitely not mere
messages; they constitute the very system itself," and the secret
power of pseudo-gentry consumption lies in her rank's calculated
acceptance of that truth.[35] The puzzling shock that Edmund and
Fanny register at Mary Crawford's allusions to the adulterous life of
Admiral Crawford makes excellent sense in these terms. The
Admiral's generous gift to Henry of his fortune carries much more
weight with Edmund and Fanny than Mary's plain-spoken truths
about his immoral life. "But was there nothing in her conversation
that struck you Fanny, as not quite right?" Edmund asks. "Oh!
yes," Fanny replies, "she ought not to have spoken of her uncle as she
did. I was quite astonished. An uncle with whom she has been living
so many years, and who, whatever his faults may be, is so very fond
of her brother, treating him, they say, quite like a son. I could not
have believed it!" Edmund agrees, "I thought you would be
struck," he says, and calls Mary's remarks "indecorous." Fanny
adds a more powerful source of complaint: "And very ungrateful I
think" (p. 63).

Fanny herself is "grateful" for all the leftovers of family bric-à-
brac that end up in the meagerly furnished and near-freezing East
room, but as her eyes pass over some "work-boxes and netting-boxes,
which had been given her at different times, principally by Tom ...
she grew bewildered as to the amount of debt which all these kind
remembrances produced" (p. 153). Nothing could be in greater

contrast than Mary Crawford's cavalier relinquishment of a necklace given her by her brother. "It is very pretty – but I never think of it," she says to Fanny. Independent of Fanny's suspicion of Henry's part in the gift of the necklace, Fanny is horrified at Mary's principles of consumption: "To take what had been the gift of another person – of a brother too – impossible! – It must not be!" (pp. 259–60).

Gift-giving can be a kind of genteel extortion, one of Austen's bitter truths in *Mansfield Park*. What return does *gratitude* dictate for a pseudo-gentry sister when her brother has received the gift of a major career promotion? Henry Crawford turns the gratitude screw with skill. Through his influential uncle the Admiral, he secures a promotion for Fanny's brother William in the navy, from midshipman to lieutenant, a classic instance of pseudo-gentry advancement through family connections. Austen's own father rose by the same route. "Prove yourself grateful," says Edmund encouraging her to accept Henry's hand (p. 347).[36] The conflict between individual desire and responsibility to her family, especially to William's advancement, is a crisis indeed: "Poor Fanny's mind was thrown into the most distressing of all its varieties. The recollection of what had been done for William was always the most powerful disturber of every decision against Mr. Crawford" (p. 364).

Fanny's decision to assert her individual will over the demands of the group is a striking act of courage for a pseudo-gentry woman. In all of Austen's novels, society exacts personal sacrifices from individual members for the sake of the group, but, paradoxically, none of her groups has any truly efficient sanction for imposing the sacrifices on maverick members. Expulsion, the ultimate measure, is really the only measure for enforcing compliance.[37] This extortionate price is one which Fanny does not have to pay. Mr. Crawford will have to find another woman to live with "in all the riot of his gratifications" (p. 123), but the crisis, as well as its blunted career, marks the line of a significant ideological dilemma in *Mansfield Park*. Fanny sails very close to the wind in refusing Henry Crawford.

Instead of absolute expulsion, Fanny is sent into the wilderness, Portsmouth, to learn her lesson, but there the plot begins to run in broken streams. The great social and moral issues of the novel yield to the lesser entanglements of consumer embarrassment. Issues of consumption dwindle to the status of a family joke, a little laugh for the author and her reader. When Henry Crawford joins the Price family for Sunday worship at the Garrison chapel, for example,

Fanny is relieved to have the family seen in their respectable Sunday finery, "their cleanest skins and best attire." It is Austen's small concession to Fanny's consumer pride: "Sunday always brought this comfort to Fanny, and on this Sunday she felt it more than ever" (p. 402). Consumer tragedy becomes consumer farce.

Austen turns away from the ethical conflicts and obsessions of the major characters to promote the more public side of her rank's implicit program of domestic economy, that is to say, a celebration of the material triumph of the Price children. In this apotheosis of pseudo-gentry success, the novel affirms their social and material advancement: in Susan's "usefulness," Austen writes in the concluding paragraphs, "in Fanny's excellence, in William's good conduct, and rising fame, and in the general well-doing and success of the other members of the family, all assisting to advance each other, and doing credit to his countenance and aid, Sir Thomas saw repeated, and for ever repeated reason to rejoice in what he had done for them all, and acknowledge the advantages of early hardship and discipline, and the consciousness of being born to struggle and endure" (p. 473). Austen's letters to Cassandra indicate how strongly this public program of consumption governs relations in her own family, but in *Mansfield Park* she allows the private and public worlds to cross paths for a devastating revelation of the moral confusions inherent in the conjunction.

If consumption represents in *Mansfield Park*, for the largest part of the novel, an essentially *private* measure of values, in *Emma* it represents a gloriously proportioned *public* measure. "When we dress the leg," says Miss Bates of a gift of pork from the Woodhouses, "it will be another thing" (p. 177). The most memorable material possession in *Mansfield Park* remains a small amber cross destined for the heroine's virgin breast; in *Emma* it becomes a Broadwood piano, large, public, and subject to the speculations of the entire village of Highbury. In sharp contrast to *Mansfield Park*, where London expense is judged to be "very much at war with all respectable attachments" (p. 433), London in *Emma* is simply a place to get a haircut, to buy a piano, or to send Harriet Smith for dental care and a renewal of spirits. Mr. Woodhouse says the worst thing that can be said of the place: "nobody is healthy... nobody can be... so far off! – and the air so bad!" (pp. 102–03).

The novel begins on a fresh wind of material acquisitions. We learn that Miss Taylor has married Mr. Weston and now has a carriage and a house of her own; that Mr. Weston has retired from trade and has bought a small estate; that Mr. Elton "has fitted up his house so comfortably that it would be a shame to have him single any longer" (p. 13). It is a society in movement, with every step marked by significant positional goods. The Coles are on the way up: they have a new dining room, more servants, a new pianoforte, and more "expenses of every sort" (pp. 207, 215). Mrs. Perry talks of Mr. Perry's setting up his carriage; Mr. and Mrs. Elton parade with unremitting vulgarity their new carriage, more servants than they can remember names, and, of course there are Mrs. Elton's lace and pearls.

The prospects of material luxury lead the imaginations of Highbury about like will-o'-the-wisps. Mr. Perry's potential carriage runs through the speculations of Mrs. Perry, Miss Bates and Mrs. Bates, the Coles, and Jane Fairfax before reaching Frank Churchill, and then resurfacing at Hartfield for the consideration of Emma, Mr. Knightley, and the Westons. Jane Fairfax's new pianoforte stimulates Emma's imagination to excesses that later return to haunt her conscience. The appearance of Mr. Knightley's carriage at the Coles' dinner party with Miss Bates and Jane Fairfax turns Mrs. Weston's mind toward matrimony. Too much of Mr. Weston's "good wine" literally leads Mr. Elton's mind astray.

Consumption in *Emma* is the order of the day. Carriages, for example, bring the Box Hill débâcle to a welcome close: "The appearance of the servants looking out for them to give notice of the carriages was a joyful sight" (p. 374). Tea saves Mr. Weston from more unwanted news of Maple Grove: "They were interrupted. Tea was carrying round, and Mr. Weston, having said all that he wanted, soon took the opportunity of walking away" (p. 310). "The saddle of mutton" sets the pace of conversation at Randalls (p. 119), and tea sets the time for departure. "Mr. Woodhouse was soon ready for his tea; and when he had drank his tea he was quite ready to go home" (p. 124). Finally, the length of a carriage ride provides the beginning and the end to Mr. Elton's declarations of "violent love" (p. 129).

For such consumer order, however, Austen trades heavily in "cultural capital," one of the pseudo-gentry's most important notes of exchange. "If a group's whole life-style can be read off from the style it adopts in furnishing or clothing," which is certainly the case in *Emma*, this is because such knowledge, writes Bourdieu, has been arrived at in one of two rather different ways: either by "birth," that is by early immersion in the culture, or later, as "educational capital," which, though useful as a working currency, can never rise to the same sterling value as "cultural capital." Mrs. Elton and Jane Fairfax illustrate the distinction to perfection. Mrs. Elton's educational capital causes her to appear with a pronounced disadvantage before the cultural capital of the heroine. Emma's low opinion of Mrs. Elton's commercial origins, "Bristol was her home, the very heart of Bristol" (p. 183), stands the test of experience. Mr. Knightley, though kinder, does not differ from Emma: "There is no saying very much for the delicacy of our good friends, the Eltons" (p. 447). As for Jane Fairfax, Mr. Knightley has nothing but praise of her cultural capital: "Every thing is in his favour," Mr. Knightley says of the Churchill–Fairfax marriage, "equality of situation – I mean, as far as regards society, and all the habits and manners that are important; equality in every point but one" (p. 428).[38] That is to say, even without a fortune, Jane's social equality is stamped on her brow by "birth," raised as she has been by Col. Campbell in those ranks of society where Mr. Knightley's cultured habits and manners, and the money to support them, reign serene.

Austen's only defense against the incursions of the *arrivistes* in *Emma* is a vigorous deployment of cultural capital. Possession of a good stock ameliorates some of the disturbances caused by the general competitive acquisition of goods. Mr. Knightley makes the terms of this cultural transaction clear when he decisively rejects Mrs. Elton's offer to plan the Donwell Abbey strawberry party. The most she can trade for is an invitation to join the party and the opportunity to display "all her apparatus of happiness, her large bonnet and her basket" (p. 358). Austen reinforces the cultural accounting system in the novel by excluding Mrs. Elton at the novel's conclusion from the Woodhouse–Knightley wedding. Mrs. Elton's poverty of cultural capital, demonstrated in her attention to material goods, lies exposed for mocking laughter as she responds to the happy event: "Mrs. Elton, from the particulars detailed by her husband, thought it all extremely shabby, and very inferior to her own. – 'Very little white satin, very few lace veils; a most pitiful business! – Selina would stare when she heard of it'" (p. 484).

Unfortunately for women without a competence, however, cultural capital does not generate an income.[39] Gifts of pork, a bushel of apples, and an invitation to play piquet do not save Miss Bates from her fears of domestic expense. Miss Bates, as a pseudo-gentry woman fallen on hard times, feels more sharply than anyone in Austen's novels the unforgiving facts of survival in a market culture. Nor does Mr. Knightley's stern lesson for Emma at Box Hill propose any real amelioration of Miss Bates' grim future: "She is poor; she has sunk from the comforts she was born to; and, if she live to an old age, must probably sink more. Her situation should secure your compassion" (p. 375).

Deep fissures open in the cheerful surface of the world of goods in *Emma*. First, rank cannot be made stable in a social system run by competitive consumption. Austen may depict Mr. Martin in a happy feudal relationship with his good friend, his landlord and adviser Mr. Knightley, but real-life Mr. Martins were rising through wartime farming prosperity to become gentlemen as fast as they could, and without the blessings of Mr. Knightley.[40] Moreover, as Austen does recognize in *Emma*, there is simply no stopping people like Mrs. Elton. Mrs. Elton, as the vicar's wife, will continue to garden the social landscape of Highbury, though always as an intruder from the "very moderate" commercial ranks of Bristol. Her exclusion from the Woodhouse–Knightley wedding cannot neutralize her presence in Highbury, nor will Jane Fairfax's rescue from the hands of the Smallridge family prevent the Smallridges and their ilk from eventually acquiring cultural capital themselves – from people like Jane Fairfax, only less fortunate.[41]

The key to getting on with life in Austen's *Emma* lies in adapting to the changes. Emma puts her finger on this in her harsh assessment of Mrs. Elton's failings: "that all her notions were drawn from one set of people, and one style of living; that if not foolish she was ignorant" (p. 272). If anything, this is Emma's own failing, her unwillingness to grant the Coles, the Coxes, and the Gilberts their undeniable advance in station; a failing to minister consistently to Mrs. and Miss Bates in their fall in station, and a self-willed blindness to Harriet Smith's realistic chances in the scramble. Mr. Knightley has no compunction about accepting dinner engagements with the Coxes, Coles, and Gilberts; he asks Harriet Smith to dance; he understands Mr. Elton, "not at all likely to make an imprudent match" (p. 66); and as for Mr. Martin, "his mind has more true gentility," he tells Emma, "than Harriet Smith could understand" (p. 65). Mr. Knightley's practical assessments of social mobility in the consumer world of *Emma* prove him the hero of the novel.

In *Persuasion*, women are excellent administrators of the domestic budget, the best. But in *Persuasion* there is something more: a powerful concern with credit that brings this novel's world of goods into a much more complex and anxious relationship with its social world than in any previous Austen novel. Credit under Lady Elliot's supervision at Kellynch Hall had been managed with "method, moderation, and economy," a regimen of domestic economy that had "just kept" Lady Elliot's spendthrift husband "within his income" (p. 9). Lady Russell explains the central relationship of credit and domestic economy: "After all," she tells Anne, "the person who has contracted debts must pay them, and though a great deal is due the feelings of the gentleman, and the head of a house, like your father, there is still more due to the character of an honest man" (p. 12). Anne subscribes completely, constructing even more rigorous plans of retrenchment: "She considered it as an act of indispensable duty to clear away the claims of creditors, with all the expedition which the most comprehensive retrenchments could secure, and saw no dignity in any thing short of it" (pp. 12–13).

Women set the tone for responsible consumption. Mrs. Croft arranges the lease for Kellynch: "And a very well-spoken, genteel, shrewd lady, she seemed to be," says Mr. Shepherd, Sir Walter's lawyer: "asked more questions about the house, and terms, and taxes, than the admiral himself, and seemed more conversant with business" (p. 22). When Captain Wentworth objects to taking women on board his ships, "from feeling how impossible it is, with all one's efforts, and all one's sacrifices, to make the accommodations on board, such as women ought to have," Mrs. Croft's response is instant and explosive: "Oh Frederick! – But I cannot believe it of you. – All idle refinement! – Women may be as comfortable on board, as in the best house in England ... I hate to hear you talking so, like a fine gentleman, and as if women were all fine ladies, instead of rational creatures" (pp. 69–70). Discomforts that had loomed large in *Emma* – the lack of a housekeeper's room at Mr. Elton's house, for example – become relative comforts in *Persuasion*. "As long as we could be together," says Mrs. Croft, "nothing ever ailed me, and I never met with the smallest inconvenience" (p. 71). A translation might read, "As long as we lived within our income ... " Admiral Croft repeats the sentiment from the husband's side as he compares their present, expensive lodgings in Bath with the quarters they shared at the beginning of his career: "We do not like our lodgings here the worse, I can tell you, for putting us in mind of those we first had at North Yarmouth. The wind blows through one of the cupboards just in the same way" (p. 170).

"Belonging to that profession," as Austen terms Anne Elliot's naval marriage to Captain Wentworth, is *Persuasion*'s image of a successful marriage, a professional partnership in which it is expected that people will pay their bills. Like Charlotte Smith, or like the despised Rachel Hunter for that matter, Austen canvasses her ranks in *Persuasion* for their spending practices. Aristocratic spending finds representation in Sir Walter Elliot and his daughter Elizabeth, whose notions of "comforts" are ruled solely by the inflexible constraints of fashion, too expensive for their budget. The unreflecting Charles and Mary Musgrove show the flag of excess for the gentry, spending to the limits of their income and agreed on only one thing, "in the want of more money, and a strong inclination for a handsome present from his father" (p. 44). Mrs. Clay's perfidy says it all for the lower end of the middle class.

Material culture mismanaged lays a deathlike hand on the world of *Persuasion*. Sir Walter considers two of his daughters "of very inferior value" (p. 5). Elizabeth invites Captain Wentworth to Camden Place because "Captain Wentworth would move about well in her drawing-room" (p. 226). Moreover, the foolish Sir Walter and his daughter Elizabeth are not singular in their opinion. It's the way of the world. Captain Wentworth describes his return to England as his own near-descent into the world of unvalued consumer objects: "We had not been six hours in the Sound, when a gale came on, which lasted four days and nights... Four-and-twenty hours later, and I should only have been a gallant Captain Wentworth, in a small paragraph at one corner of the newspapers" (p. 66).

Characters from the professional ranks in *Persuasion* must exert themselves vigorously to gain control of their possessions. When the Crofts take over Kellynch, they commence straight away to put their new-leased things in order: "We told you about the laundry-door, at Uppercross," Admiral Croft reminds Anne: "The wonder was, how any family upon earth could bear with the inconvenience of its opening as it did, so long!" (p. 127). Captain Harville and Mrs. Smith manufacture things for their health. Mrs. Smith even sells goods that she manufactures in her sickroom. In short, directed industry marks the road to success and happiness in *Persuasion*. Rightly considered, material goods have the power to open the world. The objects in the Harvilles' rooms at Lyme, "something curious and valuable from all the distant countries Captain Harville had visited, were more than amusing to Anne: connected as it all was with his profession, the fruit of its labours, the effect of its influence on his habits, the picture of repose and domestic happiness it presented, made it to her a something more, or less, than gratification" (p. 98).

One ideology of consumption in *Persuasion* rests on a simple pseudo-gentry assumption, that people who have success deserve it. Even in regard to her own father and sister at Kellynch, Anne "could not but in conscience feel that they were gone who deserved not to stay, and that Kellynch-hall had passed into better hands than its owners'" (p. 125). There is also a kind of smug satisfaction to be found in Admiral Croft telling Mr. Shepherd expansively that he "knew he must pay for his convenience" in leasing Kellynch Hall (p. 22). Even Mrs. Smith, equally delinquent with her husband in their spendthrift days, is allowed to rehabilitate herself through the manufacture of little sewing-cases to sell for the poor. As her reward, the lost West Indian estates fall back into her pocket.

It takes poor Dick Musgrove to expose the rent in this version of the economy. In dispatching that unfortunate youth, Austen herself subscribes briefly to the darkest of her revelations about consumption. She turns him into a consumer object with no apologies, a poor prize in the lottery of parenthood, "nothing better than a thick-headed, unfeeling, unprofitable Dick Musgrove" (pp. 50–51). The family owes him nothing, not even a few "fat sighings" or a Christian name. Material goods seek out *deserving* characters as their reward for industrious participation in the economy. In effect, the moral order of *Persuasion* rests on a divinely ordained guarantee of health in the British economy, an assumption not so very different from Mary Meeke's, Sarah Green's, or Rachel Hunter's in their Minerva novels, only offered up to the Austen reader from the perspective of a different rank.

Austen does not rest comfortably, however, with so simple an economic universe. At the conclusion of *Persuasion*, the thoroughly unworthy Mr. William Elliot continues in his selfish career, sexually gratified, wealthy, and secure in the inheritance of Kellynch. Sir Walter and Elizabeth remain in their fashionable Camden Place lodgings, as happy as people like themselves *can* be. Worse, good people are cut off in their careers by economic forces out of their control. "There comes old Sir Archibald Drew and his grandson," says Admiral Croft: "Ah! the peace has come too soon for that

younker" (p. 170). One can assume that the peace has come too soon
for the economic fortunes of the wounded Captain Harville and his
family as well. In fact, the Anne and Wentworth plot turns on the
unpredictability, not the predictability, of Wentworth's economic
success. Wentworth's prosperity has been the luck of the draw, as he
himself admits. "I have been used to the gratification of believing
myself to earn every blessing that I enjoyed. I have valued myself on
honourable toils and just rewards," he tells Anne. "I must learn to
brook being happier than I deserve" (p. 247). Anne agrees: "It was,
perhaps, one of those cases in which advice is good or bad only as the
event decides" (p. 246).

"Only as the event decides" is probably the key to the economic
puzzle left by Austen's unfinished *Sanditon*.[42] In *Persuasion* her
protagonists sail towards happiness on a wave of fortunate circumstance: Anne gets Captain Wentworth and a new landaulette;
Captain Wentworth gets Anne and £25,000 in prize money. In
Sanditon, in contrast, Mr. Parker engages an economy that is a far
more problematic adversary than the French Navy. Wentworth
places his courage, strength, and skill against an identifiable
opponent, but Mr. Parker, trusting to eternally fair economic
weather, sails into the uncharted investment waters of Sanditon, a
small, seaside bathing place.[43] The failure of Austen's ever-sanguine
brother Henry's bank in which her uncle, Mr. Leigh-Perrot, and her
brother Edward lost huge sums of money in March 1816 may well be
Austen's inspiration for this line of economic exploration. *Sanditon*
was roughed out less than a year after the bankruptcy, between
January and March 1817, when illness forced her to put the fragment
aside unfinished. Regardless of the inspiration, the fragility of Mr.
Parker's hold on the economy seems likely to be the central issue in
Sanditon.

There is a strong sense in reading the fragment that we are looking
at familiar Austen characters thrust into an unsettling economic
world.[44] There is Lady Denham, Mr. Parker's partner, a par-
simonious, arbitrary woman of great wealth who tyrannizes over her
poor relations with the spirit of Mrs. Ferrars and has less to say for
herself in the village than Lady Catherine de Bourgh. She may or
may not, mostly may not, continue financial support for the Sanditon
investment when bad economic weather hits. The two Miss Beauforts,
recent arrivals in Sanditon and reminiscent of the Steele sisters and
Isabella Thorpe, are no strong foundation on which to build a

fortune either. Mrs. Parker with her feeble domestic presence, rather like Lady Bertram's, will be no support in a storm. Ironically, these villains, semi-villains, and weak reeds are the very characters on whom Mr. Parker stakes his future.

As for consumer objects in *Sanditon*, they disappear into the thin air of real estate promotion. Success in the economic venture of Sanditon, as Austen suggests ominously, lies wholly at the mercy of consumer whim. In truth, Mr. Parker's Sanditon is the purest of consumer objects, almost solely an object of the imagination. Advertisements, newspapers, and word of mouth are the bricks and mortar of Mr. Parker's enterprise. The world of signs completely outruns the world of things. It is the joke of the piece, of course, but also a situation that promises to mark a fatal separation between Mr. Parker and his fortune.

In spite of the clouds on the economic horizon, however, Charlotte Heywood's view from her window offers the reader a picture of material goods in harmony with nature: "the miscellaneous fore-ground of unfinished Buildings, waving Linen, & tops of Houses, to the Sea, dancing & sparkling in Sunshine and Freshness" (p. 384). It hardly seems likely that Austen will let the investment go under completely, but all that can be predicted with confidence in this fragment is that Austen's own rank, the pseudo-gentry, will continue to exert its claims on our attention. Mr. Parker, from the traditional landowning ranks of the gentry, is clearly out of his depth in commercial investment. This is the pseudo-gentry's field of expertise (brother Henry's banking débâcle notwithstanding), and Austen provides a likely hero in Mr. Parker's businessman brother Sydney, a competent member of her own favorite social group, to set things straight. A pseudo-gentry author to the end.

In the promotion of her own rank, Austen's works follow a pattern familiar to all women's fiction of her generation. Her steady promotion of the pseudo-gentry does nothing more nor less than Meeke, Green, and Hunter do for the commercial ranks. It becomes startlingly clear in women's fiction, 1790–1820, that systems of consumption and systems of discourse are not by any means independent of one another. And as part of one system, Austen's novels get tossed onto the same tables at the circulating library with the novels of every other woman author claiming a space there. When Austen, Cassandra, and their niece Anna visited a circulating library in Alton after the publication of *Sense and Sensibility*, Anna, not yet privy to the secret of the novel's authorship, picked up her aunt's novel, looked it over, and threw it back on the table with "careless contempt, little imagining who had written it, exclaiming to the great amusement of her Aunts who stood by 'Oh that must be rubbish I am sure from the title.'"[45] The demands on Austen in the competitive marketplace of women's fiction could hardly be better illustrated. She claims her place in the commerce without shame in *Northanger Abbey*, where she reminds her readers that heroines must be "patronized," that novels are "productions," that they issue from a "literary corporation," and, unhappily, they often fall into a world intent on "undervaluing the labour of the novelist" (p. 37).

Jane Austen has long since been rescued by her admirers from the tables of the circulating library, but with a great loss, I think, to our understanding of her work, and with an even greater loss of our appreciation of the context of women's fiction in her time. "In Jane Austen's day" is a term almost irksome in its implication that anything serious in the period belongs to Austen alone. In truth, all women's fiction was a serious business: first, in the commercial sense, because it opened a door for women to participate in the economy as patrons and as readers, and second, metaphorically, in its social and ethical sense. If Austen was amused by the silliness in contemporary fiction, "We are just going to set off for Northumberland to be shut up in Widdrington Tower, where there must be two or three sets of victims already immured under a very fine villain" (*Letters*, 248), it was not a casual amusement, but the amusement of an engaged mind, alert to the underlying current of common energy that gave such fiction life.

Today, mass culture trivializes consumer passion by consigning it to actors on television commercials, but at the end of the eighteenth and the beginning of the nineteenth centuries, consumption was a serious matter, not to be taken lightly. "Cozy hearths" might at some future time become a retreat for the bourgeois where, as David Musselwhite argues, they "could indulge a nostalgia for objects stripped of commodity values,"[46] but not so for writers and readers of the early century who *wanted* to know the price of a hearth. Commodity values were the nourishment of the imagination, the foundation of culture. Women's fiction understands this, of course, and demands a place in the shop window of the age where it becomes arguably the most compelling product on offer.

Plate 5. Frontispiece, *The Lady's Magazine* (January 1789).

An elegant Female Figure seated in her Library, contemplating the Beauties of the
LADIES MAGAZINE.

CHAPTER 5

Picturing the heroine: " The Lady's Magazine," 1770–1820

The author of the beginning of the Novel, is either at liberty to send for his copy to the editor, or favour him with the whole of the narrative, prior to publication; but is desired to advert, that the correspondents of the Lady's Magazine are all *Volunteers*.

The Lady's Magazine, 1777

The frontispiece for the collected and bound *Lady's Magazine* for the year 1789 features an "elegant Female Figure," as the text explains, "seated in her Library, contemplating the Beauties of the LADIES MAGAZINE" (plate 5). This young woman, it continues, represents "Study, who is crowned by Wisdom, in the Character of Minerva, with a Chaplet of Laurel, assisted by Cupid, displaying the Torch of Hymen." A *bargain*, as the magazine regularly reminded the readers, "the plates worth *four* times the price charged for this Magazine" (January 1819). To modern readers, however, the plate reveals a rather different message. With its elegantly imagined "Library" and well-turned-out reader, a more likely title for the frontispiece might be, "Consumer Desire Ministered to by Sentimental Love and a Fine Show of Education."[1]

From the beginning in 1770 of the *Lady's Magazine*'s long life, *fashion* was its operative language.[2] In fact, its pictures and stories depend upon the negotiating power of fashion to make any sense at all. The reader of the *Lady's*, for example, receives her copy, notes its elegant frontispiece, turns rapidly through the pages to glance at the illustration of the month's story, skips to the end see if there is perhaps an illustration of Paris Dress or some sheet music or a pattern for an apron, her trip through the magazine becoming itself a kind of shopping expedition with no expectation to buy, window-shopping of the most guileless sort among the ideas and images of the *Lady's*.[3] Then and only then, after the initial pass through the magazine's plates, the reader is free to turn to the tale and peruse its columns

Lovers Vows. Act 5, Scene the last.

Publish'd as the Act directs for G.G.& J.Robinson March 1.1799.

Plate 6. From *The Lady's Magazine* (February 1799).

through the decoding lens of fashion. The space between the reader's first consumption of the magazine – its illustration of the tale, the fashion plate, the patterns, music, recipes, maps of foreign parts, etc. – and her actual reading of its fiction provides a wide arena for negotiating the contemporary social discourse inevitably embedded in the magazine's style and presentation.[4]

"Everybody" read the *Lady's Magazine*, too. That is, everybody prosperous enough to afford a ticket to the local circulating library where current issues and copies of back years in bound volumes could both be obtained.[5] It is no exaggeration to claim that the *Lady's Magazine*, in its first fifty years, from 1770 to 1820, defined public issues for women. Through its subsequent yearly appearance gathered in bound volumes, it not only had an indefinite shelf-life, but it became a magazine of reference.[6] With the readers supplying most of the *Lady's* fiction, *gratis*, as humble offerings on the altar of fame, its publication policies presented contemporaries with a genuine forum for women's issues. The pulse of eighteenth-century magazine fiction beat not only in its printed pages, but quite literally in the audience itself.[7]

The variety of consumer features in the *Lady's* gave a strong illusion of contemporaneity: sheet music of the latest songs, plates with the newest fashions – "Turbans are still the fashion. Some wear them with the part before that used to be behind" (see plate 9) – new recipes, new patterns for filigree work, new patterns for aprons and caps, and news of the latest theater productions. An "Account" in October 1798 of the play *Lovers' Vows* was published, and four months later in the issue for February 1799 the text of the play, translated by Elizabeth Inchbald and embellished with a handsome illustration (plate 6) appeared. The illustration depicts Frederick and Agatha at the moment of their warm embrace, the same dramatic scene that Henry Crawford and Maria Bertram take such pains to get right.[8] Jane Austen's connection to the *Lady's* surfaces again in the issue for April 1800, where there appears an "Account" of the trial of Austen's aunt, Mrs. Leigh-Perrot, for allegedly stealing lace from a shop in Bath, embellished by a handsome engraved portrait of Mrs. Leigh-Perrot (plate 7).[9]

Mrs. Leigh-Perrot, the *Lady's Magazine*'s embattled heroine for the April issue, looks balefully out of the frontispiece as a living witness to the dangers of consumer life.[10] The magazine's "Account" tracks the story of Austen's unfortunate aunt step by step as it follows parcels of

Mrs LEIGH PERROTT.

Plate 7. From *The Lady's Magazine* (April 1800).

black and white lace around the streets of Bath, details the complex accusations of the shopkeeper and her assistants, reports the accused woman's plea to the jury, the jury's verdict, and, finally, the charged response of the crowd attending the trial. The real-life stakes for Mrs. Leigh-Perrot were appalling: conviction for any theft over a shilling demanded a sentence of death or, with leniency, transportation to Australia. It seemed at the time, and in retrospect, that the Leigh-Perrots were the victims of an extortion scheme devised by the owners of a failing lace shop, who hoped to extract a handsome sum from Mr. Leigh-Perrot for dropping the charges against his wife. The Leigh-Perrots refused, spent seven months in confinement awaiting trial, and, at the moment the *Lady's Magazine* story commences, were facing the dramatic conclusion of their ordeal.

The "Account" is full-dress *Lady's Magazine* melodrama. After noting the "*elegant Portrait of Mrs. Leigh Perrot*" that accompanies the story, the correspondent proceeds to describe the precise fashion details of Mrs. Leigh-Perrot's costume for her day in court: "a very light lead-color pelisse, a muslin handkerchief on her neck, with a cambric cravat. Her hair of a dark-brown, curled on her forehead; a small black bonnet, round which was a purple rib band, and over it a black lace veil, which," the report notes scrupulously, "was thrown up over her head." When Mrs. Leigh-Perrot's opportunity to address the jury arrives, the reader is given the details that matter: "She was extremely agitated, and, in attempting to address the court, her voice failed her so frequently, that Mr. Jekyll, one of her counsel, was requested to sit by her, and repeat what she wished to say to the court." The address is pitched to the high-wrought style of the magazine's own fiction: "Placed in a situation the most eligible that any woman could desire, with supplies so ample that I was left rich after every wish was gratified," Mrs. Leigh-Perrot begins, "blessed in the affections of the most generous man as a husband, what could induce me to commit such a crime?" "Can you suppose that disposition so altered," she asks rhetorically, "as to lose all recollection of the situation I held in society, to hazard for this meanness [the alleged theft] character and reputation, or endanger the health and peace of mind of a husband whom I would die for?"[11]

Mrs. Leigh-Perrot admits achieving everything a *Lady's Magazine* reader could desire – a generous husband, high social position, consumer satiation: *what*, Austen's aunt asks the court, could be any conceivable advantage in stealing? "I know my own oath, in this case, is inadmissible," she concludes to the jury, "but I call upon that God whom you all adore, to attest that I am innocent of this charge, and may he reward or punish me as I speak true or false, in denying it!" "During the time of dictating this address," the magazine's correspondent reports, "the prisoner and her husband were frequently excessively affected and distressed." The verdict arrives with a flourish: "The jury having retired about a quarter of an hour, brought in a verdict of – *Not Guilty*." The magazine's correspondent records the last hurrahs, "The agitation of embraces of Mr. and Mrs. Perrot may be more easily conceived than described," with only one important postscript left for special note, that "the court was crowded with elegantly dressed women." In the end, Mrs. Leigh-Perrot returns from her heroine's pilgrimage triumphant, but with her story ruthlessly transformed by the *Lady's Magazine* from real-life suffering to fodder for the magazine's readers, a lifestyle tale of dishonest lawyers, conniving shopkeepers, heartless humiliation, an heroic speech, last-minute rescue, and the expected reward of a *Lady's Magazine* heroine: "a handsome seat at Hare-hatch, near Reading," "a handsome fortune," and "the most generous man as a husband."

The same rules that govern the relation between Mrs. Leigh-Perrot's story and her frontispiece portrait also govern the illustrated fiction of the magazine. In the illustration (plate 8) accompanying "The Careless Lover" (August 1788), an extravagantly behatted woman sits by a stream with a book in her hand as she looks out the frame of the picture, her gaze directed at the reader with a look of knowing complicity. Within the illustration, she is watched with interest by a male figure hidden in the background. In the tale, we read that the young woman is Miss Fenwick, a young heiress "in possession of a considerable fortune in various shapes." She is pursued by George Davison, "a very fashionable young fellow, of a very respectable family, but rather straitened in his circumstances, being a man of ton and taste, as he had only a small post under the government." Miss Fenwick discovers a letter left by accident in a book he has given her. "By that note it appeared that a favourite mistress had the full possession of his heart, and that a great part of the fortune arising from his marriage was destined to keep her in the most fashionable style." In the plate, Miss Fenwick exchanges an amused and sardonic smile with the reader of the magazine, mutually acknowledging their shared experience of male fecklessness. But in the written narration, she waits for revenge. On the day of the

The Careless Lover.

Plate 8. From *The Lady's Magazine* (August 1788).

wedding, when Mr. Davison is to come before her "in his bridal dress," then and only then does she confront him with the letter: "Read this note," she says to him, "and never let me see you again" – The End.

Laura Mulvey's book on cinema, *Visual and Other Pleasures* (1989), suggests an explanation for Miss Fenwick's shared glance with the reader. In the movies, Mulvey argues, there are three separate operations of "the gaze." There is, first, the camera as it records; second, the audience as it watches the final product; and third, there are the characters on the screen as they look at each other. The illusion of the movie is to suppress our consciousness of the camera and of the audience in order to emphasize the actions of the characters on the screen.[12] In contrast, the illusion of the illustration in the *Lady's Magazine* is to make the reader herself, Mulvey's "audience," the focus of the entire exercise.

The tale of Miss Fenwick and Mr. Davison is familiar enough in the columns of the *Lady's Magazine*, repeated at least once a decade, but Miss Fenwick's knowing look in the accompanying illustration brings to the old story fresh meaning.[13] As Miss Fenwick returns the reader's gaze, she demonstrates her keen awareness that both she and the reader are "other." She has the proof of it in her hand. In addition, if any more proof were needed, the male voyeur in the illustration asserts their position as "other" yet again. He might be Mr. George Davison, but the tale remains silent on his identity. He might also represent a generic reader waiting for Miss Fenwick's response, a "reader" alerted to the Mr. Davisons of the world.[14] The illustration removes the focus of discourse from Mr. Davison and his nefarious plot to Miss Fenwick's response, to her private exchange of glances with the reader. "In the absence of any coherent culture of oppression," writes Mulvey, "a simple fact of recognition has aesthetic and political importance." For women, she suggests, there is a "dizzy satisfaction" in the revelation that "sexual difference under patriarchy is fraught, explosive, and erupts dramatically into violence within its own stamping-ground, the family."[15] Miss Fenwick's triumph over Mr. Davison "in his bridal dress" is no small matter.

Amateur women's fiction in the early magazines balances on a narrow cusp of presentation, tilting between naive folklore and the modern technology of publication.[16] One would be hard-pressed indeed to attribute the force of Miss Fenwick's story to either one or the other. The expected tropes of the tradition-bearer arrive reader-supplied in the stale formulas of the tale, but through the technology of magazine publication, especially in the startlingly intimate portrait of Miss Fenwick, or Mrs. Leigh-Perrot for that matter, the yoked interests of the magazine and the reader-author find active consummation. In short, Miss Fenwick hides an unsettling merger of new technology and old anxieties beneath her fashionable hat.

In a single moment, writes Marshall Berman in his study of modernity, when Goethe's Gretchen "looks at herself in the mirror" – or when Miss Fenwick and the *Lady's Magazine* reader exchange their knowing glance – "a revolution takes place inside her. All at once she becomes self-reflective; she grasps the possibility of becoming something different, of changing herself – of *developing*."[17] Magazine fiction between 1770 and 1820 provides the self-reflecting mirror of Goethe's Gretchen that sends the *Lady's Magazine* reader on her way to modernity.

Print, as both "news" and "fashion," knocked on the door of every middle-class household in Britain through the *Lady's Magazine*.[18] A comparison of two plates in the magazine, both of them of fashionably dressed women – first, a fashion plate, next an illustration for a tale – suggests a power particular to the illustration of fiction. The fashion plate "Paris Dress" (March 1802) presents a picture of fashion detail as precisely rendered as a reader could desire (plate 9). It is a two-dimensional design intended for implementation, and, as John Styles demonstrates, is standard visual language for trade by the end of the century.[19] Clean lines, no shadows, and no distractions from the pattern. Nevertheless, there are special qualities that such an illustration cannot provide, like color, texture, and "air" that must be attended to in the accompanying text:

All the head-dresses for full-dress have a strongly-marked Asiatic character: they are perfect turbans, and are worn very far back. Some of them are decorated with strings of pearls, some shine with silver *shefs*, and a very great number are formed of shawls embroidered with gold and silver ... Rose is still the favourite color. The robes are adorned with flowers, lozenges, or very close foliage. The spencers are of white satin.

Alone, the materiality of the illustration overwhelms it. Only the anecdotal patter of the textual explanation, "worn very far back," or the specific detail, "very close foliage," can bring the dress into the focus of experience.[20] The reader is thrown back on the text for

Mutlow Sc. Rufsell Co.

PARIS DRESS.

Plate 9. From *The Lady's Magazine* (March 1802).

essential information, clues as to where she might wear such a dress, or how to make it up, or to be assured that rose is still a fashionable color. The vacuum of social context in "Paris Dress," of place, occasion, and air, balks any sense of immediate engagement.

On the contrary, the striking illustration (plate 10) to "Charlotte Bateman. A Tale" (November 1782) offers the reader another order of pleasure altogether. In "Charlotte Bateman" fashion steps into the consumer world of "modern autonomous imaginative hedonism" described by Colin Campbell.[21] Unlike the characterless mannequin of "Paris Dress," the young woman in "Charlotte Bateman" is *doing* something with her new clothes. Dashingly attired, she descends a rope ladder by the light of the moon to place herself in the arms of her vigorous, handsome, graceful, and well-dressed lover. Miss Bateman herself is calm, dignified, assured, fashionable – and, claims the story, completely justified in her elopement. "From the first time I saw Captain Melvin," she writes, "I felt a certain *je ne sais quoi* in his favor, which I cannot describe." Her angry but misguided father recognizes his error, forgives his daughter's elopement in the concluding paragraph of the tale, and lives out his declining years in the benevolent care of Charlotte and her new husband, the graceful gentleman in the picture.

In "Charlotte Bateman," the modern consumer spirit is in full operation.[22] In contrast to the particularized and distant representation of "Paris Dress," the illustration of Miss Bateman's tale offers an imaginary costume of unspecified detail, but great imaginative allure. The plate generalizes the costume, giving it the glamorous aura of being exactly right for the occasion. Miss Bateman's self-possession succeeds brilliantly in the theater of the consumer imagination as her marvelous *sangfroid* in descending her rope-ladder triumphs over any possible anxiety the reader might have as to whether her bonnet is knotted "upon or under the chin" ("Paris Dress"). Even though the reader's own experience tells her that Miss Bateman's ladder is impossible, her lover improbable, and her elopement unlikely, the grand illusion of the heroine's freedom, her ability to choose, her freedom to go anywhere, overcomes all objections. The romance of her splendid hat and dress can simply be taken-in or let-out to suit the size of the imagination.[23] The emotional charge comes from the combined effect of the story and illustration taken together. Ownership of a hat like Miss Bateman's inevitably will fall short of the happy illusion presented in the *Lady's Magazine*

Charlotte Bateman,
A Tale.

Plate 10. From *The Lady's Magazine* (November 1782).

plate, but desire will enrich both the illustration and the narrative with new pleasures; pleasures worth seeking monthly in the pages of the *Lady's*.[24]

The fashion plot

Decades are, of course, not proper historical containers, but if ever there were a claim for the packaging of historical time, it might be made for the deliberate time-watch that fashion magazines place over the images that depict relationships between people and material goods. From 1770 to 1820 in the *Lady's Magazine* there appears a year-by-year series of illustrations of women depicted in specific relations to material goods, in images self-consciously offered as "new." Decades in a discussion of fashion magazines simply make the hands of the fashion clock more visible.[25]

In the 1770s, for example, courtly fashions define the *Lady's* heroines. The illustration (plate 11) to "The Toilette" (February 1777) supplies the reader with a heroine rich and secure, sitting at a luxuriously appointed dressing table attended by an elegantly dressed suitor and a set of smartly costumed attendants. The scene appears to be one of supreme order, a measured minuet of courtship. In fact, it is a gift, a material object – the text explains it – that saves the heroine from the disorder of an ill-fated match. The relation between the illustration and the written tale marks a moment of transition in the century's concept of "luxury," as John Sekora describes the debate.[26] In the written tale, the heroine, middle-class but educated to "luxury," is saved from marriage to a dishonest aristocrat (his social rank specified by his possession of a carriage) through her father's discovery that "a large diamond" that he had unfortunately lost is the very diamond in the "costly egrette" that the aristocratic suitor has given his daughter. Thus the heroine, Prusilla, is saved from marriage into a corrupt aristocracy through the canniness of her observant, middle-class father. On the other hand, she, the middle-class girl, is depicted in a setting of great material luxury, luxury that in the written tale represents excess and corruption in the superior classes. The story concludes with an apt question from "G——," the author: "But what is the moral of this interesting story?"

A decade later, the style of clothing and the style of heroine show a pronounced change. The 1780s belong to smartly dressed heroines like Charlotte Bateman (November 1782) or Miss Fenwick (August

The Toilette.

Plate 11. From *The Lady's Magazine* (February 1777).

The Happy Escape.

Plate 12. From *The Lady's Magazine* (March 1782).

1788), to whom the world of magazine fiction grants power and choice. In the illustration (plate 12) to the "The Happy Escape" (March 1782), the heroine leans over her Venetian balcony to reject a suitor who arrives in an elegant gondola: "'No,' replied Elvira, 'I marry no one, I elope with no one – I have not my parent's consent to make an indissoluble union with you. – Be gone!'" The chagrined suitor departs just as she commands him, but in punishment for his temerity, says the author, he is "taken by an Algerine, and sent to Algiers into captivity."

The next decade, the inflationary 1790s, presents a very different world for the heroine. "The Vicissitudes of Fortune" (December 1791) and its illustration (plate 13) suggest that both choice and decision have slipped from the heroine's grasp, along with her smart dresses and dashing hats. The reader's eye courses over the illustration to find the heroine of "The Vicissitudes of Fortune" abandoned, seated by the side of a public road and in a state of great personal disarray. The narrative explains that the unhappy young woman is Miss Harcourt, whose adopted father, Mr. Harcourt, having "too long neglected legally to secure to her what he had always intended to bestow on her," is now dead and she is penniless. The legal heirs have ejected Miss Harcourt from her childhood home, leaving her to make her way in the world without friends or funds. Miss Harcourt's sad tale, in one form or another, appears time and again in the *Lady's* during the 1790s, with its leitmotif of economic loss regularly reminding the reader, as the author of "The Vicissitudes of Fortune" specifically concludes, of "the uncertainty of all human prosperity and happiness, as is but too frequently exemplified."

The next decade, 1800–1810, sets the heroine on her feet again, though not in the fashionable luxury of the 1770s or with the commanding flair of the 1780s. The heroine gradually emerges from her time of trouble arrayed modestly in the sober costume of domestic duty. She is the magazine's new woman of the decade, secure in a new role, but still strictly answerable to the grammar of fashion. Lavinia Darwell in the illustration (plate 14) for "The Reward of Charity" (December 1807) wears a simple dress and cap for her story, which has her unexpectedly coming upon a poor man in the forest, who kneels on the ground, a dagger at his side. The text explains that Lavinia, the modest young woman in the plate, was left penniless by the death of her clergyman father some years previously and had supported herself by teaching in a boarding school, where she was

The Vicissitudes of Fortune.

Plate 13. From *The Lady's Magazine* (December 1791).

The Reward of Charity.

Plate 14. From *The Lady's Magazine* (December 1807).

The Visit to the Fleet Prison.

Plate 15. From *The Lady's Magazine* (October 1812).

seen, admired, and wed by a wealthy gentleman in the neighborhood. With her new-found affluence, Lavinia now devotes her leisure hours to caring for "the indigent and unfortunate in the vicinity, to whom her liberality was almost boundless." Her liberality, claims the text, was "readily assented to by Mr. Edgecumbe, her husband; since whatever she said or did was with him, and with reason was – 'Wisest, virtuousest, discreetest, best.'" As it fortunately happens, the poor man kneeling on the ground with the dagger at his side is her very own brother, aged past recognition by business disappointments, and now contemplating suicide. In a happy turnaround of gender power, the successful sister takes the unsuccessful brother under her wing. She applies to her husband, Mr. Edgecumbe, who "soon afterwards procured a lucrative situation for Mr. Darwell, who showed himself," claims the tale triumphantly, "well worthy to be the brother of such a sister."

In the next decade, 1810–1820, the magazine heroine leaves the chrysalis of Lavinia Darwell's humble cap and gown to appear in the full splendor of new consumer powers. She regains her spendable income, her elevated station, her fine dress and fashionable hat, but with a difference. She now wears her station and finery as the costume of social responsibility. She becomes an elegant woman blessed by riches, a woman empowered to improve the lot of those unfortunates whose merits can enlist her largess. The well-dressed heroine of the *Lady's Magazine* now visits the sick, consoles the poor, and dispenses recipes for cottage soup. Charity becomes *fashionable*. At the moment when women are most eager to find a place for themselves in the economy, the *Lady's* provides the way.

"The Visit to the Fleet Prison," the illustration (plate 15) that accompanies "The Debtors" (October 1812), shows just such a heroine, Louisa Pennington, on a visit to the prison cell of an impoverished tradesman – she has been late in paying her bill owed to him – where she finds "the hapless father of the unfortunate family, sitting up in a mean pallet bed, and languidly leaning back, while his unhappy wife was endeavouring to persuade him to take a little water-gruel." Here is a gratifying story of woman's new-found domestic power. With her access to wealth and privilege, the generous and penitent Louisa Pennington saves the little family from the privations of poverty. In entering the imagined scene of "The Visit to the Fleet Prison," the reader embraces the woman-empowered world described by Nancy Armstrong: "The domestic woman exercised a form of power that appeared to have no political force at all, because it seemed forceful only when it was desired."[27] Charity in the *Lady's Magazine*, embellished with an attractive dress, a bonnet, and a fine umbrella, is truly power with a pleasing face.

The *Lady's Magazine* reinvents the world through fashion, but not always the *dress* fashion that we tend to expect. All an editor needs to set the operation in motion is a ready tale and an illustration, minimally applicable, to go with it. Designs for the plates seldom rise above traditional images, employed, one suspects, mainly with the notion of getting the job done as quickly as possible.[28] If a knife appears in the story, which is always spare on details, the artist puts a knife in the plate. If there is a ladder, the ladder finds its place. Otherwise, settings are interchangeable: pastoral, historical, Eastern, Spanish, French, whatever drops from the pattern book. A tale embellished with Eastern costumes may feature a heroine named Everina Wilson, while an illustration in contemporary dress may depict heroines named Cleora and Flavilla. As for the stories, they arrive on the editor's desk, like the stereotypical illustrations themselves, full blown and completely formed from the wellsprings of cliché.

The reader herself does the creative work, producing meaning as she goes back and forth between the plate and the story where the negotiable ground supplies ample space for daydreaming that is specific to the reader, unanticipated by either the editor or by the designer of the plate, and unsuspected even by the amateur writer of the story.[29] At the producing juncture of plate and narrative there emerges a concept very near the modern advertiser's employment of image, that is to say, a supposed version of reality teased into an imitation of life through the yearnings of desire.

Illustrating the economy

A comparison of two illustrated tales in the *Lady's Magazine* reveals the reader's complicity in joining the magazine's fiction to its illustrations. In the plate accompanying the story "The Fortunate Deliverance" (December 1788), we find an illustration (plate 16) with a typical hodgepodge of iconography: a stricken maiden, an archer, a forest, and a lion, each of which appears to have been lifted separately from a different pattern book. Questions fall upon the

The Fortunate Deliverance

Plate 16. From *The Lady's Magazine* (December 1788).

reader with few clear answers provided in the plate. The lion: is it bemused, pitying, or threatening? The archer: is he aiming his weapon at the lion or the maiden? The maiden: is that a contemporary dress she has on? Is that an English forest? What on earth is she doing in such a predicament? The illustration's caption, "The Fortunate Deliverance," offers minimal guidance, because what is it the heroine is to be "delivered" from? – The half-naked archer? The laconic lion?

The reader turns to the written text for more certain information. Emilia Crompton, she discovers, is the name of the unfortunate Englishwoman on the forest floor:

By the sudden death of her father – she had lost her mother several years before – Emilia Crompton found herself in a very distressful situation: unexpectedly, too, as she had great reason to believe, from her father's style of life, joined to the parental kindness with which he always treated her, that he would leave her a handsome fortune. How bitter therefore, was her disappointment, when, upon opening the will, she saw a sum bequeathed to her which was barely sufficient to furnish her with the decent necessaries of life.

The heroine "doubly felt, indeed, the striking change in her situation," the story continues, because as soon as her impoverishment is known to her suitor, "to whom she had been fondly attached," he withdraws his attentions and decamps.

Although Emilia draws comfort from "the generous conduct of her female friends, who joined in making up a purse for her," she concludes that she must leave England to live with an aunt married to a rich merchant in America. When Emilia arrives in America, her aunt's husband insists that she marry a "gentleman, much older than herself, possessed of a large fortune, but not very agreeable in person or behavior." Emilia refuses; the uncle dismisses her from his house; she seeks refuge at the home of a woman friend of her aunt. On the way, she becomes lost in the American forest:

Seized with terror by the advancing of a lion, she fainted, and fell: but just when she, dreadfully terrified, imagined she was going to be devoured, she was fortunately delivered from her dangerous condition.

"A brave Indian, happening to be at that moment within sight of her," saves her from the maw of the ravening beast. The Indian, "by a long intercourse with the most civilized Americans," the author claims, having "lost every thing that was savage about him," proposes marriage. Emilia accepts, although, as the author insists, "All the assiduities of the one [the brave Indian], or the pressing persuasions of the other [her aunt], would, it is probable, have had no effect, if her first lover had not so basely deserted her." Nevertheless, when she at last consents to the marriage, "she gave him – for in spite of the tincture of a skin – a heart replete with gratitude and affection."

It takes no startling powers of insight to see that Emilia Crompton's story, the one suggested between the plate and written text, makes up a specifically woman's world. The reader consults the dismaying plate; she guesses at the mystifying dangers depicted there; she reads the story, an absolute nightmare of dispossession, whence she returns to the plate to discover the archer, the lion, the forest, and the maiden in a coherent and revealing visual relationship.

In the illustration, "The Fortunate Deliverance," the lion hovering over Emilia Crompton looks suspiciously like an heraldic British lion, but now one with superadded heroine-devouring power. Other stories in the *Lady's* confirm this reading of Emilia's lion with frequent allusions to the tigers, lions, and bears that represent British institutions hostile to women. The lawyer in "Benevolence Rewarded" (September 1795), for example, glances "on the bank notes on the table" in the home of an impoverished widow and her daughter, "and rapidly, as the tiger of the Indian plains springs exulting on her prostrate prey, did he seize them in his rapacious claws, and convey them to his pocket."[30] The supposedly American forest is a stand-in, likewise, for Emilia's English economic wilderness. In fact, the sole non-English participant, the "brave Indian," in this insistently home-grown tale, also supports the local anxieties of the story. The deplorable fact that Emilia's rescue from British economic injustice comes only at the hands of a savage makes itself heard with a satisfying ring of righteous indignation. There is nothing to stop the reader – and everything to encourage her – to picture herself in Emilia's place on the forest floor.[31]

The triple relationship of story, illustration, and the woman-focused context of the periodical, forces a revelation of woman's culture into the open, or very nearly. The allegorical implications of "The Fortunate Deliverance" become irresistible only at the moment Emilia Crompton presents her hand, "in spite of the tincture of a skin," to her "brave Indian." In an instant, her psychological exile is translated into the precise value system of the market.[32] One might be tempted to consider Colonel Brandon in Austen's *Sense and Sensibility*, also conceived in the 1790s, as a "brave Indian" who rescues Marianne Dashwood, in spite of the "tincture" of middle age and a flannel waistcoat, from exile in her economic wilderness. As in allegory, both Austen's novel and the anonymous *Lady's Magazine* tale are forced beyond the closure of the narrative for their disappointingly meager resolutions. Emilia does indeed "give" her hand, gaining a legal contract that attests to her altered economic state, but, like Marianne Dashwood, she consents only for the lack of a more desirable alternative.

In the next decade, the power field is reversed. In the plate (plate 17) accompanying "Ador and Zulva; or, the Triumph of Love: a Mexican Tale" (October 1802), the reader finds an heroic young woman already on her feet and taking aim at the threatening lion. Just as in Emilia Crompton's story, loosely invoked allegory moves the tale through faraway exotic climes, here Mexico, but the reader quickly locates the familiar economic turf of the suffering English-woman. The difference in "Ador and Zulva," however, lies with Zulva, the energetic heroine, who herself slays the devouring lion to save her helpless lover, Ador, from certain death. Ador, the narrative tells us, belongs to the "old-style," that is to the defeated order of the old king, generous and good. He now lies in the power of the usurper king, under sentence of death. A ferocious lion, however, roams the usurper's kingdom terrorizing the citizens. In return for Ador's release, Zulva promises the usurper that she will go forth into the forest to find and slay the beast, "whose ferocity has already proved fatal to several of our most experienced and bravest hunters." The intrepid Zulva understands the requirements of the task. She "had been accustomed to the sports and fatigues of the field: she could send the winged shaft from the twanging bow with unerring aim, and a force seldom exceeded by the masculine arm." Determined to "go out with her arrow and her bow against the monster of the woods, and either fall by his fangs, or fulfill the condition which was to secure life to her lover,"

she traversed undauntedly the thickest of the forest, explored its gloomy recesses, and, at length, espied the furious beast. Intrepidly she fitted the arrow to the string...she took aim, and, discharging the shaft with inconceivable force, pierced the vital part where the spinal marrow joins the brain. The beast without a struggle, fell motionless before her.

Ador and Zulva.

Plate 17. From *The Lady's Magazine* (October 1802).

The Rash Attempt.

Plate 18. From *The Lady's Magazine* (May 1801).

It is a new world, a new century, and yet another image for the magazine heroine. Mrs. Winslow in the *Lady's* story "The Rash Attempt" (May 1801) of the previous year offers a helpful gloss on Zulva's accomplishment. As the long-suffering wife of a spendthrift husband, the firm-minded Mrs. Winslow, Zulva-like, rescues her "old-style" husband from bankruptcy, and, as the illustration (plate 18) reveals, she comforts him with a bank account that she has neatly balanced herself: "the violence of his feeling choaked his utterance, and he sank down in an agony of remorse." In a like spirit of triumph, Zulva delivers the head of the devouring beast to the usurper king: "'I come,' said she, 'my sovereign to claim your royal promise. A lion which ravaged our plains has fallen by my hand. I bring you his head. Let Ador live.'" The usurper king redeems the canceled Ador, and, more to the central economic point of *Lady's Magazine* fiction, he gives Ador "an important post" in the government, but only on the strength of Zulva's "twanging bow." Mrs. Winslow, likewise, confronts and defeats the ravening beast, but she does it without allegory, through thrifty ways and the household budget.

Heroines on the margin

Between 1770 and 1820, magazine illustrations regularly represent the heroine literally negotiating the margin of dry land and open sea. Time and again in the illustrations, castaways wash about her feet, barks founder in the distance, ships sail away with husbands and lovers, and, occasionally, the billows engulf the heroine herself.[33] The regular appearance of seashore texts in the *Lady's* presents a five-decade opportunity to measure the heroine's stories of her own economic marginality against the suggestive images in the plates.

In the first decade of its publication, the *Lady's Magazine* offers a tale and illustration (plate 19), "Dorilacia; or, the Fair Captive" (September 1777), that displays at first glance an horrific seashore tableau: the heroine, bound and seemingly dead, lies prostrate on a rocky strand with a group of burly men gathered around her.[34] But surprisingly, despite the threatening impact of the plate, the written tale describes a world that corresponds to the serene plate that illustrates "The Toilette" (February 1777) (see plate 11). In the heroine-centered society of both "The Toilette" and "Dorilacia" ritual courtship is the central action, and in the illustrations to both

Doralicia, or the fair Captive

Plate 19. From *The Lady's Magazine* (September 1777).

stories, helpful assistants gather around the heroine, including a waiting-maid and a musician in "The Toilette," and in "Dorilacia," a group of rough-looking but well-intentioned men who are there to guard her from harm. The written text explains that the heroine, Dorilacia, has been abducted by a passionate Saracen who gives her the choice of complying with "the whispers of an illicit passion" or of being bound and thrown into the waves. She chooses the waves and is found on the shore by her intended husband, who "fortunately arrived in his vessel on the strand": "The cords with which she was bound were unloosed, and when the measures lately revived for the recovery of drowned persons were made use of," claims the text, "she returned to life, and lived to bless the world with a numerous race of heroes."

In both "Dorilacia" and "The Toilette" the stories aim at the inspirational. The central condition for "winning" in the courtship contest demands that the heroine relinquish her will, indeed her body, the specific image in "Dorilacia," to the power of male authority. But the violence of the "Dorilacia" plate, as consolatory as its explanation certainly is, remains persistently in the mind's eye, and informs the meaning of "The Toilette" as well. The male "gaze" to which the brawny fishermen subject Dorilacia's helpless body is perceived, inevitably, as a violation. Dorilacia's entrapment is both *particular*, with the ropes that bind her, and *general*, in the public gaze of the men's eyes. Her courtship story lies beached on a decidedly ambiguous margin of violation and rescue, as is the heroine's in "The Toilette," though there much more prettied up. In confirmation of Dorilacia's disturbing marginality, the elegant women on the deck of the ship, all of them safe and dry, turn their eyes from Dorilacia's prostrate body with dismay.

The next decade, the 1780s, gives magazine readers a more gratifying vision of the heroine's life on the margin. In the plate accompanying "The Patriotic Parting" (June 1782), a well-dressed woman standing on the beach waves farewell to a man in a small boat headed, presumably, to the large ship flying the Union Jack in the bay beyond (plate 20). A smartly dressed child clings to the woman's skirts; the woman waves goodbye with an elegantly managed glove; the waves are moderate, the sky pacific, and, although a gothic castle looms behind, the woman models her large and fashionable hat with confidence. This is Mrs. Townshend, and the man in the small boat is Mr. Townshend, who, having "frequently wept over the setting

The Patriotic Parting.

Plate 20. From *The Lady's Magazine* (June 1782).

sun of England's prowess and glory," is now leaving Mrs. Townshend in order to correct this situation, intending on his return to lay "his laurels at the feet of his lady." Unfortunately Mr. Townshend is captured by the French. He escapes, is rescued by an old friend, and learns upon returning to his native shores that "during his absence, a near relation of his wife's had died, and bequeathed her an addition to her fortune." He hastens home to greet his son with "a deluge of parental tears" and to clasp his wife in his arms, which, claims the tale, is "the summit of all her wishes." In the plate, the potential threats to Mrs. Townshend's prosperity are all there: the open ocean, the martial task, the gloomy castle. On the other hand, there is a cheerful display of consumer prosperity as well: Mrs. Townshend's fine hat and dress, her elegant glove and smartly dressed child, presenting a strong point of contrast that in the event is borne out by the happiest economic conclusion imaginable for the Townshends, much enhanced by the unlooked-for inheritance received by Mrs. Townshend during Mr. Townshend's absence. The price Mrs. Townshend pays for her wait on the beach in the 1780s seems negligible indeed. Prosperity and happiness arrive to reward her confidence in a buoyant economy.

The next decade, the 1790s, brings a change in the economic weather. "Henry and Agnes," the *Lady's Magazine*'s illustrated story for November 1799, reveals an ominous development of the familiar seashore *topos* (plate 21). In the plate accompanying the story, a rustic lifts an apparently drowned heroine from the foaming waves; a kneeling female raises her arms in grief; a looming cliff and dark sky brood over the background; a gothic ruin hangs on the brow of a cliff.

The narrative describes a young married couple, from "the west of England," who unhappily find that "sincerity and affection are not alone sufficient to protect their votaries, when devoid of wealth." Henry, the husband, takes "an advantageous situation" on a West-India merchant ship bound for Jamaica, and Agnes, like Mrs. Townshend, is left to await his return. But for Agnes, unlike the confident Mrs. Townshend of the previous decade, "every gale which blew raised a storm far more violent in her breast." When rumor reaches her ears that the *Anne of Liverpool*, "the ship in which her husband was," has just gone down, and very near *her* beach, "her fears overpowered her; she sunk in a fit, and, her foot slipping, she fell from an elevated part of the shore into the waves, in which she was ingulfed." A faithful servant, Oliver, extracts her from the waves,

Henry and Agnes.

Plate 21. From *The Lady's Magazine* (November 1799).

"but in a state apparently lifeless." This is the crisis of despair depicted in the illustration.

Meanwhile Henry, who had landed "the day before at a sea-port town at a considerable distance, and travelled night and day to fly into the arms of his Agnes," arrives on the shore to find his wife senseless. Although Agnes revives with "the aid of proper applications," she loses her mind in her anxiety for her husband: "so much had the shock affected her imagination and mental powers, that she only stared wildly on him, insisting that he was not her Henry, for she had seen him perish with her own eyes." Agnes stays in this way for so long, reports the author, "that serious apprehensions began to be entertained that it would end in a settled derangement of her senses." Even though she is restored to sanity, through "the soothing caresses of her husband, and proper medical treatment," the focus of her story is not on her new prosperity, as it was with the Townshends, but on the "derangement of her senses" through her anxiety for the future.

Although the tale of "Henry and Agnes" comes heavily freighted with the distress of Agnes' imagined loss of Henry, Henry himself remains totally absent from the plate, and is in fact absent from most of the written text too. The author gives more attention to the name of the ship than she does to Henry or even to Agnes. The couple's story and their fragile happiness depends on an economy which, like the *Anne of Liverpool*, rides on stormy seas. If Henry's investment fails, the reader will understand that every member of the family goes down with the ship. Agnes fears the loss of fortune, she experiences the loss of sanity, and she is left, in the visual record of the plate at least, deprived of all her comforts and as good as drowned herself.

"The Shipwrecked Mariners" (September 1800), one year later, supplies an answer to Agnes' plight. In the plate accompanying this story, the reader finds the heroine briskly up and about (plate 22). Instead of a heroine laid low on the strand, it is the breadwinner himself who now lies there prostrate and lifeless. Jane Barton and John Mowbray, like Henry and Agnes from the previous decade, come from a "seaport town in the west of England." Although this young couple, too, "would immediately and heedlessly have rushed into the indissoluble bonds of matrimonial union, without bestowing a thought on the means whereby they were to live as well as love," their wiser relatives prevail upon them to wait until John has made his fortune. John's uncle, a ship's captain, takes him on a voyage to

The Shipwrecked Mariners.

Plate 22. From *The Lady's Magazine* (September 1800).

the West Indies and promises to "do every thing in his power, both for his instruction in the management of a vessel, and for the advancement of his interest." The voyage is "extremely prosperous," claims the author, and "when all the accounts were balanced" John is "enabled to purchase a vessel of his own, with which he made several short trips, all of which proved successful and prosperous." He starts a "private venture, in which he had embarked at once the whole of his own property, and all he could raise by credit, now by no means small," and he leaves Jane, a second time, to wait until his return from one more extended voyage so that they can marry in economic security. While John is gone, a neighboring gentleman takes a fancy to Jane, tries to seduce her, fails, then tries to marry her, with "honourable proposals," the author insists, "offering not only to make her his wife, but to settle on her a jointure of five hundred a year."

The narrative pauses portentously: "Now came the real trial of the honour and virtue of poor Jane." Jane continues to refuse "the honourable seducer," even though her busy relatives now encourage her to forget John and marry wealth, when suddenly the temptation is removed. The rich gentleman, in admiration of Jane's virtue, adds "a codicil to his will, by which he bequeathed to her five thousand pounds – the next day he expired."

Scarcely has the "honourable seducer" breathed his last, when John's vessel arrives off shore, but in horrific weather: "It blew a storm; almost a hurricane." Jane rushes to the beach where she finds two shipwrecked sailors (see plate 22), one without injury, but "– how great was the shock to her heart," the other apparently lifeless sailor is John. He awakes in Jane's arms; Jane greets him with "emotions bordering on frenzy," which, as the author claims in the usual formula of the *Lady's* fiction, "can only be conceived by those who have experienced a similar transition from despair to exstasy." John, however, despairs over "the reflection that probably all he had in the world was lost, and that he could only reward the ardent and tender affections of her he so fondly loved with extreme indigence and dependence." But Jane has the economic resolution to their joint catastrophe safely in her pocket. Like the bow-twanging Zulva in "Ador and Zulva," or the managing Mrs. Winslow in "The Rash Attempt," "Jane felt the noblest and most refined pleasure that it is in the power of wealth to bestow, by being enabled to assure him that she possessed sufficient for them both, though all he had himself should, as he foreboded, be swallowed up in the deep." She has earned it herself (with a bit of luck) by keeping the home fires going. The new decade's woman provides the way to solid land.

The next decade for the *Lady's Magazine*, 1810–1820, brings elegance, prosperity, and higher station to the illustrated heroine. Even so, the threatening waters do not retreat. "Affection Recompensed" (December 1816) reveals a handsomely dressed heroine (plate 23), who, with all her finery, lies exhausted on the beach, her feet in the waves, and a stormy sky threatening in the distance. A vigorous gentleman in top hat and agitated Regency cravat springs over the rocks to her aid. The written text explains what has brought these well-dressed people to such a pass.

Mrs. Montague and Captain Montague, happily married for several years, visit Brighton for the Season, where "the captain's rank and situation" naturally lead him to spend much time in company, so much time that Mrs. Montague is alarmed for his "health," and suggests that they return to the country. "He haughtily told her she might return whenever she pleased, but there he should stay: he had no wish to detain her." Mrs. Montague, dismayed, retires to their country estate, "a part of her own inheritance," the author carefully notes, and awaits her husband's return with a "depression of spirits." Meanwhile, in Brighton, Captain Montague is "introduced to a select society of gamblers, and in a short time lost every thing but his honor." He bitterly repines: "Had he but bestowed a small share of that confidence in her he had so profusely given to others," remarks the author, "what bitter pangs might he have been spared!" He returns home with the disastrous news: "His amiable lady forbore reproaches; cheerfully rallied him on his great losses; and observed, that as they had procured her his society, how trivial they were in comparison with a husband's affection." Captain Montague's guilty "reflections," however, render home "irksome" to him, and he procures an appointment to a ship "on a distant station." Mrs. Montague retires to a small village on the coast "where she resided in seclusion, patiently awaiting the restoration of her husband" – his "restoration" from abroad, but more poignantly and by implication, his "restoration" to the marriage and sound domestic economy.

When Mrs. Montague eventually hears of Captain Montague's ship being ordered home, it becomes her custom to walk the beach in anticipation. "On one of these evenings having ventured too far, the tide approached before she was aware of her danger; her recollection

Plate 23. From *The Lady's Magazine* (December 1816).

failed, and she sunk exhausted at the foot of a rock; when she heard footsteps rapidly approaching, and languidly opening her eyes, beheld, with joy too great for expression – her husband!" The moment of psychological crisis, of course, has been lengthened and deferred by the economic crisis, Mrs. Montague's problem remaining intractably economic: what to do with a wastrel husband, his guilt, the financial loss (fortunately the estate is "her inheritance"), and his marital defection. "Providence," announces the author, "directed him at that critical moment to the spot, where his adored wife must have perished but for his timely appearance." Mrs. Montague's meeting with her husband, the author assures the reader, "after so long an absence, and at so peculiar a juncture, endeared him if possible, still more to her, and recompensed her for all her sufferings." Mrs. Montague's patience, her sound domestic economy, her steadfast devotion are female heroism, no question about that, implies the *Lady's Magazine*. Nevertheless, it is not Captain Montague, but Mrs. Montague, the woman on the margin, who must be rescued from the dangerous waters that lap round her feet.

An immovable fear of economic loss drives the fiction, demonstrably the illustrated fiction, of the *Lady's Magazine* from one decade to the next. The separate stories of Henry and Agnes and John and Jane balance their yearnings for prosperity against the risks of never having it. The strain of economic uncertainty drives Agnes, in the 1790s, to insanity, and Jane, in the next decade, to acts of heroic self-denial. In seeming contrast, the wealthy Mrs. Montague, privileged with prosperity from the start, would appear to be far better off, but, in fact, she remains just as economically marginal as either Agnes or Jane. Her own small, "very mediocre," fortune allows her a modest seaside residence when her husband deserts her, and it keeps her in hats, but she has sunk decidedly from her former affluence through Captain Montague's gambling losses. In effect, from start to finish in the *Lady's Magazine*, from the prostrate Dorilacia in the 1770s to the prostrate Mrs. Montague in 1816, the magazine never retreats from its sobering message to women. Everywoman remains, even in the best of times, ever on the margin, continually subject to unpredictable and arbitrary storms of economic violence.

Her image, however, undergoes a long, 50-year period of developing, to return to Goethe's Gretchen and her magic mirror. From 1770 to 1820, fashion is every magazine heroine's birthright: "Fashion raises even the unimportant individual," writes Georg Simmel, "by making [her] the representative of a class, the embodiment of a joint spirit.''[35] Decade by decade, from the fashionable luxury of the 1770s, through the assertive hats of the 1780s, through Miss Harcourt's disarray by the side of the road in the 1790s, and finally, through woman's stepped investment in material goods, from humble caps to respectable bonnets during the first two decades of the new century, the heroine emerges, finally, in full consumer glory in the 1820s.

It was a dubious bargain. In March 1819, the editors of the *Lady's Magazine* began the process of eliminating reader contributions of fiction in order to prepare the way, they claimed, for a "New and Improved Series":

We respectfully inform those Correspondents who are in the habit of supplying us with occasional Tales, that no Tale can, in future, be admitted into our Miscellany which extends longer than three or four numbers: and the authors of all Novels now in progress are particularly requested to bring them to a conclusion as early as possible; as we have plans in perspective for the amusement of our readers, which we cannot mature till we have a little more space.

In effect, the editors announced the death of the "print culture" of the early women's magazines. Economic success turned them into slick, professionally managed profit-makers for their publishers. There were to be no more regular, monthly, meta-communicative chats among amateur reader–authors. No more "frank, vigorous and mentally stimulating" stories and essays in the *Lady's* by the magazines' "*Volunteers*", "representing a cross-section of feminine (and often masculine) opinion."[36] No more club of readers with "a comfortable sense of community and pride in their identity."[37] With the abrupt introduction of the "New and Improved Series" of the *Lady's Magazine*, the withering hand of modern consumer culture took possession of Gretchen's soul forever. After 1819, the writing of fiction for the women's magazines fell to professional writers, mostly men, with Sir Walter Scott leading the pack. The fiction was better, in fact, and the essays, often by women, were earnest and laudably edifying. Illustrations "By the Best Hands" continued to accompany the magazine's fiction, but now under the direction of an editorial policy catering to specific consumers. The change, in effect, created a new reader of magazines: a commodity product in her own right, no longer the producer of lively, naive, and revealing fictions about

Plate 24. Lady Pemberton instructs her sons in the duties of charity. From Amelia
Opie, *Tales of the Pemberton Family* (1825).

herself, but an elegant object shaped and designed by the magazine's editors.[38]

The illustration for Amelia Opie's children's book, *Tales of the Pemberton Family; for the Use of Children* (1825) demonstrates the change. Here we find Lady Pemberton engaged in an elegant display of motherhood with her twin sons, Harry and Edward (plate 24). The ostensible "lesson" at hand concerns giving charity to the poor: Edward does, Harry does not. However, the lesson that strikes the eye of the reader before any other is that material goods, solid furniture, a fine carpet, elegant curtains, and a handsome dress not only embellish virtue and render it pleasing to the eye, but outshine virtue itself. The illustrator devotes equal attention to the elegance of the furniture and to the elegance of Lady Pemberton. Style overwhelms and swamps the narrative of Edward and Harry.[39] So it is with the new magazines designed for women. Elegantly turned out and soulless, they become respectable, sober, profitable, and, like the New Woman herself, suitable for display.

CHAPTER 6

Fictions of employment: female accomplishments

I was as friendless as the first outcast that was driven forth a
wanderer... My own labour, therefore, was now become my
only means of obtaining shelter or subsistence; and, foreign as
the effort was to all my habits, the struggle must be made. But
how was I to direct my attempts? What channel had the customs
of society left open to the industry of woman?

Mary Brunton, *Discipline* (1814)

The clanking plots of women's fiction develop a high-pitched whine
of social dissatisfaction in Jane Austen's time. Austen acknowledges
the worst of the din in her "Plan of a Novel" where the heroine is
"often reduced to support herself & her Father by her Talents &
work for her Bread; – continually cheated & defrauded of her hire,
worn down to a Skeleton, & now & then starved to death" (*MW*,
430). But when the shoe is on the other foot, and employment
threatens one of her heroines, we hear a genuine cry of anguish: "I
would rather be a Teacher at a school (and I can think of nothing
worse) than marry a Man I did not like," cries Emma Watson in
Austen's unfinished novel *The Watsons*. Elizabeth Watson, the
heroine's older sister, replies without hesitation: "I would rather do
any thing than be a Teacher at a school... *I* have been at school,
Emma, & know what a Life they lead" (*MW*, 318).

The response to women's employment is not, however, univocal in
women's fiction. Heroines who face the dreaded trial must meet it
according to the kind of novel they appear in. Employments
appropriate to novels intended for genteel readers, that is to say for
the daughters of prosperous clergymen and the like with incomes
above £500 a year, cannot be the same as employments appropriate
to novels aimed at the daughters of petty tradesmen, minor clerks, or
even impoverished curates with incomes below £150 a year.

Women from the middling ranks learn about employment almost

Female Accomplishments.

Plate 25. From *The Female Instructor: or, Young Woman's Companion* (1822).

solely through fiction, the only widespread and easily available source of public information on the subject. Novelists of every rank consider its practical aspects. The carriage-trade publishers, for example, offer writers like Austen, Burney, and Edgeworth; the didactic trade, a separate though related market, has writers like Brunton, Ferrier, More, Plumptre, Reeve, and Pilkington. Finally, a third market, one directed to the lower ranks of the middle class with the Minerva novel leading the way, finds its leading writers on employment in Bennett, Parsons, Charlton, and Hanway. The great questions: how to secure employment, how to gauge its potential, how to deal with employers, how to establish a fair amount of pay, are surveyed. But more significantly, novels are also active proponents of employment as a respectable source of income for middle-class women. Novelists offer their readers a wailing wall for mourning their unwelcome predicament, of course, but they also provide a safe space for exploring economic reality for women.

Female employment looms as an especially nettling matter for the genteel heroine, who, when she seeks employment, unavoidably betrays her own class and all its urgent aspirations for station. As a result, when employment signs go up in this kind of novel, heroines need not apply. Even Mary Wollstonecraft in her radical novel *The Wrongs of Woman* (1798) allows employment only to those women born in the working class. The heroine's servant, Jemima, brings reports from the workplace to her interested mistress, but the heroine herself lives on inherited money, never entertaining the least notion of employment for herself.[1] Charlotte Smith considers conditions for women in domestic service in *Celestina* (1791), their lack of fresh air, their long hours, unfair mistresses, but neither does she entertain employment for her genteel heroines. Her novel *The Old Manor House* (1793) provides the sole example of a heroine who takes employment, but Monimia is born to the serving classes. After providing Monimia with marriage to a gentleman (impoverished), Smith accepts the fact that it is her heroine's proper task to contribute to the family income, but she emphasizes that is also Monimia's duty to hide her employment, sewing for a local warehouse, from her gentleman husband to protect his delicate feelings. Three genteel sisters in Smith's sixth novel *Marchmont* (1796) briefly consider trade, opening a shop in Margate, but a cash windfall saves them from the trial.

In Austen's *Emma* (1816), all but Mrs. Elton uniformly greet Jane Fairfax's option of employment as humiliating. Mrs. Elton alone waxes eloquent when she lists the economic power of Jane's "resources": "Your musical knowledge alone would entitle you to name your own terms, have as many rooms as you like, and mix in the family as much as you chose; – that is – I do not know – if you knew the harp, you might do all that, I am very sure; but you sing as well as play; – yes, I really believe you might, even without the harp, stipulate for what you chose" (p. 301). The reader can only cringe to watch the central values of Austen's novel, the hearth and domestic comforts, put up for sale. When Jane Fairfax wanders the fields of Highbury in an agony of despair, ostensibly she is mourning the end of her engagement to Frank Churchill, but the most convincing gauge of her emotional distress lies in the impulsive consent she gives to become governess to the children of Mrs. Elton's *nouveau riche* friends, the Smallridges.[2] Austen saves her from this fate by marrying her into genteel money, but it is a patched-up resolution at best, and one that confirms Jameson's claim that ideology is "in its very nature Utopian."[3] Frank Churchill, with all his claims to station, is no prize as a husband.

Frances Burney courageously sends the well-born heroine of her last novel *The Wanderer* (1814) into the world of women's employment to experience its humiliations first hand, but every attempt of the "Wanderer" to earn her own bread contributes one more addition to an unrelieved string of failures.[4] The heroine concludes bitterly that a genteelly educated, unprovided and unprotected woman may, after every earnest effort to support herself, have no place in the economy at all:

How few, she cried, how circumscribed, are the attainments of women! and how much fewer and more circumscribed still, are those which may, in their consequences, be useful as well as ornamental, to the higher, or educated class! those through which, in the reverses of fortune, a FEMALE may reap benefit without abasement! those which, while preserving her from pecuniary distress, will not aggravate the hardships or sorrows of her changed condition, either by immediate humiliation, or by what eventually, her connexions may consider as a disgrace! (II, 230–31)

In short, employment for a heroine turns the ideology of the genteel novel upside down.[5] Authors like Austen, Burney, Edgeworth, Smith, even the radical Wollstonecraft, are consistently resistant to turning their heroines into wage-earners, because, paradoxically, the heroine's successful employment would invite the hostility of the very society to which the heroine so earnestly aspires to belong.

In contrast, a second kind of heroine, the "improving" heroine, looks towards employment with the fervor of a religious convert. Didactic fiction has its own inspiring agenda for women's employment: "Where love of labour glows, / There too the stream of Independence flows" (p. 107), cries an impoverished widow in Elizabeth Bonhote's poem *Feeling, Or, Sketches from Life; a Desultory Poem* (1810).

Didactic novels stress the respectability of female employment, especially its respectability for those women from the ranks of the pseudo-gentry, the daughters of clergymen and other genteel professionals (the Jane Fairfaxes of the world), who have fallen on hard times. Thomas Longman's publishing house caters to this public, also Hookham and Carpenter, and, in Edinburgh, the firm of Manners and Miller. The fiction is earnest, frankly instructive, and often directed to a younger audience of readers.[6] Mary Brunton, Amelia Opie, Anne Plumptre, and Jane West, all published by Longman, are typical contributors to the conversation, along with others like the redoubtable Clara Reeve and the respected children's writer Mary Pilkington, both cut from the same cloth, published by different firms, but sharing the well-meaning aim of instruction.[7] The message for women in didactic fiction fairly shines with moral uplift: the trials of employment can furnish a crown of Glorious Respectability.

Mary Brunton's novel *Self-Control* (1810), published cooperatively by Manners and Miller in Edinburgh and by Longman in London, presents a typical example of the employment program of didactic fiction. The heroine, Laura Montreville, and her elderly father retire to the country after the father loses the family fortune in unwise speculation. Laura, with a keen eye on family finances, recognizes that she and her father cannot live within their lessened income, even in rural retirement, and continue to enjoy the domestic luxuries that her father refuses to relinquish. A visiting artist passes through their village and sees Laura's artwork displayed in the cottage. "If this be, as I suppose, the work of a young artist," he exclaims, "I shall not be surprised that he [*sic*] one day rise both to fame and fortune."

The stranger's last expression had excited an interest which no other earthly subject could have awakened. Her labours might, it appeared, relieve the wants or increase the comforts of her father's age; and, with a face that glowed with enthusiasm, and eyes that sparkled with renovated hope, she eagerly advanced to question the critic as to the value of her work. In reply, he named a price so far exceeding her expectations, that her resolution was formed in a moment. She would accompany her father to London, and there try what pecuniary advantage was to be derived from her talent. (I, 59)

The old father objects: "'It is hard, very hard,' said he with a deep sigh, 'that you, my lovely child, the descendant of such a family, should be dependent on your daily labour for our support.'" Laura answers him earnestly, "Oh call it not hard my dear father... Thanks, a thousand thanks to your kind foresight, which, in teaching me this blessed art, secured to me the only real independence, by making me independent of all but my own exertions." The father continues to object, "fretfully," but Laura, knowing the poor state of the family budget, presses him to consent. "'It is true,' answered Laura mildly, 'that my success depends upon taste, and that the public taste is capricious; but some, I should hope, would never be wanting, who could value and reward the labours of industry – you observe,' added she with a smile, 'that I rest nothing upon genius'" (I, 211–12). Even this modest appeal to femininity does not mollify the old gentleman, who replies capriciously, "I cannot endure to see you degraded into an artist, and therefore I desire there may be no more of this traffic": *traffic*, the ultimate genteel degradation.

The heroine wastes no sympathy on him. "Laura looked at him with affectionate concern – 'Alas!' thought she, 'if bodily disease is pitiable, how far more deplorable are its ravages on the mind'" (I, 212). She must take to employment in secret, working late into the night while her father is asleep. One evening he finds her in a dead faint from lack of food and rest:

"Merciful Heaven!" he exclaimed, "what is this?"... The whole truth flashed at once upon Montreville, and all the storm, from which his dutiful child so well had sheltered him, burst upon him in a moment... and the father wrung his hands and sobbed like an infant. (II, 77)

He bursts a blood vessel that very night, leaving her penniless and alone. The heroine can now get on with her life.

The problem with such well-intentioned literature as Brunton's *Self-Control*, of course, lies in its eagerness to show that work for women is not only their virtuous duty, but profitable as well. As Jane Austen wrote her to sister Cassandra, Brunton's book was "an excellently-meant, elegantly-written Work, without anything of Nature or Probability in it" (*Letters*, 344).

Minerva authors, in contrast to authors of both genteel and didactic novels, present a much more canny assessment of employment for women in their works. When the social rank of the Minerva author can be known at all, it tends to skirt the lower edges of the middle class: Eliza Parsons, the daughter of a wine merchant; or Elizabeth Helme, the daughter of a schoolmaster; and even farther down the social scale, Anna Maria Bennett, the daughter of a grocer.[8] Business life is not foreign to these women. Parsons took an active hand in her husband's turpentine firm after a disastrous fire; Helme boasted of contributing materially to the support of her family by her pen for seventeen years; Bennett worked in her youth as a slop-seller and later in life in a chandler's shop. In pointed distinction to a writer like Austen, Minerva writers refuse to rescue their heroines from the experience of employment. They give their heroine the usual perquisites at the conclusion of course, a husband with utopian virtues and large estates, but not until *after* the heroine has tested the waters of employment and triumphed. The measure of success, however, is totally unlike that of the Brunton-style didactic novel.

When the heroine of Elizabeth Bennet's Minerva tale *Beauty and Ugliness* (1819) loses her fortune, she too, like Brunton's Laura, looks to her accomplishments, the fruits of her expensive education, for support.[9] Faint with hunger and in great financial distress, she leaves her squalid garret room with the manuscript of a newly written novel under her arm and some needlework undertaken for a local shopkeeper. The needlework is late because of a recent illness. The unfeeling shopkeeper, Bennet indignantly reports, "told her, with a table of smoking luxuries before him, that 'Such people as earned their bread should not be overdelicate like,' and then inhumanly pushed her from the door, desiring her never to come near it again, and left her with only the slender hope of being able to dispose of her novel" (IV, 145). Unable to sell the novel, the heroine eventually finds employment in a country village where she looks after a small school. Her life passes there in "unvaried monotony," Bennet admits, but "she could not be quite indifferent to the success which attended her exertions; with a feeling of pleasure she beheld the school daily more crowded... She was now in the receipt of seven shillings a-week, her board and lodging found here, and she comparatively rich; she had few anxieties, few wishes for the future."

She assesses her situation: "I am alone, but I have strength and health, and the power of still being serviceable to my fellow-creatures: let this be my consolation" (IV, 184–85).

In the Minerva novel, employment is much more than proof of the heroine's virtue, it is her grudged triumph over an economy that has turned its back on women. Even the detail of pay, seven shillings a week, a typical Minerva specific, contrasts tellingly with the vague, genteel sums promised to Brunton's Laura in *Self-Control*. On the other hand, the high melodrama of martyrdom and suffering that informs *Beauty and Ugliness* is no different in its relationship to the economy than Jane Fairfax's agonized decision to work for the Smallridges, or Laura's anxious moments over her sewing. In Austen's, in Brunton's, and in Bennet's works the terror of a misogynistic economy appears as a fact of life, the condition of employment.

All three kinds of novel, genteel, didactic, and Minerva, see the same truth, though through a veil darkly. It is "as though we were observing the behaviour of a man urgently gesticulating," writes Terry Eagleton, "and so *intimating* an actual state of affairs only to realise that his gestures were...actions which indicated nothing immediate in his environment, but revealed, rather, the *nature* of an environment which could motivate such behaviour."[10] Employment, either vaguely or specifically imagined, represents in women's novels a hostile universe for the middle-class woman of whatever station. The genteel novel averts its face from employment; the didactic novel creates a mini-religion of it; the Minerva novel swallows its bitter pill. In the last pages of Bennet's *Beauty and Ugliness*, the heroine marries an appreciative member of the upper gentry, but, as any reader can see, Selina's real triumph over "the nature of her environment" comes through the labor of her own hands, not through any gentle assist of her author into a fairy-tale marriage.

Employment, odious (1): companion

The challenge for novelists who deal with employment is to situate their heroines happily in an employment that, as Fredric Jameson argues, is "susceptible to both a conceptual description and a narrative manifestation all at once."[11] No easy task. The professions of companion and governess, the two classically genteel employments available to contemporary women, raise universal horror across the entire range of women's fiction.[12] The two employments come up against Jameson's wall of "intolerable closure," trapped as they are between the demands of genteel station and the demands of economic survival.

"Oh misery of Dependence! – the heaviest toil, the hardest labour, fatigue the most intense – what are they compared to the corroding servility of discontented Dependence," cries a character in Frances Burney's play "The Witlings" (*c.* 1779), to which another replies, "Nothing, I grant, is so painful to endure, but nothing so difficult to shake off."[13] The position of Humble Dependent, the companion, is almost inevitably one of the severest trials suffered by a heroine, and one of the oldest, going back at least to Jane Collier's *Essay on the Art of Ingeniously Tormenting* (1753) and Sarah Fielding's *David Simple* (1744).

The woman's novel at the end of the century assumes the gothic pose: "HELENA STERNHEIM was in the humble state of a dependant [*sic*] on the Duke's family," Sophia King writes in *Waldorf; or the Dangers of Philosophy* (1798): "Her family was tolerably good, but her poverty caused her to be considered as a menial – and her beauty excited envy" (I, 104). The heroine of Matilda Fitz John's *Joan!!!* (1796) receives the same humiliating treatment: "She was called, she was blamed, like a servant," although, as her author remarks, "She looked like a being infinitely superior to the rest of the household" (I, 26). Jane West warns readers away in *The Advantages of Education; or The History of Maria Williams* (1803): "That situation which halts between the servant and the companion is generally deemed miserable" (II, 106).

The position lies particularly open to exploitation, sliding so easily as it does into the role of personal servant. Although Burney's Juliet in *The Wanderer* stoutly maintains that there is no shame in a woman earning her own bread, she finds shame enough for herself when she becomes the paid companion of the irascible Mrs. Ireton, a sadistic monster who delights in mocking Juliet's dependent position with brutal sarcasms:

And I was stupid enough to suppose, that meant a person who could be of some use, and some agreeability; a person who could read to me when I was tired, and who, when I had nobody else, could talk to me; and find out a thousand little things for me all day long; coming and going; prating, or holding her tongue; doing every thing she was bid; and keeping always at hand.

The heroine candidly admits that Mrs. Ireton's taunts are not at all an unreasonable description of the job: "Juliet, colouring at this true, however insulting description of what she had undertaken, secretly revolved in her mind, how to renounce, at once, an office which seemed to invite mortification, and license sarcasm" (III, 255). However, it is not the verbal abuse that finally defeats Burney's heroine, but two demeaning duties Mrs. Ireton insists on that Juliet considers totally unacceptable: minding a spoiled child and exercising Mrs. Ireton's bad-tempered lap-dog Bijou. These tasks cannot be deemed genteel by any stretch of the heroine's imagination.

The Minerva novelist Mary Ann Hanway represents the position as equally unsatisfactory, but with broader strokes of satire and greater fury. In Hanway's novel *Ellinor* (1798), the unspecified duties of the companion's position are also a focus of irritation, but Hanway treats them with typically specific Minerva detail. Lady Fritterfame, a wealthy woman of fashion, sighs over the "companion problem" with a guest, while poor Ellinor, her companion, must sit by and hold her tongue: "Ingratitude," says Lady Fritterfame, "is the way of them all":

I only expected her to make up my millinery and dresses, clean my laces, write my cards, answer my letters of business, superintend my house accounts, and embroider a court dress, when not employed in the avocations I have mentioned! For this I permitted her to dine with me when I had *no* company, or nobody *I cared for*, and gave her *twenty pounds* a year; she had the impertinence, because I ordered her to clean and feed my birds, and to wash and comb poor dear little Fidelle, to tell me that she did the work of all the servants in my house, without their *wages*; and that, tho' she had condescended to wait upon me, she certainly should not think it equally necessary, to *attend* my birds and beasts... I bid her take herself, and her beggarly pride out of my house directly. (I, 134–35)[14]

Jane Austen, with a more refined sensibility, simply sends her heroine, Fanny Price, to the sofa in *Mansfield Park* with a splitting headache, the result of unreasonable tasks loaded on her by her two selfish aunts. When her cousin Edmund frets that the whole family is too much accustomed to employing Fanny as a servant, Mrs. Norris supplies the attack direct: "I shall think her a very obstinate, ungrateful girl, if she does not do what her aunt and cousins wish her – very ungrateful indeed, considering who and what she is" (p. 147).

But worse, a heroine might become a companion to a parvenu. "What a terrible life is that of an humble dependent upon upstart insignificance," writes Minerva novelist Mary Elizabeth Robinson in *The Shrine of Bertha* (1794).[15] Sarah Green, also a Minerva writer, introduces just such a mortifying experience for the heroine in her generally cheerful and upbeat novel *The Fugitive, or Family Incidents* (1814).[16] The heroine, Emma Southby, leaves the employ of Mrs. Mordaunt, a moody and ill-tempered gentlewoman, to become the paid companion of the kind, but irrepressibly vulgar Mrs. Bennet:

Proud of her wealth, the very worst of all pride, and proud also of having the daughter of a gentleman in an inferior situation under her roof, she was kind to her in private, because she really loved her, as much as such a being could be capable of transferring any portion of affection from self; but, in company, her arrogance now would continually take care to proclaim her dependent state, and to exalt her own charitable feelings; and when some ladies in the garrison have kindly vied in their attentions and kindnesses to the interesting orphan, she would exclaim, "Ah! God help her, poor thing, she hasn't, as one may say, a friend in the world, nor one shilling to rub against another, if twasn't for the handsome salary I *gives* her; for I'm such a fool, only tell me a tale that's *misfortunate*, and I can't for the life of me but strive to mend matters. (II, 138–39)

Most galling, Mrs. Bennet addresses the genteel Emma as "Amy" before company: "Amy, my dear," she says, "that tart is cut, take some more of it child; it won't come to the table again, and it may as well be eat up here as in the kitchen" (II, 139). Green's inability to let Mrs. Bennet simply pass as a comic fool, and a kindly one at that, suggests an ideological dilemma that even comedy cannot resolve. Frances Burney submits her heroine in *The Wanderer* to equally mortifying table humiliations, but tells the story with even greater resentment: "At meals, the humble companion was always helped last," she writes, "even when there were gentlemen, even when there were children at the table; and always to what was worst; to what was rejected, as ill-cooked, or left, as spoilt and bad" (III, 268).

The job of companion is no joking matter. Green's Emma falls into a nervous decline: "deprived of the hope of obtaining another situation, should she quit that she then held, she was obliged to endure her lot with patience; but her health, from the conflict in her mind, began to decline, and her pallid countenance, and often humid eye, evinced the anxiety of her susceptible heart, and its secret anguish" (I, 140). The symptoms are only too common. Eliza Parsons' similarly situated heroine in *The Castle of Wolfenbach* (1793) has, "too much sensibility to be happy – she feels her dependent and unprotected state too keenly, – it preys upon her mind and injures her health."[17]

Austen, from a different ideological tack, confronts the position in her unfinished fragment *Sanditon*, but she too fails to suggest a way to unravel the social tangle. The vulgar, domineering Lady Denham in *Sanditon* takes her niece, Clara Brereton, as a companion. Charlotte Heywood, the heroine, first sees Clara, significantly, at a circulating library: "Perhaps it might be partly oweing to her having just issued from a Circulating Library – but she c^d not separate the idea of a complete Heroine from Clara Brereton. Her situation with Lady Denham so very much in favour of it! – She seemed placed with her on purpose to be ill-used. Such Poverty & Dependance joined to such Beauty & Merit, seemed to leave no choice in the business." Charlotte watches the relationship carefully, but can see nothing of the legendary hardships: "She c^d see nothing worse in Lady Denham, than the sort of old fashioned formality of always calling her *Miss Clara* – nor anything objectionable in the degree of observance & attention which Clara paid. – On one side it seemed protecting kindness, on the other grateful & affectionate respect" (*MW*, 391–92). Austen's eye focuses on her craft as novelist here, rejecting the hoary employment cliché of women's fiction, but she does not confront with any candor the difficulties that Clara would reasonably face in living with the suspicious, low-born, and arbitrary Lady Denham.

Mary Ann Hanway's Ellinor expresses the consensus of other Minerva heroines when she concludes that the companion's job is little better than forced labor, a gross betrayal of any genteel ideal that its proximity to station might seem to promise. When Ellinor is coerced by an unsympathetic employer into attending a ball, she designs a costume emblematic of her "galling yoke of dependence": "It was perfectly simple," writes Hanway, "it was of a Greek slave" – adding that it was composed of "fine clear muslin, over white silk, which fell in full graceful folds on the ground." The rest of the costume is equally genteel and as pointedly apt in displaying the paradoxical miseries of her station: "Her fine turned arms were naked above the elbow; the sleeves were full, and confined with gold: the zone about her waist was the same, from the middle of which depended a long gilt chain: the ends were fastened with clasps on her wrists" (II, 253).

Painful experience and conflicting ideology join hands "in

deformatively 'producing' the real."[18] The golden chains of rank, loyalty, and genteel necessity that in real life bound Frances Burney to Queen Charlotte as Second Keeper of the Robes netted her, finally, as she records in her letters and journals, no more than debts, loneliness, physical debility, and a near nervous breakdown. The humiliations of Juliet, Burney's "Wanderer," were learned first-hand. "Dear Heart!" cries a character in Burney's "Love and Fashion," a play written ten years after her tour of duty with the Queen, "if this is not the most extraordinary of all! So here I've been trampled upon all these years for nothing – except the Honour!"[19]

Employment, odious (2): governess

The governess trade is no better: "Our poor heroine was now almost exhausted, and had scarcely courage to knock at the door of a fourth advertiser of slaves to torture," writes Elizabeth Bennet in *Beauty and Ugliness* (IV, 128). Jane Austen uses the same image: "I did not mean, I was not thinking of the slave-trade," Jane Fairfax tells the puzzled Mrs. Elton in *Emma*, "governess-trade, I assure you, was all that I had in view; widely different certainly as to the guilt of those who carry it on; but as to the greater misery of the victims, I do not know where it lies" (pp. 300–01).[20]

Complaints about the conditions of the job are universal in women's fiction. A governess in Mary Charlton's *The Wife and the Mistress* (1802), a Minerva novel, claims, "I have been mantua-maker, milliner, sempstress, clear-starcher, nursery maid, and lady's maid, though at the same time for talents and accomplishments I was expected to be a perfect female Crichton" (IV, 302–03). A young woman in Jane West's *Ringrove* (1827), a Longman didactic product, confesses feelingly of the job, "Though accustomed to every indulgence, I have limited my wants and contracted my desires until a little world would content me; but that little I cannot procure unembittered by the gall of involuntary servitude" (II, 51–52). Mary Wollstonecraft in *The Wrongs of Woman* calls the job, "the only one in which even a well-educated woman, with more than ordinary talents, can struggle for a subsistence; and even this is a dependence next to menial" (p. 124). In the anonymously written *Rosemary Lodge; or, Domestic Vicissitudes* (*c.* 1800), a gentleman praises the courage of a young woman who is "looking out for a situation as a governess":

"How pleasing it is, when we meet with such cheerfulness as Miss St. Clare manifests, although poverty and distress await her, she does not needlessly repine, but submits to the decrees of providence with calmness and serenity" (p. 99).

Even when the profession of governess is given mild approval, the author simply drops the heroine at the door with no further enquiries or follow-up. Clara Reeve's grateful job aspirant in her novel *School for Widows* (1791) disappears into the house of a woman ominously named "Lady Haughton." And all we learn of Ann Gomersall's heroine in *Eleonora* (1789) is the provocative information that she spent nine years "happily" with the Oswalds, except for "my increasing though hopeless attachment to Mr. Carlton" (II, 9).

For the most part, novelists admit only misery. Rosa, the heroine of Anna Maria Bennett's Minerva novel *The Beggar Girl* (1797), flatters herself that it was "exactly the situation in life she considered herself able to fill with credit to her own abilities, and though a dependant [*sic*], not a servile employ" (IV, 33–34). Bennett's cheerful approach to the job reveals a typical we-can-do-it Minerva attitude, but, sadly, Rosa's employer treats her with suspicion and rudeness. Rosa is even subjected to a "gross salute" from a stable boy. Hanway's heroine in *Ellinor* leaves a job as companion to become a governess, but finds the new position no less miserable: "generally abused and laughed at" in the housekeeper's room for her pretensions to gentility, Ellinor is even less happy in the drawing-room where, at best, she is ignored or "stared out of countenance by pride-swollen dowagers," or, worse, "talked *at* by disappointed spinsters," or "satirized and laughed at by conceited misses." Turning aside from her tale, Hanway addresses her readers: "If this book should ever be read by an ill-fated female that *is*, or ever *has had* the dire misfortune to be placed in such a state of dependence, she will feel and acknowledge the truth of the drawing, that it is not too *highly* coloured, but a genuine copy from nature" (I, 96).

Emma Southby, Sarah Green's resourceful heroine in *The Fugitive* (1814), takes employment as a governess with a Lady Gavestone, who merits her name by putting off her servants when they ask for their wages, and, if pressed, threatening them with the loss of a reference for any other job. The unsuspecting Emma is shown to her room:

A bedstead, which seemed half falling down, was furnished with very ragged printed cotton furniture, a patchwork quilt, and sheets of the coarsest hemp.

Two windows, which had a very pleasant view over Hyde Park, were shaded by two drapery kind of curtains, "tape-tied, and never meant to draw," one of a striped gingham, the other formed of a piece of flowered chintz and coloured cotton sewed together. A looking glass broke at one corner, and the foot tied on with a piece of packthread; a broken china jug full of water, a yellow Staffordshire-ware bason, and a ragged towel made out of an old table cloth, completed the furniture, except one chair and a deal table, of Emma Southby's bed chamber. (III, 90–91)

When, after some months of unpaid employment, she asks for her wages, her conversation with Lady Gavestone outlines the dimensions of her ideological predicament with stark clarity: "'And,' repeated the Countess in a rage, 'it was nothing but for the sake of paltry lucre, that you engaged yourself to me. What else could I expect from an ignoble mind, unprincipled, like all those of low birth!'"

"Not so, my Lady," said Emma, with that native dignity which rather abashed the Countess, "yet when you say I came merely for the sake of what you are pleased to call lucre, till I had the honour of more particularly knowing your ladyship, is, in some part, just. A female, like myself, totally unportioned, with nothing but her talents to support her, seeks only a competence for the hard, very hard task, of transferring those talents to another." (III, 176–77)

The Countess retorts angrily that Emma has "bound" herself to teach Lady Georgiana. "My Lady," says Emma, "whatever I *bound* myself to teach Lady Georgiana, you cannot detain me against my will, I am not apprenticed here." "Apprenticed!" cries the Countess, now touching the exposed and raw nerve of Emma's gentility: "vulgarity will discover itself in all the low-born." Emma responds that she most certainly is not "low-born." "'So then, you set up for a lady of family, I suppose,' said the Countess, with contempt." Emma answers her in the same spirit that Austen's Elizabeth Bennet answers Lady Catherine de Bourgh in *Pride and Prejudice*: "'I can never rank myself amongst the low-born,' said Emma, 'my father was a gentleman, and a man of honour; and my mother was the daughter of a respectable country gentleman'" (III, 178).

The job ends badly anyway: the father, Lord Gavestone, makes improper advances, and the son, Lord Edward, falls in love with her. Unencumbered by the social pretensions of a genteel novel, Green has her Minerva heroine quit the Gavestones' elegant employ to take up a better job, embroidery for a commercial warehouse – where the heroine triumphs, both in terms of wages and her own pride.

Sophia Lee, who wrote novels and ran a successful boarding school in Bath as well, gives practical advice in her novel *The Life of a Lover* (1804) to women seeking to become governesses. Lee acknowledges the necessary humiliation of the interview, "The awkwardness of being announced in an inferior light – of becoming my own historian and panegyrist; – a thousand nameless, but overwhelming, sensations" (I, 21), but she supplies the ideological justification that allows the heroine to submit to the ordeal: "Though suddenly thrown far below the rank you have been accustomed to fill (for, alas! you never held that which you are calculated to adorn)," says the heroine's adviser, "you have resolutely avoided the humiliation of dependent gentility, by daring to apply those talents which you have delighted to cultivate" (I, 6). Lee also offers some canny instruction on how to conduct the interview:

As your acceptance in life, my dear, must a good deal depend on your appearance, (for many, many narrow souls measure merit by that standard!) let it not be too economical; it will be an erroneous humility to undervalue yourself: some dignity of carriage is likewise necessary, to obviate the objection of your youth, and impress your pupils and their parents with that respect which alone will induce them to render a subordinate situation tolerable. "Make something of your self, and the world will make something of you," is a common but useful adage. Though pride in the extreme is a most disgusting fault, in the medium you will find it a mighty useful one. (I, 9)

The heroine secures a position at the respectable salary of £40 a year, and later, in her second place of employment, receives £50 a year, high wages indeed for a woman in this position. Even so, Lee is no more reconciled to the unhappy circumstances of the governess's job than Green.[21] As she confesses in the novel, "There seems hardly any other choice for the delicate and unfortunate of our sex, than private tuition, yet that too often proves either a irksome or unpleasant occupation" (I, 6). The job comes to nothing. The son of the heroine's employer springs from the closet, like Pamela's Mr. B—, and the employment issue dissolves in intricacies of rank, title, and dastardly seduction. Lee's only resolution to the employment dilemma is to advocate a Mary Astell style of monastery for women, urging the creation of a place of refuge for "the daughters of men in

liberal professions" who are "most exposed to become thus destitute." A deep sense of defeat, however, governs Lee's project:
"some retired and tranquil home, where other sad stragglers, not
more fortunate than themselves, may unite in supplying, as far as
situation will allow, those dear and tender ties which circumstances
have robbed them all of" (1, 4–5, 8–9).[22]

Paradoxically, it is the position's traditional association with
gentility that destroys it as a desirable, genteel resource. Food,
housing, and a genteel seat in the parlor may be in the contract, but
self-respect is not. "I am treated like a gentlewoman," Mary
Wollstonecraft wrote her sister on her first evening as governess to the
daughters of the Kingsboroughs in Ireland, "but I cannot easily
forget my inferior station – and this something betwixt and between
is rather awkward – it pushes one forward to notice."[23] Wollstonecraft's "betwixt and between" produces the antinomy that
spoils this avenue of employment. We admire Jane Fairfax for
heroically, even tragically consenting to become the governess to
Mrs. Elton's friends, the Smallridges, rather than marry the trifling
Frank Churchill, but we are not forced to witness the consequences.
Austen's "poor Miss Taylor" experiences successful employment in
Emma, but everyone, except Mr. Woodhouse, admits that she is far
better off as Mrs. Weston with her own house and carriage than Miss
Taylor living as a dependent at Hartfield. We sympathize with the
fury of Mary Charlton's overworked governess in *The Wife and the
Mistress*, but Charlton can offer nothing better than anger – and a
wealthy suitor – in the final pages of her novel. We cheer the energy
of Sarah Green's plucky Emma Southby, but even Emma cannot
make a success of the position. Sophia Lee can coach the heroine of
her novel through an interview for governess, but she cannot picture
successful employment for her in the position. The governess's
position represents a dismal failure of the collective imagination. In
the women's novel, both positions, the companion and governess,
hover between two imagined worlds: one promising economic
security, long since lost and irretrievable; the other, threatening
certain disaster, already here and irreversible.

Employments, possible: schoolmistress, sempstress, actress, prostitute

As a response to the lost cause of companion and governess, women's fiction turns to female employment that ventures well beyond the ideological closure of these two genteel employments. The school-mistress, for example, gets a far warmer reception in the novels than the more prestigious governess; the sempstress is given a better chance of psychological and economic survival than the companion; even the actress and the prostitute find their defenders as emblems of the oppressed economic condition of all women. Authors, abandoning the longed-for seat in the parlor as untenable, send their heroines into the open marketplace to take their chances on finding an "independence," the single goal of employment that emerges in women's fiction as consistently "respectable."

School-keeping does not immediately suggest any cause for optimism. Nelly Weeton, a genuine veteran of the profession, records that from the moment she began to help her mother in their day school, "her life as well as mine was from this time a life of slavery."[24] When her mother fell ill, the entire responsibility landed on the child's shoulders: "I had to attend 9 hours a day to the school, to cook, to clean, to sew, and to nurse my poor unfortunate mother ... Bread and potatoes were our principle diet." Her salary was only 6 shillings per quarter for each of fourteen students, about 7 shillings a week – the same as a common laborer – out of which she felt obliged to pay the debts left by her mother at her death. Mary Wollstonecraft remembered her own experience as a schoolmistress in the bitterest of terms: "A teacher at a school is only a kind of upper servant who has more work than the menial ones."[25] The cost of supplies, rooms for the school, and the salaries for extra teachers could easily put a woman into debtors' prison if her pupils' parents or guardians should renege on the bills, as Wollstonecraft found out, her school in Newington Green failing after three shaky years through such defaulting.[26] "My creditors have a right to do what they please with me should I not be able to satisfy their demands," Wollstonecraft wrote despairingly to George Blood. Blood, in response, encouraged her to flee to Ireland.[27]

Jane Marks, "Schoolmistress," as she styled herself, informed the trustees of the Royal Literary Fund that after keeping a "Genteel Day School" for nearly thirty years in Fetter Lane, Holborn, she was driven to poverty by the "failure of several of the Parents of my Boarders in their Payments." She submitted an autobiographical poem in manuscript in support of her request for financial aid:

> No Sire nor Husband to assert her claim
> Crush'd by Oppression see the friendless Dame
>
> In Debt & famish'd sinking to the grave
> And look in vain for some kind hand to save.[28]

Nevertheless, in the face of all this economic uncertainty, school-keeping as an *idea* had powerful ideological advantages that could defeat even the certain knowledge of its dangers and rigors. With the terrifying failure of her own school behind her, Mary Wollstonecraft succumbs to its attractions in her collection *Original Stories from Real Life* (1788). Having recently eaten "the bitter bread" of the Kingsboroughs in Ireland as governess to their children, she found the precarious independence she had enjoyed as a schoolmistress more valuable in retrospect. *Original Stories from Real Life* features an idealized (and appalling) picture of a contented country school-mistress:

She lives alone, has only the society of children, yet she enjoys much ... she seems above the world, and its trifling commotions. At her meals, gratitude to Heaven supplies the place of society; she has a tender social heart, and, as she cannot sweeten her solitary draught, by expressing her good wishes, an ejaculation to Heaven for the welfare of her friends is the substitute ... This circumstance I heard her mention to her grandfather, who sometimes visits her. (p. 132)

The lack of witnesses to the schoolteacher's "solitary draught" seems to be the secret of its favor. The heroine tolerates lonely exile and demotion in station as the price to pay for avoiding the humiliation of social exposure. If shame there is, it is held in abeyance by Wollstonecraft's iconic picture of martyrdom – the anchorite caught at her solitary board in a toast to absent friends.

The same isolation holds sway in Elizabeth Bennet's *Beauty and Ugliness* (1819), in which the heroine, after disastrous failures to earn her living – as a governess, then an author, and finally a sempstress – secures the welcome position of assistant to a country schoolmistress who is in ill health. Bennet does not disguise the tedium endured by her heroine, Selina, whose life "passed in the unvaried monotony of reading and spelling," but insists that the heroine does find one solid satisfaction in the job, the delight of attracting more paying students: "With a feeling of pleasure she beheld the school daily more crowded, until at length the exulting governess," Selina's employer, "who was now able to leave her apartment, talked of getting a larger room." The heroine is now able to count a series of personal rewards in her new, if lowly, independence: "I am alone, but I have strength and health, and the power of still being serviceable to my fellow-creatures: let this be my consolation" (IV, 184–85).

A witness from Selina's former world of fashion and ease, a Mr. Moncton, discovers Selina engaged in nursing a village woman dying of cancer – "the offensive smell from the wound was so dreadful, that the poor sufferer could scarcely endure herself," he notes. A fashionable young woman later asks Mr. Moncton if Selina's smallpox, one of her abundant trials, had "quite destroyed" her beauty: "'Her face!' said Mr. Moncton – 'I never looked at it: once, I think, she said something about being frightful, but I do not remember a single feature – I heard nothing but the voice that spoke comfort to the dying, and I believe I only saw the dear little grey stuff dress'" (IV, 223). Like Wollstonecraft, Bennet legitimates employment for the middle-class woman through a picture of lonely martyrdom. Selina exchanges her fashionable dress for the "grey stuff dress" of a secular, nursing nun.

The novel concludes, of course, with Selina's marriage to her Beverley, a colorless young man with plenty of money and a landed estate, but there is a significant difference between the conclusion of Bennet's Minerva novel and Frances Burney's *The Wanderer*, written for a more genteel audience. Bennet's conclusion provides no personal fortune for the heroine and no noble blood. Also in contrast, Selina actually succeeds in supporting herself by her own hands. Burney's heroine fails with every try.

Minerva Press novelists persist in seeking an image of employment in fiction that will bring women into the economy as wage-earners. Rachel Hunter finds successful employment for the heroine of *The Schoolmistress* (1811) in a "play school," also called a "day school." "Behold me now presiding in my day school," writes the satisfied heroine, "from nine to twelve, and from three to five, every day, with a cap of wisdom, and sceptre of authority" (II, 133–34). Mrs. Hunter's lesson is very simple: women must exert themselves. In spite of the heroine's cruel reversals, "notwithstanding the utter re-nunciation of Adolphus Vernley's orphan daughter by his family connexions," she writes, "she and her mother's sister lived on the fruits of their honest labour, and by their conduct raised up for themselves friends able and willing to alleviate their difficulties; they wanted no more: their talents and industry have since provided for them a sufficiency, and a reputation beyond the reach of slander or malice" (II, 155).

Rosa, the plucky Minerva heroine in Anna Maria Bennett's *The Beggar Girl* (1797), is orphaned while she is at boarding school. The headmistress, who experiences an attack of the gout, undertakes a search for an additional teacher: "Rosa knew herself competent to the situation, and offered to fill it – not in the language of solicitation of distress, nor humiliation, but with a frank and just confidence, that the arrangement would be mutually beneficial." She rejoices in finding respectability so near to hand: "Miss Buhanan [Rosa] took her seat at the tea table relieved, to the infinite joy of Mrs. Harley, for a thousand painful circumstances, that must have attended such an arrangement, between people less attached to each other, and less at peace with themselves" (II, 128–29).

Didactic novelists, however, are not so quick as Minerva novelists to recommend schoolkeeping for the heroine, although Anne Plumptre in *Something New: Or, Adventures at Campbell-House* (1801) considers teaching in a country school to be at least preferable to prostitution. A curate's daughter in Plumptre's novel, seduced by the local squire, loses every respectable way of getting a living: "In this situation, driven almost to despair, and seeing herself nearly reduced to the dreadful alternative of starving or prostitution, her story accidentally became known to Miss Campbell," the heroine of the novel, who makes the seduced woman the mistress of a little school – "and the children have improved rapidly under their [hers and her helpful mother's] tuition" (I, 96–97). Nor can Mary Robinson bring herself to countenance schoolteaching as an employment for her heroine in *The Natural Daughter* (1799). The heroine thinks "of gaining a livelihood by the dull drudgery of diffusing knowledge in a seminary of fashionable education," tries it, and fails: "Here indeed her patience was put to the test, by the stupidity of some; the infantine impertinence of others; the budding pride of the high-born; the pert vulgarity of the low" (II, 52–53).

Nonetheless, if the sacrifice must be made, didactic authors have practical advice on how to go about it. Mrs. Darnford, an impoverished widow who desires to set up a school in Clara Reeve's

The School for Widows (1791), asks advice. "Do not hazard your little pittance in any great undertaking," her benevolent sponsor tells her:

Do not take a share of any other person's school: partnerships are dangerous, unless you are perfectly acquainted with the temper and qualities of the person you engage with. Hire a lodging ready furnished: let it be a genteel one; that may give you some credit. Ask a handsome price, such as may pay you for your trouble. You shall not keep a dame's school, like Shenstone's, though you use the poetical license in describing it, but such as may induce the principal people in the place to send you their children. (II, 96–97)

But for Reeve, as for Plumptre, only magdalens and poor-but-virtuous widows are allowed to prove the point that a woman can achieve dignity and respect through teaching in a school. The heroine's preferred dispensation in the didactic novel remains the same as it does for Jane Austen, who cannot abide the smug assertion that employment for wages is a satisfactory alternative to a genteel seat in the parlor. The economic dilemma that keeps Austen's heroines out of the schoolroom, as it does Reeve's, is first that the position cannot guarantee sufficient economic security or even reasonable comfort. Second, at the very best, it demotes a woman into that group Austen calls "the second set," the company, for example, of Mrs. Goddard, the successful schoolmistress in *Emma*, who runs "a real, honest, old-fashioned Boarding-school, where a reasonable quantity of accomplishments were sold at a reasonable price" (pp. 21–22). Mrs. Goddard is fit enough company for old Mr. Woodhouse, when no one better is "come-at-able," but she most certainly is not qualified to be the heroine of an Austen novel.

Needlework emerges as the universal solvent in women's fiction. No matter how grueling or financially unrewarding, no matter how finely it teeters on the line between genteel work and common labor, authors consistently offer needlework as a fit employment for their heroines.[29]

Among heroines of genteel station, Ellena in Radcliffe's *The Italian* (1797) makes copies in embroidered silks of designs from Herculaneum that the nuns at a nearby convent sell for her. Burney's Juliet in *The Wanderer* (1814) and her friend Gabriella likewise take up fine muslin-work in their shared private quarters, but with much harsher working conditions than Radcliffe's heroine. "The two friends," writes Burney, "soon had more employment than time, though they limited themselves to five hours for sleep; though their meals were rather swallowed than eaten; and though they allowed not a moment for any kind of recreation, of rest, or of exercise" (II, 47). When Gabriella must leave the partnership, needlework unsweetened by friendship turns bleak indeed. Juliet finds that there are "continual and vexatious" delays of payment: "Her work was frequently, when best executed, returned for capricious alterations; or set apart for some distant occasion, and forgotten; or received and worn, with no retribution but by promise." Juliet "had concluded," writes Burney, "that, in consecrating her time and her labours to so simple an employment as needle-work, she secured herself a certain, though an hardly earned maintenance." She eventually must confess that "neither talents" nor "patronage" are enough to make her successful in the business. The most important precondition of success, the one regularly denied to women, is missing: "Capital – also was requisite, for the purchase of frames, patterns, silver and gold threads, spangles, and various other articles; to procure which, she was forced, in the very commencement of her new career, to run into debt" (II, 51–53).

When Juliet's debts are unexpectedly called in, the heroine must turn to the town's shops for employment, but as soon as she takes her seat in the public room of the shop, the setting in which she is expected to do her sewing, she finds herself subject to the unwelcome attentions of a notorious rake, Sir Lyell Sycamore (III, 115). She abandons the shop for private employment with a mantua-maker, Mrs. Hart, who allows her to do her sewing in a separate apartment with other women, "her needle-sisterhood," as Burney terms it, but here she finds nothing but misery as her fellow-workers resent her for her efficiency. Warehouse employment brings the heroine, Burney writes, "calmness without contentment; dulness without society... The unvarying repetition of stitch after stitch, nearly closed in sleep her faculties, as well as her eyes" (III, 175). And it fails to bring her financial security. After three weeks, when the work runs out, Mrs. Hart terminates her employment without apology.

Charlotte Smith's novel, *The Old Manor House* (1793),[30] like Burney's, is tuned to genteel sensibilities, though it allows a carefully arranged modicum of needlework to Monimia, its servant-girl heroine. Nevertheless, Monimia's first efforts in the public workroom of a shop come to the same disastrous end as Burney's Juliet, and for the same reason, the unwanted attentions of a notorious rake (pp. 479ff). Her work at home does not remove the family from poverty, but it does keep the duns from the door. "Orlando saw her always busy; but he made no remarks on what occupied her; and, without shocking his tenderness or his pride, she was enabled to add a little to the slender stock on which depended their subsistence" (pp. 493–94). The argument, work or starve, weighs more heavily in Smith's scale of approval than the gentlemanlike blindness of Monimia's husband.

The Minerva novel justifies needlework for heroines solely for the independence it can purchase. Emma Southby, Sarah Green's heroine in *The Fugitive*, escapes Lady Gavestone's position as governess to find gratifying success as a sempstress of "fine work" – decorative needlework. She "was fortunate in immediately obtaining a single room on the second floor at the house of an eminent embroiderer, in the neighbourhood of Soho," writes Green with her usual devotion to commercial detail. The offer of "eighteen shillings a week, made her gladly enroll herself amongst the workwomen, with permission to work alone in her apartment." Again, the need for privacy, ostensibly to avoid the eyes of predatory men, guides the choice of employment. Green doesn't mince the difficulty of survival in London: "But how difficult was it for poor Emma, in this expensive town, to support this character of paying regularly every week out of her hard earned gainings; her room was half a guinea per week." Nevertheless, Emma triumphs splendidly: "She worked over hours, as it is called, and obtained twenty five shillings a week, soon after, so that, with strict economy, she did pretty well." She is also able to supplement her sewing income by delivering goods, "for which office he [her master] paid her the same price he would have given a porter" (III, 200–02). Moreover, Emma does considerably better than her brother, who is in the pay of the booksellers: "I have been employed," he tells Emma, "by an eminent bookseller in the city, correcting proofs, and poor Charlotte [his mistress] has taken work [needlework] and clear-starching, and yet we can scarce pay our lodgings, or keep ourselves from starving" (III, 211). Green's economic structure illustrates the ideological point: a kept woman and a man chained to the booksellers are joined in an doubly unholy union, a combination that stands, profit-wise, a poor second to the efforts of a determined, respectable, single woman working alone.

Needlework in fiction acts like a barometric check on employment in the outside world. Its earning power is too publicly known to be hidden by unfounded optimism. The heroine of Elizabeth Benger's Longman novel *The Heart and the Fancy* (1813), "having no other resource, took in plain-work; in which," she reports, "I persisted, till

I became afflicted with a numbness in my joints, which rendered me incapable of that exertion" (I, 38–39). The impoverished widow of a naval officer in Eliza Parsons' Minerva novel *The History of Miss Meredith* (1790) takes in needlework from among her neighbors, and is enabled "to appear decently, and lay up a little sum of money in four years," but the sum is so precariously small that all is lost on doctors' fees and medicines when her daughter falls ill (II, 47–49). A character in Jane Timbury's *The Philanthropic Rambler* (1790) speaks to the desperate condition of another respectable widow dependent upon needlework: "Why, she washes and irons, and makes shirts, and any thing she can get" (I, 84).

The magic formula that will unite women to the economy remains elusive, for all ranks of women. *La Belle Assemblée*, a popular upmarket magazine of fashion, news, and fiction, includes in its issue for November 1808, a sharply focused story-essay on women's employment entitled "Men-Milliners." The plot features a heroine who, recently deserted by her husband, "resolved to ... boldly try in what way a well educated woman could exert her abilities, so as to procure some comforts, without being held up to the eye of the world as an object of compassion or contempt." Taking a baby cap she has worked in cambric to a local shop, she offers it for sale. "May I ask what you would offer if purchasing such a one," Laura asks the shop woman. "We do not buy them so, and should only offer a few shillings," the woman replies. "'For cambric and a fortnight's constant work?' said Laura, in a tone of indignant surprise, 'do you suppose any one could subsist on such earnings?' – 'Subsist, indeed; no, Ma'am, they are chiefly worked at school, or by those who think they had better get three pence a day than nothing.'" Still determined, Laura next offers her services to a shop that farms out the sewing of shirts:

"Would you employ me if I gave you security?" – "Why, not at present, it is rather a dead time; that is worked in Scotland, they do it much cheaper than here; but if you wish for a fine shirt to make, and deposit half-guinea, you may have one." – "What do you allow for making one?" – "One shilling and nine-pence." – "I thank you," said Laura shrinking, "but must decline it."

Mary Charlton's heroine in *Grandeur and Meanness* (1824), a Minerva production, encourages well-to-do middle-class women to take a little practical, sisterly economic action. She suggests that women employ other women in needlework directly, thus by-passing the shops altogether. In doing this, the consumer performs not only an act of loyalty to her own sex, says Charlton's heroine, but "she saves money, and makes an industrious creature comfortable, instead of contributing to the luxurious habits of the opulent shopkeeper" (I, 39–41). The heroine of *La Belle Assemblée*'s "Men-Milliners" also suggests a course of united action for women. Women should refuse to patronize shops where men are employed in positions that should by rights belong to women: "Yet it is averred that many ladies prefer going to shops where these fribbles preside; – shame on them, may their likings never be consulted." Priscilla Wakefield's *Reflections on the Present Condition of the Female Sex, with Suggestions for its Improvement* (1798) and Mary Ann Radcliffe's *The Female Advocate, or An Attempt to Recover the Rights of Women from Male Usurpation* (1799), two prominent contemporary tracts, also argue that women must stand together in the economy. Frances Burney mocks male attendants in London shops in *Evelina* (1776), and women's magazines throughout the period mount continual, sporadic attacks on "men-milliners."

Didactic novelists are particularly devoted to the message that women must support other women in the economy. Mrs. Howardine, the wise matron of Mary Pilkington's children's novel *Violet Vale* (1805), has the task of educating her spoiled niece, Matilda, sent to her from India by her parents. The aunt and the niece visit the home of the Miss Middletons, their name indicative of their rank, where they find the Middleton women busily engaged with some interesting needlework: "The table at which they sat, was strewed with a variety of pieces of ornamental little paintings upon sattin; there were *pincushions, housewifes, workbags,* and *pocket-books*; in short, a sufficiency of those kind of articles to have furnished a small shop." Mrs. Howardine compliments the ladies on their work, assuming the objects are "*presents* intended for their *friend*" (pp. 27–28). The two young women blush:

"We do not occupy our time *thus*, madam, merely for ornament," said the elder Miss Middleton, in a hesitating tone of voice: "our father's income is *small*, and we could not bear the idea of being an entire burden to him; therefore, by the sale of these articles, we are enabled to support ourselves; we send them once a month to a principal shop in London, and this happens to be the day we expect the coach to pass; will you then be kind enough to excuse me a few minutes, as my sister or myself always pack them up."

Mrs. Howardine promptly gives her wholehearted approval of their employment: "'Make no apology to *me*, my dear Miss Middleton,' replied Mrs. Howardine, in an affectionate tone of voice, 'it is not possible for me to say how much admiration your ingenuousness has excited; or how amiable I think the motives which induce you to thus occupy your time" (pp. 27–28). Matilda, the Anglo-Indian niece, has reservations: "But is it not very *mean* of them, aunt, to *sell* their things?" she inquires: "'ladies never do such things in Bengal.' 'I believe it my dear girl,' replied Mrs. Howardine, 'because ladies in that country are generally as *rich* as they are *proud*. So far from its being *mean* to dispose of the fruits of their *taste* and *industry*, it is a mode of conduct for which they must be admired: their father's income, you heard, was a very confined one, and he could enjoy few of the comforts of life, if he had *them* to *support*'" (pp. 29–30). The boarding-school trifles produced by the Middleton women, in the privacy of their own home of course, give a touch of elegance to their occupation, but the system of distribution, the tastes of the shopkeepers, the amount of work involved remain unaccounted for.[31] Pilkington's optimism issues from her vision of what ought to be, not from any reflection of the realities of commerce. Genteel writers like Frances Burney and Charlotte Smith, more sensitive to the taboos of station, paradoxically have a stronger appreciation of those discouraging truths.

The theater, a profession in which privacy cannot possibly be incorporated into employment, must be rejected firmly by heroines of novels. In *The Woman of Genius* (1821), the heroine refuses out-right to entertain the proposal that she go on the stage, "a profession humiliating to pride and disgusting to delicacy" (I, 46–49). The heroine of Madame de Genlis' novel *The Young Exiles* (1799) is praised "for refusing to sing or play on the harp at public concerts" (III, 83). Burney's Juliet in *The Wanderer* (1814) consents to play in public, but only after much soul-searching in which she determines that it is the only way to be honorable and pay her bills. Although the sting is much ameliorated by the fact that it is to be a subscription performance with invited guests, even so the hero begs her not to descend to such employment, cautioning her against "deviating, alone and unsupported as you appear, from the long beaten track of female timidity" (II, 365). He admires her courageous honesty, he tells her, but his family could never welcome her afterwards. In the end, the trial is never engaged: a melodramatic interruption brings the performance to a halt before it starts and the heroine's brief career never gets off the ground.

Mary Robinson, who had a successful career on the stage before becoming a novelist, offers a lonely defense.[32] The heroine of her novel *The Natural Daughter* (1799) takes to "the boards of scenic exhibition" in search of an independence. And though she "looked not forward to any thing beyond a decent independence," claims Robinson, she fails disastrously (I, 250). When her husband returns to her arms – he had abandoned her on an unjustified suspicion of her infidelity – he asks her how she supported herself in his absence. "The exercise of those talents which heaven sometimes bestows as the substitutes for fortune," she tells him. He does not understand. She spells it out. "A strolling actress! God forbid!" he responds. "Why have you disgraced yourself – your family?" Her desperate, last-stand reply: "Rather ask me how, so pressed by poverty, so deserted, so scorned, I have prevented both my own and my family's dishonour" (II, 14–16). Robinson's brief but notorious career as the mistress of the Prince of Wales could not have lessened the general prejudice against the acting profession, but her readers' certain knowledge that there were worse things than acting could not have gone unmarked either.

Prostitution, surprisingly, receives a forgiving, even a sympathetic hearing when it is brought into the woman's novel – not as an employment for the heroine, of course, but often enough for some tempted, frail friend of the heroine. Very seldom indeed does the profession appear in women's fiction solely as an excuse for sentimental tears. That is a male prerogative. Instead, the woman's novel offers prostitution as an intentionally shocking emblem of the general, humiliating economic condition of Everywoman. It is an old tradition in women's fiction.[33] The oldest profession becomes the woman novelist's whipping-post to expose an unjust society.[34]

Prostitution is no employment anomaly, writes Mary Hays:

I have divided women, with but few exceptions, into two classes of victims, those who are necessitated by the worst kind of prostitution to exchange their persons for a subsistence: (for this traffic is no uncommon basis even of matrimonial engagements) and those whom superior spirits & taste, or the want of meretricious allurement, condemns to the severe tests of stifling every natural affection & exposing themselves, unprotected, weakened by education & habit, to insult if not to penury.[35]

That is to say, minus the angry euphemisms, Hays' world of employment is divided between the miseries of prostitution (married or otherwise) and the equal miseries of respectable employment. Between these two appalling alternatives, Hays implies, the difference is only of degree, not kind. Prostitution for Hays is merely a darkened extension of the general employment horizon for all women.

Emily Clark's heroine in *Ermina Montrose* (1800) openly sympathizes with the economic plight that drives women to the oldest profession: "Never did she deform her face as so many ladies do, by a contemptuous sneer, or haughty pout of the lip, at the sight of any of those unhappy women, who, though they have lost one virtue, may yet have many others remaining to make them more estimable, than those who haughtily deride them" (III, 187–90). In "Men-Milliners," the previously cited *La Belle Assemblée* tale, Laura, the heroine, also speaks feelingly of the "frail beauties" on the London streets as she responds to an intolerant young woman, Miss Bland, who has just called them "disgusting wretches." "You have a comfortable home, and are well protected," Laura tells Miss Bland, "therefore so shielded you cannot feel the necessities of your fellow-creatures, nor even know their tortures; the state of women obliged to subsist by their own industry is most deplorable." Remembering her own unavailing search for employment at the linen-drapers' shops, Laura adds pointedly, "Had wages proportionate to the wants of the times been allowed them," they would not have become such "hapless victims."[36]

Turning to Miss Bland, Laura poses the central question of all contemporary women's fiction: "Pardon me for a blunt question, suppose yourself for a moment deprived of friends and fortune, how would you endeavour to support yourself?"

Miss Bland, turning up her lip proudly, replied, – "I might perhaps be a governess, or teacher." – "As situations of every description," said Laura, "are soon filled by accomplished women, suppose one not to be met with." – "Why, then I should make fancy things." – "Alas! the trade is over-stocked, you would not earn bread and water." – "Why, then I suppose I must work at my needle." – "No doubt," said Laura, pensively smiling, "you would undertake to work cambric habit-shirts at eight shillings that would take you twelve days to complete."

Laura then sets up a hypothetical situation for an underpaid sempstress: "'Suppose a gay seducer spreads his wiles, and promises not merely peace, but every thing the world terms pleasure, say, is it any wonder she quits her solitary room? Alas! so forlornly situated I would not answer for myself.' – 'Nor I,' said Ellen. – 'And I,' said the severe censor, 'should not think it any sin to run off with the first that would take me from such a scene of misery.'"

Women's struggle for economic independence is nowhere more clearly visible in women's fiction than in its angry representations of the economic temptations of prostitution. When Mrs. Darnford, a character in Clara Reeve's *School for Widows* (1791), refuses a settlement of a farm on "her and her heirs forever" in return for her virtue, the rake's retort is a brutally clear statement of the general economic plight of single, unprotected women: "You are a proud, ungrateful, saucy woman, unworthy of my love or esteem. I leave you to your fate; to that Poverty, which you prefer to my friendship" (II, 21–22). A rake in Charlotte Smith's *Ethelinde* (1789) offers the heroine an annuity of £600 pounds a year for her sexual favors: "And I think that's a devilish handsome price," says the rake, "for a girl that has not a sixpenny piece in the world, and a little crack in her character with that story of Sir Edward. Come, come," he tells her, "don't affect all these violent airs; but remember 'tis not an offer you'll have every day" (V, 44). In Robinson's *The Natural Daughter*, when the respectable Mrs. Morley fails at getting a living by her pen, a gentleman offers to take her into keeping: "Two thousand pounds for present exigencies, and three hundred pounds per annum, were proferred as the price of her degradation; by one, who not many weeks before, had refused to aid her literary toils by the subscription of a single guinea!" Robinson, with her own bitter experience as a kept woman, writes with feeling: "Mrs. Morley's indignation was strong, but her necessities were powerful… The trial was a severe one; she was trembling, fearful, perplexed, distressed, and wounded by the insults of unfeeling persecutors. The man of wealth was selfish, ignorant, and ostentatious: she was oppressed and humbled" (II, 70–71).

Charlotte Smith, always skeptical of the virtues of employment, speaks plainly and repeatedly of the powerful temptations of becoming a kept woman. In *Ethelinde* (1789), the hero's mother, Mrs. Montgomery, relates her own mother's unfortunate history: "On one side, affluence, with the man whom she already loved more than she was aware of, and a certain provision on the infant on whom she doated," explains Mrs. Montgomery, and "on the other, poverty, dependence, and contempt; her child torn from her, and herself sent to service. The contrast was too violent" (I, 141).

In Smith's *Celestina* (1791), Emily, the fallen younger sister of Mrs. Elphinstone, rescues her older sister and her family with money she has made as a kept woman. Mrs. Elphinstone, frantic and in search of a doctor for her ailing infant, meets Emily in a London street riding "in an elegant vis-a-vis," notes Smith. "In my anxiety for the life of my infant," explains the desperate mother, "I forgot the culpable conduct of my sister ... A strange stupor overwhelmed me" (II, 294). The "stupor," reminiscent of that which accompanies the rape in *Clarissa*, afflicts Mrs. Elphinstone just at the moment she takes the money of her fallen sister, a scarcely disguised version of her own economic rape. Emily sends her, "by a porter, the next day, a forty pound note." "As soon as I was capable of reading and understanding this, all that had passed came back to my recollection. I had been supported, then, for many days, by the wages of shame; and now had nothing but a gift from the same hand, to save my husband, my brother, and myself, from actual hunger." When Mrs. Elphinstone later visits Emily to expostulate with her on her way of life, "she owned all her guilt, and all her folly; without having the power, or, at that time, perhaps, the wish to quit a manner of life, where she possessed boundless splendour and luxury, for such a precarious subsistence as women can earn in business" (II, 298). The implicit comparison between the respectable Mrs. Elphinstone's miserable life as the long-suffering wife of a wastrel and Emily's luxurious life as a much-loved mistress is *not* a moot point for Smith. It lies there for angry contemplation. Emily dies, but her keeper, the volatile, unsteady rake Vavasour, receives the blame, and Smith spares Emily any hint of an obligatory scene of repentance.

At the last stand, all these fictions of employment fail. First of all, the nostalgic subtext of Peter Laslett's "world that was" must be squared to an economic reality more powerful than any fiction that the novelists can invent.[37] In the upmarket novels of Austen, Smith, Burney, and Edgeworth, echoes of a threatening economy reach the reader through the bitter language of loss. The dispossessed heroine of the genteel novel walks in the dual shadow of an indifferent traditional economy and a hostile market economy. In the didactic novels of Pilkington and Brunton, fantasies of employment fail as earnest, but patently impractical, plans for implementation. Finally, among the Minerva writers, a kind of grim, stoic buoyancy runs the employment show. Here the reader finds arguable success for women in the economy, with an especially good example in Sarah Green's heroine Emma Southby. If happiness can be found on 25 shillings a week, then Emma Southby will certainly have it.

Nevertheless, employment for middle-class women remains a profoundly conjectural proposal in the woman's novel. The novelists circulate their tales in a Bakhtinian marketplace of discourse with one eye turned to the economy of pounds, shillings, and pence, but with the other on the more important negotiation for station and self-respect. As the discourse of employment in women's fiction "weaves in and out of complex interrelationships, merges with some, recoils from others" on its Bakhtinian route, it produces a chorus of discords and harmonies.[38] The gauge of tension can be measured by the almost complete impenetrability of the only employment that authors can be guaranteed to know first-hand: novel-writing itself. The hedges and thickets that women novelists throw up around their own profession furnish out the terrain of the final chapter.

CHAPTER 7

Writing for money: authors and heroines

An unexpected change of fortune, suggested the idea of authorship; those talents, which were cultivated for *amusement*, have become the means of *support*; and through their exertion, an aged mother has been supplied with the common comforts of existence, for upwards of eleven years.

Mary Pilkington, *Violet Vale* (1805)

Publication for profit is the admitted goal of women novelists like Charlotte Smith and Jane Austen, and many other women besides. "Men very seldom write pleasing novels," Charlotte Smith confided to her friend Sarah Rose.[1] Jane Austen acknowledged the competition of male authors more directly: "Walter Scott has no business to write novels, especially good ones. – It is not fair. – He has Fame and Profit enough as a Poet, and should not be taking the bread out of other people's mouths" (*Letters*, 404). Lady Morgan's writer heroine in *Florence Macarthy* (1818) makes no apology for her need for money either: "Necessity has urged me to trace so much nonsense, that I may live and others may laugh" (III, 264–65).

Although the fear of "traffic," of selling home and hearth to any stranger with the price of a library ticket, kept the title page of Jane Austen's novels "By a Lady" all her life, it is not the risk of social prejudice that accounts for the most pressing anxiety of women authors, including Austen, but the much graver economic risks that they ran in putting pen to paper. Certainly a woman with pretensions to rank might be exposed by her writings to a fall from station, but women who depended upon novels for their livelihood faced a more palpable terror: the double prospect of poverty and debtors' prison. In their novels, authors of all ranks cast an obscuring veil over the economic dangers of the writing profession.

Genteel novelists almost never make their heroines authors;[2] didactic novelists must have a very pressing moral justification

191

Accept O Cyprian Queen our joint Essay,
And Smile propitious on the FEMALE *Lay.*

Plate 26. From *The Lady's Magazine* (February 1773).

indeed for them to chance it; and Minerva novelists embrace it for heroines only in utter desperation. Perhaps an older woman, *not* the heroine herself, may be driven in a genteel novel to turn her pen to fiction for the support of a sick husband or fatherless children; and for the same reason, the heroines of didactic novels and Minerva novels might possibly try their pens for a living, but no character in any woman's novel, with rare exception, ever seeks to be an author.[3] The steady reluctance of women authors to turn their heroines into authors constitutes a telling gauge of women's position in the writing profession.

For Charlotte Smith, the irksome contrast between the real-life troubles of authorship and the fictional troubles of heroes and heroines, opens the study door on the creative process. Mrs. Denzil, Smith's woman author (a matron who must support her family) in *The Banished Man* (1794), describes a hard day of writing. In the midst of her morning's composition she receives a note from Mr. Humphrey Hotgoose, a lawyer, on behalf of Mr. Thomas Tough demanding immediate payment of a debt of "sixty-two pounds, nine shillings and eleven-pence." A "precious recipe," Smith herself interjects, "to animate the imagination and exalt the fancy!"

After a conference with Mr. Tough, she must write a tender dialogue between some damsel, whose perfections are even greater than those "Which youthful poets fancy when they love," and her hero, who, to the bravery and talents of Caesar, adds the gentleness of Sir Charles Grandison, and the wit of Lovelace. But Mr. Tough's conversation, his rude threats, and his boisterous remonstrances, have totally sunk her spirits; nor are they elevated by hearing that the small beer is almost out; that the pigs... have broke into the garden, rooted up the whole crop of pease, and not left her a single hyacinth or jonquil.

Worse yet, her maid comes in to tell her that "John Gubbins's children over the way, and his wife, and John his-self, have all got the *scarlot favor*; and that one of the children is dead on't, and another like to die." Mrs. Denzil sends the Gubbinses what little wine she has in the house, and she presses on with her story:

The rest of the day is passed as before; her hero and her heroine are parted in agonies, or meet in delight, and she is employed in making the most of either; with interludes of the Gubbins' family, and precautions against importing the distemper into her own. (II, 224–29)

Sophia King sees no future in writing at all. In the "Preface" to her novel *The Fatal Secret, or Unknown Warrior* (1801), "printed for the

Author," she maintains that, "If only she possessed the wealth of the mines of Potosi, never should the drooping child of intellect, with fatal MS be seen prowling in melancholy solitude, seeking relief in the shape of some extortionate bookseller" (I, ii). Mary Robinson's heroine, the protagonist of *The Natural Daughter* (1799), a Longman novel, does give novel-writing a try, although warned by a wise older woman that "There is no harder labour ... The toils of intellect are more severe than even the miseries of adversity" (I, 78):

She had employed her pen, till her health was visibly declining; she had denied herself the comforts of existence, till existence itself was scarcely to be valued. All that her honourable, her incessant industry could procure, was insufficient for the purposes of attaining a permanent independence; and she was at length so deeply involved, so menaced with destruction, that nothing but an effort of despair could save her. (II, 69–70)

Reality matches Robinson's picture.[4] A correspondent of the *Lady's Magazine* (October 1796), in an essay, "On the Superiority of Female Talents," asks wryly: "Which requires greater abilities, – to govern a kingdom, or to cajole a bookseller?" (p. 439). Despite the common fame of Frances Burney's impressive commercial success with *Camilla* (1796) and Hannah More's triumph with *Coelebs* (1809), truly, there was nothing for women authors to celebrate.[5] The highly touted successes of Burney and More, or Maria Edgeworth and Susan Ferrier, two other women who took profits in four figures on individual novels, must be put in terms of lifetime earnings to become significant.[6] Maria Edgeworth's meticulous accounts show her lifetime's income from writing, mostly fiction, to come to exactly £11,062 8s 10d, certainly a magnificent showing, but not a genteel competence for life. In fact, Edgeworth's money was never used for living expenses at all, but was set aside to provide personal luxuries outside the family budget.[7]

Frances Burney received 20 guineas for *Evelina*, £250 for *Cecilia*, around £2,000 for *Camilla*, and £3,000 for *The Wanderer*, all this stretched over a 36-year period. If, hypothetically, Burney's money had been invested in the government funds at 5 percent interest, which it was not because it was needed for immediate expenses, it would have brought her, hypothetically, a yearly income of only around £160, the income of a country curate, though without the benefit of his house or glebe. If Burney's total income is computed as annual earned income for the thirty-six years, it averages out to less than £150 a year, again not much of a competence. Susan Ferrier received a total of £2,850 for her writings over a 13-year period. Again, the income that this figure hypothetically could have generated for her, invested in the government funds at 5 percent interest, is only £142 a year; computed as annual earnings for the thirteen years, it would amount to little more than £200 a year; again, meager funds indeed for a gentlewoman.

Charlotte Smith's earnings over a 19-year period of constant production and desperate labor come to only £4,500 or £5,000 total, most of it consumed as soon as it was received, often before.[8] Jane Austen's records of profit in her publishing history read as a series of unfortunate misjudgments of the business. She published *Sense and Sensibility* with Egerton on commission, made £140, but judged it too dangerous an experiment to try with her next novel, *Pride and Prejudice*. This novel she sold to Egerton outright for £110: "I would rather have had £150," she wrote Cassandra, "but we could not both be pleased, & I am not at all surprised that he should not chuse to hazard so much" (*Letters*, 501). The second edition of *Mansfield Park*, published on commission with Murray, in 1816, brought severe disappointment, producing a loss of £182 8s 3d for the year, and reducing her profits on *Emma* to only £38 18s.[9] In the end, her entire lifetime's income from writing amounted to only about £670, approximately a single year's income for her clergyman father at Steventon.[10]

There were, in general, four ways to publish a novel, none of them without serious financial drawbacks for the author: first, to sell the copyright to the publisher; second, to publish at the author's own expense; third, to publish on commission; and fourth, to publish by subscription. Sale of the copyright to the publisher had the obvious disadvantage of depriving the author of future profits if the work should prove popular. The author would receive her fixed sum and be entitled to no further money from her work. Frances Burney's loss from her sale of the copyright of *Evelina* was famous in its day, but lesser authors knew the sting as well.[11] Mary Robinson alludes to the bitter experience in her novel *The Natural Daughter* (1799) when the impoverished heroine of her novel, a struggling novelist, is taken to a madhouse where she must beg for reading material. Her keepers bring her a novel, her own, one she had sold outright for £10, and now in its sixth printing.[12]

The second route into print, to publish at one's own expense, held obvious risks. Although Hannah More succeeded brilliantly with this

publishing tactic for *Coelebs in Search of a Wife* (1809), the great danger
was that the profits on the book might not equal the costs.[13] The
Marchesa Cattarina Hyde Broglio Solari found herself in the Fleet
Prison for the sum of £17: "a debt contracted for a work she printed
in honour of H. G. the D. of Wellington ... but for the want of the
means of news paper promulgation, the sale has been obstructed, for
which she has been imprisoned by the printer, in consequence of not
having been able to satisfy his demand."[14]

Publishing on commission (closely related to publishing at one's
own expense) was, according to John Trusler in *Modern Times* (1785),
a notoriously unrewarding way for an author to seek print. In this
arrangement, the bookseller-publisher would agree to pay for the
costs of producing and selling the book in return for his expenses and
a percentage of the profits. "If you give a bookseller a work to get
printed," writes Trusler, "and conclude an edition of five hundred;
they will order seven hundred and fifty, and more, to be printed, call
all above five hundred their own, sell all their own first, and account
you with the remainder."[15] Samuel Paterson in *Joineriana* (1772)
provides mock instructions to an imaginary bookseller on how to
discourage the sale of books to which he does not own the copyright
himself: "Be sure you say, there's none bound! – And, if he would
take it in sheets – tell him the rat-catchers are in the warehouse, and
you dare not go in for fear of disturbing them – but he may have one
a week hence, if he'll call."[16]

In the absence of independent financial resources, the choice of
publishing either at one's own expense or on commission remained
risky business indeed. Catherine Bayley received a bill and a laconic
explanation from Longman and Company, 14 February 1812, for a
work of hers that they had printed at the author's expense: "The sale
of 'On Vacation Evenings,'" Longman wrote Bayley, "is £87. 19. 3.
short of expenses. If this amount be paid to Messrs Longman and Co.
they will with pleasure deliver up all the copies which remain."[17]
Amelia Opie and Mary Robinson found limited satisfaction in a
commission arrangement with Longman. A 50 percent profit-sharing
between author and publisher was Longman's preferred method for
introducing new fiction. The writer would share profits equally with
the publisher in return for the publisher's taking on the decisions of
what to print and when, and for absorbing any losses. No risks to the
author. The disadvantage was that if the book sold well, the author
made 50 percent less than she might if she had run the risks herself.[18]

Subscription, the final way into print, could bring an author enormous profits, as for Frances Burney with *Camilla*, but there was the major disadvantage, as Charlotte Smith and Burney both confessed, of its being personally humiliating: "*I* also feel *myself* much hurt," wrote Smith, "as in cases of Subscription A Author is always consider'd as a kind of literary beggar, & is open to all the insidious reflections of arrogant prosperity."[19] For the most part, as a writer for the *Critical Review* observed in 1794, subscriptions for novels were seldom successful anyway, since an adequate number of subscribers was "a circumstance rarely attendant on Novels" because of their inexpensive availability at the circulating libraries.[20] Jean Marishall published her novel *Alicia* by subscription, from which she made about 100 guineas, but complained that "not one in twenty were disposed to throw away a crown on what they could get a reading of when published for a few pence" (II, 193). Mary Goldsmith was reduced to destitution by the failure of the subscription to her novel *Casualties* (*c.* 1804), aptly named, not collecting enough money "sufficient to answer the encreased Expense of Printing and Publishing."[21]

First novels, even those purchased by the grandest publishers, scarcely met even the low standard of remuneration set by William Lane's Minerva Press. Crosby gave Jane Austen £10 for *Susan* (published posthumously as *Northanger Abbey*), never published it, and sold it back to the author years later for the same price. The famous Noble was engaged by Jean Marishall through a friend's help to publish her first novel *Clarinda Cathcart* (1766):

She told me, that Mr. N——le was highly delighted, and desired her to tell the lady, that if she kept up the same spirit throughout the work, he would give a very genteel price; but could not ascertain what it would be till he saw it fully completed. Now the question was, what could Mr. N——le consider to be a very genteel price to be offered to a lady? ... Nothing less to be sure, than a few hundreds; nay, we concluded with all the positive presumption of ignorance, that a novel of two volumes, although ever so insignificant, if thought fit to be printed, could never bring less than a hundred guineas.[22]

In due time, the response from Mr. Noble arrived: "PETRIFIED with astonishment, I stood motionless for a few seconds. When, endeavouring to recover myself, in a faint and low key I repeated – *five guineas*!'" Marishall took the 5 guineas, and, with her author's copies was able to extract an additional £12 from the deal, and, with the 10 guineas contributed by the Queen, to whom she dedicated the novel, she garnered a grand total of £27 15s for her first novel[23] – rather good actually, a sum that equalled the price that Lane paid established authors for novels at the Minerva Press.

Women authors burdened with debts and home duties stood little chance of lessening their troubles through the publishers, these "Turks and Tartars," as Lamb called them.[24] Charlotte Lennox, a highly respected novelist (celebrated by Dr. Johnson, admired by Jane Austen), confessed in the last years of her life that she was "in great distress for the common necessaries of life & ... too ill & now too old to be able to assist herself in any way."[25] Mary Pilkington, a respected author of children's literature, reported that the pressure to produce fiction had driven her to "a Nervous Disorder [that] has totally incapacitated me for every species of Composition."[26]

The Royal Literary Fund, the charity established to aid destitute authors, was little more than an institutional repository of abandoned hope. Echoes of a mythic golden age, the lost circle of hearth and family, are heard again and again in the desperate appeals for financial help that fill its records. Ann Burke, a prolific but destitute novelist, writes the charity's trustees:

I have now another work in hand, which unhappy circumstances, and an afflicted mind deprives me of the power of finishing, and I am distracted by the want of daily bread, and am a Widow, with a little boy to support, who is just recovering from the small pox, and at present in very ill health: and I have been obliged to part with the greatest part of my apparel to support him in his illness.[27]

Two years later, she remains in urgent need,

not now having one article of property left, even to produce a single shilling. The cloaths I now wear to deliver this letter, are borrowed of a humane Friend, whose power of assistance cannot extend farther ... I hourly expect to be obliged to quit my lodgings for the rent due, which is two guineas, and in my present state, destitute of cloaths and money, with a child the sharer of my deep Distress, my Life must be the Victim, unless speedy relief be extended.[28]

Maria Hunter, whose novel *Fitzroy: or, Impulse of the Moment* (1792) had been well received by *The Gentleman's Magazine*, wrote the Literary Fund from the Fleet Prison: "I have not a room to myself therefore cannot write or Employ my self in any manner to procure the least Subsistence." A year and a half later, still in prison for debt, she wrote, "I have had a very Severe Illness & have not had Money or necessaries – but am indebted for my recovery to the kindness of the prisoners."[29]

Elizabeth Helme, a prolific Minerva writer whose works were reprinted throughout the nineteenth century and were favorably reviewed in both the *Critical Review* and the *British Critic*, expressed a mixture of both pride and despair in reviewing the course of her literary career:

For seventeen years I have written for the press, and by that means supported myself respectably, and materially assisted a large family, but a very close application for the last three years, rendered necessary by the failure of all other means, has intirely distroyed [*sic*] my health and for the two past plunged me into a complicated, and hopeless, dropsical and liver complaint from which I can flatter myself with no relief but Death.[30]

The edge of the economic abyss was a working fact of life for the woman writer. Mary Robinson and Amelia Opie, both well-received writers earning around £500 a year from their writing, ended their careers in debt.[31] "This struggle, this perpetual warfare must have an end," lamented Eliza Fenwick, burdened with a drunken husband and employed in keeping a shop in Penzance. "I cannot write," she confessed to her friend Mary Hays, "perpetually surrounded with my family even were I assured that I have talents to make writing profitable & I possess no such confidence."[32] The mythic family hearthside, a pitifully contracted version, haunts Fenwick's imagination: "I long to have a house," she wrote Hays,

I wish I could be sheltered under the same roof & had some regular & quiet pursuit which could provide my subsistance & allow us generally to join our hours of recreation. I really contemplate (only to myself remember) Eliza [her daughter] & I colouring prints together for a living in some cheap lodging. I know the respect that several people hold me in would prevent the solitude and obscurity from growing on my heart. I confess to you, but to you alone, that some such combination presents itself whenever I think of happiness.[33]

Time was not on the woman author's side. Mr. Crisp, Frances Burney's literary adviser in her early years, counselled an amused Burney that she could simply "sit by a warm Fire, and in 3 or 4 months...only putting down in black and white whatever comes into her own head, without labour drawing simply from her own Fountain, she need not want money."[34] The truth, as Burney knew

from experience, was quite another matter. The pressure of composition was simply too great, even for the most prolific woman
writer, to succeed in getting a steady and comfortable living by her
pen alone.

Mary Ann Hanway confessed to her readers in the preface to
Falconbridge Abbey (1809) that "four years it has been procrastinated,
from a series of ill health, having laid dormant in my desk for six
months together!" (I, ix–x). As Charlotte Smith complained to a
friend, "I was compelled to finish the three volumes of 'Letters of a
Solitary Wanderer,' which I had been two years about, & I do assure
you that there were times when the anxiety of my mind & the labour
I was notwithstanding oblig'd to go thro, so entirely overcame me,
that I thought I must have given all up, & desisted from so vain &
hopeless an attempt as resisting any longer so overwhelming a
destiny."[35] Elizabeth Inchbald's story is no different: "I do not
shrink from labour," she wrote William Godwin, "but, I shrink from
ill health, low spirits, disappointment, and a long train of evils which
attend on a laborious, literary work." "I was ten months unceasingly
in finishing my novel, notwithstanding the plan (such as you saw
it)," she explained to him, "was formed and many papers written.
My Health suffered much during this confinement."[36] It is just as
Sarah Scadgell Wilkinson confessed to the Royal Literary Fund:

All that industry can do I have tried, but I am of that sex whose earnings at
the best of times are comparatively small, and a weak state of health joined
to a painful tumour under my right arm renders me incapable of any
exertions beyond my pen and needlework, and except one pound a month
which I received for conducting a part of the Ladies Monthly Museum my
employ is casual and latterly very inadequate to the support of myself and
Fatherless child.[37]

Lady authors, that is those women with genteel pretensions,
suffered economic stress in publishing too – different from Sarah
Wilkinson's, but significant and troubling nonetheless. Susan Ferrier's correspondence with the publisher John Blackwood illustrates
their dilemma. In the early years of her career, Ferrier's brother
carried on her business dealings with Blackwood the publisher, while
Ferrier herself closely guided the negotiations from behind the scenes.
Blackwood's letters to his lady author supported the genteel charade
by avoiding all mention of money and by supplying a regular
allotment of well-pointed flattery. Over the years, Blackwood paid
£150 for the copyright of Ferrier's first novel, *Marriage* (1818), an

extraordinary price for a first effort, and £1,000 for her second novel, *The Inheritance* (1823), an outstanding price for any novel.[38] Balking, however, at the third novel, *Destiny*, on account of the poor sales of *The Inheritance*, Blackwood apparently cast aside the airs of gentleman patron for the plain-speaking idiom of trade, a lower order of communication altogether. The mere whiff of the tradesman in Blackwood's language was enough to send Ferrier to the ramparts:

The last time I had any conversation with you regarding my works I clearly understood from you that "The Inheritance" at least had proved unsuccessful, or, as it seems I had erroneously termed it, *unfortunate*, and I never should have thought of *offering* a future work to you after being told the second edition of my former one was "dead stock" upon your hands.[39]

Jane Austen takes similar care to distance herself from the gentleman-like posings of the great John Murray. "Mr. Murray's letter is come," she writes Cassandra. "He is a rogue of course, but a civil one ... He sends more praise however than I expected. It is an amusing letter. You shall see it." In her next letter on the interesting subject: "He is so very polite indeed, that it is quite overcoming ... In short, I am soothed & complimented into tolerable comfort." Two days after, not quite so amused or comforted by Murray's flattery and concerned with the slow progress of the printing of *Emma*, she reports, "I *did* mention the P. R [the Prince Regent, to whom *Emma* was to be dedicated] – in my note to Mr. Murray, it brought me a fine compliment in return; whether it has done any other good I do not know ..." (*Letters*, 425, 433, 436).

Mary Brunton, who had an independent income of her own, felt the need to justify her occupation: "I do not need to write for bread," she reminds her sympathetic brother: "A moral therefore is necessary for me ... A *lofty* moral, too." However, when Brunton's novel received poor reviews, it was not the "lofty moral," but the "bread" that rescued her self-esteem. "Nevertheless, the book is both read and bought," she wrote defensively: "In spite of all these faults, and a hundred more, (many of them contradictory) there is not a copy to be had in Edinburgh or in London." Lady Morgan (Sydney Owenson) offers the same justification for her heroine, Lady Clancare, in *Florence Macarthy* (1818), and in the same phrases: "With all these vices and faults they have been so read and bought, as to realize an independence for their author ... It would appear, that in spite of professional criticism, the public are *always* with her"

(IV, 37). Susan Ferrier demonstrates the same ladylike attraction to and repulsion from the money she earns: "As for the money, I'm surprised how little I care about it," she writes. Not true: in practice she was a tough bargainer, refusing to release *The Inheritance* until Blackwood doubled his original offer of £500. Jane Austen's candid delight with the profits of her novels comes as a refreshing contrast, though her love of the money is still touched by the diffidence of the lady author: "People are more ready to borrow & praise, than to buy – which I cannot wonder at; – but tho' I like praise as well as anybody, I like what Edward calls *Pewter* too" (*Letters*, 419–20).

Nevertheless, money was the name of the game, and if a lady author chose to throw in her lot with the publishing business, she was forced to confront its still undetermined social status. Her difficult task was to stay afloat financially, keep her attachment to her station and rank intact, and to preserve, if possible, some shred of personal dignity and self-esteem in the bargain.

Charlotte Smith: the genteel dilemma

Born to a life of comfortably appointed, genteel luxury, Charlotte Smith found herself in her middle years totally dependent on her pen for a livelihood.[40] Virtually penniless, abandoned by her husband, and responsible for the education and rearing of nine children – her jointure and a large inheritance were kept from her by impenetrable lawsuits – the necessary charade of gentility was her crown of thorns. With the help of a small £70-a-year annuity and, in later years, occasional gifts of cash from her two oldest sons, she pieced together a living by selling, on the average, a novel a year for ten years from 1788 to 1798 – "I love novels," she wrote a friend, "no more than a Grocer does figs."[41] In addition, she published a considerable body of poems, translations, and children's literature. She generally received £50 a volume for her novels, that is £150 to £200 each. If she had not been hamstrung by pretensions to gentility, as her biographer Judith Stanton suggests, she might have negotiated for still more.[42] With the contributions of her elder two sons included, Smith's income in her best years could range from £370 to £570 a year, modest enough and with none of the stability of the regularly paid £500 a year that Austen allows the Dashwood women in *Sense and Sensibility*, though far better than the frightening poverty of her worst writing years.

The comparison with her former income of £2,000 a year, when she was first married, was an embittering fact for Smith, but, more seriously, her writer's income was simply too small to meet the demands of a large family, and especially insufficient to command the education needed to maintain station for her sons, and *never* enough to maintain the style of life to which she herself laid claim: "I have the character of being expensive, when perhaps no Woman brought up as I was, was ever so *little* expensive."[43] Her correspondence over two decades reveals her struggle to keep the duns at bay, to persuade booksellers to give her advances and loans, to ward off depredations regularly made on her income by her husband, and to claim the social rank for her children that she believed them entitled to by birth.

Physical and emotional collapse overtook her in early 1794. She wrote from Bath, "I have found the waters of very great service to me in removing that excessive lowness and depression which render'd me unfit for every thing, & is perhaps the most distressing of all evils to a person situated as I am – who must live to write & write to live."[44] But later, in October of that year, financial pressures mounted again and she reported to her friend the Reverend Joseph Cooper Walker that her affairs had become desperate:

tho I often sit up all night to write, I cannot obtain wherewithal to support my family – There is now an Execution in my house at Storrington for 25£ – & my books the only things I had been able to reserve, are seized for rent & will be sold. This is so much a blow to me, that added to the inconveniencies I suffer here for want of Money, I am unable to support my courage.[45]

Only a month later she confessed to Cadell and Davies, her publishers, that she was behind in her work for them:

tho I have finish'd the first Volume of the Novel I had begun, and have received the money for it £50, from a Bookseller in Soho – it is quite impossible that the most incessant labor on my part, can entirely support a family of seven persons in the requisites of existence, & my daughter's four months illness – & five Medical Men, who have continually attended her have really reduced me to more cruel exigencies that I have ever known.[46]

Life got no easier for Smith over the years, even with steady publication. Near the end of her career – one daughter home from India with a dangerous fever, another recently widowed and penniless – she confessed to Joseph Cooper Walker:

Amidst all this, I was compelled to finish the three volumes of "Letters of a Solitary Wanderer," which I had been two years about; & I do assure you that there were times when the anxiety of my mind & the labour I was notwithstanding oblig'd to go thro, so entirely overcame me, that I thought I must have given all up, & desisted from so vain & hopeless an attempt as resisting any longer so overwhelming a destiny.[47]

Charlotte Smith died in 1806. The estate upon which she had pinned all her hopes for economic security did not reach settlement until seven years after her death, in 1813. The original fortune, plentiful stock in the East India Company and two plantations in the West Indies, by then reduced through delay, trustees, and litigation to a mere £4,000, was divided among the surviving children.[48]

Eliza Parsons: the Minerva struggle

Eliza Parsons, a Minerva writer, the daughter of a Plymouth wine merchant and the widow of a turpentine distiller, also found only distress and poverty in her publishing career, mainly with William Lane's Minerva Press. The price Lane would pay for a complete novel could go as low as £5, but could cover a spread of figures, before 1800, that ran from £5 to £20. After 1800, the rate increased to £30 for Lane's best novelists, and even £40 for a popular novelist like Parsons,[49] whose novels *The Castle of Wolfenbach* (1794) and *The Mysterious Warning* (1796) feature, as has been noted, in Isabella Thorpe's list of "horrid novels."

In 1792, widowed, burdened with the responsibility for eight children, and bedridden for six months with a broken leg, she applied to the Royal Literary Fund for financial aid. As she explained her career to the Fund's trustees, "I had no recourse but my needle and pen ... I was compelled to avail myself of the fashion of the times and write novels." Four years later she applied again for help: "In the course of five years I have written five and twenty volumes, under all the disadvantages of a disordered body and mind." In seven more years there was yet another application, this time from debtors' prison: "These two years past I have been a prisoner, at 62 years of age, I have experienced the loss of liberty and every attendant mortification." Her fragile hold on economic stability strikes terror to the heart: "In these Melancholy Circumstances I have to write Works of Fancy for my daily Subsistence, and hitherto have supported myself Tolerably, but a recent Illness 6 weeks since which took me from my Pen near 3 weeks have involved me in fresh difficulties."[50]

Pretensions to gentility run thin with Minerva writers. Parsons, who aspired to publish with "a BURNEY, a SMITH, a REEVE, a BENNET,"[51] never approached the economic success of either Burney or Smith, although her lifetime output was enormous, nineteen multi-volume titles. She did achieve in her publishing career, however, demonstrable success in maintaining the station to which she laid claim. She was able to start three daughters in teaching or mantua-making, put two sons in the navy, and send the rest to school, a marked triumph in keeping her children established in the lower ranks of the middle class, but one bought at the crushing price of physical debility, grinding economic anxiety, and personal humiliation.[52]

Heroine authors: the case in fiction

In a startling paradox, Amelia Beauclerc, a Minerva writer, provides a heroine in her novel *Husband Hunters!!!* (1816) who demonstrates the same genteel confusions about female authorship that distress Mary Brunton and Susan Ferrier, two authors far more comfortably situated in society than Beauclerc herself ever was.[53] Heroines are genteel by definition, but the significant difference in Beauclerc's novel lies in the Minerva-style frankness that she brings to her task of a public exploration of female authorship. *Husband Hunters!!!* presents three clearly articulated, and competing, opinions about women authors. Of three sisters in the novel who have "retired from the world" after the loss of their family fortune, the middle sister, Louisa, becomes a published novelist. Beauclerc, as omniscient narrator, remains thoroughly ambivalent throughout the novel about the motivations and the results of her heroine's enterprise. "She had talents, but she overrated them," she reports early of Louisa: "She was unpleasant amongst ordinary acquaintance, silent, and absent; and her gravity created an idea that she was proud and ill-natured" (1, 29–30). In effect, Louisa's novel-writing is represented as both undermining her moral character and foiling her ability to negotiate general society as well.

The youngest of the three sisters, Dorothy, the low-bred and outspoken half-sister of their late father's second marriage, warns Louisa emphatically that female authorship and marriage can never be reconciled:

I can tell you one thing, *Miss*... you will never get married if such are your plans... Who do you think would be acquainted with a *petticoat author*? All men run away from them; men never like women who are wiser than themselves – they are dangerous; for one is never sure but at the moment they condescend to speak to one, they are taking us [*sic*] off to clap us into their book in some ridiculous point of view to be a laugh for their readers.[54]

The best justification that Louisa, the aspiring author, can muster for herself, one that echoes uncannily Brunton's and Ferrier's real-life protestations, is that she is not "a *known* author," that she writes for her "*own* amusement," and that her satire is "*useful*" and may "warn the young and unwary from treading the same path of idiotism" (I, 35–36).

Even Louisa's genteel elder sister, Emily, who receives financial support from Louisa's literary efforts, has no good words for her sister's authorship either. She chastises Louisa for her over-delicate behavior to a wealthy, respectable suitor, Sir Lucius Fitzgerald, who disapproves of all women authors. Such punctilious behavior, Emily asserts, is all brought about by spending too much time with novels, both reading them and writing them. Louisa, in response to Emily's damaging charge, offers a passionate defense of female authorship, one that is implicitly buttressed by the economically obvious situation: the destitute and suffering Emily, together with her infant son, are living off the bounty of Louisa's hard-earned profits:

I was once a common, every-day character; till I commenced author, I was a vain, inconsiderate, giddy creature; myself was my first object on all occasions, and the roots of goodness nature had bestowed lay without the aid of culture, making no progress to fruition... In portraying perfection in my imagination, I strove to subdue every disposition that should contradict the feelings I myself theorized; if I could not attain the perfect character, I strove to get as near as my feeble nature allowed of; I shook off my thoughts of self; and you are indebted for all you say I have done and sacrificed for you, to that warm friendship and tenderness I bear you, and the devotion to you of my future life, singly and solely to that elevation of soul you choose to ridicule as the spirit of romance. (IV, 166–67)

The banner of family loyalty unfurls to justify Louisa's writing: the protection of the hearth sanctifies female authorship, since the produce of Louisa's sentimental imagination, an imagination that Beauclerc herself had deemed "unpleasant," is the single resource that stands between the little family and destitution.

Louisa's wealthy suitor, Sir Lucius Fitzgerald, loathes Louisa's profession on principle. He expresses horrified disbelief when he discovers that a respectable older woman whom he had previously admired, the Countess d'Esterre, is a novelist too.[55] But he is forced to admit, grudgingly, that the Countess,

> had been an excellent wife, had always acted with fortitude and energy, and that very energy had put her on the means, by turning author, to gain a living, when otherwise she would have starved from necessity.

And he can even apply the lesson to Louisa's case, with, however, a single important reservation:

> And was not Louisa of a strong mind? was not she the guardian angel of her sister? did not she manage all the domestic concerns, and was not every thing arranged with a niceness peculiar to herself? But the countess was in part a Frenchwoman. The French encourage female authors; but in England, so humiliating was that profession, that the men shrunk from them, and the cypress shades of celibacy usually twined over their heads. (II, 224–25)

Beauclerc shifts the argument to France where the problem becomes cultural, not moral. But when Sir Lucius wavers towards condemnation, unconvinced by his own argument, Beauclerc must provide a higher-ranking character, Lord William, to defend the principle of female authorship: "'This is prejudice in the extreme,' replied Lord William; 'I am a great novel-reader, and I assure you that great talents are required, and thorough knowledge of the world also, to make what I call an interesting work of fancy, such as to amuse and to instruct'" (II, 226). Jane Austen offers a similarly high-minded justification in *Northanger Abbey*, where "performances" are praised "which have only genius, wit, and taste to recommend them" (p. 37). But as Catharine Macaulay notes plainly and roundly in her "Modest Plea for the Property of Copyright" (1774), these arguments for quality are really beside the point: "Literary merit will not purchase a shoulder of mutton, or prevail with sordid butchers to abate one farthing in the pound" (p. 15).

Sir Lucius concedes the argument over the respectability of female authorship to the higher-ranking Lord William, he has no choice, but Beauclerc herself remains unsure. She allows Louisa to marry Sir Lucius, but only on the condition that she give up her writing: "matrimony outrivalled the witching charms felt by 'an author,'" claims Beauclerc (IV, 229).

There are at least two plausible explanations for Beauclerc's decision to have Louisa forego authorship, especially after the heroine has defended it so warmly through four volumes. First, the landed money represented by Sir Lucius reaffirms life as it ought to be. Second, and thorniest, Beauclerc can never satisfactorily justify the social dislocations implied by female employment. The Countess d'Esterre's success notwithstanding, in England the Countess remains a freak of nature. The novel's last word on the subject belongs to the wife of a local merchant, who comes to the sisters' house to congratulate the vulgar half-sister, Dorothy, on her marriage to a medical quack. Louisa and Emily fairly run from the room to avoid the guest's parvenu contagion: "'Heaven defend me from pride!' thought she [the merchant's wife]; 'why I could buy them all out and out. I have my carriage and six servants, while the *Mortimers* tramp it summer and winter. Dolly did right to take up with a quack-doctor; I'll warrant she will ride too in good time'" (I, 110–11).

Charlotte Smith explores the writing profession in her novels, but she uses male authors in *Celestina* (1791), *The Wanderings of Warwick* (1794), and *Marchmont* (1796), to reveal the business of Grub Street with more exactness than she finds appropriate to her one female author, the genteel Mrs. Denzil in *The Banished Man* (1794). In *Celestina*, Mr. Cathcart, a minor figure, writes for the journals in order to support his sister and her children. Exactly as in all other Smith novels, the careers of the sentimental heroine and hero are set to one side for more pressing stories of upper-middle-class people, who, like Smith herself, suffer the ills of a market economy.

"I am unhappy," the author-brother says, "not because I was born and educated a gentleman, and am now reduced to a condition worse than absolute servitude, but because those I love and feel for more than for myself are fallen with me; because my labour – and yet I am sacrificing my life to follow it – my labour is insufficient to support a woman, delicately brought up, and her four infant children!" (I, 160). The phrase "delicately brought up" holds the key to the distress of the passage. The memory of a lost golden age for genteel women governs Smith's angry response to the labors of the pen. The maid in the house where Cathcart has his garret room describes the working conditions he endures:

"Ah! Madam," replied the weeping Jessy, "he still remains writing for the existence of his sister and her children: at his pen from early morning, to eleven or twelve at night. By such assiduous application he is enabled indeed to earn double the money he would otherwise do; but his dear health is fast declining, and God only knows," continued she, clasping her hands together, "whether I shall ever see him more." (1, 169–70)

The profits Smith was making from her own work, far greater than Mr. Cathcart's garret room would suggest for him, reflect the bitterest feelings of a woman who, herself "delicately brought up," also grieves over her own lessened expectations.

When the hero of Smith's *The Wanderings of Warwick* (1796) turns to writing reviews of novels for a living, he confronts an insoluble dilemma, he confesses, "when I reflected that I was sometimes compelled, in the execution of justice to crush the hopes of industrious indigence – of a mother, perhaps, who had recourse to her pen to supply bread to a family for whom she had no other resource – of a daughter endeavouring to assist in the support of a helpless superannuated parent, whom she could not leave to engage in any of the few occupations for which women are qualified" (pp. 274–76). For Smith, the real injustice in woman's lot runs far deeper than the unrelenting demands of the publishing industry. If it is sad, but "just" to *crush* an industrious woman for writing badly, is there any salvation at all in this world, she asks implicitly, for unprovided women?

The futile attempt to bring together the dreams of an older, family-oriented economy and the real-life economy makes novel-writing, for heroines at least, a pre-judged failure. Even when the rare novelist, like Beauclerc, can imagine success for an author heroine, it does not produce any truth-telling ring of experience, only the echo of a distant fantasy. The Countess d'Esterre in *Husband Hunters*!!! serves as an exemplary case of a woman who saves her family from poverty by her novel-writing, but Beauclerc keeps her safely out of the reach of inspection, across the channel in France. We never see her do it, nor do we hear anything of her booksellers, her critics, or how much she earned, whether she was paid in advance, on time, or too late to help. Louisa's career is equally a blank in these respects. In fact, not one of the fictionalized authors in women's novels, successful or unsuccessful, reveals any sum of money he or she gets from novels, not a shilling. Paradoxically, these are presumably the only professional earnings that a reader could be guaranteed that the author knows with certainty. These much-too-familiar figures are concealed by the author's own sleight of hand, in a calculated attempt to obscure and explain at the same time her own participation in the market.

The experiences of Elizabeth Bennet's Minerva author heroine in *Beauty and Ugliness* (1819) produce an echo of the Royal Literary Fund's dolorous files. "The fictitious sorrows of her heroine had just reached their climax, and the manuscript was drawing to a conclusion, when her labours were suspended by a very severe illness, which confined her for some time to her chamber" (IV, 139–40). Finishing the novel in great financial distress, she must exert herself to sell it:

It was cold day in the month of December that Selina, for the first time after her illness, quitted her home: her dress was thin, and ill-calculated for the season, and her recent suffering had nearly reduced her to the feebleness of infancy; but she was now in want, for her money was all gone, and a piece of stale bread, the last of her store, she had taken previous to setting out.

...

But here no success awaited her; she was unknown as an author, therefore her wit and fine sentiments were of little value to that part of the world which appreciates by fashion. Had she no patron? they inquired; was there no exalted person to whom she might dedicate this first effusion? (IV, 144, 145)

As if to underscore the futility of the whole novel-writing enterprise, Bennet has her heroine, "faint, weary, and forlorn, with only five shillings," encounter a mob in the streets: she is "violently pushed against the wall, and the manuscript, her last resource and hope, rudely snatched from her feeble grasp" (IV, 148). A futile effort doomed from the start.

As Rachel Hunter confessed sadly in the preface to *Family Annals* (1808), "From having been a novel reader in my youth, I am become a novel writer." The same galling transformation leads Anna Maria Bennett to confront the fatuous demands of her imagined Gentle Readers of *Ellen, Countess of Castle Howel* (1794) with a sudden display of brutal cynicism about her task: "In short, as in duty bound," she writes, "the author leaves all parties who have been friends to her favourites, rich, happy and respectable":

The few readers who have had patience to accompany the author thus far, will be apt to exclaim, "Aye! those are the monsters we meet at the end of all LANE's collections, men without error! and women without faults!"

LADIES AND GENTLEMEN,

The truth is, notwithstanding all that has been said to the contrary, the Honorable and Right Reverend Bishop Claverton and Countess of Castle Howell, are quite as subject to the common frailties of human nature as the reader, or even the writer of this delightful history, but as they are among the most noble, the most affluent and most admired pairs, in the most flourishing kingdom, of the most enlighten'd world, it would be very rude to pry into secrets at parting we have hitherto so carefully avoided, particularly such secrets as never have, nor ever will be exposed, when concealed, as in the present instance, by the impenetrable veil of

IMMENSE RICHES. (IV, 230)

Jane Austen's peremptory endings to *Lady Susan* and *Northanger Abbey* direct their own tongue-in-cheek observations about money towards the same disjunction of fiction and experience that bothers Bennett, though not with Bennett's ferocity, but with a forgiving wink to those readers who are themselves in on the fraud.[56]

As for mandatory wedding bells at the conclusion, Elizabeth Hamilton ends her *Memoirs of Modern Philosophers* (1800) with the following mock concern: "But how could we have the heart to disappoint the Misses, by closing our narrative without a wedding? A novel without a wedding is like a tragedy without murder, which no British audience could ever be brought to relish":

First, then, with regard to the disposal of our heroine. We are very sorry to confess that she is still unmarried. But this is far from being our fault; and if you will have the goodness to recollect that she is neither *rich* nor *handsome*, it will cease to appear so very extraordinary. (II, 356, 361)

At the end of the eighteenth century, as Q. D. Leavis so grudgingly admits, "though the circulating library conventions are in full possession yet there is something alive in the body of the book." This "something alive," she proposes, consists "in the absence of romantic idealism, and in consequence the presence of a rational code of feeling; words really mean something, and a particular vocabulary is at the novelist's disposal that enables him [*sic*] to deal with the situation with dignity."[57] Although Mrs. Leavis' tastes lead her to Jane Austen and not to the Minerva novel for her examples, the same "something real" that controls the Minerva novel controls Jane Austen's as well.

The economic anxieties of female authorship at every social level get muted in women's novels through a contract of polite avoidance agreed upon between the writer and the reader, a conspiratorial relationship that has the tragi-comic effect of containing both the problem and the fiction of the problem as well. Language literally becomes "constitutive of reality, rather than merely reflective of it."[58] Charlotte Smith's suffering characters rehearse such powerful stories of distress, humiliation, and passionate resentment of women's economic fate that they simply fade from memory in favor of the author herself. In *Marchmont* (1796), where the hero tries writing novels for support, Smith complains, "If I painted my hero an unfortunate wanderer, existing by his own efforts, I understood that I should be accused of egotism, and of having represented my own adventures" (II, 226–27). But the critic for the *Universal Magazine* (April 1802) approved of the personal allusions: "Her experience, her afflictions, and the fluctuating course of her life, have evidently contributed, not less than the native strength and vivacity of her genius, to enable her to make her works, to a degree so remarkable, a great exhibition of the varieties in human nature, and of genuine English life."

Minerva writers in their turn create heroines like those of Eliza Parsons, whose gothic rambles rehearse every middle-class woman's midnight terrors of the economy. As the heroine's mother in Agnes Musgrave's Minerva novel *The Solemn Injunction* (1798) tells her, "Alicia, thou must, my daughter, become as hard as the unfeeling world thou hast to encounter" (I, 99). "Miserable child that I am, (exclaimed Alicia) thus are all my friends torn from me! thus am I left abandoned – desolate – alone, as it were, in the world" (I, 148).

Money remains the common language of women's fiction through-out the period, although the voices that employ this language are not, of course, in perfect agreement. The readers' circles that supported Jane Austen's aspirations as a novelist could not be the same circles that sustained the careers of Eliza Parsons or Anna Maria Bennett. Nevertheless, the pressures of the economy drew readers and writers of novels together in the shared dream of an "independence" for women. They conspire in promoting a female fiction because, in truth, neither readers nor writers had a choice. Women's fiction existed, after all, not only to secure the *author's* means to a seat in the parlor, but to confirm the *reader's* right to a seat there as well.

Notes

INTRODUCTION

1 Maria Edgeworth, *The Parent's Assistant, or Stories for Children* (London: J. Johnson, 1796). The story originated in *The Parent's Assistant*, a collection of nursery stories for children, but was moved to the pedagogic series *Early Lessons* (1801) as the founding text of a whole sub-series called "Rosamund" after its heroine. Plots in *The Parent's Assistant* regularly turn on money, usually the need of the protagonist, as often a girl as a boy, to earn it or better manage it. See Marilyn Butler, *Maria Edgeworth: A Literary Biography* (Oxford: Clarendon Press, 1972), for an account of this story's successful career (pp. 158–59).

2 Hoh-Cheung Mui and Lorna H. Mui's major study, *Shops and Shopkeeping in Eighteenth-Century England* (London: Routledge, 1989), describes the relations of shopkeepers, the "great" shopkeepers and the "petty" shopkeepers, to their customers, expanding our knowledge of the completeness of retail coverage in all the middling ranks. Carole Shammas, *The Pre-Industrial Consumer in England and America* (Oxford: Clarendon Press, 1990), is especially helpful in setting the history of retail trade in the context of formerly persuasive "revolution" theories of change. Lorna Weatherill, *Consumer Behaviour and Material Culture in Britain, 1660–1760* (London and New York: Routledge, 1988), exposes the limitations of theories of "emulation" by citing multiple social reasons beyond emulation for the growth in the consumption of domestic goods during the century.

3 Chandra Mukerji, *From Graven Images: Patterns of Modern Materialism* (New York: Columbia University Press, 1983), p. 8.

4 See Scott Sanders, "Towards a Social Theory of Literature," *Telos*, 18 (1973–74), 107–21: "The significance of a literary work does not reside in details of style or character, but in the mental structures which bind it together ... collective solutions to common problems, collective responses to a common social situation" (116). See also Levin L. Schucking, *The Sociology of Literary Taste* (London: Kegan Paul, 1944), who argues that, "there is no such thing as a spirit of the age; there are only, so to speak, a series of Spirits of the Age. It will always be necessary

to distinguish entirely different groups, with differing ideals of life and society" (p. 7).

5 The defense of "lesser writers" comes from Robert Colby, *Fiction with a Purpose* (Bloomington: Indiana University Press, 1967), p. 27. The classic condemnation of this fiction comes from George Saintsbury – "Only to a taste so crude as their own can they give any direct pleasure now" – in "The Growth of the Later Novel," *The Cambridge History of English Literature*, 15 vols., eds. A. W. Ward and A. R. Waller (Cambridge University Press, 1953), XI, p. 299.

6 Works that have been especially formative in the study are the following: Terry Eagleton, *Criticism and Ideology: a Study in Marxist Literature* (London: Verso, 1976), and *Literary Theory: An Introduction* (Oxford: Blackwell, 1983); Fredric Jameson, *The Political Unconscious: Narrative as a Socially Symbolic Act* (Ithaca: Cornell University Press, 1981); M. M. Bakhtin, *The Dialogic Imagination*, trans. Caryl Emerson and Michael Holquist (Austin: University of Texas Press, 1981); Elizabeth Janeway, *Man's World, Woman's Place: A Study in Social Mythology* (New York: Dell, 1971); Terry Lovell, *Consuming Fiction* (London: Verso, 1987); Mary Poovey, *The Proper Lady and the Woman Writer* (University of Chicago Press, 1984); Nancy Armstrong, *Desire and Domestic Fiction: A Political History of the Novel* (Oxford University Press, 1987); Teresa De Lauretis, *Alice Doesn't: Feminism, Semiotics, Cinema* (Bloomington: Indiana University Press, 1984); two thought-provoking essays in Tania Modleski, *Studies in Entertainment: Critical Approaches to Mass Culture* (Bloomington: Indiana University Press, 1986), one by Judith Williamson, "Woman is an Island: Femininity and Colonization," and the other by Kaja Silverman, "Fragments of a Fashionable Discourse"; Jean Baudrillard's essays, "The System of Objects" (1968) and "Consumer Society" (1970), in *Jean Baudrillard: Selected Writings*, ed. Mark Poster (Stanford University Press, 1988); Pierre Bourdieu, *Distinction: A Social Critique of the Judgement of Taste*, trans. Richard Nice (London: Routledge & Kegan Paul, 1984); Colin Campbell, *The Romantic Ethic and the Spirit of Modern Consumerism* (Oxford: Basil Blackwell, 1987). This short list by no means exhausts my debts, but I think it reflects the works that have been most influential in helping me bring together my ideas.

7 Weatherill, *Consumer Behaviour*, p. 196.

8 For the important distinctions between the terms see Campbell, *The Romantic Ethic*, pp. 56–57. See also Amanda Vickery, "Women and the World of Goods: a Lancashire Consumer and Her Possessions, 1751–81," in *Consumption and the World of Goods*, eds. John Brewer and Roy Porter (London and New York: Routledge, 1993), pp. 274–301, for a revealing account of recent scholarship as it has moved away from "emulation" theories of consumption (pp. 274–78).

9 For a description of the *Lady's Magazine*, see Alison Adburgham, *Women in Print: Writing Women and Women's Magazines From the Restoration to*

the Accession of Victoria (London: George Allen and Unwin, 1972), pp. 128–58; 276.

10 In 1820, when the editors of the *Lady's* decided to upgrade fiction in the magazine by publishing the work of professionals only, an era of a vigorous and revealing reader-author culture in the magazine came officially to an end.

11 Amanda Vickery, "Women and the World of Goods," supplies an account of the mythologies of women as consumers that have dominated, and still influence, studies of consumer history (pp. 276–78).

12 Shammas, *The Pre-Industrial Consumer*, pp. 186–88.

13 Weatherill, *Consumer Behaviour*, p. 138.

14 Amanda Vickery, "Women and the World of Goods," analyzes "the family and estate papers, social correspondence, and personal manuscripts" of Elizabeth Shackleton, mistress of Browsholme Hall, in the West Riding of Yorkshire. The "ultimate control of financial resources ... remains opaque," Vickery writes, but it is clear that Shackleton was in charge of the "*management* of consumption" when it came to "routine decision making" (pp. 278–301).

15 Hoh-Cheung Mui and Lorna H. Mui, *Shops and Shopkeeping in Eighteenth-Century England*, pp. 201–20. See also Carole Shammas, "The Domestic Environment in Early Modern England and America," *Journal of Social History*, vol. 14, no. 1 (Fall 1980), 3–24: Shammas argues that as the century wore on, "women's labor in behalf of home consumption gradually ceased being spread thinly over primary, intermediary, and final processes and become concentrated on the last stage ... While female participation in primary and intermediary processes hardly disappeared, more and more it occurred within the context of market production" (p. 17). Lorna Weatherill, "A Possession of One's Own: Women and Consumer Behavior in England, 1660–1740," *Journal of British Studies*, vol. 25, no. 2 (April 1986), 131–49, finds that women were numerous in the trades "of intermediate status," and "especially in retailing ... Half of these economically active women were shopkeepers, and a further sixth were innkeepers or victuallers. These, taken with the miscellaneous dealers, meant that almost three-quarters of this group of presumably independent women were in the retail and dealing sectors" (p. 148).

16 Royal Literary Fund, case number 266, 27 March 1811. The Royal Literary Fund, a private charity constituted in 1788 for the aid of indigent authors, assigned each applicant for aid a case number under which all correspondence pertaining to the applicant was filed. See Nigel Cross, *The Royal Literary Fund, 1790–1918* (London: World Microfilms Publications, 1984), for an account of the cataloging of applicants.

17 Royal Literary Fund, case number 256, 2 June 1811.

18 Royal Literary Fund, case number 266, 12 November 1817.

19 Joseph Wiesenfarth, *Gothic Manners and the Classic English Novel* (Madison: University of Wisconsin Press, 1988), pp. 3–22.

20 Charlotte Smith was clear on who was and who was not a respectable publisher. She wrote the publisher George Robinson, 18 June 1789, that she would stay with her present publisher, Thomas Cadell, Sr.: "Mr Cadells respectability cannot be denied– & if I am compelled to change, it must be only for a Gentleman of equal respectability" (New York Public Library, Berg Collection). Smith was mortified, as she confessed in a letter to William Hayley, late 1788–89 (copy by Hayley, no address or postmark, Fitzwilliam Museum, Cambridge), by a visit and a letter from William Lane, the Minerva Press publisher: "But I am such a proud fool, that I feel humbled & hurt at being supposed liable to his negociations ... But I think I have done right in repulsing forever his pert advances." These quotations from Smith's letters were supplied to me by Judith Phillips Stanton, editor of Charlotte Smith's *Letters* (Indiana University Press, forthcoming). Professor Stanton traces, in "Statistical Profile of Women Writing in English from 1660 to 1800," *Eighteenth-Century Women and the Arts*, eds. Frederick M. Keener and Susan E. Lorsch (Westport, Conn.: Greenwood Press, 1988), pp. 249–54, "the steady emergence of women writers in the early eighteenth century, followed by their explosive increase in its final three decades." In "The Production of Fiction by Women in England, 1660–1800: A Statistical Overview" (paper delivered at the International Society for Eighteenth-Century Studies, Bristol, July 1991), Stanton notes that the statistics suggest that the customary selection by women of publishers according to social respectability begins to fragment at the end of the century under the great numbers of one-time-only publishers of women's works.

21 Elizabeth Jenkins in her biography *Jane Austen*, 1st ed. 1949 (New York: Minerva Press, 1969), notes that in *La Belle Assemblée* (March 1810) there are listed two Hampshire marriages with names including Elizabeth Steele and Edmond Ferrers (p. 64). In my essay, "Money Talks: Jane Austen and the *Lady's Magazine*," in *Jane Austen's Beginnings: the Juvenilia and Lady Susan*, ed. J. David Grey (Ann Arbor: UMI Research Press, 1989), I note that Brandon and Willoughby appear in a *Lady's Magazine* story entitled "The Ship-Wreck" (in the "Supplement" for 1794), and Mr. Knightley shows up in "Guilt Pursued by Conscience," in the *Lady's Magazine* (Nov. 1802). In the magazine story, Mr. Knightley marries the lovely girl from the boarding school despite her low origins.

22 Marilyn Butler, *Jane Austen and the War of Ideas* (Oxford: Clarendon Press, 1975); Gary Kelly, *The English Jacobin Novel* (Oxford: Clarendon Press, 1976) and "Jane Austen and the English Novel of the 1790's," in *Fetter'd or Free? British Women Novelists, 1670–1815*, eds. Mary Anne Schofield and Cecilia Macheski (Athens: Ohio University Press, 1986), pp. 285–306.

23 Jane Spencer, *The Rise of the Woman Novelist: From Aphra Behn to Jane*

Austen (Oxford: Basil Blackwell, 1986); Dale Spender, *Mothers of the Novel: 100 Good Women Writers Before Jane Austen* (London and New York: Pandora, 1986); Ann H. Jones, *Ideas and Innovations: Best Sellers of Jane Austen's Age* (New York: AMS Press, 1986).

24 David Daiches' classic essay, "Jane Austen, Karl Marx, and the Aristocratic Dance," *American Scholar*, 17 (1948), 289–96, has been an influence on all subsequent generations of Austen scholars. Nor could any study of money in Austen be conceived without confessing major debts to Alistair M. Duckworth, *The Improvement of the Estate: A Study of Jane Austen's Novels* (Baltimore and London: The Johns Hopkins University Press, 1971).

25 Michael Fores, "The Myth of a British Industrial Revolution," *History*, vol. 66, no. 217 (June 1981), 181–98.

26 Maxine Berg and Pat Hudson, "Rehabilitating the Industrial Revolution," *Economic History Review*, vol. 45, no. 1 (1992), 24–50. Berg and Hudson call attention to the testimonies of contemporaries who "had little doubt about the magnitude and importance of change in the period, particularly industrial change" (p. 26).

27 See David Cannadine's essay, "The Past and the Present in the English Industrial Revolution 1880–1980," *Past and Present*, no. 103 (1984), 131–72, for an historicizing analysis of former accounts of the "industrial revolution."

28 Royal Literary Fund, case number 266, 21 January 1819.

29 Charlotte Smith to Joseph Cooper Walker, 16 October 1794, Henry E. Huntington Library, HM 10816, San Marino, California.

30 Royal Literary Fund, case number 173, 6 July 1805.

31 For the century's debates on luxury, see John Sekora, *Luxury: The Concept in Western Thought, Eden to Smollett* (Baltimore and London: The Johns Hopkins University Press, 1977), pp. 110–31.

32 Adam Smith, *An Inquiry Into the Nature and Causes of The Wealth of Nations* (1776), 2 vols., ed. Edwin Cannan, first published 1904 (University of Chicago Press, 1976), II, p. 399.

33 Letter from Charlotte Smith to Sarah Farr Rose, *c.* 1800, Henry E. Huntington Library, HM 10825, San Marino, California.

34 Nancy Armstrong, *Desire and Domestic Fiction: A Political History of the Novel* (Oxford University Press, 1987).

35 David Spring, "Interpreters of Jane Austen's Social World: Literary Critics and Historians," ed. Janet Todd, *Jane Austen: New Perspectives* (New York and London: Holmes & Meier, 1983), pp. 59–63.

36 "Letter to Lord Byron," *Collected Poems*, ed. Edward Mendelson (New York: Random House, 1976), p. 79.

37 Q. D. Leavis, *Fiction and the Reading Public* (London: Chatto & Windus, 1939), p. 140.

1 THE GENERAL CALAMITY: THE WANT OF MONEY

1 Mary Poovey, *The Proper Lady and the Woman Writer* (University of Chicago Press, 1984), explores the ideological significance of this troubling paradox. See especially pp. 3–47. The quotation from "The Witlings" comes from a holograph, unsigned and undated, 126 pages, the Berg Collection, New York Public Library.

2 Frances Burney [Madame D'Arblay], Queen's Lodge, Windsor, August, 1790, *Diary and Letters*, ed. Charlotte Barret, with Preface and Notes by Austin Dobson, 6 vols. (London: Macmillan and Co., 1904), iv, pp. 416–17.

3 Letter to Eliza Bishop [London] Saturday [late 1790], in *Collected Letters of Mary Wollstonecraft*, ed. Ralph M. Wardle (Ithaca and London: Cornell University Press, 1979), p. 198.

4 Letter to Charles Beauclerk, 8 December 1807, Richmond. Quoted by Mrs. Steuart Erskine, *Lady Diana Beauclerk: Her Life and Work* (London: T. Fisher Unwin, 1903), p. 305.

5 *The Journals and Letters of Fanny Burney (Madame D'Arblay)*, ed. Joyce Hemlow, 4 vols. (Oxford: Clarendon Press, 1972). See vol. ii, no. 80, 4–5 May 1793, fn.; also no. 93, 31 May [1793], for examples of suppressed references to money.

6 Letter to Joseph Cooper Walker, 20 January 1794, Henry E. Huntington Library, HM 10811, San Marino, California.

7 Letter to Doctor Burney, 27 April 1800, *Journals and Letters*, ed. Hemlow. D. Grant Campbell offers a compelling analysis of the effects of inflation and credit in Frances Burney's work in, "Fashionable Suicide: Conspicuous Consumption and the Collapse of Credit in Frances Burney's *Cecilia,*" *Studies in Eighteenth-Century Culture*, 20 (East Lansing: Colleagues Press, 1990), pp. 131–45.

8 Humphry Repton's verse from *Odd Whims* (1804) also bemoans the shift in the economy: "In England the value of lives is computed / By Annuities granted transferred or commuted; / Our glory and pride with stocks rise and fall" (ii, pp. 163–64). Quoted by Stephen Daniels in "The Political Landscape," *Humphry Repton, Landscape Gardener, 1752–1818*, eds. George Carter, Patrick Goode, Kedrun Laurie (London: Sainsbury Centre for Visual Arts, 1982), pp. 114–15.

9 For the legal explanation, see Susan Staves, *Married Women's Separate Property in England, 1660–1833* (Cambridge, Mass.: Harvard University Press, 1990); Staves, "Pin Money," *Studies in Eighteenth-Century Culture*, 14 (Madison: Wisconsin University Press, 1985), pp. 47–77; and Ida Beatrice O'Malley, *Women in Subjection: A Study of the Lives of Englishwomen before 1832* (London: Duckworth, 1933), pp. 22–26.

10 Letter to The Rev. Joseph Cooper Walker, 16 Oct. 1794, Henry E. Huntington Library, HM 10816, San Marino, California.

11 See Staves, *Married Women's Separate Property*, for the definitive account of the legal disabilities of women in the economy, especially chapter 5.

12 Caroline Austen, *Reminiscences of Caroline Austen*, ed. Deirdre Le Faye (Guildford: The Jane Austen Society, 1986), p. 27.

13 According to R. S. Neale, *Bath, 1680–1850: A Social History* (London: Routledge & Kegan Paul, 1981), a woman in the late eighteenth century would have been unlikely to contribute more than 5 or 6 shillings a week to a household budget through employment: "Consequently, if, as was common, a woman through death or desertion should find herself the sole support of a family the impoverishment of the family was virtually certain" (pp. 279–80).

14 Letter to Mary, Countess Jenison of Walworth, 19 October 1800. Quoted by Mrs. Steuart Erskine, *Lady Diana Beauclerk*, p. 278.

15 John Sekora, *Luxury: The Concept in Western Thought, Eden to Smollett* (Baltimore and London: The Johns Hopkins University Press, 1977), pp. 95–100.

16 Phyllis Deane and W. A. Cole, *British Economic Growth 1699–1959: Trends and Structures*, 2nd ed. (Cambridge University Press, 1969), p. 17.

17 John Burnett, *A History of the Cost of Living* (Harmondsworth: Penguin Books, 1969), pp. 28–29, 137.

18 Burnett, *A History of the Cost of Living*, pp. 198–99.

19 Burnett, *A History of the Cost of Living*, pp. 200–01.

20 The *Universal Magazine* tale might also refer to "mutability" in the form of economic depression, a recurrent economic distress of the period. Deane and Cole, *British Economic Growth 1699–1959*, for example, record a depression and revival in 1801 and a deep depression in 1811 (pp. 162–73).

21 Letter to the Rev. Joseph Cooper Walker, 20 Jan. 1794, Henry E. Huntington Library, HM 10811, San Marino, California.

22 Letter to Mrs. Phillips, December 1797, *Journals and Letters*, ed. Hemlow. For a discussion of the hardships caused to consumers by taxation during the war years, see Clive Emsley, *British Society and the French Wars, 1793–1815* (London: Macmillan, 1979), especially, pp. 41–64.

23 Such rags-to-riches phenomena were not uncommon. Eric J. Hobsbawm, *The Age of Revolution* (New York: New American Library, 1962), cites Robert Owen's career: "In 1789 an ex-draper's assistant like Robert Owen could start with a borrowed £100 in Manchester; in 1809 he bought out his partner in the New Lanark Mills for £84,000 *in cash*. And his was a relatively modest story of business success" (p. 36).

24 See Sekora, *Luxury*, pp. 100–09.

25 John Trusler, *The Master's Last Best Gift* (London, 1812), pp. 21–22.

26 Quoted by F. M. L. Thompson, *English Landed Society in the Nineteenth Century* (London: Routledge & Kegan Paul, 1963), p. 19.

27 Anna Lefroy, Jane Austen's closest friend besides her sister Cassandra, is hardly less frank: "I have not seen Miss Andrews," she writes her son Edward, "but hear from everyone that she is very pretty and very amiable. Her fortune is said to be about £70,000. It is entirely at her disposal. Her Father and Mother are dead and she has no relation nearer

than a first cousin." Canterbury, 24 September [1804]. Transcript, letter no. 162, private collection of Miss Helen Lefroy.

28 From Mary Berry's *Social Life in England and France from ... 1789 to 1830* (1831). Quoted by M. D. George, *English Social Life in the Eighteenth Century*, Part I (London: The Sheldon Press, 1923), pp. 121–22.

29 *The Way to Be Rich and Respectable*, 7th ed. (London, 1796), p. 24.

30 Letter to Susanna Burney Phillips, 18 January 1798, *Journals and Letters*, ed. Hemlow.

31 John Trusler, *Domestic Management*, "a new edition" (Bath, 1819): "Wealth is comparative: that which would make one man rich, another shall be poor with. Every man should be able to live, and make an appearance in life, equal to his station in it" (pp. 10–11).

32 David Spring, "Interpreters of Jane Austen's Social World: Literary Critics and Historians," in *Jane Austen: New Perspectives*, ed. Janet Todd (New York and London: Holmes & Meier, 1983), pp. 53–72. "The pseudo-gentry were 'pseudo,'" writes Spring, "because they were not landowners in the same sense as the gentry and aristocracy were. They cannot be said to have owned landed estates. But they were gentry of a sort, primarily because they sought strenuously to be taken for gentry" (p. 60).

33 Jane West, *Letters to a Young Lady* (London, 1806), III, 259–60.

34 The only exception in Jane Austen's works occurs in *Pride and Prejudice*, where Mr. Collins uses the 4 percents to calculate Elizabeth Bennet's future inheritance (p. 106). Mrs. Bennet in that novel, however, appears unsure of which to use, the 5 percents or the 4 percents, in calculating Mr. Bingley's annual income from his £100,000 fortune: "four or five thousand a year," she tells Mr. Bennet (p. 4).

35 Deborah Kaplan argues in "Representing Two Cultures: Jane Austen's Letters," *The Private Self: Theory and Practice of Women's Autobiographical Writings*, ed. Shari Benstock (London: Routledge, 1988) that women participated in "a general, male-dominated culture and at the same time in a woman's culture." The discourse of this "woman's culture," writes Kaplan, "often focuses enthusiastically on what Austen refers to as 'particulars,' the details of everyday life" – including the prices of clothing and food (p. 221).

36 Anna Laetitia Barbauld and John Aikin wrote *Evenings at Home: Or, the Juvenile Budget Opened* between 1793 and 1796. See Betsy Rodgers, *Georgian Chronicle: Mrs. Barbauld & Her Family* (London: Methuen, 1958) for an account of their authorship; most of the stories were by John Aikin (p. 122). The edition cited above is *Evenings at Home: Or, the Juvenile Budget Opened*, 2 vols. (Philadelphia: James Kay, Jun. and brother [1846]), I, 229–30.

37 Hannah More, "The Way to Plenty; or, the Second Part of Tom White," in *Cheap Repository Tracts Published during the Year 1795*, vol. I (London: J. Marshal, 1795 [?]), pp. 25–26.

38 "It should be remembered," writes Eric J. Hobsbawm, "that around

1800 less than 15 per cent of British families had an income of more than £50 per year, and of these only one-quarter earned more than £200 a year." In *The Age of Revolution*, p. 36.

39 Deirdre Le Faye, *Jane Austen: A Family Record* (London: The British Library, 1989), p. 131.

40 "Considerations of the Expedience of Raising, at This Time of Dearth the Wages of... Clerks in Public Office" (1767). Quoted by M. D. George, *English Social Life in the Eighteenth Century*, pp. 77–78.

41 Letter to Frances Burney from Susanna Burney Phillips, 4 April 1793, *Journals and Letters*, ed. Hemlow.

42 Letter from Doctor Burney to M. D'Arblay, 11 July 1793, *Journals and Letters*, ed. Hemlow.

43 Royal Literary Fund, case number 116, 2 January 1802, and 30 April 1812. The Royal Literary Fund, a private charity constituted in 1788 for the aid of indigent authors, assigned each applicant for aid a case number under which all correspondence pertaining to the applicant was filed. See Nigel Cross, *The Royal Literary Fund, 1790–1918* (London: World Microfilms Publications, 1984), for an account of the cataloging of applicants.

44 *The Castle of Wolfenbach* (1793) ed. Devendra P. Varma (London: The Folio Press, 1968), p. 97.

45 Domestic economists differ in their estimates on the two-servant household: James Luckcock in his *Hints for Practical Economy* (Birmingham and London, 1834) maintains that it would take £400 a year (£30 more than Trusler's estimate of 1774) to support a household with two servants, a difference possibly stemming from the 60-year gap between their works. However, Luckcock's contemporaries Samuel and Sarah Adams, in *The Complete Servant* (London, 1825), award two servants to a family with an income of only £300 a year (p. 5).

46 James Woodforde (Parson Woodforde) did rather better on £400 a year, living in rural Norfolk, his house and a substantial garden provided with his living. He kept two maidservants, two menservants, a boy, and three horses. See John Beresford, "Introduction," *The Diary of a Country Parson, 1758–1802* (Oxford University Press, 1979), p. ix.

47 See Samuel and Sarah Adams, *The Complete Servant* (1825), p. 5. John Trusler, in *The Master's Last Best Gift*, claims that for a prosperous tradesman "a clear income of from four to seven hundred pounds a year, with economy, is sufficient for every comfort in life, and enough to make some provision for children" (p. 49).

48 *Jane Austen's Letters*, ed. R. W. Chapman, 2nd ed. (Oxford University Press, 1979): "We plan having a steady Cook, & a young giddy Housemaid, with a sedate, middle aged Man, who is to undertake the double office of Husband to former & sweetheart to the latter" (p. 99). "My father is doing all in his power to encrease his Income by raising his Tythes &c., & I do not despair of getting very nearly six hundred a year" (p. 103).

49 *Memoir and Correspondence of Susan Ferrier (1782–1854)*, ed. John A. Doyle (London: John Murray, 1898), p. 169.

50 In Jane West's *The Church of Saint Siffrid* (1798), Charles Harwood, a married gentleman with £500, fixes "on a small but comfortable house in a solitary and beautiful situation" in the Welsh mountains, where he firmly resolves that "the example of his more opulent neighbours should never lead him into expenses" (1, 7). John Trusler, in *A System of Etiquette* (1804), claims, "It matters not, whether a man possess 5,000l. a year or 500l. if he is truly a gentleman" (pp. 4–5).

51 Quoted by Le Faye, *Jane Austen*, p. 131. For a complete account of the Austen women's financial situation on the death of Mr. Austen, see Le Faye, ibid., pp. 130–32. See also Emma Austen-Leigh, *Jane Austen and Steventon* (London: Spottiswoode, Ballantyne and Co., 1937). During the life of Austen's father, the family possessed a yearly income between his two parishes of Steventon and Deane of between £500 and £600 a year. With his death in 1805, Jane, Cassandra, and Mrs. Austen were left in "straitened circumstances," according to Le Faye, "for most of Mr. Austen's income had been derived from the livings of Steventon and Deane, and his small annuity from the Hand-in-Hand Society died with him." Austen's brothers Henry, Frank, and James each pledged to send £50 annually to the three women, and Edward promised £100 a year. Mrs. Austen herself had, presumably, about £160 a year from property, and Cassandra £50 a year from the interest on Tom Fowle's legacy to her of £1,000. In 1805, Jane Austen had no income at all of her own to contribute to domestic expenses.

52 John Trusler, in *The Way to be Rich and Respectable* (1777), gives specific figures for keeping a carriage, a clearly extravagant expense for the Dashwood women: "The expence of keeping a Post Coach and Four, in a gentleman's own stable, if he is obliged to buy his provender. £287 14 6." Note: "These expences may be reduced, but not to make a genteel appearance. No allowance is here made for the occasional death of a horse, nor waste of hay and corn" (pp. 44–46).

53 Tract quoted by George, *English Social Life in the Eighteenth Century*, pp. 112–13.

54 G. E. Mingay, *English Landed Society in the Eighteenth Century* (London: Routledge & Kegan Paul, 1963), p. 26.

55 W. Bence Jones, "Landowning as a Business," *The Nineteenth Century*, vol. 11 (1882), p. 254. Cited by F. M. L. Thompson, *English Landed Society in the Nineteenth Century*, pp. 25–26.

56 F. M. L. Thompson, *English Landed Society in the Nineteenth Century*, pp. 25–26.

2 GOTHIC ECONOMICS: THE 1790S

1 This reading of women's fiction is shared by Eva Figes, in *Sex and Subterfuge: Women Novelists to 1850* (London: Macmillan, 1982): "Whatever their personal life styles or conscious political ideas, the fact is that

there was very little difference in attitude between the Jacobin and anti-Jacobin stance as far as women's fiction is concerned ... Reality proved too strong a fetter" (p. 60). Gary Kelly's essay, "Jane Austen and the English Novel of the 1790's," in *Fetter'd or Free? British Women Novelists, 1670–1815*, eds. Mary Anne Schofield and Cecilia Macheski (Athens: Ohio University Press, 1986), pp. 185–206, explores links between women novelists of different political persuasions. In *The English Jacobin Novel, 1780–1805* (Oxford: Clarendon Press, 1976), Kelly notes the influence of the Jacobin Elizabeth Inchbald on Maria Edgeworth and other women novelists, "who were also interested in the relationship between society and the individual, but who were not Jacobins" (p. 64).

2 David Punter, in *The Literature of Terror* (New York: Longman, 1980), notes that Clara Reeve's *The Old English Baron* (1777), "is despite appearances, the world of the eighteenth-century middle class" (p. 54). See also Punter's essay, "Social Relations of Gothic Fiction," in *Romanticism and Ideology: Studies in English Writing 1765–1830*, eds. David Aers, Jonathan Cook, David Punter (London: Routledge & Kegan Paul, 1981), where he argues for a social program in gothic fiction: "The concern of the authors is to produce fear in a form in which it can be immediately neutralized: to act as lightening conductors for social transition" (p. 117). The easy translations between the gothic tropes of novels and the ordinariness of everyday life was a common joke: C. L. Pitt, in *The Age* (1810), suggests, "Where you find A Castle ... put An house"; "A giant ... A Father"; "A midnight murder ... put A marriage." Cited by E. F. Bleiler, *Three Gothic Novels* (New York: Dover Press, 1966), p. 4.

3 Page references are to *The Romance of the Forest*, ed. Chloe Chard (Oxford University Press, 1986).

4 Page references are to *The Castles of Athlin and Dunbayne*, "Foreword" by Frederick Shroyer (New York: Arno Press, 1972).

5 Patricia Meyer Spacks, in *Desire and Truth: Functions of Plot in Eighteenth-Century English Novels* (Chicago University Press, 1990), notes that Radcliffe distinguishes between "phallic power," imaginary, in her villains and "social power, [which] remains both real and dangerous" (p. 160).

6 Ellen Moers, in *Literary Women* (London: The Women's Press, 1976), recognizes that Emily's "struggle with the villain Montoni is essentially legalistic, [and] concerns her property rights" (p. 207). Emily herself "determined to preserve those estates, since they would afford that competence by which she hoped to secure the comfort of their [hers and Valencourt's] future life" (*Udolpho*, p. 136).

7 *The Italian*, ed. Frederick Garber (Oxford University Press, 1981), p. 220.

8 Michael Sadleir's sympathetic treatment of Austen's five "horrid novels," in *Things Past* (London: Constable, 1944), pp. 167–200, similarly insists on a contemporary frame of reference for at least four of

the Austen horrors: Roche's *Clermont*, "stripped of its Gothic trappings ... is really a novel of the time"; Parsons' *Wolfenbach* and *Mysterious Warnings* are "portraiture of mature ladies of the upper-middle class"; Sleath's *Midnight Bell* is "stay-at-home stuff."

9 The differences between gentlemen and tradesmen are contested by John Trusler in his encouragement of trade in *The Way to be Rich and Respectable* (1796): "Frugality and economy have put many upon a footing with men of larger fortunes, and often made them far more respectable" (p. 9). The same assertion appears in an edition of 1775. Dorothy Marshall, in *Eighteenth Century England* (London: Longman, 1962), draws the lines of "the solid mass of the middling sort" more like Trusler's plan than Reeve's: "substantial tenant farmers, the smaller freeholders, the millers, the inn keepers ... the traders, shopkeepers, middlemen ... In addition they were invading the lower ranks of the professions: they became apothecaries, attorneys and men of business, school masters, clerks and civil servants, customs and excise men" (p. 35). See Harold Perkin, *The Origins of Modern English Society, 1780–1880* (Toronto University Press, 1969), for further permutations on the distinction between gentlemen and others (p. 24).

10 See John Sekora, *Luxury: The Concept in Western Thought, Eden to Smollett* (Baltimore and London: The Johns Hopkins University Press, 1977), pp. 100–09, and pp. 110–31.

11 Luckcock suggests in *Hints for Practical Economy* (1834) that an income of £150 a year could support £2 12s. for "subscriptions" (p. 11), and that an income of £200 a year would allow £8 for "subscriptions and amusements" (p. 12). Trusler, in *The Economist* (Dublin, 1774), confirms the sum Luckcock allows for the £200 a year income by advising a similar sum, £7 12s. for these purposes: £5 for the master, and £2 12s. for the mistress and children. A subscription to Lane's Minerva Library in Leadenhall Street cost a guinea (£1 1s.) a year in 1798, a guinea and a half in 1802, and two guineas in 1814. This expense would be almost prohibitive at Luckcock's £150 a year income, but far easier at the £200 a year income. For confirmation, see Dorothy Blakey, *The Minerva Press, 1790–1820* (Oxford: The Bibliographical Society at the University Press, 1939), pp. 117–18. John Trusler, in *The London Adviser and Guide* (1786), lists six leading circulating libraries in London: "At these libraries you may have new publications, in volumes, to be read at 3d. a volume, have the reading of all new books, and that of their whole library, of which they have catalogues at 6d. each, for 12s. a year, or 4s. a quarter, and have two books at a time, and change them every day; but at Bell's, for one guinea a year, you may read all the new pamphlets and books of any value" (p. 121).

12 The use of gothic imagery to describe the economy is a commonplace. The radical writer Thomas Spence in his tract, *The Rights of Infants; or, the imprescriptable right of mothers to such a share of the elements as is sufficient to enable them to suckle and bring up their young in a dialogue between the aristocracy*

and a mother of children (1797) addresses the landed interest: "O, you bloody landed interest! you band of robbers! Why do you call yourselves ladies and gentlemen? Why do you assume soft names, you beasts of prey? Too well do your emblazoned arms and escutcheons witness the ferocity of your bloody and barbarous origin! But soon shall those audacious Gothic emblems of rapine cease to offend the eyes of an enlightened people, and no more make an odious distinction between the spoilers and the spoiled" (p. 7).

13 The list of subscribers to Parsons' *History of Miss Meredith* includes the Prince of Wales, the Duke of York, the Duke of Gloucester, followed by the Earl and Countess of Abingdon, with the remaining subscribers in order of rank, then alphabetical. The last group includes, "Mrs. Fitzherbert, Pall-Mall," "Mrs. Montague, Portman-Square," and "The Hon. Horace Walpole."

14 Elizabeth Bonhote grew up near the ruins. She and her husband, a solicitor, eventually bought them and converted them for domestic use, selling them to the Duke of Norfolk in 1800. See the entry in *The Feminist Companion to Literature in English*, eds. Virginia Blain, Patricia Clements, Isobel Grundy (London: B. T. Batsford, 1990).

15 Citations are to *The Mysterious Warning*, ed. Devendra P. Varma (London: The Folio Press, 1968).

16 Bennett's work pleased Scott and Coleridge (see *The Feminist Companion*, eds. Blain, Clements, and Grundy). Mary Mitford preferred Bennett's novel *The Beggar Girl* to Edgeworth's "do-me-good air": "a freshness and truth... which I never found in any fiction except that of Miss Austen. 'Vicissitudes' and 'Ellen' are almost equally good." Cited by Dorothy Blakey, *The Minerva Press*, p. 55.

17 In *Pride and Prejudice*, Wickham takes Lydia Bennet to London with every intention of abandoning her when he tires of her. Her sister Jane is appalled when she finds that he is "a gamester" as well (p. 298).

18 Parsons published first with Hookham, then in the 1790s with William Lane, at the Minerva Press, then with Longman, and, after 1800, with Norbury in Brentwood. See her entry in *The Feminist Companion*, eds. Blain, Clement, and Grundy.

19 Quoted by Nigel Cross from the files of the Royal Literary Fund, *The Common Writer: Life in Nineteenth-Century Grub Street* (Cambridge University Press, 1985), p. 171.

20 Citations are to *The Castle of Wolfenbach*, ed. Devendra P. Varma (London: the Folio Press, 1968).

21 Pierre Bourdieu, *Distinction: A Social Critique of the Judgement of Taste*, trans. Richard Nice (London: Routledge & Kegan Paul, 1984), p. 7.

22 Letter to Joseph Cooper Walker, 29 May 1796. Henry E. Huntington Library, HM 10818, San Marino, California.

23 Letter to Sarah Farr Rose, 14 Feb. 1804. Henry E. Huntington Library, HM 10834, San Marino, California.

24 At present the only full-length biography of Smith is that by F. M. A.

Hilbish, *Charlotte Smith, Poet and Novelist* (Philadelphia: University of Pennsylvania Press, 1939), written without the benefit of Smith's letters. I am indebted to Smith's present biographer and editor of her correspondence, Judith Phillips Stanton, for sharing with me her vast knowledge of Smith's correspondence and career.

25 As Ida Beatrice O'Malley explains in *Women in Subjection: A Study of the Lives of Englishwomen before 1832* (London: Duckworth, 1933), "She [the married woman] had no power or standing in regard to [her household or children]. The husband might squander his own fortune or hers or his own earnings and hers; he might take her children away from the hour of their birth; he might place them in undesirable hands; he might refuse to let her see them; in the eyes of the law they were not her children but his." She quotes Blackstone: "By marriage the very being or legal existence of a woman is suspended, or at least it is incorporated into that of the husband, under whose wing, protection and cover she performs everything and she is therefore called in our law a feme-covert" (pp. 22–26).

26 As Jane Spencer reports in her entry on Charlotte Smith in *A Dictionary of British and American Women Writers 1660–1800*, ed. Janet Todd (Totowa, New Jersey: Rowman & Allanheld, 1985), Smith's "compassion for victims of oppression, which formed the basis of her political ideas, remained constant" (p. 289).

27 Citations of this novel are from *Emmeline, The Orphan of the Castle*, ed. Anne Henry Ehrenpreis (Oxford University Press, 1971).

28 Jane Austen proposes an analogous situation in *Mansfield Park*, but with significant alterations in the resolution.

29 Quotations are from the 2nd edition (London: Printed for T. Cadell, 1790).

30 Jameson discusses the appearance in Balzac's *La Vieille Fille* (1836) of the Comte de Troisville, such an "horizon figure," who appears to be a "solution" to Mademoiselle de Cormon's problem of a suitable match: his background is both aristocratic (Russian) and Napoleonic military. Unfortunately, like Sir Edward Newenden, he is already married. The near-miss solution, writes Jameson, is "explicitly marked by the narrative as a merely 'ideal' one, as a Utopian resolution in the narrower and empirically unrealizable sense." *The Political Unconscious: Narrative as a Socially Symbolic Act* (Ithaca: Cornell University Press, 1981), p. 168.

31 Quotations are from *The Old Manor House* (Oxford University Press, 1969).

32 Nina Auerbach, in "Jane Austen and Romantic Imprisonment" in *Jane Austen in a Social Context*, ed. David Monaghan (Totowa, New Jersey: Barnes & Noble, 1981), argues that women's imprisonment is the central fact of life in Austen's novels: "Inexorable denial mingles with the unique unimpeachable comfort of Austen's settings" (p. 10). In the

same collection of essays Ann Banfield, in "The Influence of Place: Jane Austen and the Novel of Social Consciousness," recognizes Austen's connection to the gothic novel through her integration of the novel of consciousness (Richardson) and the novel of place (gothic), "to become the novel of consciousness of class and society" (p. 30).

33 Ellen Moers, in "Money, the Job, and Little Women," *Commentary*, 55 (January 1973), 57–61, suggests that "Austen's realism in the matter of money was in her case an essentially female phenomenon, the result of her deep concern with the quality of a woman's life in marriage" (p. 58).

34 Anne Henry Ehrenpreis, "*Northanger Abbey*: Jane Austen and Charlotte Smith," *Nineteenth Century Fiction*, 25 (1970), 343–48, finds any number of echoes of Charlotte Smith in Jane Austen's work, both assent and protest, some implicit, "lying at various depths."

35 Christopher Gillie, in "*Sense and Sensibility*: An Assessment," *Essays in Criticism*, 9 (1959), 1–9, asserts that Marianne Dashwood, "has the misfortune to be in love with a man who cannot live without two thousand a year, and this comes to be the whole of her tragedy" (p. 3).

36 A thorough account of finances and their implications in *Sense and Sensibility* is found in Alistair Duckworth's *The Improvement of the Estate: A Study of Jane Austen's Novels* (Baltimore and London: The Johns Hopkins University Press, 1971), pp. 85–91.

37 Marilyn Butler, in "Disregarded Designs: Jane Austen's Sense of the Volume," *Jane Austen in a Social Context*, ed. David Monaghan, notes that Austen favors Elinor's economic choice, a competence and an independence in a country vicarage, but that "Lucy's success in achieving *her* aims is meanwhile a decided comment on the state of the rest of the nation" (p. 60).

38 Mark Schorer's essay, "Pride Unprejudiced," *Kenyon Review*, 18 (Winter, 1956), recognizes the dangers of the economic world represented by Wickham, "the acquisitive, the materialistic impulse at its worst, which is to say when it moves out beyond all social restraint whatever" (pp. 72–91). P. B. S. Andrews, in "The Date of *Pride and Prejudice*," *Notes & Queries*, 15 (1968), argues for a 1790s' date for the setting and most of the composition of the novel (pp. 338–42). Ralph Nash, in "The Time Scheme for *Pride and Prejudice*," *English Language Notes*, 4 (1967), 194–98, finds that "the events of the first autumn reflect the calendar of 1799," and "the events of spring and summer reflect the calendar of 1802," and that the time-scheme gives little support to conjectures of extensive revisions in 1811–1812.

39 See Ivor Morris, *Mr Collins Considered: Approaches to Jane Austen* (London and New York: Routledge & Kegan Paul, 1987), for an account of Mr. Collins' close adherence to general social opinion.

40 Cecil S. Emden, in "The Composition of *Northanger Abbey*," *Review of English Studies*, 19 (1968), 279–87, places the largest part of the composition in 1794, with additions in 1798, 1803, and even in 1816.

3 THE GIFTS OF HEAVEN: CONSUMER POWER, 1800–1820

1 See Amanda Vickery, "Women and the World of Goods: a Lancashire Consumer and Her Possessions, 1751–81," *Consumption and the World of Goods*, eds. John Brewer and Roy Porter (London and New York: Routledge, 1993), pp. 274–301; Carole Shammas, *The Pre-industrial Consumer in England and America* (Oxford: Clarendon Press, 1990), pp. 180–81, 186–88; Lorna Weatherill, *Consumer Behaviour and Material Culture in Britain, 1660–1760* (London and New York: Routledge, 1988), pp. 137–39; Hoh-Cheung Mui and Lorna H. Mui, *Shops and Shopkeeping in Eighteenth-Century England* (London: Routledge, 1989), pp. 133–72.

2 Lady Sarah Pennington, *An Unfortunate Mother's Advice to her Absent Daughters* (1761), p. 63; John Gregory, *A Father's Legacy to His Daughters* (1774), pp. 52–53; and Elizabeth Griffith, *Essays Addressed to Young Married Women* (1782), pp. 109–10.

3 Women's magazines, too, had included for some years the occasional story of a female economist, especially magazines, like the *Universal Magazine*, with an evangelical tendency. In "Aspasia and Flavilla," a story in the *Universal* (May 1784), Aspasia gives a lengthy account of her daily schedule, beginning with morning prayers and her first task: "I walked to inspect the charity school I have established in the next village ... At two, enjoyed a sweet walk through some of the pleasantest fields in England (In one of which I luckily saved the life of a dying lamb) ... In the evening ... Miss S— and I retired into the alcove in the grove, the weather being hot, and amused ourselves with working [sewing] for a distressed family." The *Universal* for September 1788, offers a story of married economy in "Female Gratitude; or the History of Eliza Bentley": Eliza Bentley, left destitute by improvident parents, marries Henry Nugent (she proposes to *him*: "He was almost frantic with joy"), her only dowry being her piety and her turn for domestic economy, "and though their income is not large, they bring up their family with elegance and propriety; educating them at home, and observing the strictest economy in all their affairs."

4 Gary Kelly, *English Fiction of the Romantic Period, 1789–1830* (London and New York: Longman, 1989), p. 19.

5 John Vernon, *Money and Fiction: Literary Realism in the Nineteenth and Early Twentieth Centuries* (Ithaca and London: Cornell University Press, 1984): as paper money became more common, Vernon argues, "fiction was becoming not only more profitable, not merely more concerned with economic themes, but also more mediated, more representational, more omniscient – in a word, more realistic" (pp. 17–18).

6 Nancy Armstrong, *Desire and Domestic Fiction: A Political History of the Novel* (Oxford University Press, 1987), pp. 3–27.

7 See Hoh-Cheung Mui and Lorna H. Mui, *Shops and Shopkeeping*, pp. 212–13; also, Lorna Weatherill, *Consumer Behaviour*, pp. 105, 137–9, 182;

also, Carole Shammas, *The Pre-industrial Consumer in England and America*, pp. 186–88, 246.

8 Eric J. Hobsbawm, *Industry and Empire* (Baltimore: Penguin Books, 1968), connects the attitude to the effect of the Industrial Revolution on the upper classes: "Those classes whose lives were least transformed were also, normally, those which benefited most obviously in material terms ... Nobody is more complacent than a well-off or successful man who is also at ease in a world which seems to have been constructed precisely with persons like him in mind" (pp. 61–62).

9 Quoted by Marshall Berman, in *All That Is Solid Melts Into Air: The Experience of Modernity* (New York: Simon and Schuster, 1982), p. 48.

10 Jean Baudrillard, "The System of Objects" (1968), in *Jean Baudrillard: Selected Writings*, ed. Mark Poster (Stanford University Press, 1988), p. 22.

11 As Janet Todd writes in *The Sign of Angellica: Women, Writing and Fiction, 1660–1800* (London: Virago, 1989), "Providing they had sufficient means ... both spinsters and married women could participate in one clear growth area of female economic involvement: philanthropy and charity, which masquerading as service, could give women all the dignity that men were deriving from their ideals of work and independence" (p. 205).

12 For a lively discussion of the issues raised by the participation of women in the new economy see *Feminism and Materialism: Women and Modes of Production*, eds. Annette Kuhn and AnnMarie Wolpe (London: Routledge & Kegan Paul, 1978), especially the essays, "Feminism and Materialism," by Kuhn and Wolpe (pp. 1–10), and "Patriarchy and Relations of Production," by Roisin McDonough and Rachel Harrison (pp. 11–41).

13 The movement for women to learn arithmetic has a long history. Erasmus Darwin, in *A Plan for the Conduct of Female Education in Boarding Schools* (Derby, 1797), warns that "there are situations in a married state; which may call for all the energies of the mind ... which the inactivity, folly, or death of a husband may render necessary"; a woman must be educated "to transact the business" of life (p. 11). "It is necessary for you to be perfect in the four first rules of Arithmetic – more you can never have occasion for," writes Lady Sarah Pennington in *An Unfortunate Mother's Advice to her Absent Daughters*, cited by Bridget Hill, *Eighteenth-Century Women: An Anthology* (London: George Allen & Unwin, 1984), pp. 57–58.

14 As part of the general program to educate women in the management of money, Maria Rundell's *A New System of Domestic Cookery: Formed Upon Principles of Economy* (London, 1818) urges married women to make themselves familiar with their husband's income: "Many women are unfortunately ignorant of the state of their husband's income; and others are only made acquainted with it, when some speculative project, or

profitable transaction, leads them to make a false estimate of what can be afforded" (xxix–xxx).

15 In the *Universal Magazine* (March 1789), there appears a young woman in the story "The Triumph of Nature; or, the Adventure of a Journey," whose "despotic" father refuses to let her marry her lover, "young, handsome, sensible, and virtuous." The lover counsels her: "Our first care must be to secure you from the pursuit of your father, whose intention is to immure you for life in a nunnery." After the stolen marriage produces a child, a "little mediator," the heroine's father forgives the couple.

16 See Amanda Vickery, "Women and the World of Goods," for her account of gentry women who felt that "shopping was a form of employment and one which was most effectively administered by women" (p. 280).

17 Jane Austen mocks the fiction of self-improvement, but she too participates in its ideology of useful leisure time for women. See Jane Nardin's essay, "Jane Austen and the Problem of Leisure," in *Jane Austen in a Social Context*, ed. David Monaghan (Totowa, New Jersey: Barnes & Noble, 1981), pp. 122–42.

18 Citations are to *Marriage: A Novel*, introduction by Margaret Sackville (London: Nash and Grayson, 1929).

19 Maria Edgeworth, in "Lazy Lawrence," a story in *The Parent's Assistant* (1796), describes a similar situation in which a charming lad named Jem (about 10 years old) is employed in garden work by a local gentlewoman. Edgeworth's emphasis in the story, however, is not on the economic and social advantages to the gentlewoman (and the nation) in employing children, as it is in Ferrier's novel, but on Jem's good heart and principles of honesty. The gentlewoman confirms Jem's virtues by giving him the opportunity to earn his widowed mother's rent money and thus avoid the sale of Lightfoot, the family's much-loved horse. In "Toys," *Practical Education* (1798), Edgeworth recommends a spade, hoe, rake, and wheelbarrow as appropriate tools for middle-class children, but as a recreation, not as a source of kitchen produce or a potential livelihood: "A garden is an excellent resource for children, but they should have a variety of other occupations" (p. 21). I am indebted to Marilyn Butler for reminding me of these early examples of children at work in the garden.

20 Olive Cook marks the change in architecture in *The English Country House: an Art and a Way of Life* (London: Thames and Hudson, 1974), p. 215.

21 Mitzi Myers notes in an essay on More's *Cheap Repository Tracts* that More and other women writers of didactic fiction create "from the ideological materials at hand ... a new ideal of educated and responsible womanhood." One of the heroines of More's *Cheap Repository Tracts*, Mrs. Jones "is the exemplary heroine of linked stories," writes Myers, "which graphically demonstrate how an entire community can be

remodeled through female enterprise and persuasive influence and exactly what improving impact such moral reform exerts on communal and family life." See Myers, "Hannah More's Tracts for the Times: Social Fiction and Female Ideology," in *Fetter'd or Free? British Women Novelists, 1670–1815*, eds. Mary Anne Schofield and Cecilia Macheski (Athens: Ohio University Press, 1986), pp. 264–84.

22 *Cheap Repository Tracts; Entertaining, Moral, and Religious* (London: printed by Law and Gilbert, and sold by F. C. & J. Rivington, 1812), I, 298.

23 Jan Fergus, "Women Readers of Fiction and the Marketplace in the Midlands, 1746–1800," delivered as work-in-progress at the Clark Library, Center for 17th and 18th Century Studies, UCLA (Spring 1991). I am indebted to Jan Fergus for sharing with me her knowledge of late eighteenth-century publishing practices.

24 See J. R. Oldfield, "Private Schools and Academies in Eighteenth-Century Hampshire," *Proceedings of the Hampshire Field Club Archaeological Society*, 45 (1989), 147–56. School advertisements touted the useful learning so much appreciated in the lower professional ranks: for the boys, "navigation, fortification, gauging, perspective drawing, architecture, the use of globes and 'every useful branch of the Mathematics', as well as English, writing, arithmetic and accounts"; for the girls, needlework, including "embroidery, tambour and ornamental work," as well as "writing, dancing, music and French" (p. 149).

25 The list of Mitford's borrowed novels is provided by A. S. Collins, *The Profession of Letters, 1780–1832* (New York: Dutton, 1929), p. 94.

26 Dorothy Blakey, *The Minerva Press, 1790–1820* (Oxford: The Bibliographical Society, at the University Press, 1939), p. 21.

27 Blakey, *The Minerva Press*: "The year 1800 is a convenient date to mark the height of Lane's career. During the thirty years before, he had risen from small beginnings by his own 'Industry, Attention, and Spirit.' Not only did he supervise affairs in London, the books at the Minerva Press being 'printed under the Proprietor's own inspection', but he also established circulating libraries in all parts of the kingdom for the sale of his novels, and was for many years his own traveller" (p. 21). Lane's press was called the Minerva Press from 1790, until the name was finally dropped in 1820 by A. K. Newman, his successor who was "principally interested in the issue of children's books and in remainder publishing" (p. 26).

28 W. H. Ireland, *Scribbleomania; or the Printer's Devil's Polichronicon* (1815), quoted by Dorothy Blakey, *The Minerva Press*, p. 157.

29 Sarah Green joins her voice to a much larger contemporary defense of consumer spending. If the rich man "hoards," argues John Trusler, *Luxury no Political Evil* (1780?), "his property is of no use to anyone but himself; if he spends, that is to say, if he indulges himself in Luxury, then, every agent he employs for his gratifications, receives part of his fortune, in the sums of money he pays. In distributing his income thus, he is far more beneficial to the state" (p. 36).

30 Jane West, though not a Minerva writer, leaps to the defense of merchants in *A Gossip's Story* (1797): "I glory in having stimulated the industry of thousands," says Mr. Dudley, a Great Merchant, "increased the natural strength of my country; and enlarged her revenue and reputation, as far as a private individual could" (I, 182–83). "I think I *can* be stout against any thing written by Mrs. West," writes Austen (*Letters*, 405). Mary Pilkington, best known as a children's writer, exclaims over the magnificent inventories in the Great Merchants' warehouses in her novel *The Shipwreck* (1819): "the richness of their silks and satins, the bales of beautiful shawls woven from goats' hair ... and a variety of other articles; amongst which I must not omit mentioning the *superiority* of their *opium* and pistachio-nuts" (p. 44).

31 Letter to Hannah Macaulay, 24 Dec. 1832. Quoted by Dorothy Blakey, *The Minerva Press*, p. 60. See also, *The Letters of Thomas Babington Macaulay*, ed. Thomas Pinney, 6 vols. (Cambridge University Press, 1974–81), I, 219; II, 124, 154, 216, 270, 339, 358; III, 82, for evidence of Macaulay's enthusiasm for Meeke's works.

32 Hunter's novels amused the Austen family and led Austen to parody the style in a letter to her niece: To Anna Austen [1814], *Letters*, p. 406. Deirdre Le Faye identifies and describes Hunter's novel *Lady Maclairn* (1806), read by the Austen family, in "Anna Lefroy's Original Memories of Jane Austen," *The Review of English Studies* (August 1988), 417–21.

33 Deirdre Le Faye gives a wry summary of this novel, *Lady Maclairn, the Victim of Villainy* (1806), in which the Flint family figures so largely, in "Jane Austen and Mrs. Hunter's Novel," *Notes and Queries* ns 32, no. 3 (1985), 335–36.

34 Jacques Derrida, *Of Grammatology*, trans. Gayatri Chakravorty Spivak (Baltimore: The Johns Hopkins University Press, 1976), p. 158.

4 SHOPPING FOR SIGNS: JANE AUSTEN AND THE PSEUDO-GENTRY

1 "Interpreters of Jane Austen's Social World: Literary Critics and Historians," ed. Janet Todd, *Jane Austen: New Perspectives* (New York and London: Holmes & Meier, 1983), pp. 53–72. Spring credits Alan Everitt as having invented the term "pseudo-gentry" as a "helpful substitute for the word bourgeois, having in mind the latter's misleading overtones" (p. 60). See A. Everitt, "Social Mobility in Early Modern England," *Past and Present*, April 1966; and A. Everitt, "Kentish Family Portrait: An Aspect of the Rise of the Pseudo-Gentry," in *Rural Change and Urban Growth 1500–1800: Essays in English Regional History in Honour of W. G. Hoskins*, eds. C. W. Chalklin and M. A. Havinden (London: Longman, 1979).

2 Raymond Williams, in *The Country and the City* (Oxford University Press, 1973), emphasizes the difference that this distinction makes between landed and non-landed incomes in Austen's social economy: "She is

precise and candid, but in very particular ways. She is, for example, more exact about income, which is disposable than about acres, which have to be worked ... The land is seen primarily as an index of revenue and position; its visible order and control are a valued product, while the process of working it is hardly seen at all" (p. 115).

3 Dorothy Marshall, in *English People in the Eighteenth Century* (London: Longman, Green and Co., 1956), asks whether the gentry are to be included in the "middle classes" or "to be regarded as a separate layer in the social strata" (p. 51). Peter Earle, in *The Making of the English Middle Class: Business, Society and Family Life in London, 1660–1730* (London: Methuen, 1989), writes of the professionals as "clinging valiantly to labels such as Esquire and gentlemen," though they really belonged to "the middle station in terms of income and life-style" (p. 5). Leonard Woolf rather waspishly points out that Jane Austen's "paternal grandfather was a surgeon and a surgeon was barely a gentleman; her father and her maternal grandfather were both clergymen, and therefore just within the charmed circle," in "The Economic Determination of Jane Austen," *The New Statesman and Nation*, 24 (1942), 39–41. Sir Walter Scott readily identifies Austen's characters as belonging "chiefly to the middling classes of society"; Madame de Staël termed Austen's work "*vulgaire.*" Both Scott and de Staël cited by Claudia Johnson, *Jane Austen: Women, Politics, and the Novel* (University of Chicago Press, 1988), xviii.

4 Social rank even regulates the hours of shopping, with the gentry and pseudo-gentry shopping before breakfast (between 9.0 and 10.0 in the morning), but the "wives and sisters of clerks, shop-keepers, apothecaries, and such workers, the lower middle class," obliged to shop in the evening. See Madeline Hope Dodds, "Hours of Business, 1780 to 1820," in *Notes and Queries* 194 (1949), 436–37.

5 Mary Douglas and Baron Isherwood, in *The World of Goods: Towards an Anthropology of Consumption* (Harmondsworth: Penguin, 1978), argue for the classifying power of goods: "Marking is the right word here. It draws on the meanings of the hallmarking of gold and silver and pewter ... Goods are endowed with value by the agreement of fellow consumers. They come together to grade events, upholding old judgments or reversing them" (pp. 74–76). Terry Lovell, "Jane Austen and Gentry Society," in *Literature, Society, and the Sociology of Literature*, ed. Francis Barker, Proceedings of the Conference held at the University of Essex (University of Essex, 1976), notes that the gentry were consumers first and capitalists only unwillingly. Austen's class, she argues, gets squeezed uncomfortably between traditional rural society and the up-and-coming new urban capitalist order: "A woman in this section of the gentry class in this period would be especially sensitive to the vulnerability of her class and of her sex within it" (pp. 121–22).

6 Pierre Bourdieu, *Distinction: A Social Critique of the Judgement of Taste,*

trans. Richard Nice (London: Routledge & Kegan Paul, 1984), pp. 375, 381.

7 Jean Baudrillard, "System of Objects," *Jean Baudrillard: Selected Writings*, ed. Mark Poster (Stanford University Press, 1988), p. 19.

8 Donald J. Greene, "Jane Austen and the Peerage," *PMLA* 68 (1953), 1017–31, examines Austen's divided mind – her loyalty to her own "middle-class" origins and her pride in being related to the aristocracy through her mother's family.

9 Arjun Appadurai proposes in *The Social Life of Things: Commodities in Cultural Perspective* (Cambridge University Press, 1986), that, "we regard luxury goods not so much in contrast to necessities (a contrast filled with problems), but as goods whose principal use is *rhetorical* and *social*, goods that are simply *incarnated signs*" (p. 38).

10 David Paul does Austen's letters a disservice when he remarks that, "As much as she loved Cassandra, the letters are curiously un-intimate," in "Syringa, Iv'ry Pure," *Twentieth Century*, 153 (1953), pp. 302–08.

11 See Barbara Hardy, "Properties and Possessions in Jane Austen's Novels," *Jane Austen's Achievement*, ed. Juliet McMaster (London: Macmillan, 1976), for a lively essay on the intimacy of *things* in Austen's novels (pp. 75–105). See also Hardy's essay, "The Objects in *Mansfield Park*" in *Jane Austen: Bicentennial Essays*, ed. John Halperin (Cambridge University Press, 1975), pp. 180–96. See also James Thompson, "Jane Austen's Clothing," *Studies in Eighteenth-Century Culture*, 13 (Madison: Wisconsin University Press, 1984), pp. 217–47, who explores the conflicts of morality with the social and economic demands represented in clothing.

12 See H. W. Garrod's famous remark, in *Essays by Divers Hands* (Royal Society of Literature, 1928), condemning Austen's letters as "a desert of trivialities punctuated by occasional oases of clever malice." Quoted by R. W. Chapman, *Jane Austen's Letters*, p. xlii.

13 Mary Eagleton and David Pierce, in *Attitudes to Class in the English Novel* (London: Thames and Hudson, 1979), discuss the "fine points of equilibrium" Austen must chart in establishing the relationship between the individual and class, especially in the responsible use of wealth (pp. 26–29). Oliver MacDonagh's study, *Jane Austen: Real and Imagined Worlds* (New Haven: Yale University Press, 1991), offers a sensitive and probing account of the role of money in Austen's life and novels.

14 Jan Fergus, *Jane Austen and the Didactic Novel* (Totowa, New Jersey: Barnes & Noble, 1983), argues that Austen's parody of contemporary fiction in *Northanger Abbey* is not so much concerned to debunk as to engage with "their power to engross the imagination and to create a response" (p. 37).

15 See John Sekora, *Luxury: The Concept in Western Thought, Eden to Smollett* (Baltimore and London: The Johns Hopkins University Press, 1977), pp. 63–109.

16 Tony Tanner, "Anger in the Abbey: *Northanger Abbey*," in *Jane Austen* (Cambridge, Mass.: Harvard University Press, 1986), p. 74.

17 B. C. Southam, "General Tilney's Hot-Houses: Some Recent Jane Austen Studies and Texts," *Ariel*, 2 (Oct. 1971), 52–62. General Tilney, claims Southam, is "a fairly elaborate portrait of a specific, historical type of late eighteenth-century, early nineteenth-century gentleman, whose life is engaged with some of the most important social and cultural currents of the time" (p. 61). Eric Rothstein, "The Lessons of *Northanger Abbey*," *University of Toronto Quarterly* 47 (1974), 14–30, suggests that General Tilney's property is simply a "material version of the Thorpes' fantasy life."

18 See Terry Lovell's division of social ranks in "Jane Austen and Gentry Society."

19 Colin Campbell's study, *The Romantic Ethic and the Spirit of Modern Consumerism* (Oxford: Basil Blackwell, 1987), pp. 69–76, 89. Jean Baudrillard is in agreement with Campbell on this point in "The System of Objects": "Neither the quantity of goods, nor the satisfaction of needs is sufficient to define consumption: they are merely its preconditions," he writes: "Consumption, in so far as it is meaningful, is *a systematic act of the manipulation of signs*," in *Selected Writings*, pp. 21–22.

20 As Georg Simmel observes in "Fashion," reprinted from the original English translation of 1906 (Dodd, Mead and Company) in *The American Journal of Sociology*, vol. 62, no. 6 (May 1957), "Fashion raises even the unimportant individual by making him the representative of a class, the embodiment of a joint spirit" (p. 548).

21 Eric Rothstein argues, in "The Lessons of *Northanger Abbey*," pp. 14–30, that Catherine must make the gothic modes "existentially viable, if only by rejecting them for alternative responses in dealing with her public, personal, and inner lives."

22 Pierre Bourdieu, *Distinction*, p. 68.

23 See Ivor Morris' analysis of Mr. Collins' character in *Mr Collins Considered: Approaches to Jane Austen* (London and New York: Routledge & Kegan Paul, 1987).

24 "Goods are ritual adjuncts... and consumption is a ritual process whose primary function is to make sense of the inchoate flux of events." Douglas and Isherwood, *The World of Goods*, p. 65.

25 "The world of play," as sociologist Don Handleman suggests, presents a "cognitive bridge [which] permits messages, which arise within the world of play to comment on the ordering of ordinary life, on its arbitrariness, and on the subjectivity of its experience," "Reflexivity in Festival and Other Cultural Events," in *Essays in the Sociology of Perception*, ed. Mary Douglas (London: Routledge & Kegan Paul, 1982), pp. 162–63.

26 Arjun Appadurai, ed., *The Social Life of Things*, p. 12.

27 The Thorpes from Fulham, in *Northanger Abbey*, also qualify.

28 Mark Schorer's remarks in "Fiction and the 'Analogical Matrix,'" in *Critiques and Essays on Modern Fiction, 1920–1950*, ed. John W. Aldridge (New York: Ronald Press Company, 1952), pp. 83–98, have special resonance for *Mansfield Park*, though he writes of *Persuasion* here: "We are in a world of substance, a peculiarly material world ... In this context certain colorless words, words of the lightest intention, take on a special weight. The words *account* and *interest* are used hundreds of times in their homeliest sense, yet when we begin to observe that every narration is an *account*, and at least once 'an *account* ... of the *negotiation*,' we are reminded that they have more special meanings" (p. 85).

29 Appadurai argues in *The Social Life of Things* that "Modern consumers are the victims of the velocity of fashion as surely as primitive consumers are the victims of the stability of sumptuary law ... In both cases demand is a socially regulated and generated impulse, not an artifact of individual whim or needs" (p. 32).

30 For the year 1807, writes Deirdre Le Faye, "the largest item of expenditure was £13.19s.3d. on 'Cloathes & Pocket', followed by 'Washing' at £9.5s.11 1/2d." In *Jane Austen: A Family Record* (London: The British Library, 1989), p. 145.

31 The "consumer," writes Baudrillard, "must constantly be ready to actualize all of his potential, all of his capacity for consumption," *Selected Writings*, pp. 48–49.

32 Fanny intends to avoid the "modern world" as it is defined by Stuart and Elizabeth Ewen, *Channels of Desire: Mass Images and the Shaping of American Consciousness* (New York: McGraw-Hill, 1982), the same world that belongs to Mary and Henry Crawford, "a world defined by the retail (individualized) consumption of goods and services; a world in which social relations are often disciplined by the exchange of money; a world where it increasingly *makes sense* that if there are solutions to be had, they can be bought" (p. 42). Fanny is caught in Igor Kopytoff's paradox, "The Cultural Biography of Things: Commoditization as Process," *The Social Life of Things*, ed. Arjun Appadurai: "One perceives ... a drive inherent in every exchange system toward a maximum commoditization ... The counterdrive to this potential onrush of commoditization is culture." The "individual," Fanny Price in this case, "is often caught between the cultural structure of commoditization and his own personal attempts to bring a value order to the universe of things" (p. 65).

33 Douglas and Isherwood, *The World of Goods*, pp. 57, 60.

34 Baudrillard, *Selected Writings*, p. 30.

35 Douglas and Isherwood, *The World of Goods*, p. 72.

36 A. O. J. Cockshut, *Man and Woman: a Study of Love and the Novel, 1740–1940* (Oxford University Press, 1978), discusses the role of mentors in *Mansfield Park* and the degrees of worldliness and materialism at the heart of this novel (pp. 54–71).

37 See Mary Douglas, *Cultural Bias* (London: Royal Anthropological Institute of Great Britain and Ireland, 1978), for her explanation of "social cosmologies" (pp. 19–20).

38 G. Armour Craig, "Jane Austen's *Emma*: The Truths and Disguises of Human Disclosure," *A Defense of Reading*, ed. Reuben A. Brower and Richard Poirier (New York: E. P. Dutton & Co., 1962), pp. 235–55, writes that rank in *Emma* "in this society is what one character stands on when he defines the motives for the actions of another or of himself. Rank, in the fullest sense, is dramatic position" (p. 242).

39 "Cultural capital" could generate income for Jane Fairfax through a paid position as a governess, though the prospect does not promise much to her advantage.

40 David Aers, "Community and Morality: Towards Reading Jane Austen," in *Romanticism and Ideology: Studies in English Writing 1765–1830*, eds. David Aers, *et al.* (London: Routledge & Kegan Paul, 1981): "The neo-feudal, static ideology conceals the class's immersion in the practices and values of agrarian capitalism pursued so decorously by Mr. Knightley and Mr. Martin in *Emma*" (p. 127). See also Beth Fowkes Tobin, "The Moral and Political Economy of Property in Austen's *Emma*," *Eighteenth-Century Fiction*, vol. 2, no. 3 (April 1990), 229–54, who argues that Mr. Knightley's gentlemanly virtues are the center of Austen's defense of the landed classes.

41 Thomas Brian Tomlinson, *The English Middle-Class Novel* (London: Macmillan, 1976), argues that in *Emma* "there are moments in the novel when one feels the presence of a slightly too easy reliance on the myth of Donwell and Hartfield as all-embracing, protective" (p. 32). E. Rubinstein, "Jane Austen's Novels: The Metaphor of Rank," *Literary Monographs*, 2, ed. Eric Rothstein and Richard N. Ringler (Madison: Wisconsin University Press, 1969), has a different interpretation, suggesting that in Highbury, Austen deliberately creates "the closest approximation of an idyllic world that the novel will permit, and brings into contrast with it the actualities of the social world, of the modern self" (p. 168).

42 B. C. Southam, "*Sanditon*: the Seventh Novel," in *Jane Austen's Achievement*, ed. Juliet McMaster (London: Macmillan, 1976), recognizes the "newness" of the economic world captured by Austen in the fragment. Austen's sympathies are with the conservative Mr. Heywood, claims Southam, but she is willing to explore a new society (pp. 1–26).

43 F. P. Lock, in "Jane Austen and the Seaside," *Country Life Annual* (1972), 114–16, calls attention to the fact that inflation first enters Austen's novels as a focus of interest in *Sanditon*.

44 B. C. Southam suggests, in "A Source for *Sanditon*?" *Collected Reports of the Jane Austen Society, 1966–75* (Folkestone: Wm. Dawson & Sons, 1977), a novel by Thomas Skinner Surr, published in 1815, as a possible inspiration for *Sanditon*: "Surr's story is set around the town of

Flimflamton, 'a new and rising watering place, created, as it were by magic, out of a few fishing huts, by the power and wealth of a certain rich banker.'" Surr shows "how the power of money can be corrupting and destructive" (p. 122).

45 Le Faye, *Jane Austen: A Family Record*, pp. 170–71.
46 David Musselwhite, "The Novel as Narcotic," in *The Sociology of Literature*, Proceedings of the Essex Conference on the Sociology of Literature, July 1977, ed. Francis Barker (University of Essex, 1978), pp. 207–24.

5 PICTURING THE HEROINE: *THE LADY'S MAGAZINE*, 1770–1820

1 Shelley M. Bennett, in "Changing Images of Women in Late-Eighteenth-Century England: 'The Lady's Magazine,' 1770–1810," *Arts Magazine* 55 (May 1981), 138–42, analyzes the changing messages of illustrations in the *Lady's Magazine*.
2 *The Lady's Magazine, or Entertaining Companion for the Fair Sex*, with name alterations and mergers with other magazines, ran from 1770 to 1832. See Alison Adburgham, *Women in Print: Writing Women and Women's Magazines From the Restoration to the Accession of Victoria* (London: George Allen and Unwin, 1972), p. 276.
3 See Colin Campbell, *The Romantic Ethic and the Spirit of Modern Consumerism* (Oxford: Basil Blackwell, 1987), who argues that the pleasure of window-shopping is essentially a pleasure of the imagination: "the pleasure which comes from the imaginative use of the object seen; that is, from mentally 'trying on' the clothes examined, or 'seeing' the furniture arranged within one's room" (p. 90).
4 See Stuart Ewen, "Marketing Dreams: The Political Elements of Style," *Consumption, Identity, and Style*, ed. Alan Tomlinson (London: Routledge, 1990): "Style," claims Ewen, is "an essential, inescapable instrument of cultural and political discourse" (p. 47). It "negotiates" between "the objective power and interests of ruling elites on the one hand, and rising popular democratic aspirations on the other" (p. 53).
5 The readership would have included households with incomes of around £150 a year (prosperous shopkeepers, lesser professionals, clerks in office) and up. The masses provided no significant market for fiction in the late eighteenth century. See Terry Lovell, *Consuming Fiction* (London: Verso, 1987), p. 49.
6 Alison Adburgham, *Women in Print*, pp. 148–50, 218–35. See also Cynthia L. White, *Women's Magazines, 1693–1968* (London: Michael Joseph, 1970), pp. 31–32, 35–36; and Melvin M. Watson, *Magazine Serials and the Essay Tradition, 1746–1820* (Baton Rouge: Louisiana State University Press, 1956), who writes, "For over a half century, the *Lady's* stood up under fierce competition ... *The Lady's* is significant for quality and attempted variety. Ordinarily, three or four, and occasionally as

many as five, series [of stories] would be running simultaneously" (p. 21).

7 Robert D. Mayo, *The English Novel in the Magazines, 1746–1815* (Evanston: Northwestern University Press, 1962), pp. 307–21. When in 1820 the editors of a "New Series" announced plans to replace all amateur, reader-supplied fiction with fiction written by professionals only, this 50-year public forum for women came to an end. See Cynthia White, *Women's Magazines*, pp. 39–40.

8 In fact, the entire cast of suspects from the Austen theatricals appear in the plate: from left to right, Mary Crawford as she witnesses it all, Mr. Rushworth helplessly watching Henry Crawford at his business, and Edmund Bertram blessing the unsavory proceedings with his presence. "The Report for the Year 1973," in *Collected Reports of the Jane Austen Society, 1966–75* (Folkestone: Wm. Dawson & Sons, 1977), pp. 194–96, reprints the *Lady's* "Account" as it appeared in the issue for October 1798.

9 A full account of the Leigh-Perrots' experience is found in Deirdre Le Faye, *Jane Austen, A Family Record* (London: The British Library, 1989), pp. 105–10.

10 David Gilson, *A Bibliography of Jane Austen* (Oxford: Clarendon Press, 1982), cites three printings of *The Trial of Mrs. Leigh Perrot* in 1800, which, he notes, "evince the curious notoriety of an event of local and ephemeral interest" (xiii). *The Bath Chronicle*, Thursday, 3 April 1800, printed an account of the trial, reporting that a crowd of 2,000 people were present, "though many hundreds of them could not possibly hear a word that was said, and were almost pressed to death, and suffocated by the heat." Quoted by Frank Douglas MacKinnon, *Grand Larceny, Being the Trial of Jane Leigh Perrot, Aunt of Jane Austen* (Oxford University Press, 1933).

11 Frank Douglas MacKinnon, in *Grand Larceny*, is of the opinion that Mrs. Leigh-Perrot's address was probably written by her counsel (pp. 118–19).

12 Laura Mulvey, *Visual and Other Pleasures* (London: Macmillan, 1989), p. 25.

13 For other versions of the familiar story see, in the *Lady's Magazine*, "The Negligent Suitor" (August 1794), "The Careless Sportsman" (September 1795), and "The Careless Lover" (November 1808).

14 Illustrations of fiction in the magazines regularly provide such unremarked watching figures in the background, most often men watching women, but sometimes women watching men.

15 Mulvey, *Visual and Other Pleasures*, p. 39. Natalie Zemon Davis argues in "Women on Top: Symbolic Sexual Inversion and Political Disorder in Early Modern Europe" that the act of reading a woman's magazine in itself alone "could operate to widen behavioral options for women," that it could could lead to a festive inversion of the "disorderly woman,"

in *The Reversible World: Symbolic Inversion in Art and Society*, ed. Barbara A. Babcock (Ithaca and London: Cornell University Press, 1978), pp. 154–55.

16 Roger Abrahams recognizes the indeterminacy of the exact point of alteration from one state to another in "The Complex Relation of Simple Form," *Genre* 2 (1969), 104–128: "At some point of the maker-user relationship spectrum, the removal between the two becomes so pronounced we call it a product of technology, not material folklore."

17 Marshall Berman, *All That Is Solid Melts Into Air: The Experience of Modernity* (New York: Simon and Schuster, 1982), pp. 53–54.

18 Chandra Mukerji notes, in *From Graven Images: Patterns of Modern Materialism* (New York: Columbia University Press, 1983), that the magazines of the late eighteenth century shared "print culture" with the "print culture" of the cheap, new printed textiles of the consumer revolution (pp. 3–17).

19 John Styles, "Manufacturing, Consumption and Design in Eighteenth-Century England," in *Consumption and the World of Goods*, eds. John Brewer and Roy Porter (London and New York: Routledge, 1993), pp. 527–54, discusses the circulation of illustrations to manufacturers at mid-century in the dissemination of new fashions (pp. 544–45). The *Lady's Magazine* picks up on an established practice, bringing it conveniently to consumers themselves.

20 John Styles, "Manufacturing, Consumption and Design in Eighteenth-Century England," in *Consumption and the World of Goods*, also discusses the general acceptance of a standard language of description for commodities as it was formalized for manufacturers, shopkeepers, and consumers during the century (pp. 545–46).

21 Colin Campbell, *The Romantic Ethic*, pp. 78–95. Doris Langley Moore, *Fashion through Fashion Plates, 1771–1970* (London: Ward Lock, 1971), distinguishes between true fashion plates and the illustrations for plays and fiction that also include elegant clothing (pp. 14–15). Moore's research on magazine illustration is cited by Neil McKendrick in *The Birth of a Consumer Society*, eds. Neil McKendrick, John Brewer, and J. H. Plumb (London: Europa Publications, 1982), pp. 47–48.

22 "Charlotte Bateman" supports Colin Campbell's paradox in *The Romantic Ethic* that "the spirit of modern consumerism is anything but materialistic." "Individuals," he writes, "do not so much seek satisfaction from products, as pleasure from the self-illusory experiences which they construct from their associated meanings" (p. 89). Campbell contrasts "modern hedonism," primarily concerned with "a degree of control over meaning," to "traditional hedonism," primarily concerned with control over "the manipulation of objects and events in the world" (p. 76).

23 Don Handleman suggests in "Reflexivity in Festival and Other Cultural Events," in *Essays in the Sociology of Perception*, ed. Mary Douglas (London: Routledge & Kegan Paul, 1982), that messages of play

"take apart the clock-works of reality, and question their organization, and indeed their very validity as human and as cultural contexts" (pp. 162–63).

24 See Campbell, *The Romantic Ethic*, p. 90.

25 Stuart Ewen argues in "Marketing Dreams," in *Consumption, Identity, and Style*, that "the past can be evoked through the assembly of style... Roosevelt, Bogart, and Hitler; each captures the styles of the thirties and forties in a different way. Together they embody the spirit of a decade" (p. 50).

26 John Sekora, *Luxury: The Concept in Western Thought, Eden to Smollett* (Baltimore and London: The Johns Hopkins University Press, 1977), pp. 110–31; see especially pp. 119–24.

27 Nancy Armstrong, *Desire and Domestic Fiction: A Political History of the Novel* (Oxford University Press, 1987), pp. 18–19.

28 Thomas Stothard, the best known of the illustrators for the magazines, is easily the most accomplished of the lot, but the editor of the *Lady's Magazine* in a "Notice to Correspondents" (January 1817) cites not only Stothard, but Burney, Corbould, Westall, and Brighty as contributors to the *Lady's*. According to Neil McKendrick, in *The Birth of a Consumer Society*, Henry Moses and J. Stevenson also can be identified as illustrators for the magazine. Stothard, claims McKendrick, could demand a guinea a piece for his plates (pp. 47–48). Nevertheless, most illustrators remain nameless, and the work itself hack work. For an account of Stothard's participation in the *Lady's Magazine*, see Shelley M. Bennett, *Thomas Stothard: The Mechanisms of Art Patronage in England circa 1800* (Columbia: Missouri University Press, 1988), p. 65.

29 As Michael Butor observes, in *Inventory*, trans. Richard Howard (New York: Simon and Schuster, 1961), "We might emphasize the importance of a given moment by its obverse, by the study of its surroundings, thus making the reader feel there is a lacuna in the fabric of what is being narrated, or something that is being hidden"; once the task of overcoming the "lacuna" is undertaken by the reader, as Butor suggests, women's magazine fiction escapes the hands of its producers to join forces with its more creative readers (p. 21). Susan Stewart's *On Longing: Narratives of the Miniature, the Gigantic, the Souvenir, the Collection* (Baltimore: The Johns Hopkins University Press, 1984), employs a traditional term to describe the phenomenon: "In allegory the vision of the reader is larger than the vision of the text; the reader dreams to an excess, to an overabundance. To read an allegorical narration is to see beyond the relations of narration, character, desire. To read allegory is to live in the future, the anticipation of closure beyond the closure of narration" (pp. 3–4).

30 Susan Stewart, *On Longing*, argues that the "gigantic" in the context of miniature art represents "the abstract authority of the state and the collective, public, life" (p. xii).

31 The "tableau," according to Susan Stewart, draws together "signifi-

cant, even if contradictory, elements," at the same time as it grants the viewer a "simultaneous particularization and generalization of the moment." *On Longing*, p. 48.

32 Susan Stewart, *On Longing*, suggests a like analysis in *Robinson Crusoe*: "If *Robinson Crusoe* is an eschatological work, its eschaton is the moment when the ship (and not the naked footprint) appears on the horizon and use value is transformed into exchange value" (p. 15).

33 The following stories are accompanied in the magazine by plates: "Dorilacia; or, The Fair Captive" (September 1777); "Omrah Restored" (July 1779); "The Shipwreck; or the Unhappy Lovers" (June 1780); "The Patriotic Parting" (July 1782); "The Fortunate Affliction" (April 1784); "The Wreck" (October 1788); "The Unexpected Recovery" (September 1790); "The Power of Compassion" (October 1790); "The Shipwreck" (Supplement, 1794); "Henry and Agnes" (November 1799); "The Shipwrecked Mariners" (September 1800); "The Hermit of the Cliff" (January 1801); "The Shipwrecked Boy" (Supplement, 1812); "The Lady of the Rock" (February 1816); "Affection Recompensed" (December 1816).

34 In the title to the story, the heroine's name appears as "Dorilacia"; in the title to the engraving, it is "Doralicia."

35 Georg Simmel, "Fashion," reprinted from the original English translation of 1906 (Dodd, Mead, and Company), in *The American Journal of Sociology*, vol. 62, no. 6 (May 1957), p. 548.

36 Cynthia White, *Women's Magazines*, p. 38.

37 Janice Winship, *Inside Women's Magazines* (London: Routledge & Kegan Paul, 1987), p. 7.

38 Cynthia White confirms this view in *Women's Magazines*: "By 1825, however, significant changes in the context and tone of women's magazines had occurred consistent with a much narrower view of the role and status proper to women... All signs of reader-involvement in the magazines of 1800 [were gone]" (pp. 38–39).

39 Vineta Colby, in *Yesterday's Woman: Domestic Realism in the English Novel* (Princeton University Press, 1974), describes the intensely consumer-oriented "silver-fork novels" that appeared between the death of Jane Austen and the novels of George Eliot, Dickens, and Thackeray (p. 52).

6 FICTIONS OF EMPLOYMENT: FEMALE ACCOMPLISHMENTS

1 The heroine's funds have been sequestered by her husband, which explains why she spends most of the novel in a private madhouse, but in terms of her income she remains firmly within the pale of gentility.

2 I am indebted to Jan Fergus for reminding me that Jane Fairfax wanders the meadows because she is in agony over losing Frank Churchill. No doubt this is true, but the horror of her future at the Smallridges, wax

candles in the schoolroom notwithstanding, hovers over her future with a persistence that no contemporary reader would have missed.

3 Fredric Jameson, *The Political Unconscious: Narrative As a Socially Symbolic Act* (Ithaca, New York: Cornell University Press, 1981), p. 289.

4 Margaret Anne Doody, *Frances Burney: The Life in the Works* (New Brunswick, New Jersey: Rutgers University Press, 1988), gives a thorough account and analysis of the heroine's unsuccessful experiences at employment (pp. 350–61).

5 In Charlotte Lennox's early novel *Henrietta* (1758), the heroine takes employment to make this very point, to spite her family: "What a triumph would be mine if any of my relations should happen... to behold me in the character of Miss Cordwain's servant!" *Novelists Magazine*, vol. 23, book 3, p.88. Quoted by B. G. MacCarthy, *The Female Pen: The Later Women Novelists, 1744–1818*, vol. II (Cork University Press, 1947), p. 56.

6 See Henry Curwen, *A History of Booksellers, the Old and the New* (London: Chatto and Windus, 1873), for an account of Longman's other contemporary educational projects (pp. 92–93).

7 See Jan Fergus and Janice Farrar Thaddeus, "Women, Publishers, and Money, 1790–1820," in *Studies in Eighteenth-Century Culture*, 17 (East Lansing, Michigan: Colleagues Press, 1987), pp. 191–207, for cases of payments to writers by Hookham and Carpenter and by Longman during the period.

8 For useful biographies of early women novelists, see *A Dictionary of British and American Women Writers, 1660–1800*, ed. Janet Todd (Totowa, New Jersey: Rowman & Allanheld, 1985), and *The Feminist Companion to Literature in English*, eds. Virginia Blain, Patricia Clements, Isobel Grundy (London: B. T. Batsford, 1990).

9 From *Emily, or the Wife's First Error; and Beauty and Ugliness, or, The Father's Prayer and the Mother's Prophecy* (London: A. K. Newman & Co., 1819). The British Library Catalogue attributes this novel to Agnes [Anna] Maria Bennett, the popular Minerva Press author. Since A. M. Bennett died in 1808 and since it would have been to Newman's advantage to use her name if it were possible, it seems unlikely that the attribution is correct. Nothing is known of Elizabeth Bennet [spelled Bennett here] who also appears to be the author of *Faith and Fiction; or Shining Lights in a Dark Generation: a Novel*, 5 vols. (London: printed at the Minerva Press for A. K. Newman & Co., 1816).

10 Terry Eagleton, *Criticism and Ideology: A Study in Marxist Literary Theory* (London: Verso, 1976), p. 75.

11 Jameson, *The Political Unconscious*, p. 87.

12 For a survey of the governess's position in fiction, see E. V. Clark, "The Private Governess in Fiction," *Contemporary Review*, 186 (1954), 165–70.

13 The Berg Collection, New York Public Library, holograph, unsigned and undated, 126 pages.

14 Hanway takes aim at a common contemporary confusion. "Usually the title of companion meant little more than its bearer was a lady's maid of a superior sort. Her work was lighter than that of the ordinary lady's maid and far less well defined; she was used with more respect and accorded a greater degree of formal courtesy, as is indicated by the 'Mrs.' generally placed before her surname when addressed. In all other respects her position was indistinguishable from that of a lady's maid." From J. J. Hecht, *The Domestic Servant Class in 18th-Century England* (London: Routledge & Kegan Paul, 1956), pp. 62–63.

15 M. E. Robinson was the daughter of Mary Robinson, the novelist and mistress, briefly, of the Prince Regent.

16 Green was a regular Minerva Press writer, although this early work was published by Black, Parry, and Company.

17 Eliza Parsons, *The Castle of Wolfenbach*, ed. Devendra Varma (London: The Folio Press, 1968), p. 97.

18 Eagleton, *Criticism and Ideology*, p. 69.

19 The Berg Collection, New York Public Library, holograph, unsigned and undated, 235 pages, accompanied by 29 pages of preliminary notes.

20 Igor Kopytoff chooses the "slave" as the ultimate image of consumer culture in "The Cultural Biography of Things: Commoditization as Process," in *The Social Life of Things: Commodities in Cultural Perspective*, ed. Arjun Appadurai (Cambridge University Press, 1986), pp. 64–91: Kopytoff describes slavery as simply part of a process he calls "commoditization," a fluid social phenomenon, in which "slavery is seen not as a fixed and unitary status, but as a process of social transformation that involves a succession of phases and changes in status." The process of "commoditization," the "up for hire" that threatens to turn Jane Fairfax and Bennet's unfortunate heroine into market commodities, becomes the darkest side of the economy for Austen and for Bennet. Charlotte Brontë's Jane Eyre, a generation later, bemoans the fate of her Rivers' cousins, both governesses, "slaving amongst strangers!"

21 Mary Wollstonecraft received 40 guineas a year from the Kingsboroughs, Emily Sunstein reports in *A Different Face* (New York: Harper and Row, 1975), p. 118. Wollstonecraft informed her sister Everina about a position that paid 25 guineas a year, but later wrote her that the sum appeared "mean," in Wollstonecroft, *Collected Letters*, ed. Ralph M. Wardle (Ithaca and London: Cornell University Press, 1979), pp. 193, 195. Nelly Weeton, a former schoolteacher, reported that she met a woman on Manx who "has a governess for her girls, a Miss Maddocks, to whom she gives only £12 a year!" *Miss Weeton: Journal of a Governess: 1807–1811*, ed. Edward Hall, 2 vols. (Oxford University Press, 1936–39), II, p. 21. Charlotte Brontë's Jane Eyre received £30 a year from Mr. Rochester for tutoring little Adele.

22 Ruth Perry describes the tradition of the female monastery in English

letters in *The Celebrated Mary Astell: An Early English Feminist* (Chicago University Press, 1986), pp. 132–35.

23 Letter to Eliza W. Bishop, 5 November 1786, *Collected Letters of Mary Wollstonecraft*, p. 124.

24 Weeton, *Miss Weeton, Journal of a Governess*, II, p. vii.

25 Wollstonecraft, *Thoughts on the Education of Daughters* (1787), p. 71.

26 A Mrs. Disney, with three children, left without paying her children's sizable debts. See Emily Sunstein, *A Different Face*, p. 98.

27 Quoted by Ralph M. Wardle, *Mary Wollstonecraft: A Critical Biography* (Lincoln: University of Nebraska Press, 1966), p. 47. See also Eleanor Flexner, *Mary Wollstonecraft: A Biography* (Baltimore, Maryland: Penguin, 1972), for an account of the school (pp. 45–54).

28 Royal Literary Fund, case number 298, April 1813. The Royal Literary Fund, a private charity constituted in 1788 for the aid of indigent authors, assigned to each applicant for aid a case number under which all correspondence pertaining to the applicant was filed. See Nigel Cross, *The Royal Literary Fund, 1790–1918* (London: World Microfilms Publications, 1984), for an account of the cataloging of applicants.

29 Mary Wollstonecraft considered needlework for herself, her sister Eliza, and Fanny Blood as a joint project in living together and supporting themselves. Fanny, who had tried needlework herself, rejected the plan: "Half a guinea a week ... would just pay for furnished lodgings for three persons to pig together. As for needle-work, it is utterly impossible they could earn more than half a guinea a week between them, supposing they had constant employment, which is of all things the most uncertain." They opened the school instead. Cited by Eleanor Flexner, *Mary Wollstonecraft*, p. 46.

30 The first edition of *The Old Manor House* was published in 1793 by J. Bell, in four volumes. Quotations here are taken from the single-volume Oxford University Press edition of 1969.

31 Barbara Hofland's Minerva novel, *A Father As He Should Be* (1815), values the privacy of at-home work for women as well, but reports failure for a widow with an infant child who must do her sewing at home; the novel predicts success, however, for a woman who plans to open a boarding school (with the help of friends) in her own home.

32 Katherine Rogers, in *Feminism in Eighteenth-Century England* (Urbana: Illinois University Press, 1982), reports that Mary Robinson's father, who left his family for his mistress, was furious to find that his wife had disgraced the family by starting a small school to support herself. He forced her to give it up. When Mary went on the stage, he was equally outraged. In fact, Robinson's entire family were grieved by her decision, though Robinson herself felt differently: that "the consciousness of independence is the only true felicity in this world of humiliations" (p. 18, n. 35). Quoted from Mary Darby Robinson, *Memoirs of Mrs. Robinson, "Perdita"*, ed. by her daughter (London: Gibbings and Co.,

1895). Rogers also notes that when Richard Brinsley Sheridan married the singer Elizabeth Linley, he refused to allow her to sing for pay, even though the young couple was penniless (p. 18).

33 Sarah Fielding employs the metaphor in *David Simple* (1744) to describe marriage for money: "*for I shall always call it prostitution, for a woman who has sense, and has been tolerably educated, to marry a clown and a fool.*" Quoted by Bridget G. MacCarthy, *Women Writers: Their Contribution to the English Novel, 1621–1744* (Cork University Press, 1944), p. 261. John Moir, however, in *Female Tuition: or, An Address to Mothers, on the Education of Daughters* (London, 1784), attributes prostitution to women's venery, their "love of forbidden joys." Economic necessity does not enter Moir's argument (pp. 260–62).

34 Real-life conditions of prostitution seldom make it into the woman's novel. Jonas Hanway, *Domestic Happiness, Promoted; in a Series of Discourses from a Father to His Daughter, on Occasion of Her Going into Service* (1786), writes, "Among abandoned women, I can tell thee, that intemperance and disease bring on consumptions and decay, and few of them live beyond the age of twenty-five" (p. 230).

35 Letter from Mary Hays to William Godwin, 1 October 1795. Carl H. Pforzheimer Library, New York.

36 The anonymous author of the tract *On Monopoly and Reform of Manners* (London, 1795), writes, "And it is known that many of our female countrywomen are, through mere necessity and want of employ, drove [*sic*] to an unfortunate state of prostitution, which would not have been the case had an honest means been left them of getting a livelihood, so it is proposed to exclude men from employs disgraceful to them, by laying a tax of ten guineas per annum, by licence, on every man employed in a milliner's, haberdasher's or silk-mercer's shop … And in general that encouragement be given to the employment of women in all businesses where they can render equal service with men" (pp. 51–52).

37 Peter Laslett, *The World We Have Lost* (New York: Charles Scribner's Sons, 1965), pp. 16–19.

38 M. M. Bakhtin, *The Dialogic Imagination*, trans. Caryl Emerson and Michael Holquist (Austin: University of Texas Press, 1981), p. 276.

7 WRITING FOR MONEY: AUTHORS AND HEROINES

1 Letter to Sarah Farr Rose. *c.* 1803, Henry E. Huntington Library, HM 10826, San Marino, California.

2 Lady Morgan (Sydney Owensen) in her novel, *Florence Macarthy* (1818), features a genteel heroine, Lady Clancare, who writes. There is little in the novel about the conditions of publication, in spite of lively satire directed against the critic John Coker, one of Lady Morgan's enemies. The reader simply learns that Lady Clancare has been successful some time in the past. Lady Clancare does, however, reflect with feeling on the woman writer's social isolation and with spirit on the unfair criticism

directed against herself: "a wild beast, *the woman that writes the books*" (III, 268); "this *mad woman, this* audacious worm" (IV, 37). Otherwise, I have not found any other examples of novels with genteel pretensions where the heroine herself gains a living by her pen. I am grateful to Mitzi Myers for pointing out this one to me.

3 Amelia Beauclerc's novel *Husband Hunters*!!! (1816), discussed below, may be that exception.

4 Although Robinson did well comparatively in her profits, she died in debt. See Jan Fergus and Janice Farrar Thaddeus, "Women, Publishers, and Money, 1790–1820," *Studies in Eighteenth-Century Culture*, 17 (East Lansing, Michigan: Colleagues Press, 1987), p. 197.

5 Fergus and Thaddeus, "Women, Publishers, and Money, 1790–1820," offer the best account of women authors' earnings during the period. See also Jan Fergus, *Jane Austen: A Literary Life* (New York: St. Martin's Press, 1991), especially pp. 1–27, for the fullest account to date of publishing conditions for women. Janet Todd, *The Sign of Angellica: Women, Writing, and Fiction 1660–1800* (London: Virago, 1989), writes that "To keep herself respectably... an indifferently successful woman novelist would have had to produce as many as ten books a year" (p. 220). Judith Phillips Stanton, in "The Production of Fiction by Women in England, 1660–1800: a Statistical Overview," a paper presented at the International Society for Eighteenth-Century Studies, Bristol, July 1991, notes that, "the mean length of a career was 9 years, a figure much inflated by a few lengthy successes. The median length of career of 4 years seems to be a more representative description of women's careers as novelists."

6 None of these four women depended solely upon her pen for her livelihood. Burney had a £100-a-year annuity from the Queen and the help of influential friends to advance the subscription publication of *Camilla*, and later there was the income, such as it was, from her husband's employment. Maria Edgeworth had family money. Ferrier had an independent income. Hannah More ran a successful school, had a small annuity of £200 a year, and, like Burney, had powerful friends to forward her literary career. She left a fortune of around £30,000 derived from her various enterprises. For information on More's fortune, see Mary Alden Hopkins, *Hannah More and Her Circle* (New York and Toronto: Longman, Green and Co., 1947), p. 276.

7 Marilyn Butler, *Maria Edgeworth: A Literary Biography* (Oxford: Clarendon Press, 1972), pp. 492–93.

8 Judith Phillips Stanton, "Charlotte Smith's 'Literary Business': Income, Patronage, and Indigence," *The Age of Johnson*, ed. Paul Korshin (New York: AMS Press, 1987), pp. 389–90.

9 Jane Aikin Hodge, "Jane Austen and Her Publishers," *Jane Austen: Bicentenary Essays*, ed. John Halperin (Cambridge University Press, 1975), pp. 75–85.

10 John Halperin, *The Life of Jane Austen* (Baltimore: The Johns Hopkins

University Press, 1984), p. 326. Jan Fergus, *Jane Austen: A Literary Life*, calculates that in Austen's lifetime she received around £630, and that from posthumous sales the total earnings after her death came to £1,625 17s 1d. Austen's father, according to Fergus, was worth about £600 a year (pp. 171, 193).

11 Burney sold the copyright of *Evelina* to Lowndes for 20 guineas, a fair price for a first novel by an unknown writer, but a hard fate for the author. "Oh, ma'am, what a book thrown away was that!" the owner of a circulating library in Brighton, not aware of her identity, told Burney: "All the trade cry shame on Lowndes. Not, ma'am, that I expected he could have known its worth, because that's out of the question; but when its profits told him what it was, it's quite scandalous that he should have done nothing! quite ungentlemanlike indeed!" Letter to Susanna Burney, 12 October 1771, *Diary and Letters of Madame D'Arblay*, ed. Austin Dobson, 6 vols. (London: Macmillan and Co., 1904), I, 281.

12 Mary Robinson went to debtors' prison with her husband where she, "did all the work of the prison apartment, including the scouring of floors, and undertook literary hackwork her husband was too grand to accept." From L. M. Hawkins, *Anecdotes and Biographical Sketches* (1822); cited by Ida Beatrice O'Malley, *Women in Subjection: a Study of the Lives of Englishwomen Before 1832* (London: Duckworth, 1933), p. 80.

13 More assumed all the expenses herself for *Coelebs* (1809), saw eleven editions in nine months, and claimed that though she spent £5,000 in publishing the novel, she cleared £2,000 and, moreover, retained the copyright to herself. A brilliant achievement, but one dependent upon having enough capital to mount such an ambitious project, a condition rare indeed for a woman author. See the *Dictionary of National Biography*.

14 Royal Literary Fund, case number 435, May 1821. The Royal Literary Fund, a private charity constituted in 1788 for the aid of indigent authors, assigned each applicant for aid a case number under which all correspondence pertaining to the applicant was filed. See Nigel Cross, *The Royal Literary Fund, 1790–1918* (London: World Microfilms Publications, 1984), for an account of the cataloging of applicants.

15 Dorothy Blakey, *The Minerva Press, 1790–1820* (Oxford: the Bibliographical Society, at the University Press, 1939), pp. 77–78.

16 Blakey, *The Minerva Press*, p. 76.

17 Royal Literary Fund, case number 317, 14 Feb. 1812.

18 A further disadvantage of commission publishing was that an author could not predict her income. With profit-sharing, she had to wait at least a year from the time of publication for distribution of the profits. I am much indebted to Jan Fergus for making clear to me the subtle differences in an author's choice of routes to publication and for sharing with me the histories of Amelia Opie's and Mary Robinson's publishing careers with Longman.

19 Letter to Thomas Cadell, Jr. and William Davies, 14 May 1799. Beinecke Rare Book and Manuscript Library, Yale University, New Haven, Connecticut.
20 Quoted by Blakey, *The Minerva Press*, pp. 75–76.
21 Royal Literary Fund, case number 155, June 1804.
22 *A Series of Letters* (Edinburgh: printed for the Author, and sold by C. Elliot, 1789), II, 151–52.
23 Jean Marishall, *A Series of Letters*, II, 157.
24 Charles Lamb, quoted by Arthur Simons Collins, *The Profession of Letters: A Study of the Relation of Author to Patron, Publisher, and Public, 1780–1832* (New York: Dutton, 1929), pp. 11–12.
25 Royal Literary Fund, case number 12, 20 Jan. 1802.
26 Royal Literary Fund, case number 256, 16 Jan. 1815.
27 Royal Literary Fund, case number 35, 9 Oct. 1795.
28 Royal Literary Fund, case number 35, 30 Aug. 1797.
29 Royal Literary Fund, case number 25, 8 Oct. 1796.
30 Royal Literary Fund, case number 97, 20 Oct. 1803.
31 This was partly because they lived fashionable lives in London, but also because of the relatively small and fixed number of buyers for their fiction. See Fergus and Thaddeus, "Women, Publishers, and Money, 1790–1820," p. 200.
32 Letter to Mary Hays, 22 October 1798, in *The Fate of the Fenwicks: Letters to Mary Hays (1798–1828)*, ed. A. F. Wedd (London: Methuen & Co. Ltd., 1927).
33 Letter to Mary Hays, 17 December 1802, in *The Fate of the Fenwicks*.
34 Joyce Hemlow, *The History of Fanny Burney* (Oxford: Clarendon Press, 1958), p. 148.
35 Letter to Joseph Cooper Walker, 14 April 1801. Henry E. Huntington Library, HM 10829, San Marino, California.
36 Letter to William Godwin, 3 November 1792. Pforzheimer Library, New York.
37 The Royal Literary Fund, case number 375, 12 Dec. 1821.
38 As widely read as they were, novels rarely brought authors rewards comparable to non-fictional works. Robertson, for example, received £4,500 for his *History of Charles V*; Hume's *History* brought around £5,000; John Hawkesworth was paid £6,000 for his *Account of voyagers ... in the Southern Hemisphere* by Cadell and Davies, Charlotte Smith's publishers; Hugh Blair had £1,100 for his *Sermons*; and William Smellie received 1,000 guineas for his *Philosophy of Natural History*. H. G. Aldis, "Book Production and Distribution, 1625–1800," *The Cambridge History of English Literature*, eds. A. W. Ward and A. R. Waller, 15 vols. (Cambridge University Press, 1953), XI, 326.
39 Susan Ferrier, *Memoir and Correspondence of Susan Ferrier (1782–1854)*, ed. John A. Doyle (London: John Murray, 1898), p. 213.
40 The best account of Charlotte Smith's economic history is by Judith

Phillips Stanton, "Charlotte Smith's 'Literary Business': Income, Patronage, and Indigence," in *The Age of Johnson*, ed. Paul Korshin (New York: AMS Press, 1987), pp. 375–401.

41 Letter to Joseph Cooper Walker, 9 October 1793. The Henry E. Huntington Library, HM 10809, SAN MARINO, CALIFORNIA.

42 Judith Phillips Stanton, "Charlotte Smith's 'Literary Business,'" *Age of Johnson*, pp. 385–88.

43 In this letter, she wrote her friend Sarah Farr Rose, "My house is indeed triste & what is worse, I have embarrassed myself in getting into it, by paying for pictures & having furniture still to pay for. But it has always been my lot to be the victim of circumstance. I could not help it. My family is *such*, that a small house will not hold us – nor a small number of servants suffice" *c.* 1800 (Incorrectly dated. Should be mid-August, 1805. Judith Phillips Stanton.) Henry E. Huntington Library, HM 10825, San Marino, California.

44 Letter to Joseph Cooper Walker, 30 Apr. 1794. Henry E. Huntington Library, HM 10813, San Marino, California.

45 Letter to Joseph Cooper Walker, 16 Oct. 1794. Henry E. Huntington Library, HM 10816, San Marino, California.

46 Letter to Thomas Cadell, Jr. and William Davies, 6 Nov. 1794. Beinecke Rare Book and Manuscript Library, Yale University, New Haven, Connecticut.

47 Letter to Joseph Cooper Walker, 14 Apr. 1801. Henry E. Huntington Library, HM 10829, San Marino, California.

48 "Introduction to Charlotte Smith's Letters," in *Charlotte Smith's Letters*, ed. Judith Phillips Stanton, Indiana University Press, forthcoming.

49 These figures are reported by Blakey in *The Minerva Press*, p. 74.

50 Royal Literary Fund, case number 21: 17 Dec. 1792; 7 July 1796; 30 May 1803.

51 "Preface," to *The History of Miss Meredith* (1790).

52 See entry for Eliza Parsons in *The Feminist Companion to Literature in English*, eds. Virginia Blain, Patricia Clements, Isobel Grundy (London: B. T. Batsford, 1990), and in *A Dictionary of British and American Women Writers, 1660–1800*, ed. Janet Todd (Totowa, New Jersey: Rowman & Allanheld, 1985).

53 Beauclerc's, Brunton's, and Ferrier's fears about the subversive taint attached to female writing were general among women authors. Frances Burney's complex relationship to authorship represents a common dilemma for women, according to Susan C. Greenfield, "'Oh Dear Resemblance of Thy Murdered Mother': Female Authorship in *Evelina*," *Eighteenth-Century Fiction*, 3, no. 4 (July 1991), 301–20: "[A]t the same time that women had more opportunities to publish than ever before, those who published necessarily subverted feminine rules" (p. 318).

54 It seems likely that this passage was written originally for a male

character (Sir Lucius Fitzgerald most probably) and transferred to the younger sister without the necessary alterations for sense and gender.

55 In Lady Morgan's novel *Florence Macarthy* (1818), the respectable Judge Aubrey is likewise surprised to find that Lady Clancare is an author: "I have had opportunities of knowing something of this young lady; but I did not know before that she labours under the *odium* of writing books, for there is certainly no personification of authorship about her – no pretension at all" (III, 111). Note, too, that Lady Morgan's female author is shifted to Ireland, where she still remains a marvel.

56 Lloyd W. Brown, "The Business of Marrying and Mothering," in *Jane Austen's Achievement*, ed. Juliet McMaster (London: Macmillan, 1976), argues that Austen's happy marriages celebrate a moral ideal which "for that very reason is unreal – a felicitous contrivance… Hence the very *unreality* of a happy marriage… becomes a satiric reflection on the very real limitations of society and individuals" (p. 42). In "The Comic Conclusion in Jane Austen's Novels," *PMLA*, 84 (1969), 1582–87, Brown argues that Austen's conclusions "accentuate her own comic form and meaning through implied contrasts with inferior fiction" (p. 1582).

57 Q. D. Leavis, *Fiction and the Reading Public* (London: Chatto & Windus, 1932), p. 140.

58 Jane P. Tompkins, "The Reader in History: The Changing Shape of Literary Response," *Reader-Response Criticism: From Formalism to Post Structuralism*, ed. Jane P. Tompkins (Baltimore: The Johns Hopkins University Press, 1980), p. 226.

Bibliography

SELECTED CONTEMPORARY SOURCES

Adams, Samuel and Sarah, *The Complete Servant* (London: Knight and Lacey, 1825).

Anon., *The Blind Child, Or Anecdotes of the Wyndham Family*, 5th ed. (London: E. Newberry, 1798).

Anon., *Caroline*, 3 vols. (London: Hookham and Carpenter, 1798).

Anon., *The Complete Governess... Intended to Facilitate the Business of Public Establishments, and Abridge the Labour of Private Education* (London: Knight and Lacey, 1826).

Anon., *Craigh-Melrose Priory; Or, Memoirs of the Mount Linton Family. A Novel*, 4 vols. (London: C. Chapple, 1815).

Anon., *Domestic Economy, and Cookery, for Rich and Poor* (London: Longman, Rees, Orme, Brown, and Green, 1827).

Anon., *Economical Cookery, for Young Housekeepers; Or, the Art of Providing Good and Palatable Dishes for a Family Without Extravagance* (London: Harvey and Darton, 1824).

Anon., *Edward and Harriet, Or The Happy Recovery; a Sentimental Novel*, 2 vols. (London: G. Allen, "and may be had at every Circulating Library in the Kingdom," 1788).

Anon., [Improbably attributed to Clara Reeve], *Fanny; or, The Deserted Daughter. A Novel*, 2 vols. (London: printed for J. Bew, 1792).

Anon., [Improbably attributed to Clara Reeve], *Fatherless Fanny; Or A Young Lady's First Entrance Into Life, Being the Memoirs of A Little Mendicant and Her Benefactors* (London: J. Wallis, 1819).

Anon., *The Female Instructor: or Young Woman's Friend & Companion... And Directions to Servants of Every Description* (London: Henry Fisher, Sons, and P. Jackson, 1830).

Anon., *Females of the Present Day, Considered as to Their Influence on Society* (London: John Hatchard and Son, 1831).

Anon., *How to Keep House: Or, Comfort and Elegance on £150 to £200 A-Year. Containing Tables for Marketing*, 7th ed. (London: Thomas Griffiths, 1832).

Anon., *The Invasion; or What Might Have Been. A Novel*, 2 vols. (London: H. D. Symonds, 1798).

252

Anon., *The Ladies' Companion for Visiting the Poor: Consisting of Familiar Addresses, Adapted to Particular Occasions* (London: J. Hatchard, 1813).

Anon., *The Ladies' Library: or, Encyclopedia of Female Knowledge, In every Branch of Domestic Economy*, 2 vols. (London: J. Ridgeway, 1790).

Anon., *The Meteors*, "Number 7" (London: A. and J. Black, 1800).

Anon., *On Monopoly and Reform of Manners* (London, 1795).

Anon., *The New Female Instructor: Or, Young Woman's Guide to Happiness* (London: Thomas Kelly, 1824).

Anon., *The Old Woman's Letter to Her Respected and Valued Friends of the Parish of—* (Barnstaple: "Sold by Messrs. Baldwin, Cradock and Joy of London; W. Syle of Barnstaple," 1819).

Anon., *The Parson's Wife. A Novel*, 2 vols. (London: Printed at the Logographic Press, and sold by J. Walter, 1789).

Anon., *The Pleasures of Benevolence; or, The History of Miss Goodwill; Intended as a Companion to "The Sorrows of Selfishness"* (London: J. Harris, Successor to E. Newberry, 1809).

Anon., *The Quaker. A Novel*, 3 vols. (London: William Lane, 1785).

Anon., *Rainsford Villa, Or Juvenile Independence. A Tale* (London: J. Harris and Son, 1823).

Anon., *Rosemary Lodge; or, Domestic Vicissitudes* (London: T. Harvey [British Library catalogue, 1800?]).

Anon., *Selina, A Novel, Founded on Facts*, 3 vols. (London: C. Law, 1800).

Anon., *The Twin Sisters; Or, The Effects of Education. A Novel in a Series of Letters*, 3 vols. (Dublin: H. Colbert, 1792).

Anon., "To the Unfortunate Female," *The Religious Tract Society* [1810].

Anon., *Woman As She Is, And As She Should Be*, 2 vols. (London: James Cochrane and Co., 1835).

Anon., *The Woman of Colour, A Tale*, 2 vols. (London: Black, Parry and Kingsbury, Booksellers to the Honourable East India Company, 1808).

Anon., *The Woman of Genius*, 3 vols. (London: Longman, Hurst, Rees, Orme, and Brown, 1821).

Anon., *Woman; or Minor Maxims. A Sketch*, 2 vols. (London: A. K. Newman & Co., 1818).

Anon., *Woman, Sketches of the History, Genius, Disposition, Accomplishments, Employments, Customs and Importance of the Fair Sex...* (London: G. Kearsley, 1790).

Anon., *Women As They Are; Or, The Manners of the Day*, 2nd ed., 3 vols. (London: Henry Colburn and Richard Bentley, 1830).

Anon., *The Young Woman's Companion: or, Frugal Housewife* (Manchester: printed by Russell and Allen, 1811).

Austen, Caroline, *Reminiscences of Caroline Austen*, ed. Deirdre Le Faye (Guildford: The Jane Austen Society, 1986).

Austen, Jane. All references are to *The Novels of Jane Austen*, ed. R. W. Chapman, 6 vols., 3rd ed. (Oxford University Press, 1982).

Jane Austen's Letters, ed. R. W. Chapman, 2nd ed. (Oxford University Press, 1979).

Baillie, Joanna, *A Series of Plays In Which It Is Attempted to Delineate The Stronger Passions of the Mind Each Passion Being the Subject of a Tragedy and A Comedy*, 3 vols. (London: T. Cadell, Jun., and W. Davies, 1798).

Ballin, Miss [Rosetta], *The Statue Room; an Historical Tale*, 2 vols. (London: H. D. Symonds, 1790).

Barbauld, Anna Laetitia, *Civic Sermons to the People* (London: J. Johnson, 1792).

Eighteen Hundred and Eleven, A Poem (London: J. Johnson, 1812).

"Epistle to William Wilberforce, Esq. on the Rejection of the Bill for abolishing the Slave Trade" (London: J. Johnson, 1791).

"From Mutual Want Springs Mutual Happiness," from *Civic Sermons to the People*, number II (London: J. Johnson [1792?]).

Lessons for Children from Four to Five Years Old (Wilmington, Delaware: P. Brynberg, 1801).

Barbauld, Anna Laetitia, and John Aikin, *Evenings at Home: Or, the Juvenile Budget Opened* (written 1793–96), 2 vols. (Philadelphia: James Kay, Jun. and brother, 1846).

Barret, Eaton Stannard, *The Heroine, or Adventures of a Fair Romance Reader*, 3 vols. (London: Henry Colburn, 1813).

The Bath Chronicle, January 1800 to December 1803.

Beauclerc, Amelia, *Alinda, or the Child of Mystery. A Novel*, 4 vols. "By the Author of Ora and Juliet, Castle of Tariffa, &c." (London: B. and R. Crosby & Co., 1812).

The Deserter. A Novel, 4 vols. (London: Minerva Press, A. K. Newman, 1817).

Disorder and Order, 3 vols. (London: Minerva Press, A. K. Newman and Co., 1820).

Husband Hunters!!!, 4 vols. (London: Minerva Press, A. K. Newman, 1816).

Montreithe; or The Power of Scotland. A Novel, 4 vols. (London: Minerva Press, A. K. Newman & Co., 1814).

Beckford, William, *Modern Novel Writing, or, the Elegant Enthusiast*, 2 vols. (London: G. G. and J. Robinson, 1796).

Benger, Elizabeth, *The Female Geniad: a Poem "Written at the Age of Thirteen"* (London: T. Hookham and J. Carpenter, and C. and G. Kearsley, 1791).

The Heart and the Fancy; or Valsinore, 2 vols. (London: Longman, Hurst, Rees, Orme, and Brown, 1813).

Memoirs of Elizabeth Stuart, Queen of Bohemia, Daughter of King James I, 2 vols. (London: Longman, Hurst, Rees, Orme, Brown, and Green, 1825).

Memoirs of the Life of Anne Boleyn, 2 vols. (London: Longman, Hurst, Rees, Orme, and Brown, 1821).

Memoirs of the Life of Mary Queen of Scots, 2 vols. (London: Longman, Hurst, Rees, Orme, and Brown, 1823).

Memoirs of Mrs. Elizabeth Hamilton, with a Selection from her Correspondence and Other Unpublished Writing, 2 vols. (London: Longman, Hurst, Rees, Orme, and Brown, 1818).

"A Poem, Occasioned By the Abolition of the Slave Trade in 1806," in *Poems on The Abolition of the Slave Trade* (London: R. Bowyer, 1809).

Bennett, Anna Maria, *Anna; or Memoirs of a Welch Heiress. Interspersed with Anecdotes of a Nabob*, 4 vols. (London: William Lane, 1785).

The Beggar Girl and Her Benefactors, 7 vols. (London: William Lane, at the Minerva Press, 1797).

Ellen, Countess of Castle Howel, 4 vols. (London: William Lane, at the Minerva Press, 1794).

Juvenile Indiscretions. A Novel, 5 vols. (London: W. Lane, 1786).

Vicissitudes Abroad: a Novel, 6 vols. (London: printed at the Minerva Press for Lane, Newman, & Co., 1806).

Bennet [*sic*], Elizabeth [Agnes Maria Bennett, British Library catalogue], *Emily, or The Wife's First Error; and Beauty & Ugliness, or, The Father's Prayer and the Mother's Prophecy. Two Tales*, "By Elizabeth Bennet, Author of *Faith and Fiction*, &c." (London: A. K. Newman & Co., 1819).

Bennett, Elizabeth [A. M. Bennett, British Library catalogue], *Faith and Fiction; or Shining Lights in a Dark Generation: a Novel*, 5 vols. (London: printed at the Minerva Press for A. K. Newman and Co., 1816).

Bonhote, Mrs., *Bungay Castle: a Novel*, 2 vols. (London: William Lane, at the Minerva Press, 1796).

Feeling, Or, Sketches from Life; a Desultory Poem, "By a Lady" (Edinburgh: A. Constable & Co.; London: Longman, Hurst, Rees, & Orme, 1810).

Olivia; or, the Deserted Bride, 3 vols. (London: W. Lane, 1787).

The Parental Monitor, 2 vols. (London: William Lane, 1788).

The Rambles of Mr. Frankly, 2 vols. (Dublin: Messrs. Sleater, *et al.*, 1773).

Brunton, Mary, *Discipline: A Novel*, 3 vols. (Edinburgh: printed by George Ramsay & Co., for Manners and Miller; London: Longman, Hurst, Rees, Orme, and Brown, 1814).

Emmeline. With Some Other Pieces: "To Which is Prefixed A Memoir of Her Life, Including Some Extracts From Her Correspondence" (Edinburgh: Manners and Miller; London: John Murray, 1819).

Self-Control. A Novel, 2nd ed., 3 vols. (Edinburgh: printed by George Ramsay & Co. for Manners and Miller; London: Longman, Hurst, Rees, Orme, and Brown, 1811). The first edition appeared in 1810.

Burney, Frances, *Camilla; or, A Picture of Youth*, 5 vols. (London: T. Payne, 1796).

Cecilia, or Memoirs of an Heiress, 5 vols. (London: T. Payne and Son, and T. Cadell, 1782).

Diary and Letters, ed. Charlotte Barret, 6 vols. (London: Macmillan, 1904).

The Early Diary of Frances Burney, 1768–1778, ed. Annie Raine Ellis, 2 vols. (London: George Bell and Sons, 1889).

Evelina: or the History of a Young Lady's Entrance into the World (London: T.Lowndes, 1778).

The Journals and Letters of Fanny Burney (Madame D'Arblay), ed. Joyce Hemlow, 4 vols. (Oxford: Clarendon Press, 1972).

The Wanderer; or, Female Difficulties, 5 vols. (London: Longman, Hurst, Rees, Orme, and Brown, 1814).

Burney, Sarah Harriet, *Traits of Nature. A Novel*, 6 vols. (London: Henry Colburn, 1812).

Carlisle, the Countess Dowager of, *Thoughts In the Form of Maxims: Addressed to Young Ladies, On Their First Establishment in the World*, 2nd ed. (London: T. Cornell, 1790).

Charlton, Mary, *Grandeur and Meanness; or, Domestic Persecution. A Novel*, 3 vols. (London: A. K. Newman and Co., 1824).

The Parisian; or Genuine Anecdotes of Distinguished and Noble Characters, 2 vols. (London: William Lane, at the Minerva Press, 1794).

Past Events; An Historical Novel of the Eighteenth Century, 3 vols. (London: R. P. Moore, 1824).

Pathetic Poetry for Youth: Calculated to Awaken the Sympathetic Affections (London: Whittingham and Arliss, Juvenile Library, 1815).

Phedora; or The Forest of Minski, 4 vols. (London: William Lane, at the Minerva Press, 1798).

The Wife and the Mistress. A Novel, 4 vols. (London: printed at the Minerva Press, for Lane and Newman, 1802).

Clark, Emily, *Ermina Montrose; or, The Cottage of the Vale*, 3 vols. (London: printed for the Author, and sold by James Wallis, 1800).

The Esquimaux; or Fidelity. A Tale, 3 vols. (London: A. K. Newman & Co., 1819).

Ianthe, or The Flower of Caernarvon, A Novel, 2 vols. "By Emily Clark, Grand-daughter of the Late Colonel Frederick, Son of Theodore, King of Corsica" (London: printed for the Author, and sold by Hookham and Carpenter, 1798).

Poems: Consisting Principally of Ballads (London: F. C. and J. Rivington, 1810).

Cockle, Mrs., *Important Studies For the Female Sex, In Reference to Modern Manners; Addressed to A Young Lady of Distinction* (London: C. Chapple, 1809).

Collier, Jane, *An Essay on the Art of Ingeniously Tormenting* (London: A. Millar, 1753).

Colquhoun, Patrick, *A Treatise on the Police of the Metropolis*, 3rd ed. (London: H. Fry and C. Dilly, 1796).

Cullen, Margaret, *Home. A Novel*, 5 vols. (London: J. Mawman; York: T. Wilson, and R. Spence, 1802).

Mornton. A Novel, 3rd ed., 3 vols. (London: Saunders and Otley, 1829).

Darwin, Erasmus, *A Plan for the Conduct of Female Education in Boarding Schools* (Derby: Printed by J. Drewry for J. Johnson, London, 1797).

Davenport, Selina, *An Angel's Form and a Devil's Heart*, 4 vols. (London: A. K. Newman, Minerva Press, 1818).

Donald Monteith, The Handsomest Man of the Age. A Novel, 5 vols. (London: A. K. Newman, Minerva Press, 1815).

The Hypocrite; or The Modern Janus, 5 vols. (London: A. K. Newman, Minerva Press, 1814).

Leap Year; or Woman's Privilege, 5 vols. (London: A. K. Newman, Minerva Press, 1817).

The Sons of the Viscount, and the Daughters of the Earl. A Novel, 4 vols. (London: Henry Colburn, 1813).

Edgeworth, Maria, *Belinda* [1st ed. 1801], 2nd ed. (London: J. Johnson, 1802).

Castle Rackrent (London: J. Johnson, 1800).

Moral Tales for Young People, 2 vols. (London: J. Johnson, 1801).

The Parent's Assistant, or Stories for Children (London: J. Johnson, 1796).

Patronage, 2nd ed., 4 vols. (London: J. Johnson, 1814).

Tales from Fashionable Life, 3 vols. (London: J. Johnson, 1809).

Tales from Fashionable Life, 6 vols. (London: J. Johnson, 1812).

[Fenwick, Eliza] Rev. David Blair, *The Class Book: or Three Hundred and Sixty-Five Reading Lessons, adapted to the Use of Schools for Every Day in the Year. Selected and Arranged from the Best Authors* (London: Richard Phillips, 1806).

Fenwick, Eliza, *The Fate of the Fenwicks: Letters to Mary Hays (1798–1828)*, "Edited by her Great-Great-Niece," A. F. Wedd (London: Methuen & Co. Ltd., 1927).

Lessons for Children: or, Rudiments of Good Manners, Morals, and Humanity, "a new edition" (London: M. J. Godwin, at the Juvenile Library, 1811).

Ferrier, Susan, *The Inheritance*, 2nd ed., 3 vols. (Edinburgh: Blackwood; London: T. Cadell, 1825).

Marriage (Edinburgh: Blackwood, 1818).

Memoir and Correspondence of Susan Ferrier (1782–1854), ed. John A. Doyle (London: John Murray, 1898).

Fielding, Sarah, *The Adventures of David Simple* (London: A. Millar, 1744).

Fitz John, Matilda, *Joan!!! A Novel*, 4 vols. (London: Hookham and Carpenter, 1796).

de Genlis, Madame, *Adelaide and Theodore; or, Letters on Education*, 3 vols. (London: C. Bathurst, and T. Cadell, 1783).

Alphonsine: or Maternal Affection, 2nd ed., 4 vols. (London: J. F. Hughes, 1807).

Alphonso; or, The Natural Son, 3 vols. (London: printed for Henry Colburn, English and Foreign Library, 1809).

The Child of Nature. A Dramatic Piece in Four Acts (London: G. G. J. and J. Robinson, 1788).

The Knights of the Swan; or The Court of Charlemagne: an Historical and Moral Tale (London: J. Johnson, 1796).

Lessons of a Governess to her Pupils, "Published by Herself," 3 vols. (London: printed for G. G. J. and J. Robinson, 1792).

The New Aera; Or, Adventures of Julien Delmour: Related by Himself, 4 vols. (London: Henry Colburn, 1819).

The Rival Mothers, 2 vols. (Dublin: printed for G. Burnet, *et al.*, 1801).

Sainclair, Or the Victim of the Arts and Sciences, A Novel, 2 vols. (Georgetown, D. of C.: Richards and Mallory, November 1813).

A Selection from the Annals of Virtue of Madame Sillery (Bath: printed by S. Hazard, for the Author, 1794).

The Siege of Rochelle; Or, The Christian Heroine, 3 vols. (London: printed by Cox, Son, and Baylis, for B. Dulau, 1808).

The Young Exiles, or, Correspondence of Some Juvenile Emigrants (London: J. Wright and H. D. Symonds, 1799).

Gomersall, Ann, *The Citizen, A Novel*, "By Mrs. Gomersall of Leeds, Author of *Eleanor*," 2 vols. (London: Scatcherd & Whitaker, 1790). Includes a list of English subscribers and a separate list of Jamaican subscribers.

Eleanora, A Novel, In a Series of Letters, Written By a Female Inhabitant of Leeds in Yorkshire, 2 vols. (London: printed for the Authoress by the Literary Society at the Logographic Press [Brit. Library d. 1789]).

Gooch, Elizabeth Sarah, *An Appeal to the Public, On the Conduct of Mrs. Gooch, the Wife of William Gooch, Esq.*, "Written by Herself" (London: G. Kearsley, 1788).

The Beggar Boy, A Novel, 3 vols. "By the Late Mr. Thomas Bellamy," 3 vols. (London: Earle and Hemet, 1801).

The Life of Mrs. Gooch, "Written by Herself. Dedicated to the Public," 3 vols. (London: printed for the Authoress, sold by C. and G. Kearsley, 1792).

Poems on Various Subjects (London: J. Bell, at the British Library, 1793).

Sherwood Forest; or, Northern Adventures. A Novel, 3 vols. (London: S. Highley, 1804).

The Wanderings of the Imagination, 2 vols. (London: B. Crosby, 1796).

Grant, Anne, *Letters from the Mountains, being the real correspondence of a Lady, between the years 1773–1807*, 3 vols. (London: Longman, Hurst, Rees, & Orme, 1807).

Memoirs of an American Lady: with Sketches and Scenery in America, As They Existed Previous to the Revolution, 2 vols. (London: Longman, Hurst, Rees, and Orme, 1808).

Green, Sarah, *The Festival of St. Jago. A Spanish Romance*, 2 vols. (London: printed at the Minerva Press for A. K. Newman and Co., 1810).

The Fugitive, or Family Incidents, 3 vols. (London: Black, Parry, & Co., 1814).

Gretna Green Marriages; or The Neices [sic], A Novel, 3 vols. (London: A. K. Newman, 1823).

Mental Improvement for a Young Lady, on Her Entrance into the World; *Addressed to A Favourite Niece* (London: William Lane, at the Minerva Press, 1793).

Parents and Wives; or, Inconsistency and Mistakes. A Novel, 3 vols. (London: A. K. Newman & Co., 1825).

The Reformist!!! A Serio-Comic Political Novel, 2 vols. (London: printed at the Minerva Press for A. K. Newman and Co., 1810).

The Royal Exile; or Victims of Human Passion, 4 vols. (London: Joseph Stockdale, 1811).

Scotch Novel Reading; or Modern Quackery. "A Novel Really Founded on Facts" (London: A. K. Newman, 1824).

Who is the Bridegroom? or, Nuptial Discoveries. A Novel, 3 vols. (London: A. K. Newman & Co., 1822).

Gregory, John, *A Father's Legacy to His Daughters* (1774).

Griffith, Elizabeth, *Essays Addressed to Young Married Women* (1782).

Gunning, Elizabeth [later Plunkett], *The Exile of Erin, A Novel*, 3 vols. (London: T. Plummer, 1808).

Malvina, "By Madame C**** [Cottin] ... Translated from the French, by Miss Gunning," 4 vols. (London: T. Hurst, *et al.*, 1804).

The Man of Fashion: a Tale of Modern Times, 2 vols. (London: M. Jones, 1815).

The Packet: a Novel, 4 vols. (London: J. Bell, 1794).

Gunning, Susannah, *Delves, a Welch Tale*, 3rd ed., 2 vols. (London: Lackington, Allen, and Co., 1797).

Fashionable Involvements: a Novel, 2nd ed., 3 vols. (London: Longman and Rees, 1800).

Gunning, Susannah and Margaret [sisters], *The Histories of Lady Frances S—, and Lady Caroline S—*, "Written by the Miss Minifies, of Fairwater, in Somersetshire," 4 vols. (London: R. and J. Dodsley, 1763).

Hamilton, Elizabeth, *The Cottagers of Glenburnie; a Tale for the Farmer's Ingle-Nook* (Edinburgh: printed by James Ballantyne and Co. for Manners and Miller, 1808).

Letters Addressed to the Daughter of a Nobleman, on the Formation of Religious and Moral Principles, 2nd ed., 2 vols. (London: T. Cadell and W. Davies, 1806).

Letters on the Elementary Principles of Education, 2nd ed. (Bath: printed by R. Cruttwell for G. G. & J. Robinson, London, 1801).

Memoirs of the Late Mrs. Elizabeth Hamilton. With a Selection from her Correspondence and other Unpublished Writings, "By Miss Bengur," 2 vols. (London: Longman, Hurst, Rees, Orme and Brown, 1818).

Memoirs of Modern Philosophers, 2 vols. (Bath: printed by R. Cruttwell, for G. G. and J. Robinson, London, 1800).

Translation of the Letters of a Hindoo Rajah; written Previous to, and During a Period of Residence in England, 2 vols. (London: G. G. and J. Robinson, 1796).

Hanway, Jonas, *Domestic Happiness, Promoted in a Series of Discourses From a Father to His Daughter, on Occasion of her Going into Service* (London: Dodsley, 1786).

Thoughts on the Plan for a Magdalen-House for Repentant Prostitutes, 2nd ed. (London: J. and R. Dodsley; James Waugh, 1759).

Hanway, Mary Ann, *Andrew Stuart, or the Northern Wanderer. A Novel*, 4 vols. (London: William Lane, at the Minerva Press, 1800).

Christabelle, The Maid of Rouen. A Novel, Founded on Facts, 4 vols. (London: Longman, Rees, Orme, and Brown, 1814).

Ellinor; or, The World As It Is. A Novel, 4 vols. (London: William Lane, at the Minerva Press, 1798).

Falconbridge Abbey. A Devonshire Story, 5 vols. (London: Lane, Newman & Co., at the Minerva Press, 1809).

Hawkins, Laetitia Matilda, *Rosanne; or a Father's Labour Lost*, 3 vols. (London: F. C. and J. Rivington, 1814).

[Hays, Mary] Eusebia, *Cursory Remarks on an Enquiry into the Expediency and Propriety of Public or Social Worship*, 2nd ed. (London: T. Knott, 1792).

Hays, Mary, *Female Biography; or Memoirs of Illustrious and Celebrated Women, of all Ages and Countries*, 6 vols. (London: Richard Phillips, 1803).

Letters and Essays, Moral, and Miscellaneous (London: T. Knott, 1793).

The Love Letters of Mary Hays (1779–1780) ed. A. F. Wedd [her great-great niece] (London: Methuen, 1927).

Memoirs of Emma Courtney, 2 vols. (London: G. and J. Robinson, 1796).

Hofland, Barbara, *A Father As He Should Be* (London: Minerva Press, A. K. Newman, 1815).

Hunter, Rachel, *Family Annals: or, Worldly Wisdom. A Novel*, 5 vols. (London: J. Hughes, 1808).

Lady Maclairn, the Victim of Villany [*sic*], 4 vols. (London: W. Earle and J. W. Hucklebridge, 1806).

Letters from Mrs. Palmerstone to her Daughter, 3 vols. (Norwich: W. Robberts; sold by Longman and Rees, London, 1803).

The Schoolmistress; a Moral Tale for Young Ladies, 2 vols. (London: A. K. Newman and Co., at the Minerva Press, 1811).

Imlay, Gilbert, *The Emigrants, &c. or the History of An Expatriated Family, being a Delineation of English Manners, Drawn from Real Characters* (Dublin: C. Brown, 1794).

Inchbald, Elizabeth, *Nature and Art*, 2 vols. (London: G. G. and J. Robinson, 1796).

A Simple Story, 4 vols. (London: G. G. and J. Robinson, 1791).

Kelly, Isabella [afterwards Hedgeland], *The Baron's Daughter*, 4 vols. (London: J. Bell, 1802).

Instructive Anecdotes for Youth (London: printed by Weed and Rider, for G. and W. B. Whittaker, 1819).

A Modern Incident in Domestic Life, 2 vols. (Brentford: printed by and for P. Norbury, 1803).

The Ruins of Avondale Priory, 3 vols. (London: William Lane, at the Minerva Press, 1796).

The Secret. A Novel, 4 vols. (Brentford: P. Norbury, 1805).

King, Sophia, *The Fatal Secret, or Unknown Warrior: A Romance of the Twelfth Century* (London: printed for the Author, 1801).

Waldorf; or The Dangers of Philosophy, A Philosophical Tale, 2 vols. (London: G. G. and J. Robinson, 1798).

Knight, Ellis Cornelia, *The Autobiography of Miss Knight*, ed. Roger Fulford (London: William Kimber, 1960).

Dinarbas; a Tale: Being a Continuation of Rasselas, Prince of Abissinia (London: C. Dilly, 1790).

Marcus Flaminius; or, A View of the Military, Political, and Social Life of the Romans: In a series of letters from a Patrician to his Friend, 2 vols. (London: C. Dilly, 1792).

Lackington, James, *The Confessions of James Lackington in a series of letters to a friend* (London, 1804).

Lee, Harriet, *Canterbury Tales for the Year 1797* (London: G. G. and J. Robinson, 1797).

The Errors of Innocence, 5 vols. (London: printed for G. G. J. and J. Robinson, 1786).

Lee, Sophia, *Almeyda; Queen of Granada*, "A Tragedy in Five Acts..." (London: printed by W. Woodfall for Messrs. Cadell and Davies, 1796).

A Hermit's Tale, "Recorded by his Own Hand and Found in His Cell," 2nd ed. (London: T. Cadell, 1787).

The Life of a Lover, "In a Series of Letters," 6 vols. (London: G. & J. Robinson, 1804).

The Recess; Or, a Tale of Other Times, "By the Author of the Chapter of Accidents," 3 vols. (London: T. Cadell, 1785).

Lennox, Charlotte, *Euphemia*, 4 vols. (London: T. Cadell, J. Evans, 1790).

The Female Quixote, 2nd ed. (London: A. Millar, 1752).

Henrietta, 2 vols. (London: A. Millar, 1758).

The History of Sir George Warrington; or, the Political Quixote, 3 vols. (London: J. Bell, 1797).

Sophia (London: James Fletcher, 1762).

Luckcock, James, *Hints for Practical Economy* (Birmingham: James Drake; and London: Longman, Rees, Orme, Brown, and Green, 1834).

Macaulay, Catharine, *An Address to the People of England, Scotland, and Ireland on the Present Important Crisis of Affairs* (Bath: printed by R. Cruttwell, for Edward and Charles Dilly, London, 1775).

Letters on Education (London: C. Dilly, 1790).

"A Modest Plea for the Property of Copyright" (Bath: printed by R. Cruttwell, for Edward and Charles Dilly, London, 1774).

"Observations on the Reflections of the Right Hon. Edmund Burke on the *Revolution in France* In a Letter to the Right Hon. the Earl of Stanhope" (London: C. Dilly, 1790).

Mackenzie, Anna Maria, *The Gamesters. A Novel*, 3 vols. (London: printed by H. D. Steel and sold by R. Baldwin, 1786).

Martin & Mansfeldt, or The Romance of Franconia, 3 vols. (London: Lane and Newman, at the Minerva Press, 1802).

Mysteries Elucidated. A Novel, 3 vols. (London: William Lane, at the Minerva Press, 1795).

Marishall, Jean, *The History of Miss Clarinda Cathcart and Miss Fanny Renton*, 2 vols. (London: printed by W. Haggard for Francis Noble; and John Noble, 1766).

A Series of Letters (Edinburgh: printed for the Author, and sold by C. Elliot, 1789).

Meeke, Mary, *Conscience. A Novel*, 4 vols. (London: A. K. Newman & Co., at the Minerva Press, 1814).

Ellesmere. A Novel (London: William Lane, at the Minerva Press, 1799).

Midnight Weddings. A Novel, 3 vols. (London: William Lane, at the Minerva Press, 1802).

The Spanish Campaign; or The Jew. A Novel, 3 vols. (London: A. K. Newman, at the Minerva Press, 1815).

There Is a Secret, Find it Out! A Novel, 4 vols. (London: Lane, Newman, and Co., at the Minerva Press, 1808).

The Veiled Protectress; or, The Mysterious Mother, 5 vols. (London: A. K. Newman, at the Minerva Press, 1819).

What Shall Be, Shall Be. A Novel, 4 vols. (London: A. K. Newman, 1823).

Which Is the Man? A Novel, 4 vols. (London: William Lane, at the Minerva Press, 1801).

Moir, John, *Female Tuition; or, An Address to Mothers, on the Education of Daughters* (London: J. Murray, 1784).

More, Hannah, *Cheap Repository Tracts, 1795–98* (London: R. White; Bath: S. Hazard; Edinburgh: J. Elder, 1795–98).

Cheap Repository Tracts; Entertaining, Moral, and Religious, vol. 1 (London: printed by Law and Gilbert, and sold by F. C. & J. Rivington, 1812).

Coelebs In Search of a Wife, "Comprehending Observations on Domestic Habits and Manners, Religion and Morals," 3rd ed., 2 vols. (London: T. Cadell and W. Davies, 1809).

Essays on Various Subjects, Principally designed for Young Ladies (London: J. Wilkie and T. Cadell, 1777).

Hints to All Ranks of People (London: J. Marshall and R. White, 1795).

Strictures on the Modern System of Female Education with a View of the Principles and Conduct Prevalent Among Women of Rank and Fortune, 7th ed., 2 vols. (London: printed by A. Strahan for T. Cadell Jun. and W. Davies, 1799).

Thoughts on the Importance of the Manners of the Great to General Society (London: T. Cadell, 1788).

"The Way to Plenty; or, the Second Part of Tom White," in *Cheap Repository Tracts Published during the Year 1795*, vol. 1 (London: J. Marshal, 1795 [?]).

Morgan, Sydney (Lady Owenson), *Florence Macarthy*, 4 vols. (London: Henry Colburn, 1818).

Murray, Hugh, *Morality of Fiction; Or, An Inquiry into The Tendency of Fictitious Narratives, With Observations on Some of the Most Eminent* (Edinburgh: printed by Mundell and Son, for Longman, Hurst, Rees, and Orme, London; and A. Constable and Co. and J. Anderson, Edinburgh, 1805).

Musgrave, Agnes, *The Solemn Injunction. A Novel*, 4 vols. (London: William Lane, at the Minerva Press, 1798).

Opie, Amelia Alderson, *Adeline Mowbray, or the Mother and Daughter: A Tale*, 3 vols. (London: Longman, Hurst, Rees, & Orme, 1805).

The Black Man's Lament; or, How To Make Sugar (London: Harvey & Darton, 1826).

The Father and the Daughter: A Tale in Prose, 2nd ed. (London: Longman and Rees, 1801).

Happy Faces; or, Benevolence and Selfishness, and The Revenge (London: S. O. Beeton, [1830?]).

Madeline, A Tale, 2 vols. (London: Longman, Hurst, Rees, Orme, and Brown, 1822).

Poems (London: T. N. Longman and O. Rees, 1802).

Tales of the Heart, 4 vols. (London: Longman, Hurst, Rees, Orme, and Brown, 1820).

Tales of the Pemberton Family (London: Harvey & Darton, 1825).

Tales of Real Life, 3 vols. (London: Longman, Rees, Orme, and Brown, 1813).

Valentine's Eve, 3 vols. (London: Longman, Hurst, Rees, Orme, and Brown, 1816).

Parsons, Eliza, *Castle of Wolfenbach* (1793), ed. Devendra P. Varma (London: The Folio Press, 1968). Citations are to this edition.

The History of Miss Meredith; A Novel, 2 vols. (London: "Printed for the Author," and sold by T. Hookham, 1790).

The Intrigues of a Morning, "In Two Acts. As Performed at Covent Garden. By Mrs. Parsons*, Author of the Errors of Education, and Miss Meredith" (London: William Lane, 1792).

Love and Gratitude; or, Traits of the Human Heart. "Six Novels translated From Augustus La Fontaine," 3 vols. (Brentford: printed by and for P. Norbury, 1804).

Lucy: A Novel, "In Three Volumes. By Mrs. Parsons." (London: William Lane, at the Minerva Press, 1794).

The Miser and His Family, 4 vols. (Brentford: printed by and for P. Norbury, 1800).

Murray House. "*A Plain Unvarnished Tale*", 3 vols. (Brentford: printed by and for P. Norbury, 1804).

The Mysterious Warning: A German Tale "In Four Volumes" (1796), ed. Devendra P. Varma (London: The Folio Press, 1968).

The Voluntary Exile, 5 vols. (London: William Lane, at the Minerva Press, 1795).

Pennington, Lady Sarah, *An Unfortunate Mother's Advice to her Absent Daughters* (1761).

Pilkington, Mary, *Biography For Girls; or, Moral and Instructive Examples, for Young Ladies* (London: Vernor and Hood, 1799).

The Calendar; or Monthly Recreations: "Chiefly Consisting of Dialogues Between an Aunt and her Nieces, Designed to Inspire the Juvenile Mind With a Love of Virtue, And the Study of Nature" (London: J. Harris, successor to E. Newberry, 1807).

Celebrity; or The Unfortunate Choice. A Novel, 3 vols. "By Mrs. Pilkington, Author of Crimes and Characters; Sinclair, or the Mysterious Orphan; Novice, or the Heir of Montgomery Castle, &c. &c." (London: A. K. Newman and Co., 1815).

Crimes and Characters; or, The New Foundling, 3 vols. (London: W. Earle and J. W. Hucklebridge, 1805).

The Disgraceful Effects of Falsehood, and the Fruits of Early Indulgence; exemplified in the Histories of Percival Pembroke, and Augustus Fitzhue (London: J. Harris, successor to E. Newberry, 1807).

Historical Beauties for Young Ladies, "Intended to Lead the Female Mind to the Love and Practice of Moral Goodness. Designed principally for the use of Ladies' Schools" (Dublin: printed by W. Porter, 1800).

The History of the Rockinghams. Interspersed with a Description of the Inhabitants of Russia, and a variety of Interesting Anecdotes of Peter the Great, "By Mrs. Pilkington, Author of The Ill-fated Mariner; Sinclair; Crimes and Characters, &c." (London: A. K. Newman and Co., at the Minerva Press, 1812).

"Memoirs of Mrs. Pilkington," *The Lady's Monthly Museum*, [signed by "C"], vol. 12, number 8 (August 1812).

Mentorial Tales, for the Instruction of Young Ladies Just Leaving School and Entering Upon the Theatre of Life (London: J. Harris, 1802).

A Mirror for the Female Sex: Historical Beauties for Young Ladies. Intended to Lead the Female Mind to the Love and Practice of Moral Goodness. Designed principally for the Use of Ladies' Schools (London: Vernor and Hood, 1798; also Dublin: W. Porter, 1800).

New Tales of the Castle; or The Noble Emigrants, a Story of Modern Times, 2nd ed. (London: J. Harris, 1803).

Obedience Rewarded, and Prejudice Conquered; or the History of Mortimer Lascelles, "Written for the instruction and amusement of young people" (London: Vernor & Hood, 1797).

"On the Mortification Arising From a Reverse of Fortune," *Miscellaneous Poems*, "Dedicated By Permission to Her Grace The Dutchess [*sic*] of

Marlborough," 2 vols. (London: T. Cadell, Jun. and W. Davies, 1796).

Original Poems (London: printed for the Author and sold by Vernor, Hood, and Sharpe, 1811).

A Reward for Attentive Studies; or, Moral and Entertaining Stories (London: J. and E. Wallis [n.d.]).

The Shipwreck; or Misfortune the Inspirer of Virtuous Sentiments (London: William Darton, Jun., 1819).

The Sorrows of Caesar; or the Adventures of a Foundling Dog (London: G. and J. Robinson, 1813).

Tales of the Cottage; or Stories, Moral and Amusing, for Young Persons, "Written on the Plan of that celebrated work, Les Veillees du Chateau, By Madame la Comptesse de Genlis" (London: Vernor and Hood, 1798).

Tales of the Hermitage, "Written for the Instruction and Amusement of the RISING GENERATION" (London: Vernor and Hood, 1798).

Violet Vale; or, Saturday Night (Dublin: printed by William Watson, 1805).

Pinchard, Elizabeth, *Family Affection. A Tale for Youth* (Taunton: J. W. Marriott and sold by Longman, Hurst, *et al.* in London, 1816).

The Ward of Delamere. A Tale, "Inscribed, by Permission to Mrs. G. A. Robinson," 3 vols. (London: Black, Parry, & Co., "Booksellers to the East India Company," 1815).

The Young Countess: A Tale for Youth (London: C. Chapple; sold also by J. Harris & Son, 1820).

Plumptre, Annabella, *Stories For Children,* "Intended to Be Read or Recited to them in the Early Periods of Infancy" (London: J. Mawman, 1804).

Plumptre, Anne, *The History of Myself and My Friend: A Novel,* 4 vols. (London: Henry Colburn, 1813).

Narrative of a Residence in Ireland During the Summer of 1814, and that of 1815 (London: Henry Colburn, 1817).

A Narrative of A Three Years' Residence in France, 3 vols. (London: J. Mawman, 1810).

The Rector's Son, 3 vols. (London: Lee and Hurst, 1798).

Something New; Or, Adventures at Campbell-House, 3 vols. (London: printed by A. Strahan…for T. N. Longman and O. Rees, 1801).

Porter, Anna Maria, *Don Sebastian; or The House of Braganza: An Historical Romance,* 4 vols. (London: Longman, Hurst, Rees, and Orme, 1809).

The Fast of St. Magdalen: A Romance, 3 vols. (London: Longman, Hurst, Rees, Orme, and Brown, 1818).

Honor O'Hara. A Novel, 3 vols. (London: Longman, Rees, Orme, Brown, and Green, 1826).

The Hungarian Brothers, 2nd ed., 3 vols. (London: Longman, Hurst, Rees, and Orme, 1808).

Lake of Killarney (1804). A "new edition" (London: Thomas Tegg, 1836).

Walsh Colville: Or, A Young Man's First Entrance Into Life. A Novel (London: Lee and Hurst, 1797).

Radcliffe, Ann, *The Castles of Athlin and Dunbayne, A Highland Story* (London: T. Hookham, 1789). Modern edition, "Foreword" by Frederick Shroyer (New York: Arno Press, 1972). Citations are to this edition.

Gaston De Blondeville: Or The Court of Henry III Keeping Festival in Ardenne. A Romance, written 1802 (London: Henry Colburn, 1826).

The Italian, or The Confessional of the Black Penitents. A Romance (London: Thomas Cadell, Jun., and W. Davies, 1797). Modern edition, ed. Frederick Garber (Oxford University Press, 1981).

The Mysteries of Udolpho (London: G. G. and J. Robinson, 1794). Modern edition, ed. Bonamy Dobree (Oxford University Press, 1970).

The Romance of the Forest (London: T. Hookham and J. Carpenter, 1791). Modern edition, ed. Chloe Chard (Oxford University Press, 1986).

Radcliffe, Mary Ann, *Manfrone Or The One-Handed Monk. A Romance* (London: J. F. Hughes, 1809). Page references to "The Third Edition," 4 vols. (London: A. K. Newman and Co., 1828). Photo reproduction, ed. Coral Ann Howells (New York: Arno Press, 1972).

The Memoirs of Mrs. Mary Ann Radcliffe. In Familiar Letters to Her Female Friend (Edinburgh: printed for the Author, and sold by Manners and Miller, 1810).

Reeve, Clara, *The Exiles; or, Memoirs of the Count de Cronstadt*, "Author of Old English Baron, Two Mentors, &c. &c." 3 vols. (London: T. Hookham, 1788).

The Old English Baron, 2nd ed. (London: E. and C. Dilly, 1778). First published, 1777, as *The Champion of Virtue. A Gothic Story*.

Original Poems on Several Occasions (London: printed for T. & J. W. Pasham, for W. Harris, 1769).

Plans of Education; With Remarks on the Systems of Other Writers In a Series of Letters Between Mrs. Darnford and Her Friends (London: T. Hookham and J. Carpenter, 1792).

The School for Widows. A Novel, 3 vols. (London: Hookham, *et al.*, 1791).

Robinson, Mary, *The Natural Daughter*, 2 vols. (London: T. N. Longman, 1799).

Walsingham; Or, The Pupil of Nature, 2nd ed., 4 vols. (London: Minerva Press, for Lane, Newman & Co., 1805).

Robinson, Miss M. E. [Maria Elizabeth, daughter of Mary], *The Shrine of Bertha. A Novel, in a Series of Letters*, 2 vols. (London: printed for the author, by W. Lane at the Minerva Press, 1794).

Robinson, Mary Darby, *Memoirs of Mrs. Robinson*, "*Perdita*" (London: Gibbings and Co., 1895).

[Rundell, Maria Eliza], "By a Lady," *A New System of Domestic Cookery: Formed Upon Principles of Economy* (London: John Murray, 1818).

Sleath, Mrs. [Eleanor], *The Nocturnal Minstrel; or, The Spirit of the Wood. A Romance* (London: Minerva Press, A. K. Newman and Company, 1810).

The Orphan of the Rhine (London: Minerva Press, 1798). Modern edition, ed. Devendra Varma (London: The Folio Press, 1968).

Smith, Adam, *An Inquiry Into the Nature and Causes of The Wealth of Nations* (1776), 2 vols., ed. Edwin Cannan, first published 1904 (University of Chicago Press, 1976).

Smith, Charlotte, *The Banished Man. A Novel*, 4 vols. (London: T. Cadell, Jun. and W. Davies, 1794).

Beachy Head: With Other Poems (London: printed for the author; and sold by J. Johnson, 1807).

Celestina: A Novel, 4 vols. (London: T. Cadell, 1791).

Desmond: A Novel, 2 vols. (Dublin: F. Wogan, *et al.*, 1792).

The Emigrants, a Poem, "in Two Books" (London: printed for T. Cadell, 1793).

Emmeline, The Orphan of the Castle, 4 vols. (London: T. Cadell, 1788). Modern edition, ed. Anne Henry Ehrenpreis (London and Oxford: Oxford University Press, 1971).

Ethelinde, or the Recluse of the Lake [first edition, 1789], 2nd ed., 5 vols. (London: T. Cadell, 1790).

Marchmont. A Novel, 4 vols. (London: printed by and for Sampson Low, 1796).

Minor Morals, Interspersed with Sketches of Natural History, Historical Anecdotes, and Original Stories (Dublin: printed by H. Colbert, 1800).

Montalbert. A Novel, 3 vols. (London: printed by S. Low, for E. Booker, 1795).

The Old Manor House, 4 vols. (London: J. Bell, 1793). Modern edition (Oxford University Press, 1969).

The Wanderings of Warwick (London: J. Bell, 1794).

"What Is She? A Comedy in Five Acts" (1799). Holograph copy, Henry E. Huntington Library, San Marino, California.

The Young Philosopher. A Novel, 4 vols. (London: T. Cadell, Jun. and W. Davies, 1798).

Spence, Thomas, *The Rights of Infants; or, the Imprescriptable Right of Mothers to Such a Share of the Elements As Sufficient To Enable Them To Suckle and Bring Up Their Young in a Dialogue Between the Aristocracy and a Mother of Children* (London: printed for the author, 1797).

[Sykes] Sikes, Henrietta, "ECONOMY," in *Hymns and Poems on Moral Subjects: Addressed to a Youth* (London: Bowdery & Kerby, 1815).

Margiana, or Widdrington Tower. A Tale of the Fifteenth Century (London: Lane, Newman & Co., at the Minerva Press, 1808).

Sir William Dorien, 3 vols. (London: A. K. Newman, at the Minerva Press, 1812).

Timbury, Jane, *The Male Coquette; or, the History of the Hon. Edward Astell*, 2 vols. (London: Robinson and Roberts, 1770).

The Philanthropic Rambler (London: printed for and sold by the Author, 1790).

Tomlins, Elizabeth, *Tributes of Affection: with The Slave; and Other Poems* (London: printed by H. and C. Baldwin; for T. N. Longman, *et al.*, 1797).

Trimmer, Mrs., *The Economy of Charity* (London: printed by T. Bensley, 1787).

Trusler, John, *Domestic Management, or the Art of Conducting a Family, with Economy, Frugality & Method*, "a new edition" (Bath, 1819).

The Economist (London: printed for the author, and sold by J. Bell, 1774; 1776; Dublin, 1777).

Family Tables (London, 1781).

The London Adviser and Guide (London: for the Author, 1786).

Luxury no Political Evil (1780?).

The Master's Last Best Gift, to His Apprentice, on His Outset in Life, Pointing Out His Way to Wealth and Reputation (London, 1812).

A System of Etiquette (Bath: printed by M. Gye, 1804).

The Way to be Rich and Respectable, Addressed to Men of Small Fortune, 7th ed. (London: printed by the author, 1796). Also referred to: editions of 1775, 1777, 1786.

Weeton, Nelly, *Miss Weeton: Journal of a Governess: 1807–1811*, ed. Edward Hall (Oxford University Press, 1936).

West, Jane, *The Advantages of Education; or The History of Maria Williams, A Tale for Very Young Ladies* [first published 1793], 2nd ed., 2 vols. (London: printed at the Minerva Press, for T. N. Longman and O. Rees, 1803).

Alicia de Lacy, an Historical Romance (London: Longman, Hurst, Rees, Orme, and Brown, 1814).

The Church of Saint Siffrid, 2 vols. (Dublin: printed for William Porter, and Nicholas Kelly, 1798).

An Elegy on the Death of The Right Honourable Edmund Burke (London: T. N. Longman, 1797).

A Gossip's Story, and A Legendary Tale [first published 1797], 2nd. ed., 2 vols. (London: T. N. Longman, 1797).

The History of Ned Evans, 2nd ed., 4 vols. (London: G. G. and J. Robinson, 1797).

The Infidel Father, 3 vols. (London: printed by A. Strahan for T. Longman and O. Rees, 1802).

Letters Addressed to a Young Man On His First Entrance Into Life, And Adapted to the Peculiar Circumstances of the Present Time, 3 vols. (London: printed by A. Strahan for T. Longman and O. Rees, 1801).

Letters to a Young Lady, in Which the Duties and Character of Women Are Considered, Chiefly with a Reference to Prevailing Opinions, 2nd ed., 3 vols. (London: Longman, Hurst, Rees, and Orme, 1806).

The Mother: A Poem in Five Books (London: Longman, Hurst, Rees, and Orme, 1809).

The Refusal, 2 vols. (London: Longman, Hurst, Rees, and Orme, 1810).

Ringrove; Or, Old Fashioned Notions, 2 vols. (London: printed for Longman, Rees, Orme, Brown, and Green, 1827).

A Tale of the Times, "Dedicated to Mrs. Carter," 2 vols. (Dublin: printed by William Porter, 1799).

Wollstonecraft, Mary, *Collected Letters of Mary Wollstonecraft*, ed. Ralph M. Wardle (Ithaca and London: Cornell University Press, 1979).

Mary, A Fiction (London: J. Johnson, 1788).

Original Stories From Real Life (London: J. Johnson, 1788).

Posthumous Works of the Author of a Vindication of the Rights of Woman, 4 vols., ed. William Godwin (London: Joseph Johnson, 1798). [Vols. 1 and 2 contain *The Wrongs of Woman, or Maria; a Fragment*. Vols. 3 and 4 contain *Letters to Imlay*, some letters to Johnson, *The Cave of Fancy* and other fragments, including some specimen lessons for Wollstonecraft's daughter Fanny.]

Thoughts on the Education of Daughters (1787).

A Vindication of the Rights of Woman [first published 1792], ed. Carol H. Poston (New York: W. W. Norton, 1975).

SELECTED CRITICAL STUDIES

Abrahams, Roger, "The Complex Relation of Simple Form," *Genre* 2 (1969).

Adburgham, Alison, *Shops and Shopping, 1800–1914*, reprint 1981 (London: George Allen and Unwin, 1964).

Shopping in Style: London from the Restoration to Edwardian Elegance (London: Thames and Hudson, 1979).

Women in Print: Writing Women & Women's Magazines From the Restoration to the Accession of Victoria (London: George Allen and Unwin, 1972).

Aers, David, "Community and Morality: Towards Reading Jane Austen," in *Romanticism and Ideology: Studies in English Writing 1765–1830*, eds. David Aers, Jonathan Cook, David Punter (London: Routledge & Kegan Paul, 1981).

Aldis, H. G., "Book Production and Distribution, 1625–1800," *The Cambridge History of English Literature*, eds. A. W. Ward and A. R. Waller, XI (Cambridge University Press, 1953).

Alexander, David, *Retailing in the Industrial Revolution* (London: Athlone Press, 1970).

Altick, R. D., *The English Common Reader: A Social History of the Mass Reading Public, 1800–1900* (University of Chicago Press, 1957).

Andrews, P. B. S., "The Date of *Pride and Prejudice*," *Notes and Queries*, 15 (1968).

Appadurai, Arjun, ed., *The Social Life of Things: Commodities in Cultural Perspective* (Cambridge University Press, 1986).

Armstrong, Nancy, *Desire and Domestic Fiction: A Political History of the Novel* (Oxford University Press, 1987).

Ashton, T. S., ed., *An Economic History of England: the 18th Century* (London: Methuen, 1955).

Aspinall, Arthur, "The Circulation of Newspapers in the Early Nineteenth Century," *Review of English Studies*, 22 (1946).

Auerbach, Nina, *Communities of Women: An Idea in Fiction* (Cambridge, Mass.: Harvard University Press, 1978).

"Jane Austen and Romantic Imprisonment," in *Jane Austen in a Social Context*, ed. David Monaghan (Totowa, New Jersey: Barnes & Noble, 1981).

Austen-Leigh, Emma, *Jane Austen and Bath* (London: Spottiswoode, Ballantyne, 1939).

Jane Austen and Steventon (London: Spottiswoode, Ballantyne, 1937).

Bakhtin, M. M., *The Dialogic Imagination*, trans. Caryl Emerson and Michael Holquist (Austin: University of Texas Press, 1981).

Banfield, Ann, "The Influence of Place: Jane Austen and the Novel of Social Consciousness," in *Jane Austen in a Social Context*, ed. David Monaghan (Totowa, New Jersey: Barnes & Noble, 1981).

Bateson, Gregory, "A Theory of Play and Fantasy," in *Steps to an Ecology of Mind* (London: James Aronson, 1972).

Baudrillard, Jean, "Consumer Society," in *Jean Baudrillard: Selected Writings*, ed. Mark Poster (Stanford University Press, 1988).

"The System of Objects," in *Jean Baudrillard: Selected Writings*, ed. Mark Poster (Stanford University Press, 1988).

Bell, Quentin, *Virginia Woolf, a Biography* (New York: Harcourt, Brace, Jovanovich, 1972).

Bennett, Shelley M., "Changing Images of Women in Late-Eighteenth-Century England: 'The Lady's Magazine,' 1770–1810," *Arts Magazine* 55 (May 1981).

Thomas Stothard: the Mechanisms of Art Patronage in England circa 1800 (Columbia: Missouri University Press, 1988).

Berg, Maxine and Pat Hudson, "Rehabilitating the Industrial Revolution," *Economic History Review*, vol. 45, no. 1 (1992).

Berglund, Birgitta, *Woman's Whole Existence: The House as an Image in the Novels of Ann Radcliffe, Mary Wollstonecraft, and Jane Austen* (Sweden: Lund University Press, 1993).

Berman, Marshall, *All That Is Solid Melts Into Air: The Experience of Modernity* (New York: Simon and Schuster, 1982).

Besterman, Theodore, *Selected Records of Cadell and Davies, 1790–1830* (Oxford University Press, 1938).

Blakey, Dorothy, *The Minerva Press, 1790–1820* (Oxford: The Bibliographical Society at the University Press, 1939).

Bleiler, E. F., *Three Gothic Novels* (New York: Dover Press, 1966).

Bourdieu, Pierre, *Distinction: A Social Critique of the Judgement of Taste*, trans. Richard Nice (London: Routledge & Kegan Paul, 1984).

Bradbrook, Frank W., *Jane Austen and Her Predecessors* (Cambridge University Press, 1967).

Briggs, Asa, *The Age of Improvement* (London: Longman, Green, 1959).

How They Lived: An Anthology of Original Documents Written Between 1700 and 1815 (Oxford: Basil Blackwell, 1969).

Brophy, Bridget, "Jane Austen and the Stuarts," in *Critical Essays on Jane Austen*, ed. Brian Southam (London: Routledge & Kegan Paul, 1968).

Brown, Lloyd W., "The Business of Marrying and Mothering," in *Jane Austen's Achievement*, ed. Juliet McMaster (London: Macmillan, 1976).

Brownstein, Rachel M., *Becoming a Heroine: Reading about Women in Novels*, first printed 1982 (Harmondsworth: Penguin, 1984).

Burke, Peter, *Popular Culture in Early Modern Europe* (London: Temple Smith, 1978).

Burnett, John, *A History of the Cost of Living* (Harmondsworth: Penguin, 1969).

Butler, Marilyn, *Jane Austen and the War of Ideas* (Oxford: Clarendon Press, 1975).

   Maria Edgeworth: a Literary Biography (Oxford: Clarendon Press, 1972).

   "Disregarded Designs: Jane Austen's Sense of the Volume," in *Jane Austen in a Social Context*, ed. David Monaghan (Totowa, New Jersey: Barnes & Noble, 1981).

Butor, Michael, *Inventory*, trans. Richard Howard (New York: Simon and Schuster, 1961).

Campbell, Colin, *The Romantic Ethic and the Spirit of Modern Consumerism* (Oxford: Basil Blackwell, 1987).

Campbell, D. Grant, "Fashionable Suicide: Conspicuous Consumption and the Collapse of Credit in Frances Burney's *Cecilia*," *Studies in Eighteenth-Century Culture*, 20 (East Lansing: Colleagues Press, 1990).

Campbell, Mary, *Lady Morgan: the Life and Times of Sydney Owenson* (London: Pandora, 1988).

Cannadine, David, "The Past and the Present in the English Industrial Revolution 1880–1980," *Past and Present*, no. 103 (1984).

Cecil, David, "Jane Austen's Lesser Works," in *Collected Reports of the Jane Austen Society, 1949–1965*, reprint, 1967 (London: Wm. Dawson and Sons, 1967).

Chapman, Robert William, "*Sense and Sensibility*," *Times Literary Supplement*, 6 July 1946.

Clark, E. V., "The Private Governess in Fiction," *Contemporary Review* 186 (1954).

Cockshut, A. O. J., *Man and Woman: A Study of Love and the Novel, 1740–1940* (Oxford University Press, 1978).

Colby, Robert, *Fiction with a Purpose* (Bloomington: Indiana University Press, 1967).

Colby, Vineta, *Yesterday's Women: Domestic Realism in the English Novel* (Princeton University Press, 1974).

Collected Reports of the Jane Austen Society, 1949–1965, reprint, 1967 (London: Wm. Dawson and Sons, 1967).

Collected Reports of the Jane Austen Society, 1966–75 (Folkestone: Wm. Dawson & Sons, 1977).

Collected Reports of the Jane Austen Society, 1976–85 (Chippenham, Wiltshire: Antony Rowe, Ltd., 1989).

Collins, Arthur Simons, *Authorship in the Days of Johnson, being a study of the relation between author, patron, publisher, and public, 1726–1780* (London: R. Holden, 1927).

The Profession of Letters: A Study of the Relation of Author to Patron, Publisher, and Public, 1780–1832 (New York: Dutton, 1929).

Cook, Olive, *The English Country House: an Art and a Way of Life* (London: Thames and Hudson, 1974).

Copeland, Edward, "The Economic Realities of Jane Austen's Day," in *Approaches to Teaching Jane Austen's Pride and Prejudice*, ed. Marcia McClintock Folsom (New York: The Modern Language Association, 1993).

"Money Talks: Jane Austen and the *Lady's Magazine*," in *Jane Austen's Beginnings: the Juvenilia and Lady Susan*, ed. J. David Grey (Ann Arbor: UMI Research Press, 1989).

"What's a Competence? Jane Austen, her Sister Novelists, and the 5%'s," *Modern Language Notes*, 9, no. 3 (Fall, 1979).

Court, W. H. B., *A Concise Economic History of Britain from 1750 to Recent Times* (Cambridge University Press, 1965).

Coward, Rosalind, *Female Desires: How They Are Sought, Bought and Packaged* (New York: Grove, 1985).

Craig, G. Armour, "Jane Austen's *Emma*: The Truths and Disguises of Human Disclosure," *A Defense of Reading*, eds. Reuben A. Brower and Richard Poirier (New York: E. P. Dutton, 1962).

Cross, Nigel, *The Common Writer: Life in Nineteenth-Century Grub Street* (Cambridge University Press, 1985).

The Royal Literary Fund, 1790–1918 (London: World Microfilms Publications, 1984).

Curwen, Henry, *A History of Booksellers, the Old and the New* (London: Chatto and Windus, 1873).

Daiches, David, "Jane Austen, Karl Marx, and the Aristocratic Dance," *American Scholar*, 17 (1948).

Daniels, Stephen, "The Political Landscape," in *Humphry Repton, Landscape Gardener, 1752–1818*, eds. George Carter, Patrick Goode, Kedrun Laurie (London: Sainsbury Centre for Visual Arts, 1982).

Davidoff, Leonore and Catherine Hall, *Family Fortunes: Men and Women of the English Middle Class, 1780–1850* (London: Hutchinson, 1987).

Davidoff, Leonore and Ruth Hawthorne, *A Day in the Life of a Victorian Domestic Servant* (London: Allen and Unwin, 1976).

Davis, Dorothy, *A History of Shopping* (London: Routledge & Kegan Paul, 1966).

Davis, Lennard J., *Resisting Novels: Ideology and Fiction* (New York and London: Methuen, 1987).

Davis, Natalie Zemon, "Women on Top: Symbolic Sexual Inversion and

Political Disorder in Early Modern Europe," in *The Reversible World: Symbolic Inversion in Art and Society*, ed. Barbara A. Babcock (Ithaca and London: Cornell University Press, 1978).

Deane, P. and W. A. Cole, *British Economic Growth, 1688–1959: Trends and Structures*, 2nd ed. (Cambridge University Press, 1969).

De Lauretis, Teresa, *Alice Doesn't: Feminism, Semiotics, Cinema* (Bloomington: Indiana University Press, 1984).

A Dictionary of British and American Women Writers, 1660–1800, ed. Janet Todd (Totowa, New Jersey: Rowman & Allanheld, 1985).

Derrida, Jacques, *Of Grammatology*, trans. Gayatri Chakravorty Spivak (Baltimore: The Johns Hopkins University Press, 1976).

Dodds, Madeline Hope, "Hours of Business, 1780 to 1820," *Notes and Queries*, 194 (1949).

Doody, Margaret Anne, *Frances Burney: The Life in the Works* (New Brunswick, New Jersey: Rutgers University Press, 1988).

Douglas, Mary, *Cultural Bias* (London: Royal Anthropological Institute of Great Britain and Ireland, 1978).

Douglas, Mary and Baron Isherwood, *The World of Goods: Towards and Anthropology of Consumption* (Harmondsworth: Penguin, 1978).

Duckworth, Alistair M., *The Improvement of the Estate: A Study of Jane Austen's Novels* (Baltimore and London: The Johns Hopkins University Press, 1971).

"Games in Jane Austen's Life and Fiction," in *Jane Austen: Bicentenary Essays*, ed. John Halperin (Cambridge University Press, 1975).

"*Mansfield Park* and Estate Improvements: Jane Austen's Grounds of Being," *Nineteenth-Century*, 26 (1971–72).

Eagleton, Mary and David Pierce, *Attitudes to Class in the English Novel* (London: Thames and Hudson, 1979).

Eagleton, Terry, *Criticism and Ideology: a Study in Marxist Literature* (London: Verso, 1976).

Literary Theory: An Introduction (Oxford: Blackwell, 1983).

Marxism and Literary Criticism (London: Methuen, 1976).

Myths of Power: A Marxist Study of the Brontës (New York: Barnes & Noble, 1975).

"Ecriture and Eighteenth Century Fiction," in *Literature, Society, and the Sociology of Literature*, Proceedings of the Essex conference on the Sociology of Literature, July 1977 (University of Essex, 1978).

Earle, Peter, *The Making of the English Middle Class: Business, Society and Family Life in London, 1660–1730* (London: Methuen, 1989).

Ehrenpreis, Anne Henry, "*Northanger Abbey*: Jane Austen and Charlotte Smith," *Nineteenth Century Fiction*, 25 (1970).

Eliot, George, "Silly Novels by Lady Novelists," *Westminster Review* 66 (1856).

Emden, Cecil S., "The Composition of *Northanger Abbey*," *Review of English Studies*, 19 (1968).

Emsley, Clive, *British Society and the French Wars, 1793–1815* (London: Macmillan, 1979).

Erskine, Mrs. Steuart, *Lady Diana Beauclerk: Her Life and Work* (London: T. Fisher Unwin, 1903).

Evans, Mary, *Jane Austen and the State* (London: Tavistock Publications, 1987).

Everitt, A., "Kentish Family Portrait: An Aspect of the Rise of the Pseudo-Gentry," in *Rural Change and Urban Growth 1500–1800: Essays in English Regional History in Honour of W. G. Hoskins*, eds. C. W. Chalklin and M. A. Havinden (London: Longman, 1979).

"Social Mobility in Early Modern England," *Past and Present* (April 1966).

Eversley, D. E. C., "The Home Market and Economic Growth in England, 1750–80," from *Land, Labour and Population in the Industrial Revolution*, eds. E. L. Jones and G. E. Mingay (London, 1967), in *Population and Industrialization* (London: Adam and Charles Black, 1973).

Ewen, Stuart, "Marketing Dreams: The Political Elements of Style," in *Consumption, Identity, and Style*, Alan Tomlinson, ed. (London: Routledge, 1990).

Ewen, Stuart and Elizabeth, *Channels of Desire: Mass Images and the Shaping of the American Consciousness* (New York: McGraw-Hill, 1982).

Feather, John, *The Provincial Book Trade in Eighteenth-Century England* (Cambridge University Press, 1985).

The Feminist Companion to Literature in English, eds. Virginia Blain, Patricia Clements, Isobel Grundy (London: B. T. Batsford, 1990).

Fergus, Jan, *Jane Austen and the Didactic Novel* (Totowa, New Jersey: Barnes & Noble, 1983).

Jane Austen: A Literary Life (New York: St. Martin's Press, 1991).

"Sex and Social Life in Jane Austen's Novels," in *Jane Austen in a Social Context*, ed. David Monaghan (Totowa, New Jersey: Barnes & Noble, 1981).

"Women Readers of Fiction and the Marketplace in the Midlands, 1746–1800," delivered as work-in-progress at the Clark Center for 17th and 18th Century Studies, UCLA (Spring, 1991).

Fergus, Jan and Janice Farrar Thaddeus, "Women, Publishers, and Money, 1790–1820," in *Studies in Eighteenth-Century Culture*, 17 (East Lansing, Michigan: Colleagues Press, 1987).

Figes, Eva, *Sex and Subterfuge: Women Novelists to 1850* (London: Macmillan, 1982).

Fleishman, Avron, *A Reading of Mansfield Park: An Essay in Critical Synthesis* (Minneapolis: University of Minnesota Press, 1967).

"*Mansfield Park* in Its Time," *Nineteenth Century Fiction*, 22 (1967–68).

Flexner, Eleanor, *Mary Wollstonecraft: A Biography* (Baltimore, Maryland: Penguin, 1972).

Folsom, Marcia McClintock, *Approaches to Teaching Austen's Pride and Prejudice* (New York: The Modern Langauge Association of America, 1993).

Fores, Michael, "The Myth of a British Industrial Revolution," *History*, vol. 66, no. 217 (June 1981).

Foster, James R., *History of the Pre-Romantic Novel in England* (New York: The Modern Language Association, 1949).

George, M. D., *English Social Life in the Eighteenth Century*, Part 1 (London: The Sheldon Press, 1923).

Gilboy, Elizabeth Waterman, "Demand as a Factor in the Industrial Revolution," in *The Causes of the Industrial Revolution in England*, ed. R. M. Hartwell (London: Methuen, 1967).

Gill, Richard, *Happy Rural Seat: the English Country House and the Literary Imagination* (New Haven and London: Yale University Press, 1979).

Gillie, Christopher, "*Sense and Sensibility*: An Assessment," *Essays in Criticism*, 9 (1959).

Gillies, R. P., *Memoirs of a Literary Veteran*, 3 vols. (London: Richard Bentley, 1851).

Gilson, David, *A Bibliography of Jane Austen* (Oxford: Clarendon Press, 1982).

Goldman, Lucien, *Towards a Sociology of the Novel* (London: Tavistock, 1975).

Gorer, Geoffrey, "Poor honey: some notes on Jane Austen and her mother," *London Magazine* 4, no. 8 (August 1957).

Green, Katherine Sobba, *The Courtship Novel*, 1740–1820 (Lexington: University of Kentucky Press, 1991).

Greene, D. J., "Jane Austen and the Peerage," *PMLA*, 68 (1953).

Gregory, Allene, "Some Typical Lady Novelists of the Revolution," in *The French Revolution and the English Novel* (New York: G. P. Putnam's Sons, 1915).

Grey, J. David, ed., *The Jane Austen Companion* (New York: Macmillan, 1986).

Jane Austen's Beginnings: The Juvenilia and Lady Susan (Ann Arbor and London: UMI Research Press, 1989).

Halperin, John, *The Life of Jane Austen* (Baltimore: The Johns Hopkins University Press, 1984).

Hamlyn, Miss H. M., *Eighteenth-Century Circulating Libraries in England* (London: The Bibliographical Society, 1947).

Handleman, Don, "Reflexivity in Festival and Other Cultural Events," in *Essays in the Sociology of Perception*, ed. Mary Douglas (London: Routledge & Kegan Paul, 1982).

Handler, Richard and Daniel Segal, *Jane Austen and the Fiction of Culture* (Tucson: University of Arizona Press, 1990).

Harding, D. W., "Regulated Hatred: an Aspect of the Work of Jane Austen," *Scrutiny*, no. 8 (1940).

Hardy, Barbara, "The Objects in *Mansfield Park*," in *Jane Austen: Bicentenary Essays*, ed. John Halperin (Cambridge University Press, 1975).

"Properties and Possessions in Jane Austen's Novels," in *Jane Austen's Achievement*, ed. Juliet McMaster (London: Macmillan, 1976).

Hartwell, R. M., "The Rising Standard of Living in England, 1800–1850," *Economic History Review*, 2nd series, 13 (1960–61).

Hecht, J. J., *The Domestic Servant Class in 18th-Century England* (London: Routledge & Kegan Paul, 1956).

Hemlow, Joyce, *The History of Fanny Burney* (Oxford: Clarendon Press, 1958).

Hilbish, Florence, *Charlotte Smith, Poet and Novelist (1749–1806)* (Philadelphia: University of Pennsylvania, 1942).

Hill, Bridget, *Eighteenth-Century Women: An Anthology* (London: George Allen & Unwin, 1984).

   Women, Work, and Sexual Politics in Eighteenth-Century England (Oxford: Basil Blackwell, 1989).

Hobsbawm, Eric J., *The Age of Revolution, 1789–1848* (New York: New American Library, 1962).

   Industry and Empire (Baltimore: Penguin Books, 1968).

   "The British Standard of Living, 1790–1850," *Economic History Review*, 2nd series, 10 (1957–58).

Holbrook, David, "What Was Mr. Darcy Worth?" *The Cambridge Review*, 105 (1984).

Hollander, Anne, *Seeing Through Clothes* (New York: Penguin, 1975).

Honan, Park, *Jane Austen, Her Life* (New York: St. Martin's Press, 1987).

Hunt, Leigh, *Leigh Hunt's Autobiography: The Earliest Sketches*, ed. Stephen F. Fogle, University of Florida Monographs, No. 2, Fall, 1959 (Gainesville: University of Florida Press, 1959).

Jameson, Fredric, *The Political Unconscious: Narrative as a Socially Symbolic Act* (Ithaca, New York: Cornell University Press, 1981).

Janeway, Elizabeth, *Man's World, Woman's Place: A Study in Social Mythology* (New York: Dell, 1971).

Jauss, Hans Robert, *Towards an Aesthetic of Reception*, trans. Timothy Baht (Minneapolis: University of Minnesota Press, 1982).

Jeffreys, J. B., *Retail Trading in Britain: 1850–1950* (Cambridge University Press, 1954).

Jenkins, Elizabeth, *Jane Austen*, 1st ed. 1949 (New York: Minerva Press, 1969).

   "Some Banking Accounts of the Austen Family," in *Collected Reports of the Jane Austen Society, 1949–1965*, reprint, 1967 (London: Wm. Dawson and Sons, 1967).

Johnson, Claudia L., *Jane Austen: Women, Politics, and the Novel* (Chicago: University of Chicago Press, 1968).

Jones, Ann, *Ideas and Innovations: Best Sellers of Jane Austen's Age* (New York: AMS Press, 1986).

Kaplan, Deborah, *Jane Austen among Women* (Baltimore and London: The Johns Hopkins University Press, 1992).

   "Representing Two Cultures: Jane Austen's Letters," in *The Private Self: Theory and Practice of Women's Autobiographical Writings*, ed. Shari Benstock (London: Routledge, 1988).

Kelly, Gary, *English Fiction of the Romantic Period, 1789–1830* (London and New York: Longman, 1989).
  The English Jacobin Novel, 1780–1805 (Oxford: Clarendon Press, 1976).
  "Jane Austen and the English Novel of the 1790's," in *Fetter'd or Free? British Women Novelists, 1670–1815*, eds. Mary Anne Schofield and Cecilia Macheski (Athens: Ohio University Press, 1986).
Kent, Christopher, "'Real Solemn History' and Social History," in *Jane Austen in a Social Context*, ed. David Monaghan (Totowa, New Jersey: Barnes & Noble, 1981).
Kirkham, Margaret, *Jane Austen: Feminism and Fiction* (Brighton: Harvester, 1983).
Klancher, Jon P., *The Making of English Reading Audiences, 1790–1832* (Madison: University of Wisconsin Press, 1987).
Kopytoff, Igor, "The Cultural Biography of Things: Commoditization as Process," in *The Social Life of Things: Commodities in Cultural Perspective*, ed. Arjun Appadurai (Cambridge University Press, 1986).
Kuhn, Annette and AnnMarie Wolpe, eds., *Feminism and Materialism: Women and Modes of Production* (London: Routledge & Kegan Paul, 1978).
Landes, David S., *The Unbound Prometheus: Technological Change and Industrial Development in Western Europe from 1750 to the Present* (Cambridge University Press, 1972).
Lascelles, Mary, *Jane Austen and Her Art*, 1st ed. 1939 (Oxford University Press, 1968).
Laslett, Peter, *The World We Have Lost* (New York: Charles Scribner's Sons, 1965).
Laurenson, Diana and Alan Swingewood, *The Sociology of Literature* (London: MacGibbon and Kee, 1972).
Leavis, Q. D., *Fiction and the Reading Public* (London: Chatto & Windus, 1932).
Le Faye, Deirdre, *Jane Austen: A Family Record* (London: The British Library, 1989).
  "Anna Lefroy's Original Memories of Jane Austen," *The Review of English Studies* (August 1988).
  "Jane Austen and Mrs. Hunter's Novel," *Notes and Queries* ns 32, no. 3 (1985).
Legates, Marlene, "The Cult of Womanhood in Eighteenth-Century Thought," *Eighteenth-Century Studies* 10 (Fall 1976).
Litz, A. Walton, *Jane Austen: A Study of Her Artistic Development* (Oxford University Press, 1965).
Lock, F. P., "Jane Austen and the Seaside," *Country Life Annual* (1972).
Lovell, Terry, *Consuming Fiction* (London: Verso, 1987).
  "Jane Austen and Gentry Society," in *The Sociology of Literature*, ed. Francis Barker, Proceedings of the Essex Conference on the Sociology of Literature, July 1977 (University of Essex, 1978).
Lucas, E. V., *The Life of Charles Lamb*, 2 vols. (London: Methuen, 1905).

Mabbett, Joseph Sheldon, *Thomas James Mathias and The Pursuits of Literature* (Fribourg: Dissertation, University of Fribourg, 1964).

Macaulay, Thomas Babington, *Letters of Thomas Babington Macaulay*, ed. Thomas Pinney, 6 vols. (Cambridge University Press, 1974–81).

MacCarthy, Bridget, *The Female Pen: The Later Women Novelists, 1744–1818* (Cork University Press, 1947).

    Women Writers: Their Contribution to the English Novel, 1621–1744 (Cork University Press, 1944).

MacDonagh, Oliver, *Jane Austen: Real and Imagined Worlds* (New Haven and London: Yale University Press, 1991).

McKendrick, Neil, John Brewer and J. H. Plumb, *The Birth of a Consumer Society* (London: Europa Publications, 1982).

MacKinnon, Frank Douglas, *Grand Larceny, Being the Trial of Jane Leigh Perrot, Aunt of Jane Austen* (Oxford University Press, 1933).

Mansfield, Muriel, *Women Novelists from Fanny Burney to George Eliot* (London: Nicholson and Watson, 1934).

Marshall, Dorothy, *Eighteenth Century England* (London: Longman, 1962).

    English People in the Eighteenth Century (London: Longman, Green, 1956).

    The English Poor in the Eighteenth Century, 1st ed. 1926 (London: Routledge & Kegan Paul, 1969).

Mayo, Robert Donald, *The English Novel in the Magazines, 1740–1815* (Evanston: Northwestern University Press, 1962).

Medwin, Thomas, *Life of Shelley* (London: T. C. Newby, 1847).

Mews, Hazel, *Frail Vessels: Woman's Role in Women's Novels from Fanny Burney to George Eliot* (University of London, the Athlone Press, 1969).

Miller, Daniel, "*Things* Ain't What They Used to Be," *RAIN* (Royal Anthropological Society News), no. 59 (December 1983).

Mingay, G. E., *English Landed Society in the Eighteenth Century* (London: Routledge & Kegan Paul, 1963).

Mitford, Mary, *Letters*, ed. Henry Chorley (London: R. Bentley & Son, 1872).

Modleski, Tania, *Studies in Entertainment: Critical Approaches to Mass Culture* (Bloomington: Indiana University Press, 1986).

Moers, Ellen, *Literary Women* (London: The Women's Press, 1976).

    "Money, the Job, and Little Women," *Commentary*, 55 (January 1973).

Monaghan, David, *Jane Austen: Structure and Social Vision* (London: Macmillan, 1980).

    "Jane Austen and the Position of Women," in *Jane Austen in a Social Context*, ed. David Monaghan (Totowa, New Jersey: Barnes & Noble, 1981).

Moore, Doris Langley, *Fashion through Fashion Plates, 1771–1970* (London: Ward Lock, 1971).

Moretti, Franco, *Signs Taken for Wonders*, trans. Susan Fischer, *et al.*, 1st ed. 1983 (London: Verso, 1988).

Morris, Ivor, *Mr Collins Considered: Approaches to Jane Austen* (London and New York: Routledge & Kegan Paul, 1987).

Mui, Hoh-Cheung and Lorna H. Mui, *Shops and Shopkeeping in Eighteenth-Century England* (London: Routledge, 1989).

Mukerji, Chandra, *From Graven Images: Patterns of Modern Materialism* (New York: Columbia University Press, 1983).

Mulvey, Laura, *Visual and Other Pleasures* (London: Macmillan, 1989).

Musselwhite, David, "The Novel as Narcotic," in *The Sociology of Literature*, Proceedings of the Essex conference on the Sociology of Literature, July 1977, ed. Francis Barker (University of Essex, 1978).

Myers, Mitzi, "Hannah More's Tracts for the Times: Social Fiction and Female Ideology," in *Fetter'd or Free? British Women Novelists, 1670–1815*, eds. Mary Anne Schofield and Cecilia Macheski (Athens: Ohio University Press, 1985).

Nardin, Jane, "Jane Austen and the Problems of Leisure," in *Jane Austen in a Social Context*, ed. David Monaghan (Totowa, New Jersey: Barnes & Noble, 1981).

Nash, Ralph, "The Time Scheme for *Pride and Prejudice*," *English Language Notes*, 4 (1967).

Neale, R. S., *Bath, 1680–1850: A Social History* (London: Routledge & Kegan Paul, 1981).

Newton, Judith Lowder, *Women, Power, and Subversion: Social Strategies in British Fiction, 1778–1860* (Athens: University of Georgia Press, 1981).

O'Brien, P. K., "British Incomes and Property in the Early Nineteenth Century," in *Economic History Review*, vol. 12, no. 2 (1959).

Oldfield, J. R., "Private Schools and Academies in Eighteenth-Century Hampshire," *Proceedings of the Hampshire Field Club Archaeological Society*, 45 (1989).

Oliphant, Mrs. [M. O.], *Annals of a Publishing House: William Blackwood and His Sons*, 3 vols. (Edinburgh and London: Blackwood & Sons, 1897).

O'Malley, Ida Beatrice, *Women in Subjection: a Study of the Lives of Englishwomen Before 1832* (London: Duckworth, 1933).

Perkin, Harold, *The Origins of Modern English Society, 1780–1880* (University of Toronto Press, 1969).

Perry, Ruth, *The Celebrated Mary Astell: An Early English Feminist* (Chicago University Press, 1986).

Women, Letters, and the Novel (New York: AMS Press, 1980).

"Home at Last: Biographical Background to *Pride and Prejudice*," in *Approaches to Teaching Austen's Pride and Prejudice*, ed. Marcia McClintock Folsom (New York: The Modern Language Association of America, 1993).

Philips, Deborah, "Mills and Boon: The Marketing of Moonshine," in *Consumption, Identity, and Style*, ed. Alan Tomlinson (London: Routledge, 1990).

Poovey, Mary, *The Proper Lady and the Woman Writer* (University of Chicago Press, 1984).

Preston, John, *The Created Self: the Reader's Role in 18th Century Fiction* (London: Heinemann, 1970).

Punter, David, *The Literature of Terror* (New York: Longman, 1980).
  "Social Relations of Gothic Fiction," in *Romanticism and Ideology: Studies in English Writing 1765–1830*, eds. David Aers, Jonathan Cook, David Punter (London: Routledge & Kegan Paul, 1981).
Richards, Eric, "Women in the British Economy," *History*, 59 (1974).
Rogers, Katherine, *Feminism in Eighteenth-Century England* (Urbana: Illinois University Press, 1982).
Rothstein, Eric, "The Lessons of *Northanger Abbey*," *University of Toronto Quarterly*, 44 (1974).
Rowbotham, Sheila, *Hidden from History* (London: Pluto Press, 1973).
  Rediscovering Women in History From the 17th Century to the Present (New York: Vintage, 1976).
  Women's Consciousness, Man's World (Harmondsworth: Penguin, 1973).
Rowse, A. L., "The England of Jane Austen," in *Collected Reports of the Jane Austen Society 1966–75* (Folkestone: Wm. Dawson and Sons, 1977).
Rubinstein, E., "Jane Austen's Novels: The Metaphor of Rank," *Literary Monographs*, 2, eds. Eric Rothstein and Richard N. Ringler (Madison: Wisconsin University Press, 1969).
Saintsbury, George, "The Growth of the Later Novel," in *The Cambridge History of English Literature*, eds. A. W. Ward and A. R. Waller, xi (Cambridge University Press, 1953).
Sanders, Scott, "Towards a Social Theory of Literature," *Telos*, 18 (1973–74).
Scheuermann, Mona, *Social Protest in the Eighteeenth-Century English Novel* (Columbus: Ohio State University Press, 1985).
Schofield, Mary Anne and Cecilia Macheski, eds., *Fetter'd or Free? British Women Novelists, 1670–1815* (Athens: Ohio University Press, 1986).
Schorer, Mark, "Fiction and the 'Analogical Matrix,'" in *Critiques and Essays on Modern Fiction, 1920–1950*, ed. John W. Aldridge (New York: Ronald Press Company, 1952).
  "Pride Unprejudiced," *Kenyon Review*, 18 (Winter 1956).
Schucking, Levin L., *The Sociology of Literary Taste* (London: Kegan Paul, 1944).
Schwarz, L. D., "Social Class and Social Geography: the Middle Classes in London at the End of the Eighteenth Century," *Social History*, vol. 7, no. 2 (May 1982).
Sekora, John, *Luxury: The Concept in Western Thought, Eden to Smollett* (Baltimore and London: The Johns Hopkins University Press, 1977).
Shammas, Carole, *The Pre-Industrial Consumer in England and America* (Oxford: Clarendon Press, 1990).
  "The Domestic Environment in Early Modern England and America," *Journal of Social History*, vol. 14, no. 1 (Fall 1980).
Shevelow, Kathryn, *Women and Print Culture: The Construction of Femininity in the Early Periodical* (London and New York: Routledge, 1989).
Showalter, Elaine, *A Literature of Their Own: British Women Novelists from Brontë to Lessing* (Princeton University Press, 1977).

Silverman, Kaja, "Fragments of a Fashionable Discourse," in *Studies in Entertainment: Critical Approaches to Mass Culture*, ed. Tania Modleski (Bloomington: Indiana University Press, 1986).

Simmel, Georg, "Fashion," in *The American Journal of Sociology*, vol. 62, no. 6 (May 1957), reprinted from 1906 edition, published by Dodd, Mead and Company.

Southam, B. C., *Jane Austen: The Critical Heritage* (London: Routledge & Kegan Paul, 1968).

"General Tilney's Hot-Houses: Some Recent Jane Austen Studies and Texts," *Ariel*, 2 (October, 1971).

"Jane Austen and Her Readers," in *Collected Reports of the Jane Austen Society 1966–75* (Folkestone: Wm. Dawson and Sons, 1977).

"*Sanditon*: the Seventh Novel," in *Jane Austen's Achievement*, ed. Juliet McMaster (London: Macmillan, 1976).

"A Source for Sanditon?" in *Collected Reports of the Jane Austen Society, 1966–75* (Folkestone: Wm. Dawson and Sons, 1977).

Spacks, Patricia Meyer, *Desire and Truth: Functions of Plot in Eighteenth-Century English Novels* (Chicago University Press, 1990).

Spencer, Jane, *The Rise of the Woman Novelist: From Aphra Behn to Jane Austen* (Oxford: Basil Blackwell, 1986).

Spender, Dale, *Mothers of the Novel: 100 Good Women Writers Before Jane Austen* (London and New York: Pandora, 1986).

Spring, David, *The English Landed Estate in the Nineteenth Century: Its Administration* (Baltimore: The Johns Hopkins Press, 1963).

"Interpreters of Jane Austen's Social World: Literary Critics and Historians," *Jane Austen: New Perspectives*, ed. Janet Todd (New York and London: Holmes & Meier, 1983).

Stanton, Judith Phillips (ed.), *Letters of Charlotte Smith* (Bloomington: Indiana University Press, forthcoming).

"Charlotte Smith's 'Literary Business': Income, Patronage, and Indigence," in *The Age of Johnson*, vol. 1, yearbook, ed. Paul Korshin (New York: AMS Press, 1987).

"Statistical Profile of Women Writing in English from 1660 to 1800," in *Eighteenth-Century Women and the Arts*, eds. Frederick M. Keener and Susan E. Lorsch (Westport, Connecticut: Greenwood Press, 1988).

Staves, Susan, *Married Women's Separate Property, in England, 1660–1833* (Cambridge, Mass.: Harvard University Press, 1990).

"Pin Money," *Studies in Eighteenth-Century Culture*, 14 (Madison: Wisconsin University Press, 1985).

Steeves, Harrison H., *Before Jane Austen: The Shaping of the English Novel in the Eighteenth Century* (New York: Holt, Reinhart and Winston, 1965).

Stewart, Susan, *On Longing: Narratives of the Miniature, the Gigantic, the Souvenir, the Collection* (Baltimore: The Johns Hopkins University Press, 1984).

Styles, John, "Manufacturing, Consumption and Design in Eighteenth-

Century England," *Consumption and the World of Goods*, eds. John Brewer and Roy Porter (London and New York: Routledge, 1993).

Sulloway, Alison, *Jane Austen and the Province of Womanhood* (Philadelphia: University of Pennsylvania Press, 1989).

Sunstein, Emily, *A Different Face* (New York: Harper and Row, 1975).

Taylor, Lou, *Mourning Dress: A Costume and Social History* (London: George Allen and Unwin, 1983).

Thompson, F. M. L., *English Landed Society in the Nineteenth Century* (London: Routledge & Kegan Paul, 1963).

Thompson, James, *Between Self and World: The Novels of Jane Austen* (University Park and London: The Pennsylvania State University Press, 1988).

"Jane Austen's Clothing," in *Studies in Eighteenth-Century Culture*, 13 (Madison: Wisconsin University Press, 1984).

Tobin, Beth Fowkes, "The Moral and Political Economy of Property in Austen's *Emma*," *Eighteenth-Century Fiction*, vol. 2, no. 3 (April 1990).

Todd, Janet, *The Sign of Angellica: Women, Writing and Fiction* (London: Virago, 1989).

ed. *A Dictionary of British and American Women Writers, 1660–1800* (Totowa, New Jersey: Rowman & Allanheld, 1985).

ed. *Jane Austen: New Perspectives*, Women and Literature Series (New York and London: Holmes & Meier, 1983).

Tomlinson, Thomas Brian, *The English Middle-Class Novel* (London: Macmillan, 1976).

Tompkins, J. M. S., *The Popular Novel in England, 1770–1800*, 1st ed. 1932 (Lincoln: University of Nebraska Press, 1961).

Tranter, N. L., "Introduction" to *Population and Industrialization* (London: Adam and Charles Black, 1973).

Vernon, John, *Money and Fiction: Literary Realism in the Nineteenth and Early Twentieth Centuries* (Ithaca and London: Cornell University Press, 1984).

Vickery, Amanda, "Women and the World of Goods: a Lancashire Consumer and Her Possessions, 1751–81," *Consumption and the World of Goods*, eds. John Brewer and Roy Porter (London and New York: Routledge, 1993).

Wardle, Ralph M., *Mary Wollstonecraft: A Critical Biography* (Lincoln: University of Nebraska Press, 1966).

Watson, Melvin M., *Magazine Serials and the Essay Tradition, 1746–1820* (Baton Rouge: Louisiana State University Press, 1956).

Watt, Ian, *The Rise of the Novel* (London: Chatto & Windus, 1957).

Weatherill, Lorna, *Consumer Behaviour and Material Culture in Britain 1660–1760* (London and New York: Routledge, 1988).

"A Possession of One's Own: Women and Consumer Behaviour in England, 1660–1740," *Journal of British Studies*, vol. 25, no. 2 (April 1986).

White, Cynthia Leslie, *Women's Magazines, 1693–1968* (London: Michael Joseph, 1970).

Wiesenfarth, *Gothic Manners and the Classic English Novel* (Madison: University of Wisconsin Press, 1988).

Williams, Raymond, *The Country and the City* (Oxford University Press, 1973).

Williamson, Judith, "Woman is an Island: Femininity and Colonization," *Studies in Entertainment: Critical Approaches to Mass Culture*, ed. Tania Modleski (Bloomington: Indiana University Press, 1986).

Wilt, Judith, *Ghosts of the Gothic* (Princeton University Press, 1980).

Winship, Janice, *Inside Women's Magazines* (London: Routledge & Kegan Paul, 1987).

Woodforde, James, *The Diary of a Country Parson, 1758–1802* (Oxford University Press, 1979).

Woolf, Leonard, "The Economic Determination of Jane Austen," *New Statesman and Nation*, 24 (1942).

INDEX